"G A S !"

The Story of the Special Brigade

Photo. by Frederic Robinson, Camberley.

THE AUTHOR.

"GAS!"

The Story of the Special Brigade

BY

MAJOR-GENERAL C. H. FOULKES

C.B., C.M.G., D.S.O.

LATE ROYAL ENGINEERS AND A.D.C. TO THE KING

CHEVALIER OF THE LEGION OF HONOUR; FRENCH CROIX DE GUERRE (WITH
PALM); COMMANDER OF THE ORDER OF THE CROWN OF BELGIUM;
BELGIAN CROIX DE GUERRE (WITH PALM); COMMANDER OF
THE ORDER OF THE CROWN OF ITALY; AMERICAN
DISTINGUISHED SERVICE MEDAL

WITH AN INTRODUCTION BY

FIELD-MARSHAL THE EARL OF CAVAN

K.P., G.C.B.

INTRODUCTION

BY

FIELD-MARSHAL THE EARL OF CAVAN, K.P., G.C.B.

THE late Lord Balfour said to me one day:

> "The invasion of Belgium and the use of gas will shake the confidence of mankind in the sanctity of treaties for years to come."

He made this statement in 1922 at the Washington Conference, and I fear it is true in 1934.

It behoves us therefore to study this work if only for our protective education.

Let me acknowledge at once that I looked upon 'retaliation' only as a painful and harassing necessity. The men hated it, and I am sure that our old enemies will agree that the compulsory use of a gas mask halves your efficiency.

But it had to be. No commander can sit still and see his men murdered without taking retaliatory measures.

The decision having been made, Sir John French chose well in appointing the author of this historical book to be the man in charge of gas reprisals. His unceasing work is unfolded in the pages of this grim story. His personal bravery and untiring energy were proved nightly during the first battle of Ypres in 1914.

I can but hope that this intensely interesting and historical study of gas warfare will be translated into many languages, and that its effect may be that nations may ask themselves the question, "Is it worth it?"

The resolve not to use gas was honourably kept by the Air Forces of all the opposing armies in the late war. Why should land and sea forces be less chivalrous?

v

INTRODUCTION

Research and experiment must be continued. No nation can afford to be surprised by a new and deadly gas against which there is no known protection.

The services of Major-General Foulkes and his Special Brigade are worthy of record and close study. The author has a clear vision of what he believes would have been the character of the battle zone had the war continued into 1919.

Let this vision be translated into adequate means of defence, for if it can be shown that gas discharges contain no terrors for a well-disciplined army, its use as an offensive weapon will disappear and my question " Is it worth it ? " will receive its answer.

Perhaps this is not the place for discussion of the protection of the civil population, but in my opinion there should be—

1. An adequate supply of gas masks on the threat of war.
2. Public notices displayed on posters and in the Press of instructional classes on " How to wear a mask."
3. Scientific research for best methods for instant dispersal of gas clouds, or of raising the gas to a level above the heads of refugees in underground places such as tube stations.

The author of this book deserves well of his countrymen, for the horrors that we may have to guard against are clearly shown in these pages.

I commend it sincerely to historians as a contribution to their study, and to my fellow-citizens as education.

CAVAN,
F.-M.

PREFACE

My object in writing this book is to place on record the history of the Special Brigade, the secret unit which Sir John French raised in June 1915 to carry out gas operations against the Germans in retaliation for their introduction of this horror of modern war.

I have been frequently pressed to compile such a record by those concerned with me in the preparation and execution of our gas attacks. I think, too, that the subject will be of interest to the general public, because no other work of the kind has appeared in print, and, at any rate during the first half of the war, even in France the strictest secrecy was maintained in regard to the doings of the Special Companies. Later on it became evident that this secrecy had been overdone, and, in order to overcome the natural antipathy of our own commanders to this new weapon and to convince them that the labour which they were being constantly called upon to provide to carry out gas operations on a grand scale was not being wasted, it became necessary by means of lectures, demonstrations and secret circulars to release to staff and regimental officers a good deal of information of the methods we were employing and of the effects produced on the enemy, as learnt from various Intelligence sources.

In the course of this story I am unable to confine myself strictly to the deeds of the Special Brigade, because, apart from narrating how I first came to be connected with the conduct of the gas operations of the British Army in France, I must explain here that besides planning, organising, raising and training this special unit and commanding it until the Armistice, I was also ' Gas Adviser ' to the Commander-in-Chief for the greater part of the war, and I assumed extra responsibilities for the last eighteen months when I took over the whole of the defensive side of gas warfare, and even became, in addition, during its concluding stages President of the Chemical Warfare Committee, a body which included most of the leading scientists in this country and which sat in London, carrying out chemical, physiological and physical research.

It is impossible, therefore, to exclude all reference to such matters as our own artillery gas tactics, the various forms of German gas activity and their consequences, the developments which took place in the protection provided for our own troops and the scientific research work which was necessary at home in connection with all these subjects. But I have enlarged on these ' asides ' only as far as I believe it to be necessary for the understanding of the general reader, more especially as, at any rate in regard to the technical work carried out by the Ministry of Munitions, there are others far better qualified than myself to put it on record.

I realise that in attempting to write such a history and at the same time to interest the public, I am adding to the difficulty by including too little detail to satisfy the requirements of the former, and yet so much as to run the risk of wearying the latter; but the subject is one which has occupied a good deal of public attention lately, and there are misunderstandings which ought to be put right.

In some of the books and articles which have appeared in recent years on the subject of the use of gas in future wars there is hardly a statement about poison gas and its capabilities which is correct : the properties are confused, the effects are exaggerated and conclusions are drawn which might well horrify the reader. These writers have, in turn, been quoted by others as authorities on the subject until it has become possible to arrive at such fantastic conclusions as, for example, that a single bomb containing one of these poison gases, if dropped from the air on Piccadilly Circus, would destroy all life between Regent's Park and the Thames !

I have taken a good deal of trouble to corroborate every statement I have made concerning the losses of German units from the gas attacks carried out by the Special Brigade : they nearly all bear the authority of the skilled interrogators of our Intelligence Service in

France ; and the enemy documents from which I have quoted are still on record—many of them mud-stained letters, diaries and Divisional Orders in the original German.

I have consulted the following books on the subject :—

German.
    ' Der Chemische Krieg,' by Dr Rudolph Hanslian.
    ' My War Memories '—English translation—by General Ludendorff.
    Various German Regimental Histories.
    ' Der Grosse Krieg,' by Lieut.-General Schwarte.

English.
    ' The Riddle of the Rhine,' by V. Lefebure.
    ' Scientific Disarmament,' by V. Lefebure.

American.
    ' Gas Warfare,' by Farrow.
    ' Chemical Warfare,' by Fries and West.

French.
    ' La Guerre Chimique,' by Henri le Wita.

The photographs are my own except where the authorship is acknowledged.

I am very grateful for permission to use these photographs, and wish also to thank the following for helping me to read the proofs : Major-General Sir Louis Jackson, K.B.E., C.B., C.M.G. ; Major-General Sir Henry Thuillier, K.C.B., C.B., C.M.G. ; Professor Jocelyn Thorpe, C.B.E., D.Sc., F.R.S. ; Brig.-General Sir Harold Hartley, C.B.E., M.C., F.R.S. ; Doctor (formerly Lieut.-Colonel) Claude Gordon Douglas, C.M.G., M.C., B.Sc., F.R.S. ; and Captain Livens, D.S.O., M.C.

C. H. FOULKES.

CONTENTS.

LIST OF ILLUSTRATIONS.

LIST OF MAPS.

THE BATTLE OF LOOS
(Scale 1/100,000).

SPECIAL BRIGADE OPERATIONS, 1915 TO 13TH JUNE 1916
(Scale 1/380,160).

SPECIAL BRIGADE OPERATIONS, 24TH JUNE 1916 TO
19TH MARCH 1917
(Scale 1/380,160).

SPECIAL BRIGADE OPERATIONS, APRIL TO DECEMBER
1917
(Scale 1/380,000).

ENEMY GAS SHELL BOMBARDMENTS, 9TH-19TH MARCH
1918
(Scale 1/380,160).

ENEMY GAS SHELL BOMBARDMENTS, 7TH-9TH APRIL
1918
(Scale 1/380,160).

SPECIAL BRIGADE OPERATIONS, 1918
(1/380,160).

LIST OF GRAPHS.

GAS DISCHARGED BY THE SPECIAL BRIGADE, DAY BY
DAY

BRITISH GAS CASUALTIES

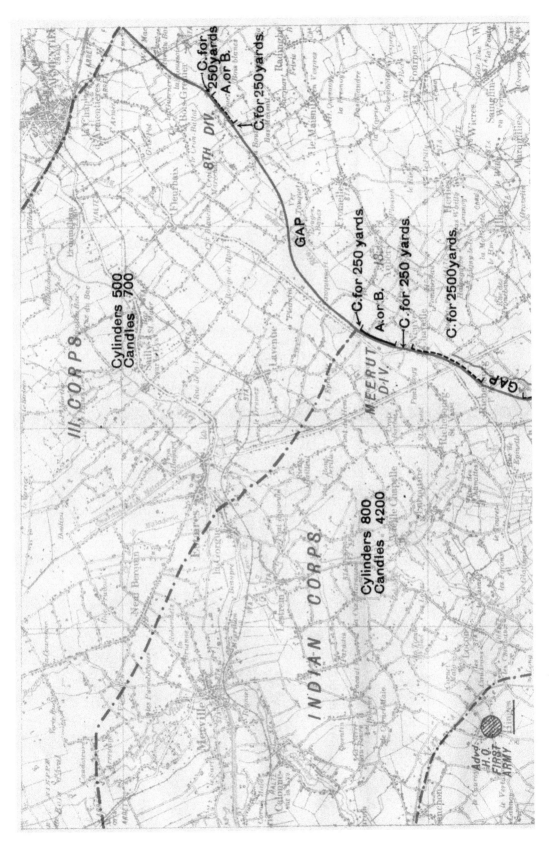

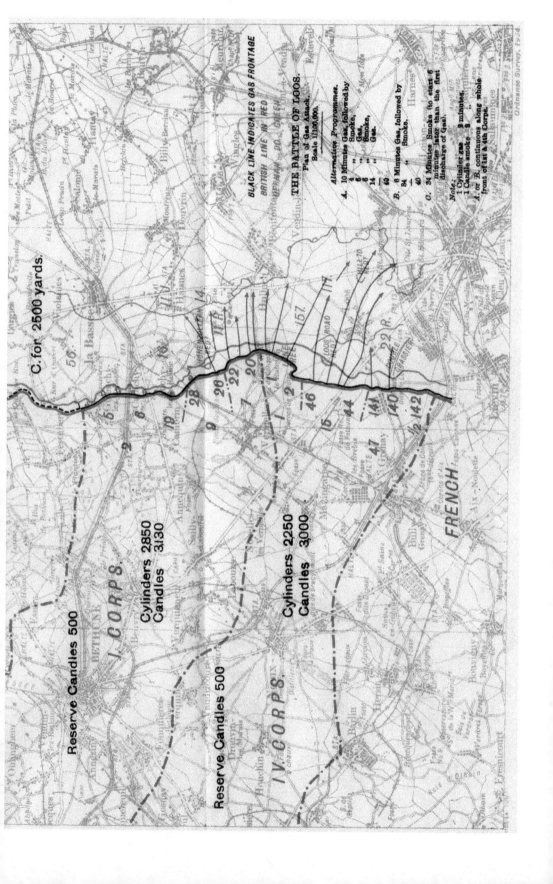

THE BATTLE OF LOOS.
Plan of Gas Attack.
Scale 1/100,000.

BLACK LINE INDICATES GAS FRONTAGE
BRITISH LINE IN RED
GERMAN DO. GREEN

Alternative Programmes.

4. 10 Minutes Gas, followed by Smoke.
4 " " Gas,
6 " " Smoke,
14 " " Gas.
40

B. 6 Minutes Gas, followed by Smoke.
B4 " "
40

C. 34 Minutes Smoke (to start 6 minutes later than the first discharge of Gas).

Note:
1 Cylinder = 2 minutes.
1 Candle smoke 3 '.

A. or B. continuous along whole front of 1st & 4th Corps.

C. for 2500 yards.

Reserve Candles 500

I. CORPS.

Cylinders 2850
Candles 3130

Reserve Candles 500

IV. CORPS.

Cylinders 2250
Candles 3000

FRENCH.

Ordnance Survey, 1914.

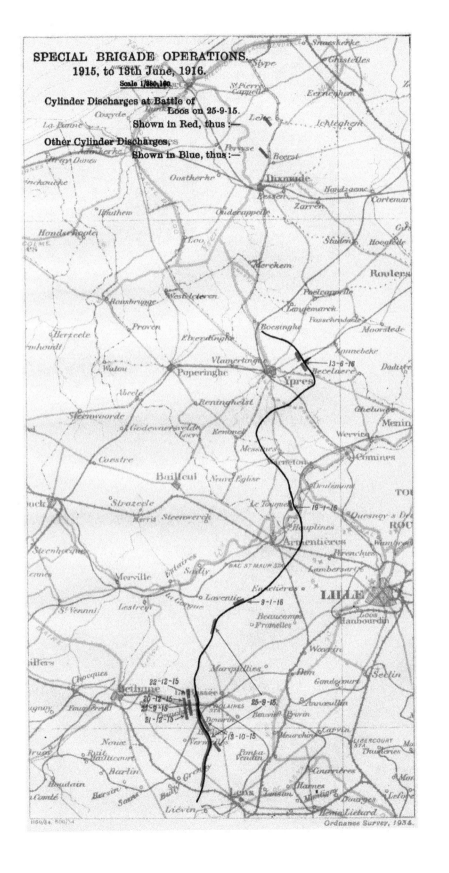

SPECIAL BRIGADE OPERATIONS.
1915, to 13th June, 1916.
Scale 1/880,160.

Cylinder Discharges at Battle of
Loos on 25-9-15.
Shown in Red, thus :—

Other Cylinder Discharges,
Shown in Blue, thus :—

Ordnance Survey, 1934.

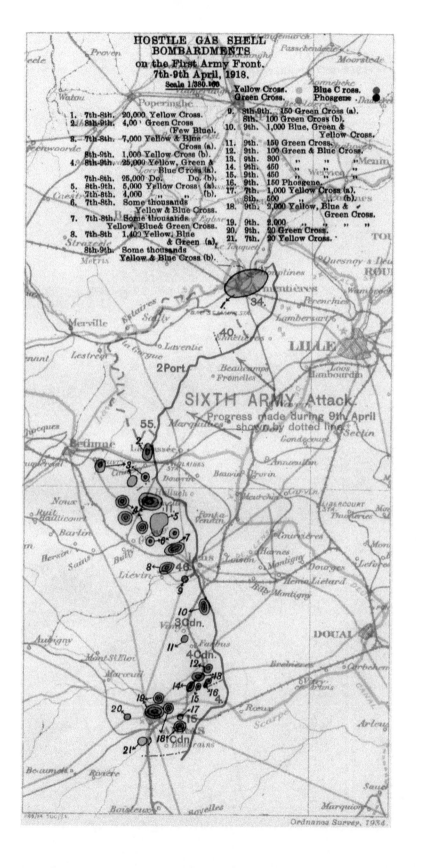

HOSTILE GAS SHELL BOMBARDMENTS
on the First Army Front.
7th-9th April, 1918.
Scale 1/380.100.

Yellow Cross.　　Blue Cross.
Green Cross.　　Phosgene.

1. — 7th-8th.　20,000 Yellow Cross.
2. — 8th-9th.　4,00` Green Cross
　　　　　　　(Few Blue).
3. — 7th-8th.　7,000 Yellow & Blue
　　　　　　　Cross (a).
　　8th-9th.　1,000 Yellow Cross (b).
4. — 8th-9th.　25,000 Yellow, Green &
　　　　　　　Blue Cross (a).
　　7th-8th.　25,000 Do.　Do. (b).
5. — 8th-9th.　5,000 Yellow Cross (a).
　　7th-8th.　4,000　,,　,,　(b).
6. — 7th-8th.　Some thousands
　　　　　　　Yellow & Blue Cross.
7. — 7th-8th.　Some thousands
　　　　　　　Yellow, Blue& Green Cross.
8. — 7th-8th　1,400 Yellow, Blue
　　　　　　　& Green (a).
　　8th-9th.　Some thousands
　　　　　　　Yellow & Blue Cross (b).

9. — 8th-9th.　150 Green Cross (a).
　　8th.　100 Green Cross (b).
10. — 9th.　1,000 Blue, Green &
　　　　　　Yellow Cross.
11. — 9th.　150 Green Cross.
12. — 9th.　100 Green & Blue Cross.
13. — 9th.　800　,,　,,　,,
14. — 9th.　450　,,　,,　,,
15. — 9th.　450　,,　,,　,,
16. — 9th.　150 Phosgene.
17. — 7th.　1,000 Yellow Cross (a).
　　8th.　500　,,　,,　(b).
18. — 9th.　2,000 Yellow, Blue &
　　　　　　Green Cross.
19. — 9th.　2,000　,,　,,　,,
20. — 9th.　20 Green Cross.
21. — 7th.　20 Yellow Cross.

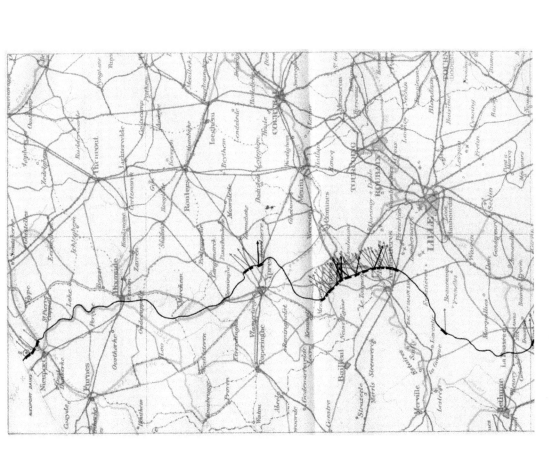

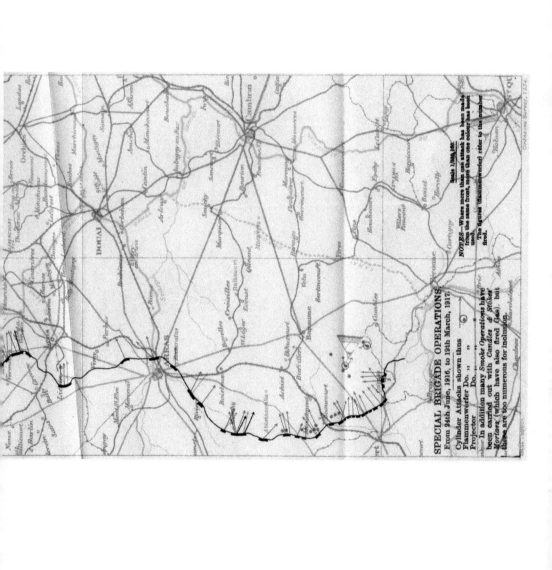

SPECIAL BRIGADE OPERATIONS

From 24th June, 1916, to 19th March, 1917.

Cylinder Attacks shown thus ●━━━
Flammenwerfer Do. „ „
Projector Do. „ „

In addition many Smoke Operations have been carried out with Candles & Stokes Mortars (which have also fired Gas), but these are too numerous for inclusion.

Scale 1/380,160

NOTES.—Where more than one attack has been made from the same front, more than one colour has been used.

The figures (flammenwerfer) refer to the number fired.

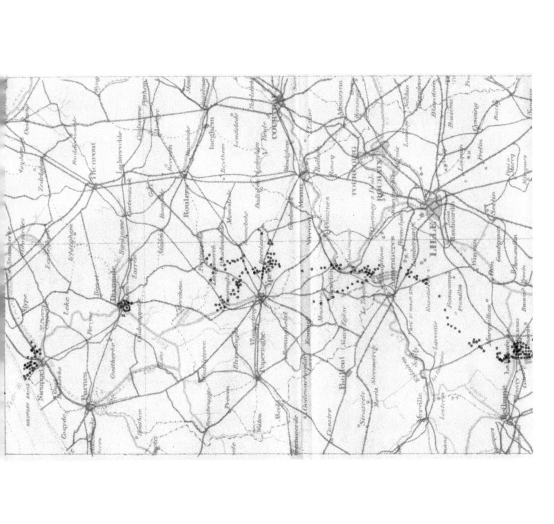

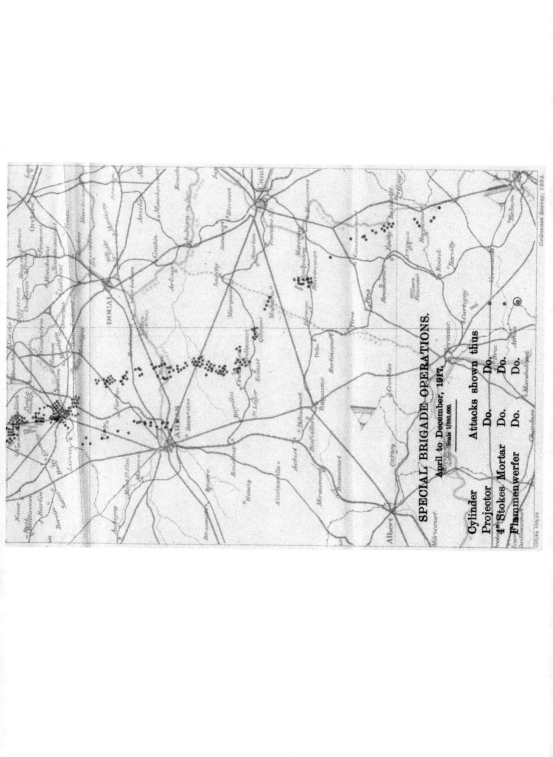

SPECIAL BRIGADE OPERATIONS.

April to December, 1917.

Scale 1/380,000.

Cylinder	Attacks shown thus
Projector	Do.
4" Stokes Mortar	Do.
Flammenwerfer	Do.

Ordnance Survey, 1924.

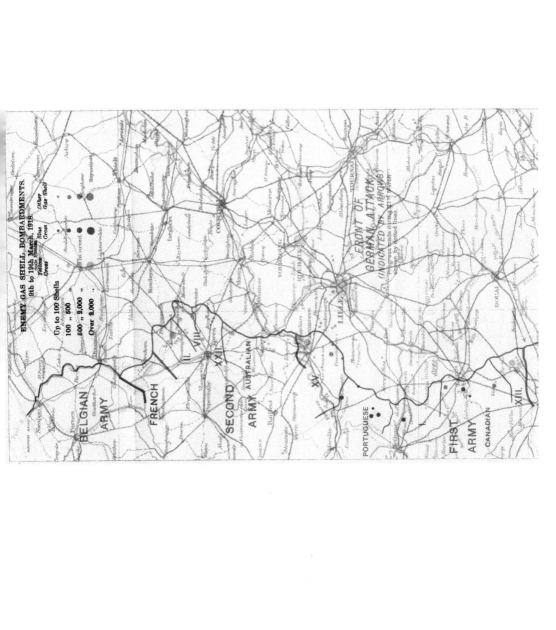

ENEMY GAS SHELL BOMBARDMENTS.
9th to 19th March, 1918.

Yellow   Blue   Other
Cross   Gas Shell   Gas Shell

Up to 100 Shells
100 " 500   "
500 " 2,000 "
Over 2,000   "

BELGIAN
ARMY

FRENCH

SECOND
ARMY   AUSTRALIAN

II. VIII.
XXII.

XV.

PORTUGUESE

FIRST
ARMY   CANADIAN

XIII.

FRONT OF
GERMAN ATTACK
(INDICATED BY ARROWS)
Progress made during attack from
shown by dotted lines.

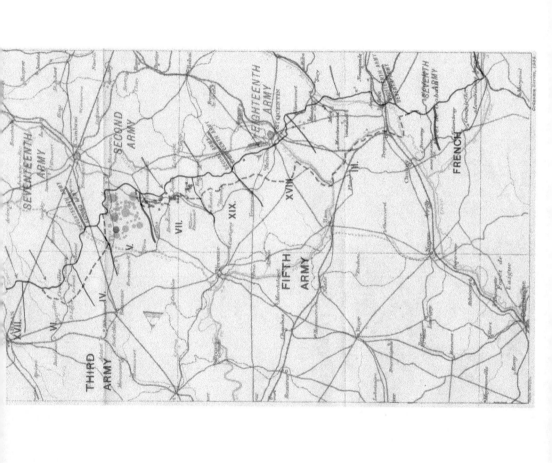

SPECIAL BRIGADE OPERATIONS—1918.

Scale 1/250,160

Each Projector Attack shown thus :

Each Cylinder Discharge shown thus:

Each 4" Stokes Mortar Bombardment
            shown thus :

                Previous After
               to Aug 1. Aug 1.

British Line 21-3-18.
  do.   1-8-18.

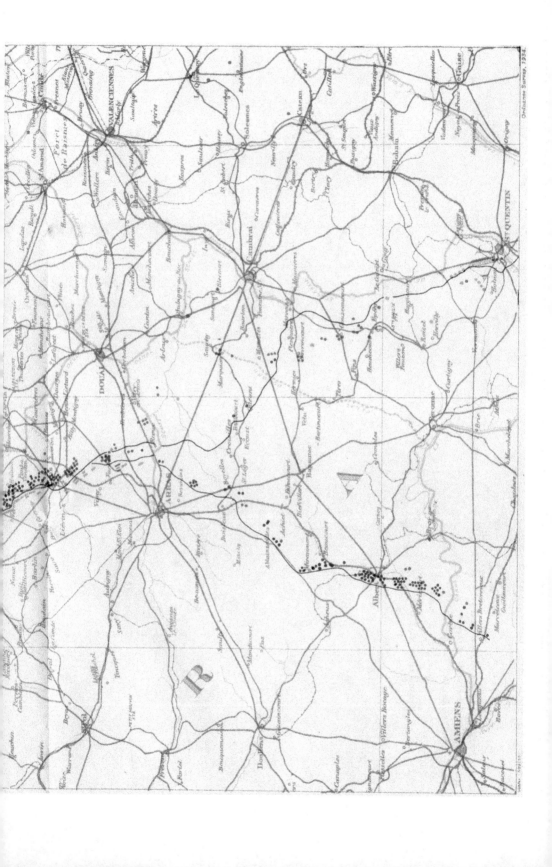

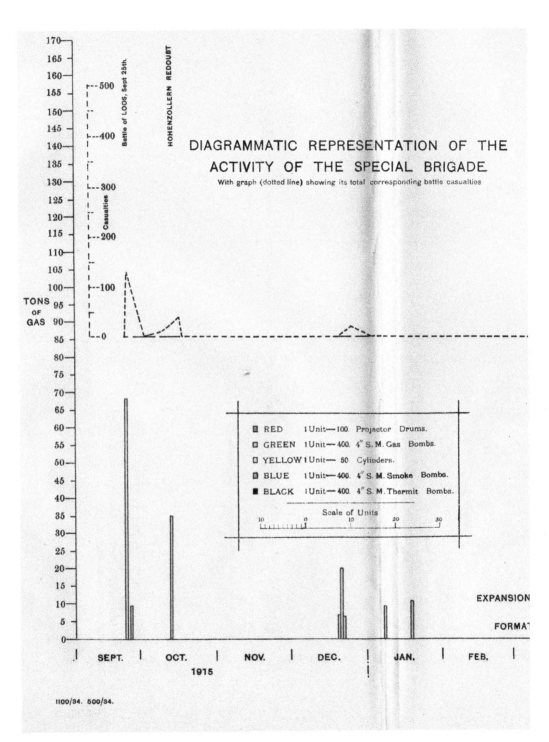

DIAGRAMMATIC REPRESENTATION OF THE
ACTIVITY OF THE SPECIAL BRIGADE

With graph (dotted line) showing its total corresponding battle casualties

Battle of LOOS, Sept 25th.

HOHENZOLLERN REDOUBT

RED   1 Unit — 100. Projector Drums.
GREEN   1 Unit — 400. 4″ S. M. Gas Bombs.
YELLOW   1 Unit — 50 Cylinders.
BLUE   1 Unit — 400. 4″ S. M. Smoke Bombs.
BLACK   1 Unit — 400. 4″ S. M. Thermit Bombs.

Scale of Units
10   0   10   20   30

TONS OF GAS

EXPANSION

FORMAT

SEPT.   OCT.   NOV.   DEC.   JAN.   FEB.

1915

1100/34. 500/34.

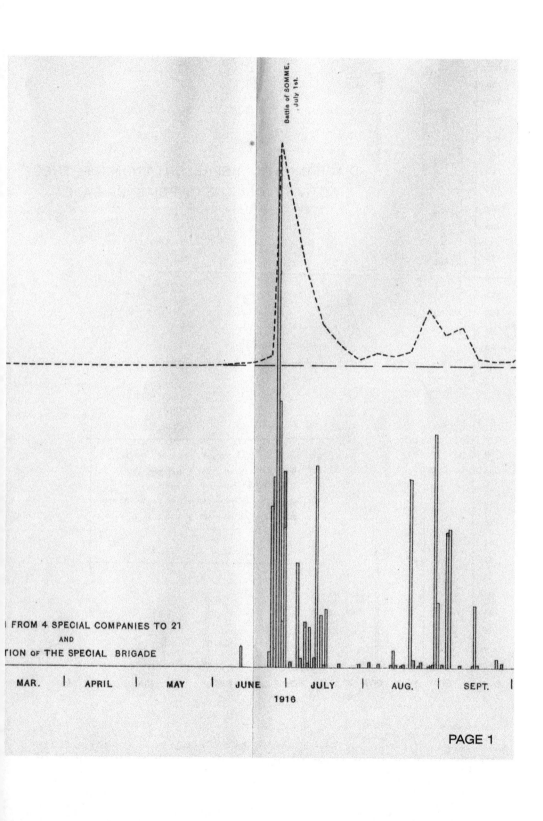

FROM 4 SPECIAL COMPANIES TO 21
AND
TION OF THE SPECIAL BRIGADE

Battle of SOMME.
July 1st.

| MAR. | APRIL | MAY | JUNE | JULY | AUG. | SEPT. |

1916

PAGE 1

DIAGRAMMATIC REPRESENTATION OF THE
ACTIVITY OF THE SPECIAL BRIGADE

With graph (dotted line) showing its total corresponding battle casualties

Battle of ARRAS. April 9th.

OCT. | NOV. | DEC. | JAN. | FEB. | MAR. | APRIL | M

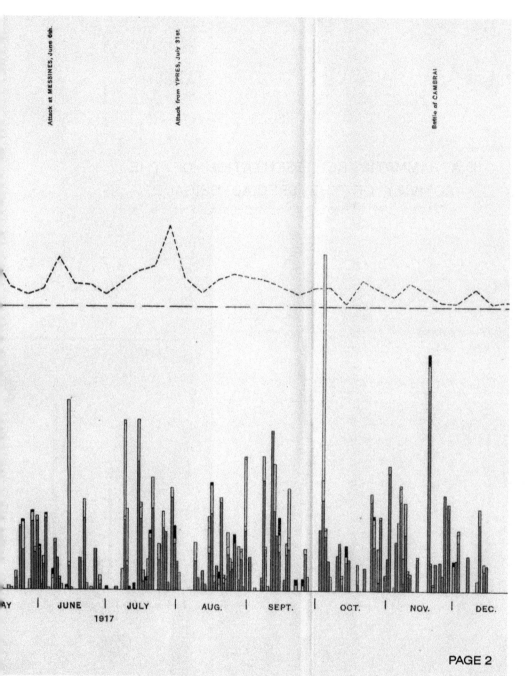

Attack at MESSINES, June 6th.

Attack from YPRES, July 31st.

Battle of CAMBRAI

MAY | JUNE | JULY | AUG. | SEPT. | OCT. | NOV. | DEC.

1917

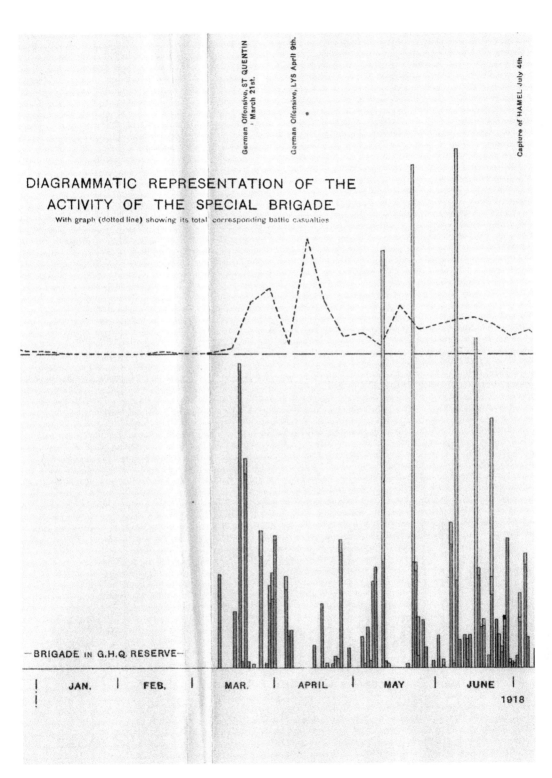

DIAGRAMMATIC REPRESENTATION OF THE
ACTIVITY OF THE SPECIAL BRIGADE

With graph (dotted line) showing its total corresponding battle casualties

German Offensive, ST QUENTIN March 21st.

German Offensive, LYS April 9th.

Capture of HAMEL July 4th.

BRIGADE IN G.H.Q. RESERVE

JAN. | FEB. | MAR. | APRIL | MAY | JUNE

1918

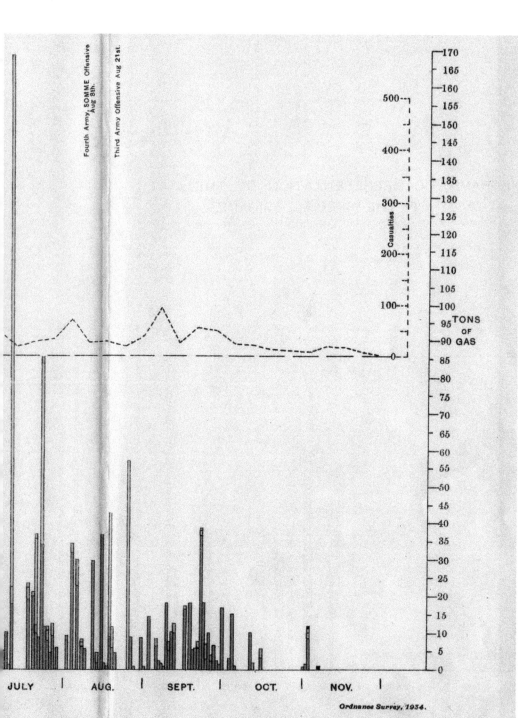

Fourth Army, SOMME Offensive Aug 8th.

Third Army Offensive Aug 21st.

500---

400---

300---

Casualties

200---

100---

JULY   AUG.   SEPT.   OCT.   NOV.

170
165
160
155
150
145
140
135
130
125
120
115
110
105
100
95 TONS
90 OF GAS
85
80
75
70
65
60
55
50
45
40
35
30
25
20
15
10
5
0

Ordnance Survey, 1934.

PAGE 3

1915

JAN.	FEB.	MAR.	APRIL	MAY	JUNE	JULY	AUG.	SEPT.	OCT.	NOV.

6 Cloud Gas Attacks
April 22 - May 24.
Number of casualties approximate
information lacking regarding
number of men casualties sustained
by enemy and number of men
killed in the field by gas.

SCALE OF CASUALTIES

— 7000

CLOUD GAS ATTACKS.   -   -   BLUE
LETHAL SHELL (Phosgene etc) PERIOD. GREEN
MUSTARD GAS PERIOD.   -   - YELLOW
PROJECTOR ATTACKS.   -   -   RED

— 6000

— 5000

— 4000

An unknown but small number of casualties caused by
lachrymatory shells   **May 1915.** ——— July 1916.

— 3000

— 2000

— 1000

— 0

JAN.	FEB.	MAR.	APRIL	MAY	JUNE	JULY	AUG.	SEPT.	OCT.	NOV.

1915

-1915 TO 1918

1916

DEC.	JAN.	FEB.	MAR.	APRIL	MAY	JUNE	JULY	AUG.	SEPT.	OCT.	NOV.	DEC.

Cloud gas attack WIELTJE. Dec 19.

Cloud gas attack HULLUGH. April 27-29.
Cloud gas attack WULVERGHEM. April 30.

Cloud gas attack WULVERGHEM. June 17.

Lethal shell first used July 14-15.

Cloud gas attack WIELTJE Aug 8.

Average mortality Cloud Gas attacks 19-12-15 TO 8-8-16.
=24·0% of casualties.

DEC.	JAN.	FEB.	MAR.	APRIL	MAY	JUNE	JULY	AUG.	SEPT.	OCT.	NOV.	DEC.

1916

1917

| JAN. | FEB. | MAR. | APRIL | MAY | JUNE | JULY | AUG. | SEPT. | OCT. | NOV. | DEC. | JAI |

Battle of ARRAS, April 9.

Battle of MESSINES, JUNE 6.

Yellow Cross first employed. July 12-13.

CAMBRAI advance. Nov 20. BOURLON WOOD Shelled. Nov 30.

Average mortality in Gas Shell
bombardments 15-7-16 TO 12-7-17.
= 6·0% of casualties.

Average mortality in Gas Shell
bombardments 13-7-17 TO 11-11-18.
= 2·5% of casualties.
Average mortality in Projector bombardments
= 18·2% of casualties.

| JAN. | FEB. | MAR. | APRIL | MAY | JUNE | JULY | AUG. | SEPT. | OCT. | NOV. | DEC. | JAI |

1917

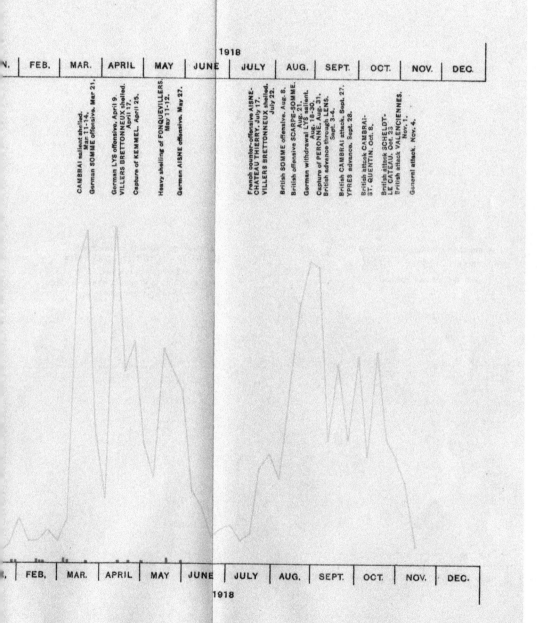

1918

N.	FEB.	MAR.	APRIL	MAY	JUNE	JULY	AUG.	SEPT.	OCT.	NOV.	DEC.

CAMBRAI salient shelled. Mar 11-14.
German SOMME offensive, Mar 21.

German LYS offensive, April 9.
VILLERS BRETTONNEUX shelled. April 17.
Capture of KEMMEL, April 25.

Heavy shelling of FONQUEVILLERS, May 11-12.

German AISNE offensive, May 27.

French counter-offensive AISNE-CHATEAU THIERRY, July 17.
VILLERS BRETTONNEUX shelled, July 22.

British SOMME offensive, Aug. 8.

British offensive SCARPE-SOMME, Aug. 21.
German withdrawal LYS salient, Aug. 18-30.
Capture of PERONNE, Aug. 31.
British advance through LENS, Sept. 3-4.

British CAMBRAI attack, Sept. 27.
YPRES advance, Sept. 28.

British attack CAMBRAI-ST. QUENTIN, Oct. 8.

British attack SCHELDT-LE CATEAU. Oct. 23
British attack VALENCIENNES, Nov. 1.

General attack, Nov. 4.

N.	FEB.	MAR.	APRIL	MAY	JUNE	JULY	AUG.	SEPT.	OCT.	NOV.	DEC.

1918

"GAS!"

THE STORY OF THE SPECIAL BRIGADE.

CHAPTER I.

1914.

By the middle of October 1914, when the Retreat from Mons was already a memory and the German armies were battering at the attenuated British line which guarded Ypres, Colonel Asser landed in France with Captain Ironside [1] as staff officer, and myself among half a dozen engineer officers as assistants, for the purpose of reoccupying Boulogne as a subsidiary base for the British Expeditionary Force. Boulogne had already been used as a base for a short period, but had been abandoned during the retreat on Paris.

The most pressing tasks before us were the extension of the landing facilities in the harbour and the creation of hospitals. The latter was simple work: leases were arranged on generous terms with the owners of all the larger hotels, already closed down, and hospital cots were crowded into them which were immediately filled from the stream of wounded men trickling down from the front. If the owners were absent, or if any delay occurred in the civil negotiations, the procedure was simpler still: the front door lock was forced and the stretchers, already waiting on the pavement outside, were carried straight in. Apologies, of course, followed, and the necessary structural alterations, such as the extemporisation of operating theatres, the provision of special lighting and so on, were carried out according to the varied require ments of the medical staff in each case.

---

[1] Now Quartermaster-General in India.

A dozen large hospitals were established in this rough-and-ready manner in the course of a week, to the astonishment and discomfort of the local contractors employed: the buildings occupied included the Casino and the Golf Hotel at Wimereux, and another on the front which was specially adapted for enteric cases, but which remained practically empty throughout the war—a monument to the genius of the Royal Army Medical Corps.

During this period a young Artillery officer with his arm in a sling described to us the fierce fighting which was going on in the Ypres Salient, and expressed the opinion that nobody could possibly go through this war without being wounded at least once. We laughed at him at the time, but he was not far wrong.

On 8th November I was ordered to the front, together with Captain Eddis who had been stationed with me at Chatham at the outbreak of war and who was destined to be closely associated with me, with only one break, until the Armistice was signed four years later. I was a junior major of nine months' standing, and we reported to the headquarters of the 2nd Division on the Menin road. With us arrived Major Tyler, who, although the senior, offered me choice of command of the two field companies in the Division, in each of which the vacancy existed: he suggested that, as he had a nephew in the 11th Company, perhaps he had better take the 5th. Eddis and I joined the 11th Company in a billet on the outskirts of Zillebeke, and the front we were working on included Shrewsbury Forest, just behind Klein Zillebeke, and the artificial knoll which later became famous as Hill 60. Lord Cavan was in command of this sector.

There seemed to be a tremendous battle going on all around, and the firing line was only about a thousand yards from our billet. The rattle of musketry was almost continuous, and, while the German artillery was extremely active, our own appeared to be non-existent: actually some of the batteries had been withdrawn, as with no ammunition to fire it was useless to keep them in action. Salvoes of German shrapnel, consisting of four shells at a time, burst in the air at unexpected moments during the day and night all over the area and swept the roads in the back regions, while howitzer shells, also fired in salvoes, searched the cross-roads; but, although well directed and accurately 'grouped,' they never appeared to hit anything worth while, as far as I could see. Human remains lay scattered on the surface in Zillebeke church-yard, and an occasional immense crater, perhaps fifteen feet deep, testified to the presence of some of the Austrian super-howitzers which had created such havoc in the Belgian frontier fortresses.

In our front line, on the other hand, the enemy's artillery was very destructive, and my first night's work consisted in re-aligning a battalion trench from the forward edge of a wood, where it had been an easy target, to a position in the interior a couple of hundred yards in rear. Leading a few score men of a Guards battalion in single file, with only the vaguest idea of the direction to be taken, we stumbled over fallen tree-trunks in pitch darkness, felt our way for three or four hundred yards, and finally emerged, to my intense relief, at about the correct connecting spot. The men were then distributed a few yards apart along the line we had followed, and each proceeded to dig a hole which he continued to enlarge for the remainder of the night. All the Chatham principles of field fortification relating to choice of field of fire and so on were necessarily ignored entirely, but the line established that night served its purpose well and was held intact for the rest of the battle.

Half my field company was on detached duty, and K. J. Martin was the only subaltern with me at the time of my arrival: when we got back that night to our farm-house towards dawn, wet through and plastered with mud, it struck me that his manner was strange and incredulous as he watched me sponge down and get into my pyjamas and 'flea-bag.' I had only assumed command just before dark, and was unaware till later that the company had been kept for days in a state of 'constant readiness,' with horses harnessed, and that the men had strict orders not even to take off their boots! A few days previously this officer and our company sergeant-major, Higgins, a noted shot on the Aldershot ranges, had picked off no fewer than forty-five Germans between them from the upper windows of a house in Klein Zillebeke, each 'spotting' for the other in turn and chalking up the score on the wall! Martin was badly wounded in the wrist on the second night after my arrival, but he had to be almost forcibly put into an ambulance and removed to hospital, where he remained for some months. I used to recall this incident when, later on, I sometimes heard men—and officers too—rejoice openly and without shame in the receipt of what was known as a ' Blighty ' wound.[1]

The 11th November was the occasion of the great attack of the Prussian Guards Division which penetrated deep into our front astride the Menin road and reached the line of our artillery. Altogether twenty-five fresh battalions of the most famous regiments of the German Army moved to the assault of that part of our line. Lord Cavan's sector adjoining it immediately to the south was also heavily attacked, but although opposed to odds of five to one, as well as a tremendous artillery bombardment, it held its front intact. The half of my company which I had not yet seen was involved in the infantry fighting and lost both its officers, young Tyler being killed. The 5th Company took part in the successful counter-attack on the Guards regiments, and Major Tyler and two of his officers were killed that day and the remaining two were wounded. This was the occasion when five cooks and duty men of the 5th Company, the very last British reserves in this sector, assaulted on their own initiative a farmhouse which had been taken by the enemy and captured the occupants. As a result of this day's fighting Eddis left me to take charge of the other half of the 11th Company, while the last subaltern remaining in the latter became commander of the 5th. We therefore had only three officers left in the two field companies, instead of twelve.

The troops in our sector were really nothing more than an outpost line and were mixed up anyhow at this period, Guards alternating with Irish battalions, the London Scottish and cavalry regiments, each unit having been reduced to about a quarter of its proper strength. All were in the front line, there being only a little wire [2] in places, and no communication trenches or dug-outs, and no supports or reserves apart from what was left of the

---

[1] It will be remembered that ' Sir Nigel,' during one of his frequent enforced absences from the front line, after he had ' stopped one,' said : " I have indeed had some small hurt, but it is shame and sorrow that I should be here if there is work for my hands."

[2] The Guards battalions refused to let us put wire in front of them, as they said that they did not need it ! They asked only for a trip wire, with tins hung on it, to give the alarm at night.

field companies. It was only at night that communication could be obtained with the troops, the sorting out of units arranged or supplies got up and the wounded removed. These sketchy fortifications were described in the German official account of the battle as " a well-planned maze of trenches behind barbed wire entanglements dug by picked troops before a single German shell arrived to disturb their work " ; and although our men were only equipped in those days with two machine-guns per battalion, half of which had already been destroyed by bombardment, their rifle fire was so effective that in the same account it was said that " over every bush, hedge and fragment of wall floated a film of smoke betraying a machine-gun rattling out bullets."

We ourselves of the Engineers were always within the immediate call of Brigade Headquarters, and got what rest we could during the daytime, besides collecting material and organising the next night's work. As soon as it was dusk we moved forward to carry out some pre-arranged task ; and with the darkness came adventure of some kind. All our work lay in No Man's Land, the limits of which were not always clearly defined. I spent some hours one night in a reconnaissance through the woods, guided only by the rifle flashes of both armies, in company with a private of the Welch Regiment, a miner called Jones. This man was a born scout, and he passed several times right through the German lines, and had spent whole nights in their rear collecting what information he could and returning in some miraculous manner before daybreak.

Once we were called upon to construct a small work for riflemen half-way between the opposing forces and a hundred yards from a German field-gun which had been established in a forward position and which had caused a lot of damage during the previous day. This little redoubt was connected at the same time to our front line by a communication trench which zigzagged among the trees ; and the sappers worked at it steadily all through the night, with a few sentries posted out beyond them, while an occasional shell burst in front and rifle bullets slapped the tree-trunks. I lost several men that night, one of whom, shot in the throat, fell up against me : we were obviously being fired at by someone from very close range, though the flash from the rifle could not be distinguished. After peering in every direction for a long while I was able at last to make out a shadowy form—not twenty yards away and well within our line of sentries—slowly and clumsily ascending the trunk of a tree with the help of what appeared to be climbing-irons : waiting till he became stationary on reaching the lower branches, I pointed my Mauser pistol in his direction, the sights and barrel being quite invisible in the darkness of the wood, and emptied the magazine. There was no comforting thud of a heavy body falling to the ground and nothing could be seen in the tree, but there was no more sniping that night. It is probable that at this period the Germans sent trained foresters prowling in the woods, the flashes from whose rifles could easily pass unobserved from the height of a tree-top ; and it seemed even possible that they were provided with powerful air-guns. Some of the enemy were supposed to have penetrated our lines and to have taken up concealed positions in haystacks and derelict windmills with a supply of food and ammunition, and to have picked off individuals in daylight whenever circumstances precluded the likelihood of discovery. There was no doubt whatever about the bravery of the German soldier, and in fact his courage did not desert him even during the final period of adversity and defeat.

At this time the village of Zillebeke was still almost intact, though it was constantly being shelled at irregular intervals, and people generally gave it a wide berth.

One night I was taking a short-cut through it when I heard the distant whine of German shells. We had quickly become expert in judging from their sound the nature of approaching projectiles ; and as the drone increased in volume and changed in tone I realised that it heralded the arrival of a salvo of big howitzer shells which would probably fall in this favourite target. I flattened myself on the roadway, opposite the church tower, and looked out sideways to see what would happen. The whine increased to a scream and then to a roar, and with a deafening explosion the shells burst all around : the air was filled with blinding flashes ; paving stones, bricks and bits of flying metal were scattered in all directions and rebounded from the walls of the houses or were flung far out into the fields ; tiles clattered from the roofs and I found myself covered with dust and débris, but without a scratch. When I picked myself up there was one shell crater in the middle of the road, still fuming, and I burnt my hand on a solid lump of jagged iron which lay on the pavement.

One of our tasks was to site a line of rifle-pits across an open space between two woods: this gap, two or three hundred yards wide, was only held by patrols at night and it was defended in the daytime by a machine-gun posted on each flank. Getting touch with the occupants of the adjoining trenches was hazardous in the extreme, as the men, suspecting a ruse, generally greeted one with rifles at the 'present' and fingers on the trigger. It was said that more than once during the preceding weeks the Germans had been able to approach our front line at night by calling out " Engineer working party."

On another night, just after we had left Brigade Head-quarters on our way to work, an infantry officer who was being carried back on a blood-soaked stretcher called out to inquire if there was an officer with my party. He begged me to return at once to the brigade commander and tell him that half an hour previously the enemy had captured the whole of his battalion's line, had mounted machine-guns on the parapet and that a break-through was a certainty. I repeated this alarming story to Lord Cavan, who inquired calmly the officer's name and regiment and whether he seemed badly wounded. I gave him this information and said that he had been shot through the groin from side to side. " Then don't believe a word of it," he said with a smile.

Under his directions I proceeded to put my men, by this time reduced in number to about twenty-five, at the disposal of the Colonel of the London Scottish, whom I found quite unperturbed and in no need of assistance: nor was there any truth in the story of the break-through. I had had a similar experience with a wounded officer in the South African campaign and have related the incident for the benefit of the youthful reader.

At dawn on the 20th November we tramped out of the Salient after a long night's work, draggled and weary: the fighting had died down, French territorials were pour-ing in to relieve our troops and we were on the way to join the Guards Brigade in reserve billets in Meteren. My men had been all through this battle, as well as the Retreat, and were in high spirits at the prospect of a rest; and as we ran the gauntlet of the Lille gate and entered the Poperinghe road they cheered derisively at the huge shells which fell four at a time in the deserted railway station, throwing up clouds of dust and débris a hundred feet into the air.

Four or five miles away in the north of the Salient a few Verey lights floated lazily in the sky and cast sharp shadows across our road: these were the first we had seen and were, if I had realised it at the time, a beacon signal to mark the spot where five months later a new phase in civilised warfare was to be staged, one which would affect me personally more than anyone else and would occupy all my energies until the conclusion of hostilities.

At the end of the first battle of Ypres the battalions which took part in it contained on an average only one officer and thirty men of their original expeditionary personnel, and a few of the units had been completely annihilated. The successful defence of the Salient was the proudest achievement of the British Army during the whole war; and among my vivid recollections of that period is one of a dapper little brigadier sitting all through the night at a table with an oil lamp in front of him and a rug over his knees, while in a corner of the farmhouse staff officers took turns to sleep on the floor; welcoming all comers with a cheery smile and listening attentively to their reports, imperturbable and lion-hearted.

The next few weeks we spent in refitting, and among the four subalterns who joined the company to make up losses was McNeile ("Sapper"), now well known as the author of 'Bulldog Drummond,' &c. We were also called upon to exercise our ingenuity in extemporising hand-grenades out of empty jam-tins and trench-mortars from any odd lengths of iron piping that could be found.

On 22nd December we marched twenty-five miles at short notice to support an Indian division which had been heavily attacked at Givenchy; and for the next five months we remained in the line without an interval, alternating between the Festubert, Givenchy and La Bassée sectors, and working with the 5th, 6th and Guards Brigades, all in the 2nd Division.

A great deal of our work consisted in putting up wire entanglements in front of the parapet at night, and as this

The Lille Gate, Ypres.
(At the time of the Armistice.)

Battle of Festubert.　The German front line.

involved driving in stakes which could not be done without noise, and the Germans were in some places only sixty yards away, we suffered a good many casualties from rifle fire which, although unaimed, was continuous. We also had a number of men hit by jumpy sentries in spite of every precaution taken to warn our own infantry that we were still working out in front of them. I lost several officers in this way : in one instance in which a subaltern was shot (he died in hospital) I was told when I went to inquire into the accident that the sentry had called out, "Who's that?" The reply was, "Engineer officer"; and so of course he fired !

On 1st February, while one section of the company was at work in the 'Railway hollow' on the La Bassée canal, the Germans suddenly launched a local attack and took the hollow from the Coldstream Guards. The Irish Guards who were in support tried to recapture it, but failed and asked for another chance the next day. The Coldstreams, however, claimed that this was their affair, and in due course advanced and retook the position. This was the occasion on which Michael O'Leary won his Victoria Cross after accounting for ten Germans, including the whole of a machine-gun crew. As soon as it was dark that night we went up to consolidate the position ; and in the course of a preliminary exploration to find out what the exact situation was I entered the German trench which had been held by the enemy all day, accompanied by a sapper orderly : leaving him posted at a fork, I proceeded cautiously in the bright moonlight and was able to get nearly half-way to the 'Brickstacks' which lay between us and the La Bassée road without meeting anyone. The Germans appeared to have abandoned this trench in a panic, together with all their rifles and equipment : I saw clips of cartridges laid out ready for use behind the parapet and rows of spiked helmets. We might have removed a hundred rifles that night without interference if there had been nothing else to do : as it was, I selected a good specimen of a pickelhaube as a trophy and a steel body-shield on my way back. Eddis was wounded that night while at work on the new defensive line, as well as one of my subalterns.

Five days later came the assault of the Guards Brigade on the 'Brickstacks' : this was a very successful little operation, well planned and executed in a manner reminiscent of the movements of a musical ride at the Military Tournament. There was an artillery bombardment of only a quarter of an hour, and from the forward position in which my company was posted, ready to break down a sand-bag barricade and join the second wave of the assaulting troops, I watched our howitzer projectiles falling into the German trenches only fifty yards away and could easily distinguish each one in the air, looking like a long black pencil, just before it struck the ground. I had one man killed on this occasion, and the Guards had a very few casualties, but we found about forty dead Germans and took twenty prisoners. The enemy must have retired a long way back because on reaching our objectives we were able to walk about in the open for an hour or two and select and adjust the exact line which it was considered best to take up : we blocked the German communication trenches with sand-bag barricades and even completed a wire entanglement in broad daylight, a feat which can have been rarely repeated in the whole course of the war.

Eight days afterwards there was further fighting in this sector which then formed the extreme right of the line held by the British Expeditionary Force and ended on the Bethune-La Bassée road. The French front line also ended on this road, but a hundred yards behind our own, and there was no communication between the two systems except at a point some way back. The German line, too, on the French side of the road ended abruptly on the latter fifty yards beyond us. In the attack of 14th February the plan was for the French to advance across the open in daylight and take the German trench in front of them, while we were to co-operate with them by fire and then move forward as soon as it was dark and dig a new line in continuation of theirs. I was put in charge of the latter operation and had a company of Grenadiers under Captain Clive to assist my own : we got plenty of barbed wire ready, so as to wire the new line the same night and do the whole thing in style.

The French advance was quite successful, but as long as there was daylight it was not possible for their supporting troops to gain touch with the infantry in the German trench, or even to find out how they had fared ; and while

Clive and I were waiting for the light to fade a French sergeant arrived to inquire if we could give his commander any news. Presently we all three walked down the La Bassée road, and on reaching the German trench we called out to ask who was there. Receiving no reply and fearing the worst we entered the trench without seeing anyone and walked along it for a little way, recognising French rifles and equipment here and there, past a dug-out in which we blew out a lighted candle, till we met a group of men to whom we repeated our question. Their reply was unintelligible to Clive and me, but as it was a long time since we had left school we thought we might be listening to some kind of patois to which our ears were not tuned.

Fortunately it was a very dark night, and the conversation proceeded at cross-purposes for a little while before the authoritative voice of an officer broke in. Clive at once said, " These are bosches : we had better clear out " ; and we turned and ran back along the trench to the road, where we were fired at point-blank by a sentry who had now appeared on the scene. We then made a hurried and undignified retreat across the open, stumbling over French corpses on the way, while Verey lights were shot in the air and rifle and machine-gun fire pursued us ; pandemonium broke loose and the firing was immediately taken up all along the line. When we got back into our own trench we found the French sergeant there, panting and minus his rifle : he had recognised the first syllable uttered by the Germans, and had bolted without warning us, probably because he did not realise that we could fail to recognise the language spoken. It appeared that the French troops had been bombed out of the position they had won and the survivors had been taken prisoner.

(An account of this adventure was written by " Eye-Witness.")

About this time we commenced some of the earliest of the mining operations, but these were soon taken over from the field companies by the tunnelling units which were being formed.

On 10th March we took part in the unsuccessful attack at Givenchy which was planned in co-operation with the assault of the 8th Division at Neuve Chapelle ; and for weeks we were employed continuously in strengthening defences and in renewing the wire entanglements. All this time, in addition to exercising general supervision over the work of the company, I had to command one or other of the sections, owing to casualties among the subalterns.

We were in support of the 1st Division in their unsuccessful attack on the Aubers Ridge on 9th May, and took over the situation from them. On the 15th May we joined the assaulting columns of the 6th Brigade when they made their night attack at Festubert and captured the German first and second lines almost without opposition. On the following morning I was accompanying my brigadier (Fanshawe) along the maze of captured trenches in an endeavour to get contact with the various units, when we reached a point from which there seemed to be no exit except across the open. Here we found Trefusis, commanding the Irish Guards, who was reconnoitring the position with a view to continuing the advance. We watched some stretcher-bearers traversing this space without being interfered with, and as chivalrous conduct of this kind was outside our previous experience of the enemy we concluded that the ground was hidden from their observation. We decided, therefore, to make a dash for it, but had not gone far before bullets zipped past our ears ; and when, after covering a couple of hundred yards in very good time, we reached cover and were able to compare notes, Trefusis pointed to a tear in the side of his jacket, just above the belt, which had been cut by a bullet during our run. This officer had had many narrow escapes, and he was killed five months later when in command of a brigade.

All the units of the 2nd Division suffered very heavily from the German artillery bombardment during this battle, and my own company had thirty-one casualties (a quarter of its strength), including two officers, one of whom was killed. I myself was nearly hit when sitting on a fire-step in a trench waiting for orders : Sim, my second-in-command, was by me, separated only by the width of his haversack which was in contact with both of us, when a large piece of shell dropped vertically between our heads and embedded itself deeply in the tin of bully-beef which was in the haversack. Previously, during the affair of the 'Brickstacks,' a portion of a spent high-

"No Man's Land."   Preparations for the assault.

Photo. by C. R. Alderson.

Draft from different line regiments arriving at Helfaut to form
the Special Brigade, 1915.

explosive shell the size of a finger-joint had dropped on my forage-cap and had stuck in there without cutting the skin. Another shell burst inside my bedroom on the top floor of the company billet in Cambrin while I was below ; and for months past I had spent nearly the whole of every night walking about among the sapper working parties, sometimes less than one hundred yards from the German line, fully exposed to rifle fire and depending only on the darkness for safety. In this type of occupation one became as expert in judging the proximity of fleeting rifle bullets as the probable fall of howitzer shells, their sound varying between the musical whine of one passing high overhead—a ' try-on ' directed more or less at random over the back area—to the vicious staccato zitt ! which indicated an aimed shot and a very narrow miss. I am quite confident that given a certain temperament a man can cultivate the absolute conviction that nothing can harm him.

In the early months of the war Engineer units were not used to the best advantage and their mechanical skill was to a large extent wasted : the reserve of regular officers was soon exhausted, and, as a consequence, after the first nine months the field companies were forbidden to do wiring, which thereupon became an infantry duty. The construction of footbridges and placing them in position across disused trenches in No Man's Land, and the destruction of wire on the German parapet with ' Bangalore torpedoes ' during the night preceding an infantry assault, were ordinary Engineer duties, and, of course, employment as infantry in times of emergency ; but wiring and the routine reconnaissance of the enemy's entanglements were not work for skilled craftsmen.[1]   It was wrong, too, to send field companies forward with assaulting columns, but when I pointed this out with some hesitation I was told that the infantry liked to have us alongside ; and as all our sympathy lay with them it was impossible to make any further protest. Some of the tasks proposed to us were fantastic : for instance, I was asked once to detail an officer to swim along the La Bassée

---

[1] In his book recently published, ' Trekking On,' Colonel Reitz says : " An order to examine enemy wire entanglements was looked upon as almost tantamount to a death sentence." It was, of course, anything but this, as we constantly did it ; but it was an infantry duty all the same.

canal, floating a load of explosives with him with which he was to destroy a small footbridge half a mile inside the German lines. The bridge itself was a temporary one and of no importance, and as the tow-path was in constant use by the enemy as a communication route the task was obviously impossible, even at night.

Four days after being withdrawn from the battle of Festubert we were sent up again to work with the Guards Brigade which was now coming into action.

I was on the road at the head of my company, with orders to report to Lord Cavan, when the driver of a motor-car stopped us and handed me a note from the headquarters of the division ordering me to go to Advanced G.H.Q. at Hazebrouck. I scribbled a reply to the effect that I had a definite rendezvous and that I would comply as soon as I had gained contact with the brigadier.

Later in the same day the driver returned with a peremptory order for me to leave the company at once, and it was evident that something unusual was afoot. I transferred my kit to the car and said good-bye to the men who had been my close companions for the last six months and to whom I was sincerely attached. There were no braver soldiers in the British Army—not even among the Guards, who are easily the best infantry in the world—and no more resolute and dependable officers and N.C.O.'s : on not one single occasion had they ever returned from a night's expedition with their set task unaccomplished, whatever the difficulties they had experienced or the intensity of the fire to which they had been exposed ; and the losses they had suffered may be judged from the fact that among the officers alone, although the establishment of the unit was only six, there had been up till now no fewer than twenty-four casualties during eight months' fighting, an experience which was shared to a similar degree by most of the other field companies in the Regular Army. Little or no engineering knowledge was required during this period of trench warfare, and by far the most important qualifications for a field company officer were a stout heart and a smiling face. The subalterns who passed through the engineering school at Chatham in the few pre-war years were, thanks largely to a remarkable commandant, (now) Sir John Capper, magnificent material, and the high percentage of loss among them in the early days of the war was a calamity.

I had no idea why I was wanted, but something told me that I was leaving these men for good, and the life I had been leading, and a scene which was anything but the nightmare of blood and horror, of depression and morbid self-pity, which it is too often represented as being by modern novelists, but one in which determined men faced discomfort and danger with a joke and a smile, found inspiration in a difficult duty well done and exaltation in the adventure. The last few months had been passed in the wettest and most active part of the line, but I had never caught a cold (except when on leave in England) or had a headache. I can honestly assert that I had thoroughly enjoyed every minute of the time ; and —what may seem still more incredible—I had never even seen a louse !

CHAPTER II.

THE FIRST GERMAN GAS ATTACK.

ON my way to Hazebrouck I had time to speculate on the object of my journey. We had heard vaguely about the German gas attacks at Ypres and of the subsequent fighting which had stabilised the situation there; but we had been far too occupied with our own affairs to think much about other people's troubles elsewhere in the line. Still, although the summons had come to me as a complete surprise, I did not exclude the subject of gas from my thoughts.

'Advanced G.H.Q.' was the title given throughout the war to the position, wherever it might be, occupied by the Commander-in-Chief and a few of his staff officers who were directly concerned with the conduct of operations. When I reached Hazebrouck I found myself in an unaccustomed atmosphere: my worn uniform with its brass buttons purposely kept dull, and its tell-tale marks of long association with mud and barbed wire, was in strong contrast with the smart kits and polished top-boots at headquarters. I was still wearing my forage-cap which had been cut with a shell splinter, and was carrying an automatic pistol strapped to my belt at which nervous glances were cast and which I was asked politely to remove a few days later. A junior staff officer met me and ushered me into the presence of General Robertson, Sir John French's Chief of Staff at that time. "You're for it!" I was told before entering the room; "we've been waiting for you all day."

There was a short silence after the door closed. "Why didn't you come when I sent for you?" I was asked. I explained the position I had been in and my personal responsibility to Lord Cavan, and added: "Besides, it's most unusual to interrupt a man in the middle of a battle" —an argument which appeared to put my redoubtable interrogator into a good humour. This was not our first meeting, as ten years previously I had amused myself during a three months' leave in visiting an important foreign fortress where I corrected the maps (which in such localities are often drawn incorrectly with intent to deceive), sketched the fortifications and took some dozens of photographs with a telescopic lens—all of which I had placed at his disposal.

"Do you know anything about gas?" he next asked, to which I replied quite truthfully, "Nothing at all." "Well, I don't think it matters," he went on; "I want you to take charge of our gas reprisals here in France. Something is going on in London, and you must cross over and find out all about it. Then come back here and tell me what you propose to do"; and with this I was dismissed.

Soon afterwards I found myself promoted to Lieut.-Colonel, with the title of "Gas Adviser"! This was now the 26th May 1915, and I reached the War Office at mid-day on the 27th with a letter to General von Donop, the Master-General of Ordnance, in which General Robertson said :—

"The employment of gas may develop into a big thing, and all branches of the staff here feel that gas may become a fifth arm and that we need some officer at G.H.Q. who will deal with the question as a whole.

"The C.-in-C. has therefore appointed Major Foulkes, R.E., for this duty. He has no pretence to technical knowledge, as far as I know, and it is not considered that he need have very much. But he has had much experience at the front, and can explain generally what we need and how we can perhaps best use it."

I was told by General von Donop to get in touch with Colonel Jackson, an Engineer officer and an old friend, who was employed at the War Office at the time under the Director of Fortifications and Works.

I did not do this immediately, as it had occurred to me when crossing the Channel that if the Germans were going to ignore the usages of civilised warfare they would certainly not hesitate to resort to bacteriological methods if better results were to be obtained with communicable disease, in which case gas might already be obsolescent.

I therefore visited the Lister Institute first, and spent

some hours there with an official who was good enough to survey the whole field of speculation for my benefit.

I decided finally that it was no use pursuing the matter, as there appeared to be no great danger in this direction in the present state of knowledge owing to the risk of infection to the side introducing germs, to the difficulty of keeping cultures of cholera, typhus, enteric and so on, alive, and of conveying them to water supplies, &c., either by projectiles, by aircraft or secret agents, and to the ease with which in modern hygienic practice almost any outbreak of disease can be suppressed at the source through the isolation of its victims.[1] (I did not know at this time that the Germans in their retreat had poisoned the wells in South-West Africa with arsenic, and had issued orders " to thoroughly infect with disease " the water in certain places. At a later stage of the war in France the poisoning of water by them was reported more than once from the Ypres district, but this was never confirmed. Such action may, however, have been considered, as General Ludendorff,[2] in describing the deliberate devastation of the country during the German retreat in March 1917, from the Somme battlefield to the Siegfried Line, says, " Poisoning of the wells was forbidden."

The " Zurich bomb and bacilli case," too, was supposed to have disclosed an intention on the part of the Central Powers to infect the Roumanian cavalry with glanders ; and the attempt was also alleged of conveying cholera cultures into Russia in fountain-pens.)

I ought, perhaps, to interrupt my story at this point in order to remind my readers of what had actually happened at Ypres in April, and to explain why a delay of five weeks had occurred before definite steps were taken to give the Germans a dose of their own medicine.

It appears from conflicting accounts that at 5 P.M. on the 22nd April a German balloon was hoisted in the north-east of the Ypres Salient, and from it three flares were dropped as a signal. The enemy then discharged their first gas cloud, which was directed on French-African troops. It was unfortunate that the latter were in the

---

[1] If the same effort had been expended during the war on bacteriological as on chemical research the situation might well have developed differently.
[2] ' My War Memories.'

line at the time, as only a few days previously they had relieved a much better French division, whereas the gas had been installed in the trenches for some weeks, ready for discharge and was only awaiting a favourable wind.

The immediate tactical effect of the gas attack was very considerable, and it was described in the following words in Sir John French's despatch of the 15th June 1915 :—

> "What followed is practically indescribable. The effect of the gas was so overwhelming that the whole of the positions occupied by the French Divisions was rendered incapable of any resistance. It was impossible at first to realise what had actually happened. Fumes and smoke obscured everything. Hundreds of men were thrown into a stupor, and after an hour the whole position had to be abandoned together with fifty guns."

This discharge was followed by a number of others against British troops during the next week or two, but in none of these cases was there any considerable loss of ground.

The Canadians who were next in line to the French on the 22nd were hardly affected by the gas on that day, but they had heavy losses in the next gas attack two days later, though they stood their ground ; while other divisions suffered more or less severely when gas was discharged against them on the 1st, 6th, 10th and 24th May. On all these last four occasions they were provided with hastily improvised respirators which were not very efficient, and in the use of which they had had little or no instruction.

On 23rd April Sir John French telegraphed an account of the first gas attack to the War Office and asked for a supply of suitable respirators ; he also urged that immediate steps be taken in retaliation to supply similar means of the most effective kind for the use of our own troops.

To this Lord Kitchener replied on the 24th :—
" The use of asphyxiating gases is, as you are aware, contrary to the rules and usages of war. Before we fall to the level of the degraded Germans I must submit the matter to the Government. These methods show to what

depths of infamy our enemies will go in order to supplement their want of courage in facing our troops."

These were hard words, but they were justified in view of the deep feeling which had been aroused and in the recollection of the conditions during the first battle of Ypres, in which, in spite of an immense superiority in numbers and of heavy and field artillery, the German attacks, carried out by their best troops and inspired by the presence of the Kaiser himself, had been brought to a standstill.

It will perhaps be remembered that at this time political interest at home was centred in the formation of the Coalition Government, which came into being on the 27th May and in which Mr Lloyd George became the Minister of Munitions. Prior to this date Government spokesmen, in reply to inquiries in Parliament, had stated that the question of gas retaliation was under consideration.

The War Minister had apparently some difficulty in obtaining Cabinet sanction [1] for undertaking reprisals, because it was not until the 18th May that he announced in public that protection must be given to our troops and the French by the employment of similar methods. Even then it was to be understood that "only gases were to be used which were as harmful, but not much more so, than those used by the enemy, though preparations and experiments might proceed for the employment of more deadly things."

As German troops were known to have suffered appreciable losses from their own gas in the course of their earliest discharges, the hesitation to retaliate on the part of our Government may have been partly due to the manifest danger to the users.

Public opinion, too, was divided on the subject (as it was later in regard to air reprisals), and one writer to the Press suggested a new convention to forbid the use of gas "so as to avert war's latest and worst horror." Lord Armstrong in another letter urged retaliation, but, in order to avoid imitation of the barbarous cruelty of the Germans, he suggested the preparation of a gas that

[1] Similarly it was only on 29th June 1915 that M. Millerand said in the French Senate : " Nous sommes décidés à suivre nos ennemis sur tous les terrains, quelles que soient les armes qu'ils emploient. Nos chimistes, ceux du Ministre, comme ceux de l'Academie, travaillent activement au problème des gaz asphyxiants."

would produce temporary unconsciousness and cause no ultimate injurious effect ; while the Bishop of Pretoria, in a patriotic and vigorous attempt to arrest the strikes at home and to rouse the nation to support the troops at the front, deprecated, in a letter to the ' Times,' descending to the level of the Germans by reprisals with gas, and added, " Perhaps next we shall hear of reprisals by poisoning water supplies ! "

The attitude of the German people at this period is also of some historical interest, as it affords an illustration of how easily—almost willingly—the conscience of a nation can be dulled and its support enlisted when the Government chooses to snap its fingers at its international obligations. Professor Wegener wrote in the ' Cologne Gazette ': " I am not going into the silly chatter about the unlawfulness of our new weapon of attack " ; and the same paper argued that the letting loose of " smoke clouds " is not only permissible by international law, but it is an exceedingly mild method of war. The introduction of " stupefying gases " into an enemy trench is similar to flooding an area with water ; and the article concluded by saying that it was only an incapacity to emulate the results of German science which had caused the enemy to raise an outcry against the employment of gas. Still another writer excused the use of gas " as it inflicted a quick and painless death " ; and a similar argument was employed in a well - known New York paper which described gas as " a real step in the direction of making war humane."

The attempt has been and still continues to be made to foist the responsibility for the introduction of gas warfare on to the Allies. In a pamphlet translated from the German and published in Stockholm in 1916, the British example was quoted of the illegal use of gas in the Boer War when " vultures feeding on horses killed by Lyddite shells invariably died." Reference was also made to the German official communiqués of the 13th, 14th, 16th and 17th April 1915, which announced that the French at Suippes and Verdun and the British at Ypres had repeatedly used gas projectiles and minenwerfer, and that the use of gas bombs and asphyxiating explosive shells was on the increase in the French Army. " To an unprejudiced mind it would appear that these official declarations coming from the German War Ministry, always known for its strict accuracy, would be ample proof of our adversaries having used asphyxiating gas." The writer went on to say: "Even the smoke device used by us in an attack at close range does in no way conflict with the law" (the Hague Convention) "as its effect is no more harmful than that produced by burning twigs or straw; besides, the rising smoke being distinctly visible even at night, a chance of evading the same in time is always possible. As the enemy has the chance to retire, why should we differentiate between water and vapour attacks?"—the reference here is to the inundations about Dixmude. "Why should they rise in indignation when we make use of air for our attacks?"

An American journal, published in May 1915 and obviously inspired, called attention to French poison shells, "the wounds from which cause death under the most dreadful agonies within four hours"; while other American papers attributed the destruction of the *Lusitania* to the fact that it was carrying a large quantity of chemicals prepared in Pittsburg for conversion into asphyxiating gases by the French Government, "who therefore had a share in the *Lusitania* disaster." One of these papers, published on the 10th May (the *Lusitania* was sunk on the 7th), claimed to have actually predicted the catastrophe on account of this cargo, and it described the dreadful scenes as the passengers, suffering from the effects of the fumes, struggled to the deck.

As the majority of the German people are still said to believe firmly that the Allies were the first to use gas, and as some ignorance on this subject perhaps still exists in this country, I want to show what little basis there is for the contention: our entire ignorance of the whole subject was particularly evident to me when the question of retaliation came to be considered, and very little help was available at the beginning, even from our most eminent scientists.

Without going far back into history it may be mentioned that a few years before the outbreak of the Great War the question was examined in this country of the possibility of poisonous gases being used in warfare; but the matter was shelved in view of the wording of the Hague Convention, which was as follows: "The con-

tracting Powers agree to abstain from the use of projectiles the sole object of which is the diffusion of asphyxiating or deleterious gases." But later on, in 1913, as the
result of an article in a foreign newspaper which indicated
that the matter was being investigated abroad, the wording of the Hague Convention was scrutinised officially;
and while it was held on high legal authority that a
"double purpose" shell—*i.e.*, one which contained a
small portion of a *lachrymatory* substance which had no
asphyxiating or deleterious effect, might not be considered
to infringe the wording of the Convention, although
contrary to its spirit, it was decided that such a projectile
was not to be used either in the British Army or Navy.
The Hague Convention made allowance for the gases
which are necessarily released by all high explosive shells,
but its intention undoubtedly was to prohibit any employment of poison gas as such; so that its deliberate use
in a shell specially designed for the purpose, or by any
other method of release, such as in a cloud, was obviously
illegal and was not even open to debate.

In December 1914, officers who had served in France
inquired privately when in England as to the possibility
of 'stink-bombs' being used for clearing dug-outs; and
a number of lachrymatory substances were examined at
the Imperial College of Science. Most of these were
rejected as contravening the Convention, but one was
indicated which experiments had shown to possess powerful
lachrymatory, without any marked asphyxiating or deleterious properties. The offer was made unofficially to
Sir John French to send "stink-bombs" containing this
substance to France "in case similar methods were
resorted to by the enemy," but it was rejected by the
Commander-in-Chief: it is, of course, impossible that the
Germans can have even heard of the proposal at the time.

Ethyl iodoacetate (known later as 'SK,' after South
Kensington) was the substance referred to, and some of it
was used for the first time ten months later at the battle
of Loos, when six hundred experimental 4.5-inch 'SK'
howitzer shells were fired into the village of Loos. Two
thousand of these shells were expended altogether in that
battle by the First Army, but as these were unsatisfactory
it was another year before properly designed 'SK' shells
were supplied for the use of our artillery; and it was only

in April 1917 that any *lethal* substance was employed by the British Army for the first time in artillery projectiles. Before this, however, in the autumn of 1916, gas trench mortar bombs were extemporised in France by the Special Brigade (I am referring to the earliest experimental 'projector' drums made from welded sheet steel), and were filled from cloud gas cylinders.

As for the French they were occupied at the same time as ourselves in similar investigations, and they were equally careful not to infringe the sense of the Hague Convention. (Professor Kling, the Director of the Municipal laboratories of Paris, who was the chief French chemist engaged in war research work, has recently (April 1933) denied vigorously the German allegation that gas was first used by the French Army, and has explained that the lachrymatory gas employed in the capture of the Bonnot gang of motor bandits was made use of for police purposes only.) Judging from the state of their experimental work when I investigated it in Paris in June 1915, they were in no better condition than ourselves to use gas either in cylinders or in bombs or artillery projectiles.

In a German history by Dr Hanslian [1] published in 1924, the 'Pall Mall Gazette' of 17th September 1914 was quoted as having contained the first reference to the preparations that were being made by the Allies to use poison gas, but when our own historians came to verify the reference it was found to be quite untrue : it was the new French *explosive* 'Turpinite' that had been mentioned in the 'Gazette,' for which, it may be remembered, the sensational claim was made that an instant and painless death would be caused to everyone within four hundred yards of the explosion of the shell. Dr Hanslian seems to have been guilty of a similar error (which, nevertheless, had its propaganda value) in stating that a French Ministerial document of 21st February 1915 contained instructions as to the employment of hand-grenades with chlor and bromacetone (lachrymator) fillings. He says that these were first filled on the 7th January 1915, and were first used at the front in March of the same year. A French writer, M. Wita ('La Guerre Chimique'), has examined this charge, but in spite of every effort made, he has been unable to find any founda-

[1] 'Der Chemische Krieg.'

tion for it whatever ; and he concludes that the rumour originated in some American periodical.

If any further evidence is required to expose the falseness of the German contention, it is supplied in a statement made by the late Doctor Haber himself, the expert responsible for the introduction of gas warfare. Speaking in Berlin on the 1st July 1926, he was reported (in the ' Times ' of 3rd July 1926) as having said : " In the early part of the war it was reported that British troops had used gas shell. He had gone forward to make an examination, and found that picric acid had been used as an explosive and the fumes (complained of in South Africa in 1899-1902) had been mistaken for gas." The German Supreme Command must, of course, have been aware of the result of this investigation, so that the pretext they employed is seen to be all the more cynical and dishonest.

It is significant, too, that the German Government attempted to conceal their use of gas from their own people, as all allusion to it was omitted from the official communiqués of the period : even in some of the popular histories published after the cessation of hostilities there is no mention of gas during the fighting at Ypres in 1915.

It is now known (from the German historian, General Schwarte, among others) that official experiments with gas were made by the Germans in October 1914 : that others had taken place still earlier was shown in a memorandum of the 2nd German Army, dated St Quentin, 16/10/14, which was captured in April 1915, and in which, among " the arms at disposal of the pioneers for fighting at close quarters," appeared " flame or asphyxiating gas projectors." [1]

It appears that gas was at first considered by the Germans for use in shells, but after debating this method Doctor Haber suggested its employment in the form of a cloud. (In May 1915 a reliable report was received from Holland to the effect that in the course of these experiments with gas clouds the Kaiser himself had been present and had forbidden the use of lethal gas, but had encouraged the use of gas which merely stupefied.)

The public memory is short, and it is important to

---

[1] Doctor Haber himself " has now admitted that he was at work on lethal substances as a means of offence in war in the laboratory of the Kaiser Wilhelm Institute in the first month of the war." (Lefebure, in ' The Riddle of the Rhine.')

bear in mind the attitude of the German Government and that of the German people in regard to the first use of gas, especially in view of the discussions that are now taking place with the object of forbidding the use of this or that weapon in future wars. And it must not be forgotten that similar pretexts were fabricated by the German Supreme Command whenever they were required: for example, when it declared that "irrefutable evidence" was available of the French intention to invade Belgium, to justify its own infringement of territorial neutrality [1]; and when it alleged mass risings of Belgian civilians, to excuse the savage measures adopted in the early days of the war [2]; and the carrying of munitions in the *Lusitania*, and troops in hospital ships, in extenuation of the submarine campaign.

Its attitude towards the first use of gas seems to have been this: "All our armaments and military preparations were based on a war of movement which has now ceased. Against troops in entrenched positions we believe that we shall gain an advantage by using poison gas. Owing to the non-existence of gas factories in France, Russia and England, it will be a long time before the enemy can retaliate—if ever. Anyhow, we are going to use it, so make the best case possible out of the loose wording of the Hague Convention: if this proves difficult, say that the enemy used it first, so that we were compelled to act in self-defence."

International agreements by formula are of little value if the desire to violate them exists and the opportunity presents itself; because it is an unfortunate fact that, owing to the mutual distrust of each other which exists among continental nations—one of which, at least, holds that "there can be no moral obligations between nations," and that "it is a point of honour to tear to pieces by force of arms treaties that are disgraceful"—the standard of conduct which it is thought necessary to observe, when large issues are at stake, is not the same as that recognised between honourable individuals. The national

---

[1] The 'Cologne Gazette' put this differently: "It was a duty for her" (Germany) "to be untrue to an obsolete treaty!"

[2] General Ludendorff, in 'My War Memories,' says: "The Belgian Government had systematically organised civilian warfare. The Belgian soldiers must also have had a special civilian suit in their knapsacks at the commencement of the war. My soldierly spirit suffered bitter disillusion."

interest is held by them to override every other consideration, and in promoting it *opportunity* is the most important factor. It is also certain that where the will exists a pretext can always be found, through the dangerous deceptions of diplomatic phraseology, to justify *any* action that is taken.

Of the gas war General Schwarte has written [1] : " Many others thought that on the German side it was very unwise for Germany to force the gas war with so much energy, as they believed that it would provoke the enemy's activities ; and this would do more harm to the Germans themselves, because the fundamental conditions for gas warfare —*i.e.*, weather conditions and the possibility of the production of materials, were more favourable for the enemy than for ourselves." (This was written in 1922 !) " But it was their opinion that it was futile to leave the leadership of this method of warfare to the enemy. Very correctly responsible persons in all countries urged the necessity of being first in the development of any kind of useful war material : whoever came late would be sure to meet surprise and reprisals. The hope that the enemy's development of the method would be slower proved to be a fallacy. The French commenced with gas grenades, but the Germans were first to recognise the tactical value of mass effect "—the cloud is evidently referred to. " The Germans were unwilling to meet the allied propaganda, partly in order to maintain secrecy and partly from conviction of right ; but there were, even in military circles, some who were in doubt about the position and who refused without any hesitation to use gas.

" From the foregoing it is evident that gas warfare originated not in Germany but in France ; but Germany took up the idea in the most effective and logical way, and led in attack and defence till the end : the lead was lost temporarily by the introduction of phosgene shells in 1916 and projectors in 1917, but it was quickly regained.

" The accusation in regard to a breach of international law and humanity was not justified according to the facts.

" The accusations were pure propaganda against Germany, and the world was easily misled ; but to-day no one should be deceived by such obvious misrepresentations."

[1] ' Der Grosse Krieg.'

Dr Hanslian uses another argument, which, being intended presumably for home consumption, is a curious aspersion on the mentality of his countrymen. "The propaganda carried out emphatically by the Allies during the war against the use of chemical warfare by the Germans was nothing but a hollow gesture intended to influence public opinion. Actually, during the whole period of the war, no enemy or neutral state protested officially to the German Government against the use of gas weapons.

"Professor Haber, in a lecture in 1925, said : 'Everyone knows that the first reply to a violation of international rights committed by an enemy consists of an official protest through a neutral power. We can conclude that all the enemy Governments preferred to adopt, as well, the new chemical methods of warfare rather than protest against their introduction.'"

From various German sources it has now been ascertained that the Supreme Command much under-estimated [1] the probable effect of their new weapon, and that the advance at Ypres was hampered by the fears of their own troops—some of whom, at any rate, were unprovided with masks—when they followed the cloud fifteen minutes after the discharge ceased. In fact, incredible as it may appear, gas was only discharged in the desire "to try it out thoroughly" at the front. After months of experiment and preparation a sector was originally selected in the south-east of the Salient, opposite Zillebeke and Hill 60, as it was erroneously believed that at the time of year southerly winds were to be expected. A major military operation was far from the enemy's intention. The digging in of cylinders began in the middle of February, and by the 10th March the whole front of the XVth German Corps had been prepared with gas. Towards the end of March, as the southerly winds did not blow, a new gas front was selected in the north of the Salient opposite Langemarck, and the cylinders were ready on 11th April : those installed on Hill 60 were left in the

---

[1] Their disbelief in the effect of the cloud attack in April 1915 was in striking contrast to the exaggerated faith placed in their bombardments with gas shells on 21st March 1918. The one showed a complete lack of imagination, while the other had no justification other than the successes previously obtained against the ill-equipped Russian Army.

trenches, but when the Hill was stormed by the British on 17th April they were not discovered. Owing to the absence of a favourable wind the discharge was postponed from day to day until it took place finally on 22nd April. Even then the tactical objective was only a limited one, though it was considered sufficient to force the evacuation of the whole Ypres Salient, and no reserves of troops were allotted for the engagement. Technically the gas discharge was not an unqualified success, as for some reason the cylinders opposite the junction of the French and the Belgians at Steenstraat were not emptied, while those opposite the Canadians east of the Poelcappelle-Ypres road were only discharged on the 24th April.

The enemy left little time (after 5.30 P.M.) to exploit his success. In the original orders issued (according to the history of the 215th Reserve Infantry Regiment of the XXIIIrd German Reserve Corps) the discharge was timed for 5.45 A.M., but at 5.30, as there was no wind, the attack was postponed. The men remained packed in their trenches all day, but fortunately for them there was no artillery fire. As the sun began to set, a wind got up, and at 4.40 P.M. definite orders were issued for the opening of the cylinders at 5 P.M. the same evening.

One of the most remarkable features about this first German gas attack, and one with which until quite recently few people were familiar, is that it came as a surprise, for there were many indications that it was about to take place. That no importance was attached to any of the reports that were received, some of which were complete in every detail, is a grave reflection on our ignorance of German mentality and on the lack of co-operation which existed at this period between the intelligence systems of the Allied Armies. Perhaps, too, the pre-war training in the war schools in Camberley and Paris had been too rigid, and in consequence staff officers failed to react to the suggestion that battle elements were about to be introduced with which they had hitherto been unfamiliar.

1. In a technical report written in the Ministry of Munitions after the war it has been stated that the Germans made their very first cloud gas attack with chlorine against the Russians at Bulimoff in February 1915 : " Our armies remained in ignorance of this information." No authority

for this story was quoted, but I have found several independent statements which seem to confirm it. According to the German historian, Hierl, cloud gas was first used on the Russian front at Skiernjewitze on the 2nd May 1915; but Dr Gertrud Woker of Berne University, in her book, 'The Coming Poison Gas War,' quotes a Polish lady doctor, Dr Budezinka-Tilinska, as having stated that poison gas was used as early as December 1914 against the Russians, that the latter had suffered severely and that 90 per cent of them died. In July 1915, Colonel Belaiew, attached to the Russian Commission in London, also made a very positive statement, which he investigated by request and subsequently corroborated, to the effect that the first cloud gas discharge against the Russians had taken place between 31/1/15 and 5/2/15; and in November 1915 two Russian delegates in London, Dr Daniel Gardner and Professor Nicholas Pouchine, confirmed this information, and added that the Germans had originally employed chlorine mixed with small amounts of bromine in their cylinders.

Further support for the supposition that gas was used against the Russians long before it was employed at Ypres is to be found in General Ludendorff's 'My War Memories,' although the wording of his reference is rather ambiguous. He writes: "The Ninth (German) Army was to attack in full force in the neighbourhood of Balimow at the end of January (1915). For the purpose our G.H.Q. placed 18,000 rounds of gas shells at our disposal. . . . The attack took place on January 31st. The weather was too cold for a gas attack, though that as yet we did not realise. Other things, too, did not turn out as we could have wished."

But whether the gas was used and its lack of effect was attributed to the cold weather, or whether the experts advised against its employment because of the temperature, is not clear from the passage. Evidence in favour of the former supposition is supplied in a later paragraph: "The Ninth Army was now to attack at Skierniewice.[1] We had received a supply of gas and anticipated great tactical results, as the Russians were not yet fully protected against gas. . . . The gas attack took place on May 2nd, and was not a success." Here the word 'fully'

[1] Skierniewice and Balimow are only half a dozen miles apart.

obviously implies that gas had been previously used, probably on 31st January, in the form of shells : on the later occasion it seems to have been discharged in a cloud.

2. But it seems probable that the Germans used gas shells even before January 1915, as there is an article in the April 1920 issue of the French periodical, the 'Revue générale des Sciences,' in which M. Daniel Florentin quotes the 'Chemiker Zeitung' (19/6/19) as admitting that the first German gas shells were fired on 27th October 1914, owing to the French having used shells containing an "irritating gas" some days previously. The excuse made is true to type, for, as will appear in the next chapter, it takes months of experiment before a gas shell can be designed and produced, so that the German employment of gas projectiles on this occasion cannot possibly have been resorted to as an improvised reprisal. They must have been manufactured long before. M. Florentin vigorously denies the accusation against the French artillery, and adds that without doubt German shells, containing benzyl and xylyl bromides (lachrymators), were used at Verdun in March 1915.

Another French writer, M. Henri le Wita, in referring to the same subject in 'La Guerre Chimique,' goes into further detail. He says that 3000 gas shells were fired by the Germans on 27th October 1914 at Neuve Chapelle. (This front was held by Indian troops at the time, but there seem to have been elements of French cavalry also present.) The shells were of a special shrapnel type : they were called 'No. 1,' and contained a sternutatory powder, but their effect was so poor that little notice was taken of them. M. Wita also states that the Germans used 'T' shells, containing xylyl bromide and similar substances, in Poland at Lodz in January 1915, and also on the French front at Nieuport at the same time. None of this information seems to have been circulated to the other Allies.

3. The 'Daily Express' published, on 1st January 1933, the following statement made by a sergeant of the Leicestershire Regiment : "It was on the morning of March 28th (1915) that, with a raiding party, I captured a German officer who spoke English very well. He wrote a statement in my carbon book to the effect that gas cylinders were in No Man's Land, to be used on us at the first

favourable wind. This statement was immediately sent to headquarters, and a party and myself were sent on patrol in No Man's Land two days later to test the truth of his statement. We found gas cylinders in dozens over a space of some hundred yards, exactly as he said. This further information was passed to headquarters. The carbon copies of both the prisoner's statement and mine I still have in my N.C.O.'s book. I have the German officer's name, his reference and his home address, but not wishing him to be punished, I withhold his name. These facts can be proved by other members of my battalion. We were on the left of Zillebeke at the time. The cylinders were like those used for blowing up balloons at fêtes, and contained, I believe, tear gas."

4. On 30th March 1915 the Bulletin of the French Tenth Army (which had recently moved from Ypres to the right of the B.E.F.) contained a report made by a prisoner of the XVth German Corps, to the effect that a large number of gas cylinders were in concealment behind Zillebeke, and a complete description was given of how the enemy proposed to use them and of the respirators with which their troops had been provided. The inventor, it was stated, had been promoted lieutenant. No action appears to have been taken in regard to this report, nor does it seem to have been brought to the notice of the British troops at Zillebeke.

5. On the 9th April, Mr Radcliffe, a chemical engineer in England, warned the War Office that the Germans were likely to use poison gas, and he suggested the provision of respirators for our troops. Serious notice was taken of this warning, but before any effective move was made the blow fell.

6. On 15th April the 2nd British Army sent G.H.Q. a report that a prisoner of the 234th Regiment of the XXVIth German Corps, taken by the French the previous day at Langemarck and carrying a gas respirator, had confirmed all the important particulars of an intended gas attack contained in the report of the Tenth Army, which has been already mentioned. The statement made by him was referred to later by "Eye-Witness," and was made the subject of a question in the House of Commons on 14th May. It also had a sensational sequel when proceedings were taken in 1920 against the prisoner concerned on a

charge of treason, as the result of the diary of a French officer having fallen into German hands. This charge was dismissed for lack of evidence; but in July 1930 the French General, Ferry, published an account of the prisoner's statement in a French periodical, and went so far as to mention his name. There was a renewal of the charge, and the German Ministry of Defence, in the course of the prosecution, maintained that the panic and shock of the first German gas attack had been weakened by its betrayal and that the casualties suffered by the German troops had been thereby increased; and, in spite of the fact that it was common knowledge that no preparations whatever were made to meet the attack, and that fifteen years had elapsed since the offence was committed, this unfortunate man was sentenced to ten years' penal servitude. According to General Ferry, he warned his Brigade Commander (in the 11th French Division), and recommended (1) the reduction of effectives in the front line, so as to reduce losses; (2) the bombardment of the cylinders; and (3) the extemporisation of respirators. He also sent an officer to warn the 28th British Division in Ypres and the Canadian Brigade in Boesinghe, and a special messenger to the XXth French Corps and the headquarters of the Groupe d'Armées du Nord, where, by a lucky chance, a representative of the Grand Quartier-Général happened to be present.

However, not only was no notice taken of these warnings, but General Ferry was told a few days later that the affair of the gas could not be taken seriously: that he had no right to communicate direct with the Allied Forces; and that the disposition of troops in the trenches was fixed by G.Q.G. and must not be varied!

7. About this time the German document was captured which was referred to on page 25 and which mentioned the intention to employ 'gas projectors' by German pioneer troops.

8. On 16th April the Belgian General Staff informed the French High Command (according to the official French history of the war) that the Germans had had tulle respirators made which, soaked in a suitable liquid, were intended to protect the men against the heavy asphyxiating gas which they proposed to discharge against the French lines. It was added that the men of the

XXVIth German Corps had just had special instruction in the handling of gas cylinders, which latter were to be disposed on the ground at the rate of a battery of twenty every forty metres.

9. On 17th April still further information came from Belgian sources, this time concerning the manufacture of twenty thousand respirators in Ghent.

10. In an account of the German gas attacks which was sent to the Americans by our General Staff (when we were placing the whole of our experience of gas warfare at the disposal of our Allies), it was stated that prior to the first attack our airmen saw gas cylinders in the German trenches at Broodseinde cross-roads : it was not, of course, realised what they contained.

11. On the occasion of the British attack on Hill 60 on 17th April, the German cylinders were actually in position in the captured trenches and had been there for some weeks.

They must have been seen by our troops, though they do not appear to have been examined; nor was their presence reported.

12. On 18th April and on the following days the Germans used lachrymatory shells in their counter-attacks on Hill 60, which were not only definitely identified, but the number of which was actually counted by an officer of the 8th Canadians.

13. And finally, to those who should have been familiar with German mentality, it ought to have been evident from the repeated references in German official reports (which were being transmitted by the Wolff wireless communiqués) to the use of gas by the Allies that the enemy proposed to use this weapon.

In view of the mass of evidence that was available beforehand it seems now almost incredible that no action was taken to meet the attack ; nor do the warnings which were received in France appear to have been brought to the notice of the War Office. I myself was quite ignorant of them until I began to collect the material for this book in December 1932.

It seems that the French were inclined to regard the reports as a ruse deliberately conveyed to their notice in order to prevent them from withdrawing troops from Ypres for the offensive which they were preparing near

Arras ; while the British appear to have been prevented from raiding the enemy's trenches to investigate the matter owing to a shortage of the ammunition required for the preliminary bombardment. Nobody realised the great danger that was threatening, it being probably considered that the enemy's attempt would certainly fail to have any important effect, and that whatever gas reached our lines could be easily fanned or borne away : nobody seems to have felt in the least uneasy, and, apart from the use of gas, its terrible effect came as a great surprise. It must be remembered, too, that the idea of gas did not convey much meaning to people in those days, and that it was associated, perhaps, with the conception of the Chinese ' stink-pot ' ; while the mistaken belief prevailed that the enemy would not depart from the recognised rules of civilised warfare.

CHAPTER III.

On the 3rd May, Lord Kitchener, in anticipation of his ability to obtain Cabinet sanction for gas reprisals, had put Colonel Jackson in charge of the preliminary investigations into the subject. Energetic action was taken by this officer, who got into touch with a number of scientists engaged in research and production, as well as with a Chemical War Committee specially constituted by the Council of the Royal Society. (It is interesting to note that the members of this Committee expressed their personal disapproval of the policy of retaliation in kind.) Colonel Jackson was relieved of his normal duties at the War Office, and was entrusted with the design and preparation of all trench-warfare appliances in addition to the study of gas : he was also called upon to investigate the numerous and, in many cases, fantastic and impracticable suggestions that reached him from the general public.

Before long a number of an elementary type of hand-grenade containing carbon disulphide and sulphur dioxide, with a small quantity of capsicine added (the active element in red pepper), were sent to France, and arrangements were made to increase their production to twenty thousand a day : an order for a hundred thousand gallons of the gases was placed in the United States. Two hundred and fifty 18-pounder shells were also filled with chlorine and sent out, though it was realised that the shooting with them would be poor.

Prior to this—in fact, immediately after the first German gas attack—Lord Kitchener had sent two eminent scientists, Dr Haldane and Professor Baker, to France to investigate the problem of protection on the spot : he had also appealed to the British public to supply pad respirators, such as were being improvised in the field, and in a very few days, thanks to the devoted efforts of

British women and the organisation of the Red Cross, every man in the B.E.F. had been supplied with some sort of protection against gas.

General Keogh, the head of the R.A.M.C. at the War Office, and Colonel Horrocks, his assistant, were in charge of this protective work, the experimental part of which was carried out in the R.A.M. College at Millbank.

About the same time Mouat Jones, who was serving in France as a private in the London Scottish, was given a commission, and he organised a small emergency chemical laboratory at St Omer, which was expanded later on and removed to Hesdin : here it became an important part of the gas organisation, with Professor Watson as its principal.

On 25th May, Sir John French, ignorant of what was going on and impatient at the delay, asked the War Office what means of using asphyxiating gas it was proposed to supply to the troops in addition to the hand bombs which had recently arrived ; and when, in reply, the War Office stated that five hundred cylinders were being made, to contain chlorine, and that bromine and sulphuretted hydrogen were also being experimented with, he decided to get into closer touch with the preparations, and my appointment was the result.

After a long consultation with Colonel Jackson at the War Office, I returned to France on the 29th May, and summarised in a note to General Robertson the preparatory work which had been carried out at home up to this time. The following is a brief résumé :—

Experiments had been made with a number of gases which came under two headings—

(a) Those suitable for a cloud attack. Chlorine was available in considerable quantities, but there was only one firm in England which possessed plant for liquefying it ; and cylinders (which were being made for the purpose) could only be filled at the rate of one ton (equivalent to fifty cylinders) a day, so that the 1500 cylinders that had been ordered could not be filled till the end of June. It was not considered certain that pure chlorine would be effective in practice, or that the Germans had used it. Attempts were being made to manufacture cylinders of a suitable size and design, but they were not very successful, as the acetylene-welded joints leaked when in contact with chlorine and the method of discharge was not yet satisfactory. Sulphuretted hydrogen was a promising cloud gas, and bromine might be procurable in the United States where inquiries were being made. The cloud gas method of attack was not favoured as it was considered too dangerous, and it was thought to be impossible under bombardment.

(b) Gases suitable for projectiles. The use of 'missiles' was recommended, but no suitable filling was yet in sight : the most promising were calcium arsenide and phosphorus and a mixture (in the form of a jelly) of prussic acid and chloroform which had been suggested by the Admiralty and with which experiments were being carried out in aeroplane bombs, under Mr Winston Churchill's instructions, by Lieut. Brock, R.N.V.R., at the Kingsnorth airship station. However, both the Admiralty and the War Office considered that Cabinet sanction would not be obtainable for the use of prussic acid or any of the more poisonous gases as fillings.

The method to be employed for projecting these missiles was by catapult ; the pattern in use could throw a 2-lb. grenade a distance of two hundred yards, and three thousand were on order : by a spring-gun of similar capabilities, of which six hundred were on order : by a pneumatic gun capable of throwing a 30-lb. shell a distance of two hundred yards ; and by the Vickers 2-inch trench-mortar which had a range of five hundred yards, and of which fifty, designed for high explosives, were already in France. The hand-grenades were to be filled with sulphur dioxide or carbon disulphide, with some capsicum extract added, and a number of them had been sent to France for trial.

As regards artillery shells, apart from those filled with chlorine which were already in France, there was great difficulty, for various reasons, in finding suitable gases : some were lighter than air and would disperse upwards when liberated ; others were unstable, and decomposed under the shock of detonation ; others, again, required glass-lined shell-cases as they attacked iron, or were too expensive to produce, or were unobtainable without interfering with the supply of explosives.

Personnel.—The War Office was getting from the principals of various universities and colleges the names of men with chemical training to deal with the offensive as well as the defensive sides of gas warfare : it was proposed to attach them to Engineer field companies as it was not thought that the formation of a special unit to handle gas would be necessary. Two officers and eighteen of these men had been already sent overseas and were employed in studying the German gas clouds.

At this time nothing whatever was known of the probable behaviour of gas discharged in quantity in the open air, and although some information was actually available, if only we had been aware of it (see pp. 29-34), nothing was known of the methods that had been employed by the enemy for storing their gas, for bringing it up into the trenches or for discharging it : even the nature of the gas they had used was still in dispute, so that I had no means of deciding how effective the gases recommended by the War Office were likely to prove, though I doubted the value of the catapults and hand-grenades. I arranged to return to England a week later, by which time it was believed that one of the newly designed syphon cylinders would be made and filled with chlorine, and I also promised to test the gas hand-grenades and 18-pounder shells in France.

I now had to formulate a gas policy for G.H.Q. This was very difficult, as from the foregoing it will be evident that there was very little on which to base it ; but time was short, as it was hoped to use gas in the offensive operations which were then being discussed. (The battle of Loos was first fixed to commence on 10th July.)

On the 31st May, therefore, I addressed the following memorandum to the C.G.S. : I have reproduced it in full because subsequent events proved my forecast to be so fortunate that if it had been written at the end of the war, after three and a half years of experience of gas warfare, there would have been no necessity to alter a word of it.

" The following are my suggestions as to the policy to be adopted for the immediate future :—

(1) Take steps to ensure that no further public mention is made of gas retaliation.

(2) Forbid the employment of gas in any form in all parts of the line for the present, until we have had the benefit of our surprise.

(3) We must not wait for further experiments, but must make use of the results already arrived at to organise a gas attack on a large scale at the earliest possible moment. The gases used may not be the best obtainable, but better will follow.

(4) The attack to be made (a) by cloud, and (b) by projectiles : the latter to be large, so as to produce appreciable effects ; long-range, to safeguard our own men ; and filled with the deadliest gases procurable.

(5) Subsequently the nature of the gases to be used to be varied from time to time so as to minimise the effectiveness of antidotes.

(6) A gas service to be organised as part of the B.E.F., its first duty to be the production of gas clouds from trenches : it will, in addition, handle all gas material, assist the medical authorities in the investigation of gases used by the enemy, and be of service to the troops in resisting gas attacks. No distinguishing badge to be worn, in view of the probability of reprisals, but the unit to assume a number as a company of Engineers. A central depot to be formed at some suitable spot for instructional purposes.

The organisation must admit of an attack being carried out anywhere, at short notice, like an artillery bombardment : the personnel to consist of professional chemists now serving in the B.E.F., suitable men from the new armies and civilians with whom the War Office is already in touch. The proportion of skilled and responsible officers must be high. Probably 25 officers and 500 men will be required.

(7) As regards the tactical employment of gas, it is possible that in the first attack in which it is successfully employed important results may be achieved, and on subsequent occasions our losses in prearranged attacks will be considerably reduced ; but it should be impressed on troops that assistance from gas cannot be depended upon, and all arrangements made for an attack should therefore be capable of fulfilment

in case the conditions for the employment of gas prove to be unfavourable.

Other developments will suggest themselves as time goes on."

The whole of these suggestions were at once accepted with the exception of No. 6, which proposed, among other things, a combination of the offensive and defensive sides of the gas organisation. As will be seen later on, the necessity for this became apparent six months afterwards without any further pressure on my part, and the War Office suggested it under rather remarkable circumstances.

As regards the size of the projectiles to be used—4 (b)—my recommendation was based merely on intuition, and it was disputed by the Inventions Committee at G.H.Q., which included the Artillery and Engineer advisers and a few scientists, to whom it was submitted: this Committee expressed the opinion that it was not advisable to ask for any artillery gas shells for the present, owing to the shortage of ordinary ammunition; and added that " so long as the required amount of gas is discharged rapidly at the desired point it is not considered to be material whether the gas is conveyed in large or small projectiles."

However, subsequent experience with trench-mortars and ' projectors ' proved abundantly that this was a very material point; and as regards artillery shells a series of experiments was carried out specially at Porton in June 1918 to investigate the matter, and the decision arrived at was that with comparable quantities of lethal gas discharged in each case the 6-inch howitzer gas shell was far superior to those of the smaller calibres.

During the next few days I found a very suitable village near St Omer (where G.H.Q. was located), well off the main roads and with a lot of rough, common ground around it on which training and small experiments with gas could be carried out without attracting attention. This was Helfaut, and it remained our depot all through the war.

I also witnessed trials of the gas hand-grenades and 18-pounder shells, and found that neither was likely to be effective. An aeroplane also dropped gas bombs, but the experiment was inconclusive owing to the high wind: this did not matter much as our Air Force decided that they would not use gas, and they refrained from doing so throughout the war. The German Air Force adopted the same policy, and although on more than one occasion gas air bombs were stated to have been employed by them, immediate investigations on the spot failed in every case to confirm the report. The Germans, on their side, also reported repeatedly the use of these bombs by the Allies, but the reports proved to be erroneous (General Schwarte).[1]

As regards the hand-grenades a number had been previously sent for trial on the Canadian front by General Seely's troops, but they were reported as being not only defective in construction but ineffective in use; and the supply which had been arranged on such a lavish scale was stopped. (Carbon disulphide and sulphur dioxide are both extremely unpleasant gases, but they have no particular lethal value; they were regarded merely as 'annoyers.')

The experiment with the new chlorine cylinders which I had been waiting for took place on 4th June at the Castner Kellner chemical works at Runcorn, on the Manchester Ship Canal: there were present, besides myself and War Office representatives, Mr Gerald Balfour, the chairman of the company, and the military attachés of Japan, Russia, Italy and Belgium. Unfortunately, there was a strong wind blowing (twenty miles per hour), but trials were carried through with cylinders of different sizes which were discharged in various arrangements; and the flexible tubes designed for attachment to them were put to a practical test. Employés of the firm were lined out to leeward of the point of discharge at measured distances, and were provided, some with protective helmets of War Office pattern and others with the respirators in daily use at the works, which consisted of many folds of flannelette held in position over the mouth and nose. These men, who were accustomed to inhaling small quantities of gas, were instructed to make a signal the moment the gas cloud reached them, but not to put on the respirators until compelled to. Paper discs, prepared to show a chemical reaction, were also pinned to poles of various

---

[1] In 1918 an order was captured which had been issued on 3rd May by the German Commandant of Wattrelos, in the Commune of Bondues, stating the precautions which were to be adopted by the civil inhabitants in case of a British attack with aerial gas bombs.

heights, and were fixed in trenches specially dug in the path of the cloud to record its action and extent. By this time the syphon idea of liberating the gas had been hit upon. A central syphon tube was fixed inside the cylinder and reached to within an inch of the bottom. When the cylinder valve was opened, the internal pressure forced the chlorine out through the syphon tube in the form of a fine spray of liquid which was converted into gas at the point of emission, the discharge taking place precisely as in the case of a soda-water syphon. It was accompanied by a slight hissing noise and a great fall of temperature, which increased the density of the cloud (chlorine itself is heavier than air) and helped to make it cling to the surface of the ground as the wind carried it along. Incidentally, this fall of temperature causes the moisture in the atmosphere to condense, so that in damp weather a visible cloud is formed ; otherwise there is hardly anything to be seen excepting at the actual point of discharge. Without the syphon tube the vaporisation of the liquid chlorine takes place inside the cylinder when the valve is opened, and as a result of the fall in temperature the valve outlet soon becomes frosted and blocked.

When I got back to France I reported that to be effective gas must be discharged from a *line* of cylinders : the cloud obtained from cylinders spaced fifty yards apart is good, but it would be better to place them twenty-five yards apart ; so grouped a very intense cloud is produced with two cylinders opened simultaneously ; the chlorine cloud clings to the ground in a remarkable manner and sinks into trenches ; it ascended a bank thirty feet high (the spoil from the canal) two hundred yards from the point of discharge, passed along the top of the bank for another two hundred yards, and was so effective when it rolled down thirty feet to the canal tow-path that when I walked into it I was compelled to put on a respirator immediately, while the bargees sailing past shouted abuse at us.

From the experiment I had witnessed I was satisfied that a discharge of five minutes' duration from cylinders spaced twenty-five yards apart would result in a continuous cloud being formed by the time the gas reached the German trench-line, and that it would disable everyone not adequately protected up to four hundred yards from the point of emission, and probably at a much greater distance; that a discharge lasting half an hour would result in the exhaustion of the chemicals in which respirators of the type which the Germans were known to possess were steeped; and that such a cloud could be followed up safely in the open by unprotected infantry a minute or two after the discharge ceased.

This report created lively interest and satisfaction at G.H.Q., and I was given practically a free hand in organising the personnel required to carry out our first gas attack. Sir John French himself anticipated that the best results from gas would be obtained from aeroplane bombs; and, while I hoped that something much more effective than chlorine would become available soon, I realised that for an attack with this gas to be successful a complete surprise would have to be achieved. Absolute secrecy was therefore necessary, and I asked for all references to gas in the Press to be suppressed, as well as the headings under gas poisoning in the casualty lists which were being published periodically. I also requested that no further use be made of the 'stink-bombs' now at the front.

From this time onwards all German respirators found on prisoners or in captured trenches were sent in to me, so that a check could be kept of the value of the German protection that had to be overcome. A few of these reached me from time to time: the first one had been taken from a dead German a month before, and consisted of a pad of tow soaked in chemicals—a primitive type that was found to be in use as late as 18th October 1915; but an improved pattern had since been issued which was known as the 'snout.' This fitted over the mouth and under the chin, and the upper edge contained a light iron spring to clip the nose; and it was carried in a small waterproof bag with a bottle containing a solution of sodium carbonate and sodium thiosulphate with which, in the presence of gas, the mask had to be moistened before adjustment. One of these 'snout' respirators was sent to Millbank to be tested, and it was found that when properly treated with the solution it held out remarkably well in a strong concentration of chlorine gas; but it took too long to adjust, it did not fit well and its resistance to breathing, when wet, was very high. Without treatment with solution it was practically useless, and many of the bottles found in the captured bags were found on examination to have been broken from rough usage. It was also ascertained that German officers and machine-gunners were equipped with oxygen mine-rescue sets which were effective for half an hour at most; so that in planning our first gas attack it was hoped that unless an improved pattern of German mask was introduced in the meantime, a gas discharge lasting forty minutes might find some of the enemy without a mask at all; others with masks that afforded inadequate protection, either owing to bad fit or to the breakage of the bottle containing the solution; while the oxygen sets would be useless, at any rate for the last ten minutes of the attack.

The personnel of the gas unit had now to be considered: as the arrangement of cylinders necessary for a forty-minute discharge required that they should be grouped in the front-line trench in batteries of seven or eight (the cylinders at Runcorn emptied themselves in five minutes), it was proposed to stand them upright on the fire-step and protect them as well as possible with sand-bags. Two men would be required at each battery to open the valves, and while one of them might be a specially enlisted chemist to supply whatever technical knowledge was needed, the other should have experience of trench warfare conditions, and ought to be an infantryman transferred from one of the battalions in the line. The front to be prepared for the gas discharge was given to me as five thousand yards, and, as I considered that an officer could not superintend a gas front of more than about two hundred and fifty yards of trench, the calculation of the strength of the unit to be created was a simple matter: twenty subaltern officers would be required, grouped in two companies of ten sections each, with myself in control of the whole operation.

I have explained this organisation in some detail, because it is necessary for the reader to understand how cloud gas attacks were staged. In the scores of such operations which we carried out in the following years hardly any modification was found necessary of the method as first planned, excepting when late in 1918 we discharged gas a number of times from lines of railway trucks which were pushed up as near the front line as possible immediately before the attack was timed to take place.

It appears, too, that almost exactly the same method was employed by the Germans; and it was also adopted by the French. I believe that the American gas companies, which were modelled on ours (and the first two of which were actually trained by me), never discharged cloud gas for lack of cylinders.

By the 16th June this organisation had been worked out and completed in the minutest detail, down to the appropriate number of cooks, batmen, &c.; and on this day Sir John French announced his policy to the War Office for the first time in the following terms :—

(a) It is desirable for the first gas attack to be a surprise, so that all preparations must be made with the utmost secrecy.

(b) The front of the attack must be such as to ensure a considerable tactical success, but it must be suitable for the number of troops likely to be available. " I consider this front to be about five thousand yards until additional divisions are sent out."

(c) The volume of gas must be adequate for a discharge lasting thirty minutes.

(d) Cylinder gas must be supplemented by gases of a more poisonous nature in aeroplane and trench-mortar bombs and artillery shells. The artillery shells (containing chlorine) already sent out for trial are unsatisfactory and further experiments are necessary; but the supply of gas shells must not interfere with the output of ordinary ammunition.

(e) The 2-inch trench-mortar, the largest available, is the most suitable owing to the amount of the gas content of the bomb, and the range, which is sufficient to safeguard our own troops from danger.

(f) Special gas units are required, and it is proposed to organise these as Engineer companies in France, with a depot for training.

Complete " War Establishments " for two companies accompanied this letter, and all the proposals in it were approved by the War Office nine days later, the War Office stating that instead of sappers the men would be enlisted as Engineer corporals, with special rates of pay, as they would be University graduates or students.

Colonel Matheson, R.E., in Colonel (by now Brigadier-General) Jackson's new department, was most useful in interviewing the chemists in London and in selecting officers from amongst them ; and with his assistance I obtained suitable men for appointment as 'Chemical Adviser' to each of the two armies for the purpose of collecting information and for advising on protective measures. A few officers already in France were transferred for service with the new units, and from these I chose Captain Monier-Williams as my technical adviser and deputy, and put him in charge of the training depot. Lieutenants Robertson, Slade and Pollitt were the first officers in France to join the Special Companies. Robertson had been employed as a research chemist in a mining company in Mexico, but he joined the army at the outbreak of war and rose to the rank of lieut.-colonel in the Special Brigade ; Slade was lecturer in Physical Chemistry at University College, London, and graduated as an officer through the O.T.C. He is now managing director of the great I.C.I. Fertiliser and Synthetic Products factory at Billingham, near Stockton-on-Tees. And Pollitt was a senior official in the firm of Brunner Mond. The last-named officer had a remarkable military career : on the outbreak of war he bought a motor-cycle, and on the same day he learnt to ride it and enlisted as a motor despatch rider, in which capacity he served during the Retreat. Owing to his knowledge of German he was then given a commission in the Intelligence Department, but office life did not appeal to him, so that on their formation I arranged for his transfer to the Special Companies at his request. He, too, rose to the rank of lieut.-colonel, and showed such a natural aptitude for leadership that towards the end of the war one of the army commanders asked me to give him up so that he might be trained for service as an infantry brigadier. He went through the mill with a Guards training unit, and was in command of an infantry battalion at the moment when he was badly wounded and taken prisoner in 1918. Although he made several attempts to escape, and almost succeeded in each case, he remained in German hands until the Armistice. He is now one of the directors of Imperial Chemical Industries.

Details of the gas apparatus considered suitable were

communicated to the Ministry of Munitions. The cylinders were to be three feet long and eight to twelve inches in diameter : they were to have a maximum weight of one hundred pounds and a gas content of sixty pounds. This was a high figure, but it was necessary to reduce the number of cylinders to a minimum, as it was hoped that it would be possible to complete their installation in trenches in a single night for the sake of preserving secrecy, so that the fewer there were to be carried up the better. Each cylinder was to be fitted with two handles for attachment to carrying-poles with rope-slings, as it was thought that two men might be detailed for this duty, with a third as a relief in the case of long carries. A ten-foot iron pipe was to be thrown over the parapet at the last moment before the discharge commenced, so as to keep the gas, when it issued, well away from the trench ; and another ten-foot flexible lead or copper pipe was to be provided to complete the connection between the parapet pipe and the cylinder outlet, allowance thus being made for variations in the depth of trenches. Stress was laid at the same time on the necessity for preventing leakage from any of the con-nections. The conviction was also expressed that chlorine would only be effective the first time it was used, so that it was necessary to find a better cloud gas for future use.

A meteorological bureau was formed in France, and seventeen observing stations were established at different points along the front for studying ground winds, and from them weather reports were sent in to G.H.Q. four times a day.

CHAPTER IV.

FORMATION OF THE SPECIAL COMPANIES.

I NOW had to wait patiently for the first chemists and cylinders to arrive in France, and had time to think about future developments: I also sought an opportunity of visiting the French Grand Quartier-Général, and the scientists who were co-operating with them in Paris, to find out what our Allies were proposing to do in the direction of gas retaliation.

I reached Paris in the middle of June and witnessed experiments with cloud gas on the artillery range at Satory, near Versailles. The French did not intend to employ liquefied gas in cylinders, probably because chlorine was not manufactured anywhere in France at that time: instead, they were proposing to generate their gas actually in the front-line trench. Iron receptacles were built into the parapet, and the gases formed by a mixture of chemicals put into them were forced out to the front of the trench through a pipe by means of rotary blowers. There was a lack of simplicity in this method, as well as danger of the fumes leaking into the trench. The apparatus was also very vulnerable to hostile bombardment, and it required much time and labour for installation, while its immobility was an additional disadvantage.

Field-gun shells were being filled with sticks of phosphorus dissolved in carbon disulphide, and from these important results were expected owing to the inflammability of the mixture. Experiments were also being made with prussic acid gas, which was considered very deadly, but which there was a hesitation to use except in retaliation; partly, too, perhaps, because it was known that large quantities of it could be produced in Germany.

I saw also on the same occasion their earliest experiments with flame projectors (the Germans had used their flammenwerfer on the French front on the 25th June 1915, but their existence was known before this : they were employed for the first time against the British at Hooge on 30th July). The French apparatus was a portable one and had a range of only about twenty yards: the oil which it discharged was ignited by an inflammable bomb thrown out a suitable distance in front beforehand.

Belgian technical officers were also present at these experiments and were awaiting developments. The visit was very interesting as showing how an entirely new problem was being approached from quite different directions by our Allies and ourselves.

On returning to G.H.Q. I resumed my inquiries, two of which had important results and are worth relating as they led to the introduction of the Stokes mortar into the British Army and to the adoption of phosgene, which became, and remained until the end of the war, our main battle gas.

At the request of General Rimington, at that time in command of the Indian Cavalry Corps, I visited him at his headquarters at Aire on 25th June. After lunch he showed me the experimental Stokes mortar which had been sent to France for trial and rejected as unsafe. This weapon was extremely simple, and consisted of a steel tube with an interior diameter of three inches, supported at an angle to the ground on a light frame.

The bomb intended for use with it fitted loosely into the barrel, and it had a central hollow projection in its base into which an ordinary twelve-bore sporting cartridge was fixed after the shot had been extracted. At the bottom of the inside of the mortar there was a sharp pin with which the cap of the cartridge came in contact when the bomb was dropped into the mortar : the cartridge was ignited in this way, and the bomb, weighing 15 lb., was ejected to a maximum distance of three hundred and fifty yards. In the original model a length of safety fuze, which led to the bursting charge in the interior of the bomb, was set alight automatically by the flash from the explosion of the cartridge ; and variations of range were obtained by fixing the mortar at different angles with the aid of a clinometer.

General Rimington suggested that I might find this mortar useful for projecting gas, and he explained that it had been rejected by a Committee at G.H.Q. because it was thought that it would be dangerous to submit bombs containing high explosive to the shock of being dropped a distance of two or three feet, and that the flame from the cartridge, when it was fired, would flash through the whole length of the safety fuze to the bursting charge inside the bomb and cause the latter to detonate prematurely. I was very impressed with the mortar and with its rate of fire and surprising accuracy, but thought that the bombs were much too small for a gas filling : however, at General Rimington's suggestion, I wrote at once to Mr Stokes to ask if he could produce a similar mortar of 6-inch diameter. He replied that a 4-inch mortar would present no difficulty in design, and three weeks later one was ready in London for trial. I saw it fired on 14th July on Clapham Common, where a trench-mortar school had been established ; and of the dozen bombs projected all fell nearly five hundred yards away within a space about the area of a good-sized room : in fact, the experiment was so successful that I asked for twenty mortars to be made at once, and for gas bombs to be provided for use in our first gas attack.[1]

The mortars arrived in France in time, but gas bombs were not supplied till a year later. However, this did not prevent the mortars from being taken into action, and they

---

[1] Mr Lloyd George, who had a genius for anticipating the requirements of the army in France, describes in his ' War Memoirs ' how, after witnessing a trial on 30th June, he gave instructions for 1000 3-inch Stokes mortars to be made.

But the date he mentions does not correspond with the entry made by Dr Addison in his diary, ' Four and a half years ' : 15th July 1915. " There was a demonstration of the working of the Stokes gun. It practically means bringing artillery into the trenches. I ordered 20 for trial."

A little later Dr Addison says : " Winston, Ll. G. and I decided " (on 13th August) " to make a plunge with regard to orders for the Stokes, in anticipation of a requisition from the Ordnance Board, and I gave instructions accordingly."

There is an amusing reference to this incident a few pages farther on, when Dr Addison describes " a rather unpleasant incident with Winston Churchill." The latter complained to Mr Lloyd George on 27th August that nothing had been done about the order for the Stokes guns ; and in a stormy interview on 8th September, Dr Addison was able to point out that " so far from the guns not having been *ordered* twenty complete guns had actually been delivered that very day and were to be sent out to France on the 11th." " The fact is that 30 guns were delivered during the week—10 more than was expected." Whereupon " Ll. G. roared with delight at Winston's discomfiture."

But the latter would have been in a position to continue the debate if he had known that these thirty guns were of the 4-inch pattern, built specially for use with gas ammunition, and that, strictly speaking, they had nothing whatever to do with the ' plunge ' that had been decided on and with regard to which Mr Churchill's complaint was made !

were all used (as well as nine others) at the opening of the battle of Loos, smoke bombs having been improvised for them by the First Army, with phosphorus contained in papier mâché cases and sent across in bulk for the purpose. They were such a success that there was an instant demand from the infantry for the three-inch pattern and high-explosive bombs : these arrived in due course with certain improvements, and thousands were in general use during the rest of the war.

As regards phosgene, the French captain, Gerschel, who was attached to the Mission at G.H.Q. and who was of invaluable service to me in many ways throughout the war, drew my attention very early to a derelict factory at Coulogne near Calais, where this substance had been manufactured in peace-time for use in the dyeing industry. We visited the place and witnessed some experiments on animals which seemed to indicate that the gas was much more toxic than chlorine. Some of it was also liberated in a closed chamber, and when I entered it, wearing the British gas helmet (the 'H,' or hypo.), I found that the latter gave no protection against the gas whatever.

Here was a valuable find ! I took a small quantity of the gas to Millbank in a cylinder, but was very disappointed to hear that it had already been tried, and that it had been found that the 'H' helmet gave complete (99 per cent) protection against it : in fact, to convince me on the point, an experiment was made in my presence, in which a rat was subjected for an hour to a measured quantity of the gas, the latter being pumped through a fold of the 'H' helmet fabric ; and when it was removed at the end of this period it appeared to be none the worse ! In spite of this I remained unconvinced, and was informed the next day that a fault had been found in the apparatus, and the penetrative value of the gas was admitted.

I reported this discovery to General Robertson and stressed its importance. Steps were at once taken to get permission from the French Government to reopen the Calais factory and to recall its employés from the trenches. All our Allies were warned at once of the danger which threatened them if the Germans made use of this new gas, and protection against it was found in London by adding a substance called phenate to the chemicals with which the 'H' helmet was being impregnated, in consequence of which the new pattern, supplies of which soon began to reach the troops, became known as the ' P.' [1]

The output of the Calais factory was greatly increased, and some of the phosgene made there was supplied for the use of the British Army in part exchange for an equal quantity of chlorine. The French built a new factory for making phosgene and enlarged the one at Coulogne, and they called the gas ' Collongite '—hence the cypher ' CG ' which we employed when referring to it. The manufacture of the gas was also undertaken in England by the United Alkali Company, but difficulties were experienced, as at Coulogne, because in making it chlorine gas combines with carbon monoxide (well known in mine accidents and in cases of poisoning from domestic gas) in a reaction, the secret of which, we were told, the proprietor of the Calais factory would not at first divulge even to his own Government.

It is interesting to note that at that period the peculiarly dangerous physiological properties of phosgene were unknown, and that its toxicity was attributed to its carbon monoxide constituent (the chemical formula of phosgene is $COCl_2$), though actually it is far more deadly.

As will appear later, thousands of tons of this gas were discharged during the war against the Germans, who also used it and a similar compound known as di-phosgene, but chiefly in a much less effective form as an artillery shell filling. This almost accidental recognition of the value of phosgene as a battle gas so early in the war proved to be of very great importance, as its manufacture by the Allies was commenced much sooner than might otherwise have been the case, while its first employment by the Germans found us fully prepared with protection against it.

On 19th June I had been sent to Boulogne with other officers to meet Mr Lloyd George at a conference on the supply of munitions. He told me that he doubted the efficacy of a gas so well known as chlorine. I agreed, but said that we ought to be able to use it effectively once if we could bring off a surprise attack, but that after that we must find something better. I referred at this interview to the discovery of the value of phosgene, and

---

[1] Later, hexamine was added to give still better protection against phosgene, and the helmet was then called the ' PH '; and finally goggles were incorporated with the helmet fabric, and the ' PHG ' came into existence.

begged him to press on with its manufacture. I also risked a rebuff by suggesting that all the scientific resources of the country that were available were not being made use of, the bulk of the research work in connection with gas being carried out at that time mainly by Professors Thorpe and Baker at the Imperial College of Science in South Kensington.

Preparations for the battle of Loos were now proceeding apace : this action, like those at the Aubers Ridge and Festubert, was forced on Sir John French so that support might be given to the French offensives in Artois and the Champagne. He was opposed to committing his troops to an attack on a large scale until the new divisions arrived in 1916, and even the front of the attack selected was considered by him as most unfavourable.

I myself was confronted with many difficulties in making the arrangements for the discharge of gas. Fortunately, those which arose in France were removed by General Robertson as soon as I found it necessary to appeal to him, which I had every opportunity of doing as I was under orders from the first to see him every day.[1] There were delays in the transfer of infantrymen from the line owing to units being below strength and the natural reluctance of commanders to part with good men, until peremptory orders were issued that the Special Companies were to have priority and that all eligible personnel were to be made available.

When the cylinders began to arrive in Boulogne, screwed up in wooden boxes and addressed to me personally by name, there was an indignant outcry because it was feared that shell-fuzes in the same store would be

---

[1] I always found him very friendly and human and anything but the dour unapproachable being of popular imagination. He sometimes expressed himself very freely and emphatically about things in general, and certain politicians in particular, who, he considered, had ruined the country ; and perhaps he found an occasional gossip with one who was comparatively young, very enthusiastic and not over-awed, a relief from the dull routine work in which he was normally engaged, with officers of high rank who took war more seriously. On one occasion I found him nursing a swollen face, and advised a visit to the dentist. " I don't believe he would do me any good," he replied doubtfully, to which I answered, " It won't hurt very much " ; and although he wagged a forefinger at me reprovingly he did not resent the insinuation.

Another time, when he was paying us a visit at Helfaut, we tried to persuade him to put on a helmet to test its efficiency in a gas cloud ; but surmising (correctly) that we were more anxious to judge his appearance in this unfamiliar head-dress than that he should satisfy himself of its adequacy, he laughingly refused.

affected by the gas, some of which inevitably leaked out. A few carefully selected officers had to be taken into confidence, and a special cylinder store was established at Audruick where sheds and railway sidings were built for the purpose.[1]

Surprise was also caused by some of the demands I made. For instance, one for three hundred watches which were necessary to synchronise the commencement of the gas discharge : such a demand was, of course, without precedent.

As regards the specially enlisted personnel, there was —probably for very good reasons—delay in their despatch to France ; and in order to hasten the approval of certain proposals I took the papers connected with them from room to room in the War Office until everybody concerned with the matter had been consulted and the matter was settled.

At one time at a later stage I found twelve of the officers earmarked for me waiting at Chatham to take their turn in conducting drafts overseas ; but, after explaining the urgent necessity for despatching them immediately to go through their training at Helfaut, I was allowed to remove them in a batch.

Although the secrecy of our preparations was a matter of the utmost importance it was disconcerting to find that questions continued to be asked in Parliament (and were reported in the Press) on the subject of gas. One Member asked in the middle of June, " whether any disabling gas, not cruel or inhuman in its effects, had been adopted by way of reprisal " ; and another inquired a month later why, up to the present, gas had not been used by our forces ; and again, " why there had been such an extraordinary delay in using chlorine gas against the enemy, and if there was still the intention to use it." He went on to suggest an inquiry into a breakdown which was alleged to have occurred in the supply of cylinders !

Fortunately, Parliament adjourned at the end of August : I also took the opportunity of enlisting Lord Haldane's help in the matter, when I was asked to meet him on the occasion of his visit to G.H.Q.

---

[1] Audruick was an open ammunition depot, and it was destroyed when a terrific explosion occurred there on 25th April 1916 ; though the gas cylinders, which were kept in a separate area, escaped damage.

There *had* actually been a breakdown in the manufacture of cylinders, as well as difficulties in the expansion of the output of chlorine at Runcorn. Cylinders were being made in all shapes and sizes, a number coming from the U.S.A., and some of them weighed, when full, as much as one hundred and thirty pounds ; while the time taken to empty them was found to be two or three minutes, instead of five as was expected. This led to the necessity of interposing smoke intervals in the period of forty minutes during which the gas discharge had been planned to last, the smoke being produced by smoke candles which were specially designed to simulate the gas. Incidentally, this was the origin of the use of smoke at the battle of Loos, and it was, I believe, the first time that smoke was used in modern civilised warfare. Hardly any British operation took place subsequently without it, though the Germans never resorted to this device, either for simulating gas or for concealing the movements of their infantry.[1]

The shortage of cylinders was so acute at one period that I was pressed to accept instead the six-foot gas cylinders of commerce, which it would have been impossible, of course, to handle in the trenches.

It was found, too, that lead and copper flexible pipes could not be supplied in quantity, and stiff iron ones with right-angle bends were substituted. Even these arrived in inadequate numbers, and they were, as might be imagined, very awkward to handle and adjust, especially when it became necessary to fit them to one cylinder after another in the course of a discharge taking place under a heavy bombardment : the number of joints, each a potential source of leakage of gas, was one of the main causes of the difficulties that were experienced when the pipes came to be used.

I myself was able to realise the difficulties which the new Ministry of Munitions had to face, but I had to bear the brunt of the dissatisfaction felt at the headquarters of the First Army when, with supplies failing to reach expectations, repeated alterations had to be made in their plan of battle. For, as the date provisionally fixed for the commencement of the action was postponed from the 10th July to the end of August, and then in turn to the

[1] " German smoke-producing methods hardly went beyond the trial stage." (General Schwarte.)

Photo. by Maj. Salt.

The "Special Brigade" in training.

Photo. by C. R. Alderson.

Helfaut.   Practice with cylinders.

Note the primitive pipe connections at first in use.

8th, the 15th and finally to the 25th September, and as divisions of the New Armies began to arrive in France, the extent of front selected for the attack was gradually increased; and, as more and more cylinders were to be expected during this extended period, the length of trench to be prepared for gas was also added to, and a corresponding increase became necessary in the number of Special Companies required for the operation, a third and eventually a fourth being authorised.

The first draft of two officers and eighty men reached St Omer on the 18th July: I met them at the station, and questioned the men as to what they had been sent out to do. It appeared that the secret had been well kept, as they had no idea of the nature of their future duties, though a few thought they would be employed in some capacity in chemical laboratories. I enlightened them, and gave every man the opportunity to return to England if he wished; but out of the five or six hundred recruits who reached Helfaut less than half a dozen took advantage of this offer.

A further draft of five officers and a hundred men arrived on the 21st, and the first two trained meteorologists appeared two days later. Lectures were given, in the course of which every officer and man was impressed with the necessity for maintaining the utmost secrecy as to the nature of their present occupation; and when the general idea of the proposed method of gas attack had been explained, sections and companies were formed and their training commenced. A little drill was, of course, necessary as most of the men had come straight from civil life; and instruction was given in revolver shooting, for it was not intended that they should carry rifles, so that greater freedom might be given for the manipulation of the gas apparatus. I paid particular attention to the necessity of finding a way across country at night, and though the men managed, naturally, to lose their way quite easily at first—and were allowed to do so—they quickly became accustomed to the new conditions.

Lines of trenches were dug on the common at Helfaut, and a few cylinders and pipes were sent out in advance for practice in making the connections and manipulating the valves. Every officer and sergeant received special training in estimating the direction and velocity of wind currents; and several excursions were arranged by motor-bus to lines of unoccupied reserve trenches for the purpose of practising schemes for organising and occupying them with a view to a gas discharge. Finally, all the officers spent a period of forty-eight hours with some infantry unit in the front line so as to accustom them to the conditions in which they would have to work; and on their return to Helfaut a general conference was held, in which the system of training they were undergoing was discussed in the light of the experiences gained.

A circular-letter was now addressed to the commanders of armies and corps by G.H.Q., in which the action of a gas cloud was explained. Of course, we had no actual experience of its behaviour, as up till the end of the war there was no experimental ground available anywhere sufficiently extensive for more than a very few cylinders to be discharged at a time with safety. Still, it was obvious that wind, the behaviour of which could be studied by watching smoke, would not act very differently when it contained one volume in a thousand or one in ten thousand of gas. If the velocity of the gas cloud was low it would be deflected by ground obstacles, would linger in hollows, flow into trenches and dug-outs and follow valleys, leaving hill-tops as islands, just as water in a slow-flowing stream swirls round the pebbles and boulders in its bed: when moving at a higher velocity it would surmount these obstacles more or less, though villages and woods might be expected to offer some resistance to penetration (see accompanying map of the observed movement of a German gas cloud). The ideal wind velocity was given as eight to twelve miles an hour, but this was a high estimate, though one on the safe side: four to six miles an hour would have been better, as representing the minimum wind velocity in which a quite definite movement of air occurs.

The safe limits of wind direction were put at 22½ degrees on either side of a line drawn at right angles to the general run of the trenches; so that if the latter ran from north to south, the safe limits of wind direction would lie between north-west to south-west. The minimum safe velocity of the wind was laid down as four miles an hour.

As regards the protection of the cylinders in the front-line trench, it was stated that nothing beyond a sand-bag

GERMAN GAS ATTACK, 19TH DECEMBER 1915.

MAP SHOWING THE DISTRIBUTION AND FLOW OF POISON GAS.

Compiled from
{
1. Observed facts.
2. Reported facts.
3. Distribution of casualties due to gas.
}

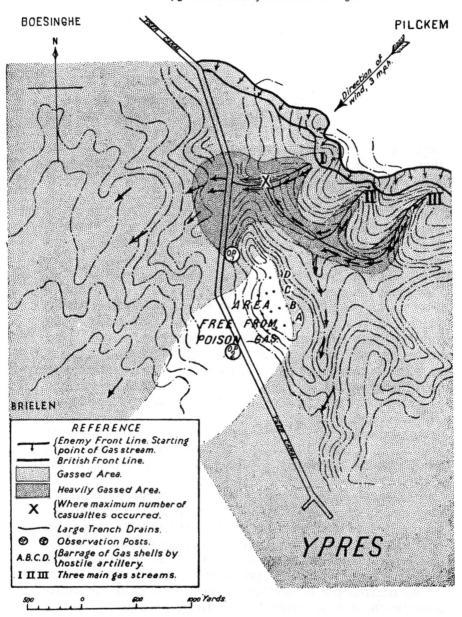

BOESINGHE

PILCKEM

N

Direction of wind, 3 m.p.h.

X

OP

D
C
AREA · B
A

FREE FROM
POISON GAS

OP

I II III

BRIELEN

YPRES

REFERENCE

┴	{Enemy Front Line. Starting point of Gas stream.
—	British Front Line.
▨	Gassed Area.
▨	Heavily Gassed Area.
X	{Where maximum number of casualties occurred.
⌐	Large Trench Drains.
⊘ ⊗	Observation Posts.
A.B.C.D.	{Barrage of Gas shells by hostile artillery.
I II III	Three main gas streams.

500   0   600   1000 Yards.

covering would be necessary provided that the installation was made soon before the cylinders were due to be discharged.

I had been put in touch with the Commander of the First Army, and learned from Sir Douglas Haig that he proposed to make the fullest possible use of gas and smoke on the first day of the infantry attack. His original plan of battle is shown on the accompanying map (at the end of Chapter V.) : the main blow was to be delivered by the Ist and IVth Corps on the front from Festubert to a point opposite Lens ; while two small subsidiary attacks were to be launched by the Indian Corps at Neuve Chapelle, and by the IIIrd Corps near Bois Grenier. Gas would be employed on the whole front of all three operations, as well as for a distance of from three to five hundred yards on both flanks of each ; and smoke, not only on the gas frontages but in the intervals between them, only two gaps being left, so that the enemy might be left in uncertainty as to where the blow would be delivered and be prevented from concentrating his artillery fire on the actual fronts selected for assault.

Fifty to a hundred cylinders were now arriving at Audruick every day, but there were fluctuations in the rate of supply : on 21st July there was already a shortage of a thousand cylinders on the number promised by the War Office for that date. A provisional maximum and minimum allotment had therefore to be made, and an order of priority of supply laid down. A gas frontage of ten thousand four hundred yards (which was increased later to fourteen thousand five hundred yards) was allowed for, in addition to twenty-eight thousand one hundred yards of smoke, making a total of twenty-two miles altogether, increased later to twenty-four and a half miles. This was an ambitious programme in view of the existing uncertainties and the novelty of the weapon.[1]

Fifteen cylinders per emplacement and five smoke candles were earmarked for the assaulting fronts, and three cylinders of gas and seventeen smoke candles for the flanks, each cylinder taking two minutes to discharge, and each candle the same time to burn out. Phosphorus hand-grenades (designed originally to set fire to the long grass

---

[1] Some weeks previously, when a gas frontage of five miles was being spoken of, Lord Kitchener suggested a less pretentious scheme.

which obscured the view in front of our parapets) were to be used in the smoke intervals, but not on the assaulting fronts, because these grenades, when they explode, scatter burning phosphorus about which was considered to be a source of danger to the infantry if they had to advance over it: phosphorus smoke, too, had less visible resemblance to gas than that issuing from the candles.

The first provisional allotment of cylinders and candles, based on estimated supplies, was as follows :—

Ist Corps	.	.	2850 cylinders and	2630 candles
IVth ,,	.	.	2250 ,,	,, 3000 ,,
Indian ,,	.	.	800 ,,	,, 2000 ,,
IIIrd ,,	.	.	600 ,,	,, 2000 ,,
Totals .	.	.	6500 ,,	,, 9630 ,,

But on 1st September there were only 3337 cylinders at Audruick, and only 900 arrived during the next fortnight ; so that it became evident that no cylinders would be available for the IIIrd Corps, and the number allotted to the Indian Corps was reduced to 160 : the fifteen cylinders per emplacement on the rest of the front were reduced to twelve, a corresponding increase being made in the number of smoke candles, the supply of which was ample, and the programme of discharge was altered accordingly.

On 22nd August we gave a demonstration at Helfaut to twenty or thirty of the senior Generals of the British Expeditionary Force, one or two alternative methods of cylinder installation being shown in the practice trenches as well as an actual discharge of gas. Sir Douglas Haig was present with his Operations Staff, as well as Generals Rawlinson (Ist Corps), Gough (IVth Corps), Pulteney (IIIrd Corps), Willcocks (Indian Corps), and their Chief Staff Officers, Chief Engineers and Divisional Commanders. Everything went well at this demonstration, and confidence in the gas and in the technique were established.

The attack was now fixed definitely for 15th September, and the next few weeks, during which I travelled on an average a hundred miles a day in a fast car, seem now like a nightmare. I had to give several other demonstrations at Helfaut to less exalted audiences ; visit all the divisions and corps in turn to make detailed arrangements ; the railway authorities to time the journeys for the special trains to carry the cylinders and pipes to their separate destinations ; the Director of Works for the construction of thousands of carrying-poles and rope-slings, and so on. I also had to make several hurried visits to England ; and all the while men for the Special Companies were arriving at the depot in driblets to receive lectures on their duties and courses of instruction, which became shorter and shorter as time went on.

On September the 9th War Office sanction was given for the formation of the fourth company, though approval for this increase had been anticipated ; but it was evident that the officers at any rate could not arrive in France in time. I therefore visited three Territorial battalions which had been withdrawn from the line into rest billets : these were the Artists' Rifles and the 5th and 13th Regiments of the London Rifle Brigade. I asked each of the Commanding Officers if they could lend me four subalterns who would care to perform a small deed outside the scope of their ordinary duties, and explained the nature of the adventure and the fix I was in. All promised without hesitation to help, and a day or two later the twelve volunteers joined at Helfaut, and they were of the greatest assistance to me in our first three gas attacks. (One of the Artists, Campbell-Smith, stayed on in the Special Brigade and rose in it to the rank of lieut.-colonel.) Even then I found myself lecturing to eight officers newly arrived from England as late as on the 18th September—seven days before our first gas attack took place ! (The longest period of training that anyone had was six weeks.) I had imagined myself to be without nerves, but I must admit that I gave instructions to the driver of my car about this time to leave his Klaxon alone and to use the motor horn only.

On 4th September the companies that had completed their training moved up to the front in sixty-eight motor-buses and eight lorries. All wore special brassards of pink, white and green, so that they might be distinguished and escape interference from infantry officers and regimental police.[1] Owing to changes in the original plan on

---

[1] These brassards were worn during the whole of 1916, but they fell into gradual disuse and were finally abandoned towards the end of the war. The German pioneer troops who handled cylinders were stated to have worn a white-and-black death's-head on their sleeves.

which my organisation had been based, it was no longer possible to adhere to the company system, and a composite company of eighteen sections went to the Ist Corps, under Captain Percy-Smith, and another of sixteen sections to the IVth Corps, under Captain Sanders. Later moves, on the 19th September, were Lieutenant Kent with two sections to the Indian Corps, and Lieutenants Pollitt and Bunker, each with two additional sections, to the Ist and IVth Corps respectively. The officers were all distributed according to a prearranged plan, and reported to the Commanders of the formations with which they had to work : they reconnoitred their fronts, selected bays in the trenches for the reception of cylinders and marked each emplacement with a number on a peg.

On this same day (4th September) I was sent by General Robertson to Sir Douglas Haig with a note to say that the opening date of the battle had been postponed to the 25th September, and this pause enabled me to spend several days in visiting practically all the emplacements along the whole front. On the morning of 15th September, the day previously fixed for the attack, there was a perfect westerly breeze blowing : I met General Robertson in St Omer, and as he passed me on the opposite pavement he raised his hand above his head to feel the wind and shrugged his shoulders in disappointment. The battle of Loos would have been far more successful if it had commenced that day.

On 17th September there were still more than a thousand cylinders fewer than the estimated number ; but after the despatch of the special trains on that date batches of cylinders were loaded into lorries every day as they arrived, and were taken up to the front direct from the ship at Boulogne. One lot, the last to arrive, left Runcorn by special train on 22nd September, reached Boulogne on the morning of the 24th and was carried into the trenches and put in position the same night !

On 18th September, Sir John French held his final conference at St Omer, at which twelve persons were present besides himself. These were Generals Robertson (the C.G.S.), Maxwell (Q.M.G.) ; the Commanders of the First, Second and Third Armies (Generals Sir Douglas Haig, Plumer and Monro ; the Commanders of the Cavalry, the Indian Cavalry and the XIth Corps (Generals Fanshawe, Rimington and Haking) ; the General commanding the Flying Corps (Trenchard) ; the Artillery Adviser (General Du Cane) ; the Engineer-in-Chief (General Fowke) ; and myself. Sir John explained his whole plan of battle on a map pinned to a blackboard, and some discussion followed, in the course of which Sir Douglas Haig mentioned the failure in the full supply of cylinders that had been promised. The Commander-in-Chief sent for me later on the same day, and told me that I was not to mind what anyone thought about this failure : I was under him personally and was to understand definitely that he was perfectly satisfied with everything that I had done, and his opinion was the only one that mattered. I had carried out a great work, and nobody living could have done more.

It had been my original intention to have all the cylinders loaded into lorries at Audruick and taken up to Helfaut. Here they were to be joined by the sections under their own officers, who would then proceed independently, each with its own allotment, to the infantry rendezvous : the cylinders and pipes would then be unboxed and carried straight into position.[1] But with the extension of the original plan of attack this method became impracticable, and railway transport had to be resorted to.

Two railheads were designated, one each for the Ist and IVth Corps : here the cylinders and pipes were unboxed by men of the Special Companies and were taken in lorries and G.S. wagons as far forward as the condition of the roads permitted. They were then carried by infantry parties into the front line, where they were received by men of the Special Companies, placed in the bays prepared for them and sand-bagged over : they were arranged in groups of eleven, twelve and thirteen on the Ist and IVth Corps fronts, excepting on the extreme right and left flanks, where only three were available at each emplacement. In the Indian Corps trenches four, five, or six cylinders were grouped together, but only in salients specially selected as suitable.

All the transport arrangements proceeded like clockwork : they were extremely well organised and there was

---

[1] Cylinders continued to be sent to France in boxes until October 1916, when the practice was discontinued owing to the cost (12s. each) and the necessity for secrecy having ceased.

not the slightest hitch anywhere, although 5500 cylinders containing 150 tons of chlorine were placed in position and about 8000 infantry took part in the carry ; nor was a single cylinder hit by a stray shot, either on the journey or when in position in the front line during the four days' bombardment which followed. The IVth Corps had even arranged for a patrol of three aeroplanes over their rail-head to prevent observation during the movement of the apparatus. These precautions met with entire success, and, as will be seen in the next chapter, the gas attack came as a complete surprise to the enemy, who had no inkling whatever of its preparation.

The meteorological office, under Captain Gold, had now been at work for some weeks. Gold was receiving reports, addressed to him direct, from stations all over Europe ; and with these and the observations made by trained men of the Special Companies established in seventeen stations behind the front of the army he was able to issue weather forecasts twice a day. He was very successful with these, but wore an air of great solemnity as he pored over his charts. I once asked him what weather he would predict if he drew the Queen of Spades out of the pack, but he denied emphatically that he made any use whatever of cards. As may well be imagined, the accuracy of his forecasts was examined with keen interest by Sir Douglas Haig, in order to estimate what faith he might put in them ; and Gold came well out of the scrutiny.

CHAPTER V.

THE BATTLE OF LOOS.

ON September the 24th the critical moment had arrived : the forecast for the following day was not very favourable for the discharge of gas, but towards evening it became more so, and from his battle headquarters at Hinges chateau Sir Douglas Haig issued the order for the gas to be discharged at dawn the next morning and for the infantry assault to follow.

There were over four hundred gas emplacements in the line, and each one was provided with a watch, accurately synchronised after midnight, and with a printed programme (one of these is reproduced on the next page) for the release of the gas and smoke, as follows : at zero hour (which was to be communicated later) six cylinders were to be discharged, one after the other : with these it was hoped to take the enemy by surprise during the first twelve minutes. Then followed in turn eight minutes of smoke, another twelve minutes of gas and a final eight minutes of smoke, during the last two of which all cylinders were to be shut off if they had not been previously emptied. At zero plus forty minutes the assault was to be delivered ; and it will be seen that it was to be preceded, for the sake of safety, by a minimum period of two minutes of smoke discharge, and probably by a good deal more if the programme was adhered to strictly.

It had been agreed that it would not be safe to depend on a message issued from Hinges and passed in turn through the Corps, Division and Brigade headquarters, being delivered to the men crowded in the front-line trench in any less period than two hours ; so that with zero hour provisionally fixed for 5.50 A.M. any alteration in the order for the discharge of the gas would have to be issued at 4 A.M. at the latest. This did not cause me anxiety, because I had given orders to all my officers that the cylinders were not to be opened unless the conditions were favourable, both in regard to the velocity and the direction of the wind. I was, of course, justified in this action on the well-known principle that an officer on the spot is not only entitled, but it is his duty in certain circumstances, to disobey orders given by higher authority.

A

SECRET.—(Not to be carried forward in the Assault).

TIME TABLE OF GAS.

ATTACKS SOUTH OF THE LA BASSÉE CANAL.

(Minutes).	
0	Start the gas and run 6 cylinders one after the other at full blast until all are exhausted.
0-12‡—0-20	Start the smoke. The smoke is to run concurrently with the gas if the gas is not exhausted by 0-12.
0-20	Start the gas again and run 6 cylinders one after the other at full blast until all are exhausted.
0-32—0-40	Start the smoke again. The smoke is to run concurrently with the gas if the gas is not exhausted by 0-32.
0-38	Turn all gas off punctually. Thicken up smoke with triple candles. Prepare for assault.
0-40	ASSAULT.

‡ On the 3-cylinder and no-cylinder fronts the smoke will be started at 0-6.

Note.—From 0 to 0-40, front system of hostile trenches will be kept under continuous shrapnel fire. Defences further in rear under bombardment of H.E. shell of all calibres.
At 0-40 artillery fire will lift as required.

The troops detailed for the assault were now in general movement towards the front line throughout the army area, and with them went the men of the Special Companies, 1404 in all, including 57 officers, carrying the pipe connections. As each officer reached his allotted station and occupied his emplacements he notified me by telephone, and at the same time sent in his first wind message thus, " 10.30 P.M., all ready, south-west four " ; and at every hour throughout the night all the forty officers in the front line took wind readings and sent reports to me personally, the messages being given priority on the line by previous arrangement with the Signal Service.

Monier-Williams and I shared a room with Gold in Sir
Douglas Haig's chateau: I had a large-scale trench-map
of the whole gas front spread out in front of me on a trestle
table, with the name of every section officer written against
his special stretch of trench. About midnight, much to my
relief, the last of the 'all ready' messages reached me,
and the line of small flags which were pinned to the map
as each message arrived was complete. This was the
culminating point of three and a half months of preparation: I had complete confidence in the courage and
determination of my officers and men, and everything
now depended on the vagaries of the wind.

Orderlies came in every few minutes with further
wind reports, and as each was received the corresponding
flag was pointed in the appropriate direction and the latest
wind reading was marked on it, there being a remarkable
resemblance throughout the night between the reports of
individual officers stationed in the same parts of the
line.

As the hours passed, General Butler, Sir Douglas
Haig's Chief of Staff, looked in from time to time, in-
spected the map and rejoined the Army Commander to
report on the conditions. Towards dawn, to the great
anxiety of everybody concerned, the wind gradually
became more unfavourable on the left front of the attack,
astride the La Bassée canal; but farther south there was
still a chance that the cylinders could be opened. Half an
hour before zero hour there was a dramatic episode: Sir
Douglas, becoming more and more doubtful of the wisdom
of his order to discharge the gas, inquired of the Corps
Commanders on the telephone whether it was still possible
to cancel it; but he was informed that it was now too
late. The conditions for a successful gas attack were more
than doubtful; but during the preceding weeks he had
formed the conviction that in the absence of sufficient heavy
artillery and an adequate ammunition supply no attack
ought to take place in any circumstances unless the conditions were favourable for the discharge of gas. He had
represented this view, but, owing to the necessity of
supporting the French attack which was due to commence
on the same day, he was overruled; so that he was prepared to take a risk with the gas, and events proved that
he was fully justified in making this decision.

Zero hour arrived at last at 5.50 A.M., and with a re-doubled artillery bombardment the gas and smoke were released all along the front. The first aeroplane report that came in a few minutes later was to the effect that the gas cloud was rolling steadily over towards the German lines; and from the top of the tall wooden tower which had been specially constructed as an observation post in the chateau grounds an awe-inspiring spectacle was visible, the whole countryside to the front, as far as the eye could reach, being enveloped in what appeared to be a vast prairie conflagration; for, apart from the fumes and dust caused by the artillery drum-fire and the clouds of gas and the smoke from eleven thousand candles, twenty-five thousand phosphorus hand-grenades were spurting out dense white fumes, and ten thousand bombs from the twenty-nine 4-inch Stokes mortars, as well as many thousands more from a hundred and thirty-five catapults, and from 95 mm. and 2-inch trench-mortars, were burning in front of all the German strong-points and were enveloping their artillery observers and machine-gunners in an impene-trable cloud.

Immediately the gas was observed the enemy opened a heavy bombardment of our front line, in the course of which a large number of gas shells were used. In parts of the front the shooting was inaccurate and the discharge of gas was not interfered with; but in others heavy shells fell in the trench or burst on the parapet. In some of the bays tons of earth were overturned, completely burying the cylinder emplacements and their crews: parapet pipes were hurled backwards, connections were snapped and a few of the cylinders were burst by fragments of shell, resulting in escapes of gas against which the Vermorel sprayers provided for such an emergency were useless. (These were apparatus similar to, but much larger than, the disinfecting sprayers often seen in places of entertain-ment.) In the din of the bombardment and in these dis-tracting circumstances the men of the Special Companies, now receiving their baptism of fire, stuck to their work with the utmost gallantry and devotion: they were further hampered by the gas helmets which they were compelled to adjust, and by defective pipes and leaky joints which were experienced by every section, without exception. But in spite of all difficulties there were some bays from which all twelve of the cylinders that had been installed were emptied, though there were others where the officers, exercising their discretion, discontinued the discharge as soon as it was evident that the cloud was likely to interfere with the movements of the infantry. At one point one of our sergeants (Barton), who had received a bullet wound through the thigh earlier in the night, insisted on super-intending his emplacements during the whole period of the gas discharge, and he repaired several defective pipes with his own hands, thereby preventing leakages of gas.

Detailed reports from every one of the forty section officers, as well as from company and other commanders, reached me in the next day or two, and I was able to con-struct a very clear picture—truer and clearer, of course, than any that has yet been recorded—of what occurred all along the front during and after the gas discharge.

Many of the officers (including myself) also followed the assaulting columns into the captured German trenches in order to ascertain what the effect of the gas had been ; while others attended wounded men or acted as escort to prisoners ; and, as a number of them could speak German, they were able to find out a good deal about what had happened on the other side.

Up to the moment when the last ' all ready ' message reached me, the preparations for the gas installation and for the infantry assault had been a model of efficient staff organisation ; but afterwards, owing to the crowded state of the trenches, there was a certain amount of confusion. Along the whole of the front of one division, as well as in certain other portions of the line, the men detailed to light the smoke candles did not reach their stations at all ; while the final message specifying zero hour was left so late that it was only received by some of the men at the cylinder bays two, three and six minutes before the moment fixed for the discharge to commence. In spite of this the gas was released punctually all along the line excepting at one emplacement, the farthest from the tele-phone on one section front, where it was half a minute late.

On the front of the Indian Corps (the Meerut Division) the wind was favourable (west, 4 m.p.h.) until one hour before zero, when it veered (see map at end of chapter). Only a few of the cylinders were opened at all, and these were shut off when it became evident that the cloud would not reach the German lines. (But see page 81.)

In spite of this the moral effect was such that some of the enemy came out of their trenches with their hands up and surrendered as soon as the gas was seen ; while the men of the 4th Black Watch were able to form up on their parapet, preparatory to the assault, without being fired at. Although the gas caused inconvenience, a good deal of ground was gained by this division at the first rush, but it had to be abandoned later in the day.

The 2nd Division was handicapped by the gas discharge more than any other. Captain Percy-Smith tried to get the order cancelled before zero hour, and the commanders of two of the three infantry brigades in the line were warned that the gas attack was impossible, as what little wind there was blew right along the trench. In spite of this the order to carry on was repeated peremptorily, the message coming from the headquarters of the division, and perhaps from still higher authority. Even then one of the section officers refused to comply until ordered to do so by the commander of one of the infantry battalions in the front trench. The discharge commenced accordingly (there were only three cylinders in each emplacement north of the canal), but it was discontinued almost at once, though not soon enough to prevent the infantry from being seriously hampered by it when the time came to deliver the assault. As the German wire was found to be intact, none of their trenches were gained excepting on the extreme right of the division front : here the gas discharged by the 9th Division on the right, drifting northwards, reached the objectives of the 1st Middlesex Regiment (of the 2nd Division), who made one of the most gallant efforts of the day, and wounded men from this battalion reported having seen many gassed Germans in this section of the German line. (Actually this drift of the gas cloud from right to left occurred all along the front of the First Army, so that even when divisions gained no advantage from the gas discharged on their own front the troops on their left had the benefit of it.)

The reports referred to above, made by wounded men, were discredited at the time ; but two letters were brought to my notice a week or two later which confirmed their statements. The first was written to a friend by a telephonist on the headquarter staff of the 1st Middlesex Regiment when in hospital in England, and it reached me through the censor's office, the following being an extract : " I don't want to see another scene like last Saturday morning. It was just Hell with the lid off. You will have read of the splendid advance we made south of the La Bassée canal. The artillery bombarded them for four days and four nights, never stopped, seven hundred guns behind us. At 5.45 on Saturday morning we turned the gas on the devils—it was an awful sight—and at 6.30 we climbed over the parapet and charged them. I carried a field telephone : four of us started ; I was the only one to reach the first German trench, which was full of dead, about three or four deep, all gassed. But they had the machine-guns in the third-line trenches and they mowed us down, and everywhere was mud and blood. When they called the roll on the 1st Middlesex, 96 answered present out of 1020. All the officers except two went down ; but that is the price of victory. Poor Baines was killed. The last I saw of him was running down after some Germans down their communication trench, bombing them as he went." [1]

On the front of the next division, the 9th, the gas attack was much more successful, though this, too, was disputed. The wind at zero was blowing from the W.S.W. at 2-3 m.p.h., and the cloud went well across to the German lines : it undoubtedly aided the attack, although some of the infantry on the extreme left advanced ten minutes too soon and ran into the cloud. On the right, on the front of the 26th Brigade, the men assembled on the parapet for the assault without anyone being hit long before they moved forward, and jocular N.C.O.'s insisted on correct dressing and sloping of arms. The 7th Seaforths walked across to the Hohenzollern Redoubt and then on to the main German line with very little loss, and advanced for nearly a mile in the first rush. A number of different individuals, including a wounded sergeant of the 6th K.O.S.B.'s, reported finding many Germans in the trenches suffering from the effects of gas ; and one in particular saw five men and two officers lying heaped in one place, blue in the face and undoubtedly gassed to death. Two gassed

---

[1] According to the official history this battalion did not pass the German wire, which they are said to have found intact.

German prisoners were brought in from their third line of defence.

Farther to the south, too, on the front of the 7th Division, the wind was favourable (S.W., 2-3 m.p.h.), though the cloud moved so slowly that some of the infantry overtook it. Three wounded officers said that the enemy were so completely demoralised that they were observed retreating from their trenches in panic. Men of the 20th Brigade (now commanded by Trefusis, mentioned on page 12) reported that there were few Germans left in their first and second lines, so that there was no need to enter them, but that many gassed were seen in the communicating trenches leading to the rear and in the third German line where whole machine-gun crews were lying gassed to death. The 2nd Gordons in this brigade moved forward for more than a mile in the first two hours, and the Divisional Commander (General Capper) expressed the opinion that the gas had been a success, and that no advance would have been made if it had not been used. Prisoners stated that the gas came to them as a complete surprise : they had never heard of their own use of gas and were unaware that our employment of it was in the nature of a reprisal.

The 1st Division next to the south was singularly unfortunate owing to the circumstance that their line formed a distinct bulge in the general trend of the position, with the result that the gas from the division on their right (the 15th) swept across their front. This, of course, affected the right brigade (the 2nd) in particular, and their attack collapsed as it encountered undamaged wire, intact parapets and a singularly gallant defence made by the German unit opposite to them (the 157th Regiment, under Captain Ritter). Nevertheless, when these trenches were occupied later in the day (opposite ' Lone Tree ') one of the regimental police reported seeing some of the enemy dead who were apparently unwounded and gassed, wearing small greenish respirators over the mouth and nose.

The 1st Brigade on the left of this division was much more successful in their attack and gained a lot of ground : they were reported to have entered Hulluch village, a mile and a half from their starting-point. For some reason, along the whole of the front of the 1st Division, the men detailed to light the smoke candles failed to appear, and all the protection from view that was afforded to the assaulting columns came from the dense gas cloud.

On the 15th Division front the wind was lighter than on either flank. On the extreme left the gas discharge went well, and it gave the infantry great confidence, some of them insisting on helping to turn on the valves. In the centre the conditions were not so favourable, though some of the gas undoubtedly reached the enemy's trenches, numbers of gassed Germans being found in the Loos road redoubt and in the dug-outs into which they retreated and died, as well as in the communication trenches farther back. The Commander of the 1st North-amptonshire Regiment told me that one of his officers (the Quartermaster) had found a German officer seated in a chair in a dug-out, unwounded, though dead. On the south-west face of this redoubt a captain in a field company found eight or ten German soldiers lying at the bottom of a trench who appeared to be unwounded and to have been killed by gas, and a corporal in the same unit took charge of a number of gassed prisoners. An infantry sergeant, who helped to bury twenty-three Germans in the village of Loos later on, noticed that some of them were wearing brownish respirators tied round the head and that they were a noticeably queer dark-green colour in the face. At the time the gas was not believed to have assisted the 15th Division in their attack, and the gas officers seem to have been influenced in their decision to open the cylinders by the conviction expressed by infantry officers that the German position in front of them was so strong that unless the gas was turned on they had a very rough time before them. At one point on this front a corporal of the Special Companies, Cousens, a science master from a Durham school, following the infantry after they had cap-tured the German trench, entered a dug-out unarmed and found a German colonel, a captain and five men, all of whom he brought back prisoners.

Finally, on the 47th Division front, the extreme right of the British line, the gas attack was an unqualified success : the cloud went well over to the German lines and none of it hung back. On the left the first two German lines were captured in fifteen minutes, and prisoners admitted that they had suffered many gas casualties, especially among their officers. They said that they did

not know what the gas cloud meant, and that it came to
them as a great surprise : fear of it kept many of them
in their dug-outs until it was too late to meet the assaulting troops. Six dead Germans were found in one dug-out
in this part of the line, sitting huddled up and apparently
unwounded ; and a German officer volunteered the information that as soon as the gas entered his trench he
lost all control over his men, although they belonged to a
good battalion, and he was unable to keep them in the
front line. He added that without the gas we would
have had no earthly chance of taking his trenches, as the
barbed wire in front was very strong and his dug-outs
had not been damaged by the bombardment. On the
right of this division, too, the gas was very effective, in
spite of the fact that for the last one thousand yards—
more than half of the division front—there were only
three cylinders in each emplacement ; and numbers of
Germans who were badly affected by it came over from the
region of the ' Double Crassier ' and surrendered shortly
after the assault. A German-speaking corporal of the
Special Companies questioned these men (of the 22nd
Reserve Infantry Regiment), and he was told that for the
last four days there had been no issue of rations owing to
the bombardment. On the morning of the 25th September
they had been completely surprised by the gas discharge ;
practically none of them had respirators and the weaker
ones were immediately overcome. The stronger members
stuffed socks into their mouths, and the married decided
to go to a place where there was no gas and await the
arrival of the British troops and surrender to them. One
of the officers of the Special Companies made a systematic
search of the German trenches after the infantry had
overrun them, and he fully confirmed the supposition
as to the nature of the protection against gas with which
the German troops had been equipped and on which our
attack was based. The enemy had gauze respirators in
the front line, tied round the back of the head, but only a
pad respirator in the support trenches, held over the mouth
and nose by pressure of the hand. Machine-gunners
were provided with the haversack form of oxygen apparatus, as was anticipated. The gas had, in consequence,
much more effect in the support line than in the front
trench, which they had abandoned only to come into our

75

artillery barrage, forty dead being counted on a small sector of fifty yards. In the front line they had apparently been more frightened than disabled, and at one point over seventy had come forward to surrender, but had been killed by their own machine-guns.

In making his report on the gas attack, the Commander of the 47th Division wrote : " The enemy opened heavy rifle and machine-gun fire immediately the gas was launched, but the fire was very wild and high and gradually died down : our assault coming up behind the thick curtain of gas and smoke practically took the enemy by surprise. There is no doubt that the success of our assault was entirely due to the gas and smoke attack, which, if it effected nothing more, formed a screen to cover the advancing troops."

It will be seen from the foregoing that the effect produced by the gas varied considerably in different parts of the front. Undoubtedly it influenced the result of the battle to a marked extent, whether the effect was material or moral ; and it is probable that in the absence of sufficient heavy artillery in the preliminary bombardment, which resulted in the inadequate destruction of wire and in many of the machine-gun emplacements and dug-outs being left untouched, no advance would have taken place anywhere if the order to release gas had been cancelled, while the casualties among the infantry would have been far heavier.

If fortune had been a little kinder, if the wind had been only slightly more favourable, there is no doubt whatever that Sir John French would have gained a smashing victory on this day.

Infantry committed to an assault are much too intent on their own immediate tasks to concern themselves with anything outside them ; nor are they likely to find many gassed men near the front. As may easily be imagined, soldiers feeling themselves suffocating in gas lose their sense of discipline, abandon their posts and struggle towards the rear, or their strength fails them in the communication trench in their retreat ; so that if I had not made special arrangements to collect information from every possible source of the actual effects of the gas, from wounded men returning from the German trenches, as well as in the dressing-stations, from prisoners and from the personal observation of the officers and men of the Special Companies who did not take part in the assault, but who watched it at close quarters, no evidence would have come to light at all from the troops, as no systematic effort was made to obtain it. At the risk of wearying my readers—and perhaps of shocking them—I have described the gas attack at the battle of Loos in some detail, partly because this was the first test to which our new 'Fifth Arm,' created with such speed and with so little choice of material at its disposal, had been put ; and partly to remove the impression which was, unfortunately, general in the army in France as well as among the public at home, that the gas discharge had been a hindrance rather than a help to our troops. This mistaken belief produced a pre-judice against the use of gas which made our future work much more difficult and which it took us a long time to overcome.

It is a well-known characteristic of our nation to belittle its own efforts and to extol those of its adversaries ; and there was a good illustration of this attitude after Loos. Our gas, it was said, was no use, though it was precisely the same as that employed by the Germans in their success-ful cloud attacks up to this time. One infantryman was reported to have said at this time : " Not only is our gas no bloody good, but it even blows back and kills our own men ! " Another story was repeated to me in proof of its futility, which ran as follows : the professor at home who was responsible for the research work on gas suddenly thought of testing the effect of chlorine on some animal ; so he put a rabbit into a closed chamber, and measured into the latter a quantity of gas which was expected to prove fatal within five minutes. But at the end of this period he found the rabbit apparently unharmed and nibbling a lettuce leaf. Puzzled at this behaviour he increased the dose of gas liberally and exposed it to the fumes for half an hour ; but even then the obstinate little animal seemed none the worse, and in his vexation he even imagined that he heard it purring. Irritated beyond measure he released all the gas at his disposal and left it to do its malignant work for six hours ; but when he went to remove the corpse—the rabbit bit him !

Subsequent experience throughout the war showed that evidence of the effects of gas attacks often only comes to hand long afterwards, the best being found in captured enemy documents ; and so it proved in this case.

The following are extracts from official British Intelligence summaries (G.H.Q. and First Army) which were published a week or two after September the 25th :—

" Prisoners of the 157th Regiment (opposite our 15th Division) taken between the Loos Road redoubt and the Double Crassier stated that the effect of the gas was not very noticeable, causing only slight inconvenience, but no permanent effect. The gas was effective from the Grenay-Lens railway to about the Hohenzollern redoubt, though owing to the light and varying breeze it was much more effective in some places than in others. The moral effect was very great. Many prisoners who were wearing masks when taken were found to be suffering from the effects of gas. The oxygen apparatus intended for the use of officers appear not to have been kept near their owners, and were usually taken and used by the man nearest them. Although the officers had warned the men that a gas attack might take place, they do not appear to have believed that gas would be used against them. Prisoners of the 11th Reserve Regiment taken near the Vermelles-Hulluch road (the boundary of our 1st and 7th Divisions) said that the gas caused considerable discomfort. Respirators were used, and goggles for the eyes. Cylinders of oxygen were kept for reviving bad cases. Prisoners of the 22nd Reserve Infantry Regiment (opposite our 47th Division) taken in the Loos area said that the gas came to them as a complete surprise."

" These men (of the 8th Coy., 11th Reserve Regiment, opposite our 9th Division) were all gassed, and crept into dug-outs on the west face of the Hohenzollern redoubt, where they remained for twelve hours before they were captured. Their experiences concerning the result of the gas are practically similar. They are all provided with small respirators which they do not consider to have been very effective. They became faint and were subjected to immediate coughing and watering of the eyes. This gradually passed off, and they do not appear to have suffered from any after effects. They are of opinion that while a good many became unconscious for the time being, they eventually recovered."

Extract from report on the examination of prisoners of the 22nd Reserve Infantry Regiment :—

" 1. The attack was not expected owing to the distance between the trenches, about seven hundred yards.

2. Soldiers' respirators proved useless. They were too loose and failed to cover the nose.

3. Soldiers had no protection for their eyes. The gas caused the eyes to smart to the extent of temporarily putting them out of action.

4. Officers had neglected to bring their masks. Some of them had just time to put on goggles.

5. Reviving apparatus (oxygen breathing sets) were too few, and they were appropriated by men nearest to them.

6. The German troops were thrown into confusion through want of preparation.

7. Men realising the shortcomings of their respirators fled into dug-outs. These were at first free from gas. Later on the gas settled in hollows of the ground and in the dug-outs, and men returned to the surface.

8. This measure of precaution, however, was to some extent thwarted by the fact that the breeze was very slight and that therefore the gas had not yet dissipated on the surface.

9. The losses of the 117th Division from gas and from the effective bombardment were very great. Prisoners could, however, give no estimate.''

Some interesting accounts of the battle were also forthcoming from the German Press. Thus Dr Scheuermann, the special correspondent of the 'Deutsche Tageszeitung,' wrote :—

" On the morning of the 25th we heard our drums frantically beating a warning, and almost simultaneously a strange unaccountable smell was noticed in the air. Then we knew that the gas attack had begun. It was only by the movements in the foremost lines of the enemy's trenches that we knew an early attack was coming. Of course, by way of precaution, all measures had been taken in expectation of a gas attack. The atmosphere was rather clouded and there was a mild west wind. By keeping an intent look-out it was possible to distinguish waves of black smoke which slowly made their way towards our positions, but which were at first undistinguishable from the light fog prevailing. Our men, having been warned, at once put on their masks while cloud upon cloud of smoke rolled towards them. It was noticeable that the British Commanders were following a certain system. First of all came a whitish kind of gas, immediately followed by a cloud of black gassy smoke. This went on for some time. This black fire-damp penetrated to the depths of our trenches, and then swept over them to the trenches beyond. It covered not merely the whole front, but even the Headquarters of the General Staff which lay far behind the lines, and it was so thick at that point that it was hardly possible to see ten paces in front of one. The effects of the gas upon those of our troops who had not provided themselves with masks were very different."

And as the description ended here in the London paper in which it was quoted (the 'Daily Telegraph'), having apparently been cut by the censor out of consideration for the feelings of the British public, I obtained the rest of the article from the editor.

"Some were killed instantaneously, but not many, comparatively speaking. Others—the greater number—were simply stupefied and lay where they fell. Most of the latter were discovered by us afterwards and brought into our lines, where they soon recovered consciousness. A good many, however, were taken prisoners by the English when in a state of coma."

Another account was published in the 'Berliner Tageblatt,' written by Bernard Kellermann, its war correspondent :—

"Then whitish fog-banks began to creep slowly nearer. Our men at first thought that the approaching bank of vapour was mist, but very soon they knew what was the matter. It was a gas attack, and the order was issued, 'Put on the gas masks.' The bank of fog passed over our trenches, then came a low bank of black-green smoke creeping towards us, and then again another bank of gas some ten minutes behind the first. Altogether three or four double waves of whitish gas and smoke swept over our trenches. Some men coughed and fell down. The others stood at the ready as long as possible. Behind the fourth gas and smoke cloud there suddenly emerged Englishmen in thick lines and storming columns. They rose suddenly from the earth wearing smoke masks over their faces and looking not like soldiers but like devils. These were bad and terrible hours. The adjoining Division also reported a gas attack, and that their first line had been stormed by the English. The smell of the gas made itself keenly noticeable. The fog was so thick, even among the staffs to the rear, that one could not see ten yards in front of one. Rumours flew about, reports circulated like wildfire. Then at last news became more definite. The British between the last gas waves had succeeded in storming the first trenches of our Division. Thus it happened."

Some accounts of the gas attack appeared, too, in the London papers, among them the following letter from an officer (regiment not stated) :—

"In our section of the advance the experiment was a great success, and was the factor instrumental in saving the lives of many of our own men. When the bombardment with high explosives had finished, and the gas had done its work and partially melted away with the favourable breeze, our incomparable infantrymen made their historic rush to the first and second lines of the German trenches. We simply walked into them without practically any loss of life. It was then we saw the deadly effect of our gas. The Germans had suffered as we too had suffered in the past. Many of them did not have time to get to their supply of respirators, and were lying around in helpless and huddled heaps. Others with respirators hastily fastened were in almost as bad a state."

It was not until Christmas 1916, fifteen months later, that any official German documents referring to the gas attack at Loos came into our possession. The following are a few brief extracts from the reports that were issued by the German Commanders :—

Second Army Headquarters, 11/10/15, signed von Bülow.

"Nothing was noticed of preparations for a gas attack. Apparently the English had not built their gas cylinders into the parapet, but had installed them in mine galleries which had been driven forward in order to prevent their being destroyed in advance by artillery fire. It is probable that these mine galleries were only opened up shortly before the attack, and the gas then discharged."

VIIth Army Corps Headquarters, 27/9/15 (covering the northern half of the British attack).

"13th Regiment (opposite our Meerut Division). Protected by these clouds the English managed to get to our trenches. The effect on different people varied. Taking it altogether, the gas caused general illness, and in some cases was slightly stupefying."

"56th Regiment (opposite our 2nd Division, north of the La Bassée canal). Up to the present 72 gas casualties have appeared in the hospitals, amongst them a number of officers. From what we can see at present, serious gas poisoning only happened to those men who for any reason had no mask or who were not trained in its use. This, for example, was the case of a few men amongst the reserves who were hurried up in reinforcement ; by officers who had raised their masks to give orders ; and in the case of men whose masks were not sufficiently moist. No deaths have been recorded so far from the gas. On the other hand, there are a large number of cases of unconsciousness, severe bronchitis and discharge of blood and yellow material from the mouth. All gas casualties treated with oxygen in the Forward Aid Posts rapidly recovered."

(*Note.*—We had not imagined that any gas could have reached the German lines on this sector.) And then in an addendum dated 6/10/15 :—

" The valves of the bottles were apparently opened by means of a time fuze. The effect varied very much. In Sectors E and F the chlorine content of the gas cloud caused unconsciousness, general illness and burning of the eyes. The A.K. has 120 gas casualties."

In spite of the wording at the head of the printed programme of the gas discharge (which forbade men to carry it forward in the assault), the following remark appeared in this German document : " A time-table of the attack was taken from an English officer south of the La Bassée canal."

Fourth Army Corps Headquarters, 27/9/15 (covering the southern half of the British attack).

" No preparations for a gas attack had been observed. The four gas clouds which were projected against our position only blew away gradually after half an hour to an hour. There was practically no wind. The gas cloud was so strong that at 6 kilometres behind the front it was only possible to see at 10 paces distance. The following new experience has been gained. At 1500 metres from the enemy trenches the artillery was in great danger from gas. Breech-blocks became unusable, and it was impossible to give orders. Anti-gas appliances must be given out in such quantity that all supports and reserves can be fitted out with them. The respirators (old type) were satisfactory at first. By the ever-recurring gas clouds they gradually became less effective."

The Chief of the General Staff of the Fifth German Army, 30/9/15, wrote : ." Among the materials used was Prussic Acid in shells and hand-grenades." (!)

And the Commander of the XIVth Reserve Corps, on 3/10/15 : " The G.O.C. of the Fourth (German) Army Corps is of the view that the temporary success of the gas attack was only made possible by the fact that the anti-gas appliances were not used in time, and that the troops lost their heads because of the unusual experience."

The following references to the gas attack at Loos have been made by German historians :—

General Schwarte : " The English succeeded in releasing gas clouds on a large scale. Their success on this occasion was due to the fact that they took us by surprise. Our troops refused to believe in the danger, and were not sufficiently adept in the use of defensive measures as prescribed by G.H.Q."

And on another page :—

" The partial break-through near Loos was chiefly due to an English cloud attack." [1]

Extract from the War Diary of the Sixth German Army :—

" Gas and smoke persisted until 10 A.M., and penetrated in great density as far as $4\frac{1}{2}$ kilometres behind the front line (Wingles). There was very little wind and the clouds dispersed slowly. In the deep trenches the gas lay very thick and persistent and the smoke prevented all visibility. In Wingles one could only see 30 paces to the front, and in the trenches 3. There were no ill-effects from the smoke. The effect of the gas on our men, who were warned in time and were able to put on their protective outfits, varied with the density and the susceptibility of individuals. It fluctuated between momentary effect and complete loss of ability to fight, but the general effect was relatively small. The smoke allowed some companies to be surprised. . . . The masks then in use broke down under the later gas waves. The formation of rust on the metal parts of the weapons, which had not been observed hitherto, made the guns and machine-guns useless. More effective was the complete absence of lower leadership, which was due to the fact that officers and under-officers could not give loud commands under their masks, and could not inspire the troops with their own example in the dense smoke and gas fog. The troops could not withstand the unusual circumstances and the numerical superiority of the enemy."

In the history of the 157th Regiment (N.W. of Loos) there is this sentence : " From Section G came news that severe losses had been caused by gas." And in that

---

[1] Dr Addison who, in ' Four and a half years,' does not often mention events in France, says : " October 7th, 1915. An interesting account has come from the front of the effect of the gas used " (on 25th September). " In some instances it was the use of gas which made the advance possible."

of the 233rd Field Artillery Regiment : " The effect of the gas caused sickness and fainting and lachrymation."

I will conclude this chapter by quoting the Commanders-in-Chief on both sides. The German official communiqué of 25th September 1915 contained these words : " Even this retirement was not the result of the English Commander's abilities, but was the consequence of a successful surprise attack with intoxicating gases." While Sir John French (who made no reference to the use of gas in his communiqué of 26th September, and first mentions it in the communiqué of 14th October : " We attacked the enemy's trenches " on the 13th, between Hulluch and the Hohenzollern Redoubt, " under cover of a cloud of smoke and gas " [1]) wrote in his despatch dated 15th October 1915 : " Owing to the repeated use by the enemy of asphyxiating gases in their attacks on our positions, I have been compelled to resort to similar methods ; and a detachment was organised for this purpose, which took part in the operations commencing on September 25 for the first time. Although the enemy was known to have been prepared for such reprisals, our gas attack met with marked success, and produced a demoralising effect in some of the opposing units, of which ample evidence was forthcoming in the captured trenches. The men who undertook this work carried out their unfamiliar duties during a heavy bombardment with conspicuous gallantry and coolness ; and I feel confident in their ability to more than hold their own should the enemy again resort to this method of warfare."

[1] The 'Times' on 5th October quoted in small print, for the first time and without comment, a reference to the gas attack on 25th September made in the German Wireless Press.

CHAPTER VI.

EXPANSION INTO THE SPECIAL BRIGADE.

On 25th September some of the British units advanced as far as 4500 yards from their original front line, and eighteen German guns were captured as well as over three thousand prisoners. So great, in fact, was the effect produced on the enemy by this thrust that convoys of their transport were formed up as far back as Douai (ten miles) ready to evacuate the area behind the battle front. But by the evening of the same day the British attack had lost its momentum, reserves were slow in moving forward to exploit the success gained, and German reinforcements, hurried forward from every direction, had arrived; so that the chance of a break-through, for which three British cavalry divisions as well as an Indian and a French cavalry corps were waiting, had passed. The attack of the French Tenth Army in Artois, on our right, had also failed. On the following days German counter-attacks succeeded in regaining much of the lost ground, mainly owing to the superiority of their hand-grenades (the Mills bomb had not yet reached us), and by 3rd October even the Hohen-zollern Redoubt had been recaptured.

In order to support the attack of the Guards Division on Hill 70 on 27th September a number of ' diversions ' were arranged elsewhere, among them being a second discharge of gas on the front of the 2nd Division astride the La Bassée canal. This discharge was very hurriedly organised, the number of cylinders in each emplacement was raised to eight (there had only been three on 25th September north of the canal), and the sections were reinforced by men transferred from farther south.

Zero was fixed for 5 P.M. (the hour at which the Guards launched their attack), but messages again reached the front line very late—a failing which was also apparent all through this infantry battle. Rain was falling, but there was a perfect wind blowing from west to north-west at five miles an hour. This was not suitable for the trench line north of the canal, or immediately south of it, and no gas was liberated there; but opposite the 'Brickstacks' 450 cylinders were emptied, and the cloud went well over to the Germans for twenty-five minutes, though when infantry patrols and bombers moved forward they were met by machine-gun fire and were driven back. For this reason the gas attack was supposed to have been a failure; but I would like to say here, quite positively, for reasons which will become clear as this story progresses, that given a favourable wind every cloud gas attack is successful, more or less, even when it takes place in daylight and the troops exposed to it are provided with efficient respirators and have been warned of its imminence and actually see it coming over. Every record we possess of all the German cloud gas attacks against British and French troops—many of which took place long after the initial advantage of surprise had disappeared—proves this statement indisputably; and some of our own attacks, which were made later on under the most disadvantageous circumstances possible, were shown subsequently to have been the most successful in the whole war in regard to the number of casualties inflicted on the enemy. Unfortunately, this was not realised by the majority of our commanders, who appeared to expect the annihilation of the enemy's troops and the elimination of all organised resistance in the area over which the clouds passed, as was the case on the occasion of the first German gas attack against unprotected troops in April 1915.[1]

The gas attacks of the 25th and 27th September had one important effect on the work of the Special Companies. It had become abundantly clear that all the gas apparatus sent over from England would have to be subjected to rigorous test before being taken into use. The difficulty that had been faced at home of providing steel containers in large numbers of a suitable size at such short notice was appreciated, but many faults in their construction had revealed themselves in addition to the

[1] It is a remarkable fact, as I will show presently, that in spite of the great effects produced by gas clouds in every instance of which a reliable record was obtained, neither the German Commanders nor our own believed in their success. See pp. 179-182.

minor practical inconvenience experienced of handling cylinders of different lengths and diameters. A number of the spanners provided for turning the valve-nuts were made of such soft material that they split open when pressure was applied, and some of the valve-nuts were found to be round instead of square. Nearly all the pipes were defective, but among them there were a few Livens made of rubber hose which had been found to be the best.

It was realised that the troops were completely ignorant of the nature and effect of gas,[1] and that they became unduly alarmed at the least leakage in the trench : many of them, moreover, had little idea of the degree of protection that the ' P ' helmet afforded, and they had been insufficiently practised in its adjustment. It was absolutely essential, therefore, for all avoidable leakage from cylinders and pipes to be eliminated in our future operations, and drastic action was necessary to prevent it.

A workshop was at once extemporised at each company headquarters in which every cylinder that was found to be defective in any way on test was at once rejected ; and, by arrangement with the Ministry of Munitions, I sent Livens over to obtain some thousands of lengths of rubber pipe and metal sockets to fit the cylinder outlets, as well as copper wire and tools for fixing the pipes to the sockets.

Livens, a civil engineer by profession, was a ' go-getter,' and his name will often appear in the following pages. He set about his mission with such energy and success that by 13th October, the date of our next gas attack, we had 3170 tested cylinders in the front line, each of which was provided with a separate rubber connection and parapet pipe of its own, every one of which had been examined under high pressure in our own workshop. We had also shortened the ten-foot parapet pipes, or had cut them in half and provided them with screw threads

---

[1] This ignorance was not confined to the troops. On one occasion a Brigade Staff, when calculating the number of men required for carrying cylinders in and out of the trenches, allowed twice as many for the latter procedure, it being thought that instead of being only half the weight the steel containers would be heavier after the gas had been let out of them !

A similar error was made a few weeks ago by one of the leading London daily papers when reporting that gas cylinders had been washed up on the shores of the Irish Channel : by way of explanation it was stated that when they were thrown into the sea at the end of the war, as an easy method of getting rid of their dangerous contents, they had been insufficiently weighted down !

for fitting together in the front line. Livens had little experience of the correct official procedure in dealing with these matters, and I had to meet many indignant protests in connection with his activities. On one occasion he brushed aside all opposition at Victoria Station and filled a Pullman car with miles of rubber pipes and boxes of heavy gun-metal castings, and on reaching Boulogne he telegraphed to the Quartermaster-General personally for the immediate supply of twenty lorries—which he got !

"Who is this damned man, Livens ? " a furious voice asked me on the telephone ; and when supplying the soft answer I could not help thinking that there was a lot more trouble to come.

After the failure of the infantry attack of the 27th September further offensive action on a large scale was postponed for one reason or another, from day to day, until 13th October, though confused fighting went on all the time all over the battle area. On this day there was a renewed attack, chiefly with the object of retaking the Hohenzollern Redoubt and the ' Quarries,' which had both been lost, and the village of Hulluch from which a few of our troops who reached it had been driven out on the opening day of the battle. Twenty cylinders were installed in each emplacement over a long front, and a programme of discharge was arranged to allow of them being emptied two at a time, so as to increase the concentration of gas.

The wind at zero (1.0 P.M.) was south-west, five miles per hour, which was perfect, excepting once again astride and south of the La Bassée canal, where very little gas was liberated and where no infantry attack was contemplated.

Opposite the Hohenzollern Redoubt the gas went well over, and there was little or no leakage in the trenches in spite of the heavy bombardment, a vast improvement being apparent in the new form of apparatus in use.

(In our Official History it is stated that though the wind was favourable the gas settled down in shell-holes and in the remains of trenches in the open, and very little of it reached the enemy ; but, of course, with such a wind velocity, which was reported all along the line, this could not have happened.)

The enemy's rifle and machine-gun fire stopped almost at once when the gas reached them, and the infantry of the 46th Division reached the redoubt at 2 P.M. with very little loss. Slade, one of the section officers on this front, went over into the redoubt an hour later and found the buttons on the German wounded and dead not much tarnished in ' Big Willie ' to the south and outside it, but in the redoubt itself they were all quite green. Pollitt, who was watching this attack at close quarters, reported :—

" There can be no question that opposite the Hohenzollern the gas put all the Germans out of action, either by killing them or frightening them away. The first party of infantry that went over had few, if any, casualties. They went slowly and spent a long time examining the first trench from the parapet. There seemed to be absolutely no rifle or machine-gun fire from the Germans on the right flank of our attack. Had the infantry advanced at the double on this occasion immediately after the gas, it is probable that they would have had no resistance at all for 1000 yards or more. By simply sending out small parties moving very slowly, they gave the Germans ample time to recover and return, or send up other troops without hindrance." [1]

Opposite Hulluch, too, the gas cloud went over perfectly and the rifle and machine-gun fire died down : when the infantry wire-cutters of the 1st Division went out at 1.50, they reached the German wire 300 yards away and returned without any casualties, though there was some opposition when the assault took place at 2.15. Here also the enemy was allowed too much time to recover, and the infantry of the 1st Brigade, discouraged, perhaps, and exhausted by the disadvantagious conditions under which they had fought during the preceding three weeks, although at first they encountered little resistance, had gained no ground whatever by the end of the day. The 2nd Brigade was in support, but it did not come into action : it was at this time under Brigadier-General Thuillier, who was to take a prominent part a little later in the development of the British Gas Service.

The battle of 13th October was even more disappointing in its results than that of 25th September, and once again nearly all the ground gained in the first assault was lost subsequently, chiefly owing to the superiority of the German hand-grenade : in view of the adverse weather

---

[1] Corporal Dawson of the Special Companies gained the Victoria Cross on this occasion for his gallant behaviour.

conditions which then set in, all hope of continuing the offensive was abandoned. A number of minor gas attacks were, however, planned, and all of these took place under favourable wind conditions. On the 20th and 21st December, on the front of the 2nd Division, just south of the La Bassée canal, 240 and 700 cylinders respectively were discharged, and the G.O.C. of the 1st British Army Corps reported : " It is probable that a certain portion of the enemy were severely gassed." On 22nd December 220 cylinders were discharged north of the canal on the front of the 12th Division, and on 9th January 300 at Fromelles, on the 20th Division front. Finally, on 19th January, 400 cylinders were discharged at Le Touquet, just north of Armentières, on the front of the 25th Division in the Second Army area. Three other operations were fully prepared, but as a time-limit was imposed to allow the Special Companies to withdraw from the line for the important reorganisation which was about to take place, no discharges were made and the cylinders were removed.

Much heavier concentrations of gas were liberated in these attacks, all of which were carried out at night ; and in the last two ' Blue star ' gas was employed instead of ' Red star ' (chlorine). This was a mixture of 80 per cent chlorine with 20 per cent of sulphur chloride, the latter ingredient having been added because it is heavier than chlorine and so tends to keep the cloud closer to the ground. It had the disadvantage of causing the deposit of a small pool of liquid from the end of the parapet pipe on the ground which continued to give off fumes for some time ; and as this was considered likely to alarm assaulting infantry unnecessarily and make them hang back, the use of ' Blue star ' was discontinued.

By this time a still further improvement had been introduced in our equipment : instead of every cylinder being connected to a separate parapet pipe by a length of rubber hose—a system which gave the front trench the appearance of a pianola—four cylinders were joined by short lengths of hose to a ' 4-way connection ' which we made up ourselves ; this consisted of a piece of iron piping about twelve inches long, which had four inlets, one at each end and two near the middle for connection to the four cylinders, and one outlet in the centre for connection to the parapet pipe.

The number of parapet pipes was thus reduced to one quarter, while the system of connections admitted of the cylinders in each emplacement being discharged according to any selected programme, from one at a time to all twenty (or more) simultaneously. Still later these ' 4-way connections ' were reduced in length and cast in gun-metal—one may be seen in the War Museum in South Kensington—and the whole equipment became so satisfactory that no further alteration was found necessary up to the end of the war. In fact, during the many cloud gas attacks which we carried out in 1916 and afterwards there was such an entire absence of leakage from cylinders and pipes that the complaint heard from the infantry now was, "Our gas is no bloody good ; you can't even smell it ! "

A little evidence was obtained of the effects of the small gas attacks which have been described : after the operation of 19th January a prisoner stated that his unit had been completely surprised by the gas and that the casualties had been extremely heavy. And in a memorandum by the Commander of the VIIth German Army Corps, dated 29/12/15 but only captured by us a year later, the following brief references appeared. Night of 21/12/15 : " A company commander who had recently attended an anti-gas course stated that the wind drove the gas direct towards the company. There was no chlorine, but a gas similar to C-stoff (a German gas used in shells) which caused for many hours bad coughing, tightness of chest and general indisposition. Thirty-eight men were made to vomit, but there were no losses. The gas cloud came over very suddenly so that very few people made use of their masks in good time. Nevertheless it appears that the gas was chlorine." On this occasion it was. Night of 22/12/15 : " Chlorine was detected in Marquilles, which is about ten kilometres from the line of discharge. Altogether there were 48 gas cases, of which 39 were in the field hospitals. Seven were left in aid-posts and two died." It may be supposed that the memoranda from which I have quoted were intended to allay alarm, so that the number of the casualties mentioned in them need not be taken too seriously. All through the war the Germans showed that they were acutely sensitive to their losses from our gas attacks, and prisoners who were ready to

PLAN OF FUTURE GAS ATTACKS, 1915.

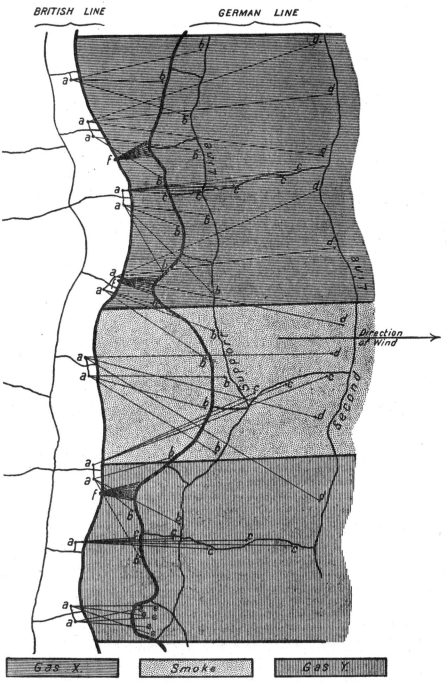

a=Stokes Mortars.   *f*=Flame Projectors.   *b*=Gas Shells in variety.
c=Flame Shells cutting off communication.   *d*=Gas Shells forming barrage,
e=Inflammable Vapour Shells ; whole area to be ignited.

Scale about 1 Inch to 250 Yards.

talk on any other subject became silent immediately the topic of gas was mentioned; in fact, many of them said that they had been specially warned not to disclose their losses from gas.

The same reticence is evident in the partial disclosures made in German books which have been published since the war. I think, however, that it will be evident from the following pages that the German losses from the weapon which they themselves introduced influenced the issue of this war of attrition far more than our own commanders believed possible at the time, or than our late enemies will ever care to admit.

As regards the gas casualties suffered by our own infantry and by the men of the Special Companies during this period of hastily extemporised effort, there was an erroneous impression in the army, and probably at home too, that our losses had been very heavy. Numerous gas casualties were certainly registered on 25th September, but for the most part they were trifling in severity. In many parts of the line there had been leakages of gas which were caused by the insufficiency of discharge pipes, necessitating their transference from one cylinder to another in succession; by faulty apparatus; by pipes being cut by hostile artillery fire; by the lightness of the wind; and by the judgment of the officers of the Special Companies being overruled. These leakages, of course, affected the men who were working at the cylinders more than any others; but the infantry were not practised sufficiently in the use of their gas helmets, and they were naturally very nervous of gas in view of the disasters to our troops in the Ypres Salient earlier in the year, and the colourful descriptions of them which appeared in our Press. Moreover, as phosphorus fumes have a distinct odour they were unable to distinguish between the sensation of gas and the smell of our smoke clouds when they reached the enemy's trenches.

In the medical returns of gas casualties for the period 25th September-14th October 1915, 2911 gas casualties were registered in the thirteen British divisions, and it is certain that the number, 550, definitely attributed to enemy gas shells was an under-estimate; so that the accidental gas casualties probably totalled about 2000. Probably at least half of the men who attended for treatment did so in ignorance, and many of them were reported as having been hardly affected by gas, if at all. Only 55 of the cases were described as severe ; and of these, 10 died from gas poisoning, including 3 men of the gas personnel.

Early in January 1916 the four Special Companies were withdrawn to Helfaut. On 25th October I had written a memorandum to the C.G.S., in which a future gas policy was sketched out. It was useless, I said, to continue employing chlorine now that the enemy was on the alert and had improved his protective appliances : new gases were being manufactured at home, but it would be a little while before sufficient quantities of them would become available, and it was inadvisable to disclose them to the enemy in any minor tactical effort. A flame-projecting apparatus had been designed which had a range far greater than that of the German portable flammen-werfer, and an improved pattern of the 4-inch Stokes mortar would soon be supplied in large numbers for throwing gas bombs.

I made a forecast in the form of a diagram (see sketch, p. 92, which is typical of our gas attacks during the whole of 1916) of the methods that we might adopt in our next series of gas operations, and suggested the creation of special units to handle the flame-projectors and mortars ; and I concluded with the sentence, " I am confident of being able to develop the use of trench-mortars for gas projection to an extent which cannot be estimated at present."

These proposals were at once approved, and I was told to reconstruct the Special Companies (which had been given the Engineer numbers 186, 187, 188 and 189) into an organisation suitable for occupying a gas frontage of 24,000 yards. In this way the original two companies, which had been increased to four for the battle of Loos, were now expanded into the ' Special Brigade,' consisting of twenty-one companies, which remained at this strength until the end of the war.

The new organisation was as simple to design as the old one had been : the frontage of 250 yards for one section under a subaltern had been found by experience to be a suitable one, and as it was desirable for a single unit (a company) to be capable of occupying the frontage usually allotted to an infantry division, which was 1500 yards on an average, six sections were necessary to form a company, and sixteen such companies, grouped for facility of control into four battalions, were required for the frontage of 24,000 yards. The only other important change was to allot three men to each cylinder emplacement, instead of two as formerly, so as to allow for casualties.

The battalions were numbered 1 to 4 : a 5th battalion consisting of four companies was given a different organisation, and was partly officered by forty gunner subalterns collected from trench-mortar and artillery units and had 192 4-inch Stokes mortars ; while the last company, with another special organisation in four sections, was formed to handle the flame-projectors. So that there were four Special *Battalions* consisting of sixteen companies, lettered from A to Q, for cloud gas enterprises ; four Special *Companies*, numbered 1 to 4, for gas projection with Stokes mortars ; and four Special *Sections*, which were later known as " Z " Company, for the flame projectors.[1] Of my four company commanders Percy-Smith (who was gassed at Loos) left me to rejoin his Indian Cavalry Regiment, and Garden was sent to Salonika, Mudros and Egypt to advise the commanders there on gas warfare, as it was feared that the Turks were about to use gas. (He took with him 3000 filled gas cylinders, but they were never used, and Garden himself rejoined the Special Brigade shortly afterwards. The Turks were believed to have been supplied with German gas, but they apparently refused to use it.[2] Our own headquarters in Egypt and Salonika both decided not to initiate gas warfare in those theatres, though this decision was reversed at a later stage in the war, when detachments of the Special Brigade were asked for, and gas shells were supplied to both armies, as well as to the army in Mesopotamia and to the troops in Archangel at the beginning of 1919.)

Monier-Williams, Sanders, Berrisford (a Natural Science and Theology student who had the distinction, after the war, of being the only president of the Oxford University Boat Club who has not awarded himself a ' Blue ' and who is now in Holy Orders) and Bunker took command of numbers 1 to 4 battalions respectively, Pollitt of the four mortar companies and Livens of " Z " Company.

[1] See Table, p. 259.
[2] General Schwarte says that there was the intention to use German gas troops in Gallipoli at the end of 1915, but this did not materialise owing to the evacuation.

I was promoted to Colonel, and I had Eddis, who by this time had recovered from his wound, sent to me as Brigade Major, and Howard as Staff Captain. Rivers, a trench-mortar expert, joined us as Brigade Artillery Officer, and his special duty was the training of the Stokes mortar detachments. Recruiting was reopened in England, but nearly all the new officers were obtained from the ranks of the four original companies. I interviewed all candidates who were brought to my notice as suitable for commissions, and of the hundreds of men who were gazetted on my recommendation not more than one or two, during the whole war, failed to justify their selection.[1]

Each of the cylinder battalions was built up on the skeleton of one of the original companies, so that with the experience already at their disposal the training of the new units proceeded rapidly. Recruits now joined as 'pioneers,' as it was found that the rank of corporal which they were given originally was incongruous for certain duties such as guards and fatigues. The men retained their revolver equipment, but the mortar companies were armed with rifles, as it was intended that they should advance with the infantry after the German line had been broken.

By the middle of May 1916 "Z" Company was still engaged in training at Hatfield, but all the other units were fit and eager to move up into the line. Each battalion had its own workshop, in which every article of gas equipment was thoroughly tested before being passed fit for use, so that leaky joints and pipes and 'dud' cylinders were now things of the past. The period of extemporised effort was over, and four thousand well-trained officers and men marched past me at Helfaut on 22nd May at a final review.

A few days later (3rd June), Sir Douglas Haig, who had, of course, replaced Sir John French as Commander-in-Chief, came to make a formal inspection of the brigade, with its mortars and transport set out in long lines and making a brave show. The Irish Guards lent us their drum and fife band for the occasion, and the Commander-

---

[1] Many of my officers were schoolmasters, and among them was Slater, one of the four Eton masters who lost their lives recently in Switzerland. On one occasion a young officer found himself at mess being waited on by his former Lecturer (at the Southampton University College) who had enlisted in the Special Brigade and had been relegated to this duty temporarily because of foot trouble.

in-Chief, after a demonstration of our new gas appliances, expressed his satisfaction at the state of efficiency which we had certainly attained. We were soon to assist in the opening stages of what became known as the battle of the Somme; but before the companies left Helfaut an important event occurred.

Earlier in the year the War Office had requested two eminent scientific men, Professors Frankland and Pope, to visit all the British gas organisations in England and France, and to make a report on what they saw. On their return from France they recommended, among other things, a closer co-ordination of the offensive and defensive services, both at the front and at home; and they suggested that an organic chemist of seniority and high standing should be appointed to spend his whole time on the organisation and direction of the technical matters connected with the offensive and defensive uses of gas.

When this report reached G.H.Q., Sir Douglas Haig agreed that it was desirable to treat gas as a distinct arm (this was what I had originally proposed, see Chapter III., page 40), and to put it entirely under one branch of the staff both at the War Office and in France; but he said that the new " Director of Gas Services " should not merely possess certain scientific qualifications, but he should be a combatant officer of experience. Gas defence in the B.E.F. was at this time the duty of the Royal Army Medical Corps (in the Adjutant-General's branch of the staff), under General Sloggett, assisted by Colonel Cummins: they corresponded in status to General Keogh and Colonel Horrocks at the War Office, both of the same corps, who carried out the research work in England in connection with the manufacture of respirators.

Sir Douglas Haig accordingly appointed Brigadier-General Thuillier (a Royal Engineer officer, in command of the 2nd Infantry Brigade) as the first Director of Gas Services in France to co-ordinate the activities of the two services of which Colonel Cummins and I were in charge, as well as that of the Central Laboratory: I was "to continue to command the Special Brigade and act as Gas Adviser," though, of course, in reality General Thuillier, as head of the service, now exercised the latter function; and I was left with full administrative freedom in regard to all dealings with the personnel of my brigade.

A similar reorganisation took place at home, but not with the same happy results, apparently ; nor were the offensive and defensive organisations united until October 1917. The Scientific Advisory Committee which had been created by Dr Addison (Secretary to Mr Lloyd George) in June 1915 was reconstituted as the Chemical Advisory Committee, but for reasons which were, no doubt, excellent the duty of *supplying* gas and its various accessories was put in charge of a separate branch, so that the scientists in General Jackson's *research* department no longer controlled the manufacture of the materials which they themselves had evolved in the laboratory and developed on the experimental field.

This resulted in a period of paralysis in one department and in serious delays in production for many months afterwards [1] ; and they were followed by frequent complaints from G.H.Q. which, fortunately for me, General Thuillier now had to voice. Although matters improved to some extent and the departments concerned in the Ministry of Munitions were again reorganised eighteen months later, when General Thuillier himself was sent from France to take charge of them, he was not successful in remedying the defect in the system referred to up till the end of the war, in spite of the fact that Mr Lloyd George " soon discovered that the separation of design and manufacture was a serious mistake and led to blunders and delays " ('War Memoirs'). Nor was the War Office to blame for this state of affairs, except indirectly, for it had never controlled the gas weapon and it was little more than an intermediary between the Ministry of Munitions and G.H.Q. in France.

This was one of the results of the friction caused by Lord Kitchener's resistance to the separation of the Ministry from the War Office when Mr Lloyd George took charge of it in 1915, of which there is ample evidence in ' Lord Riddell's War Diary.' [2] Mr Lloyd George was followed by a succession of Ministers, all of whom had powerful political influence or support.

---

[1] Dr Addison, in ' Four and a half years,' refers repeatedly to these changes of organisation in the Ministry, and to the inter-departmental friction which arose out of them.

[2] Mr Lloyd George also says in his ' War Memoirs ': The new Ministry of Munitions " was cut out of the living body of the War Office, and that hurt. . . . The War Office was surly, suspicious and hostile, and no help the new Ministry tendered or gave softened the animosity of the War Lords towards it."

CHAPTER VII.

MANY suggestions reached us at one time or another in connection with the offensive use of gas, as well as in regard to the protection of our own troops against German attacks. The most valuable of the former naturally came from officers of the Special Brigade, who had the opportunity and were given every encouragement to develop novel ideas, and who were often specially detached from duty to work them out, sometimes in England, in co-operation with the Ministry of Munitions. Among these were the Livens 'projector' and Wilson's method for the electric discharge of thousands of cylinders simultaneously, of both of which we made important use.

Other proposals, although extremely ingenious in conception, were lacking in simplicity, which is by far the most important requirement in the more or less organised chaos of the battlefield ; while still others were merely fantastic.

A great deal of attention was paid in the early days of the war to the dissipation of gas clouds by mechanical means ; thus we find in a report issued by the Chief of the General Staff of the Fifth German Army and dated 30th September 1915 : " It has not proved satisfactory to dissipate the cloud by means of artillery fire, although very large quantities of ammunition were used in the attempt. Trench-mortars and hand-grenades, &c., have also no effect." The Commander of the IVth German Army Corps wrote on 27th September 1915 : " Protective rapid fire (rifles and machine-guns) into the cloud had not the desired effect in destroying it." And the Commander of the VIIth German Army Corps, on the same date : " Fires lit on the parapet were useful in lifting the gas." This method of lighting protective fires obviously required very alert sentries and elaborate preparations as well as dry weather, and it was adopted extensively by the enemy after our attack at Loos and for a long time afterwards, though he abandoned it later. We never believed in it at all, but our French Allies apparently did, as I found the system in use when I visited their trenches on the Montdidier front on one occasion in August 1916.

To be even partially successful the fires would have to be continuous along the parapets of successive lines of trenches, and the supply of fuel adequate to keep them burning for an hour or more on occasion.

An elaboration of this idea was suggested in December 1915 by a Mr Hall, who proposed the formation of an impenetrable barrier of flame by laying down a system of pipes provided with jets all along the front trench. Fuel oil from reservoirs was to be forced into the pipes by a gas such as that obtained as a by-product in the oil works at Thames Haven, and the oil could then be ignited at will. I witnessed a demonstration of this invention in England, and although a formidable barrier of flame five or six feet high was successfully formed the proposal was, for many reasons, obviously impracticable for use at the front.

In a letter to the 'Times' (11/8/15), Sir Hiram Maxim made a similar suggestion for firing incendiary bombs in the path of the gas cloud : he anticipated that as the air became heated and rose the gas would be driven upwards out of harm's way.

A writer in 'Le Génie Civil' wanted black powder bombs to be thrown out in front of the trench, partly to dissipate the cloud and partly to form potassium sulphate fumes, which, reacting on the chlorine, would greatly minimise its harmful properties.

One inventor urged the construction of a series of steel tunnels leading from the front line to the rear. An aeroplane propeller installed in each one would, when set in motion, suck the gas into the passages and deposit it in some area behind the lines where it would do no harm.

A writer in 'Cassier's Magazine' (July 1915) went even further with this principle, and proposed using propellers for creating counter air-currents which would carry the gases back into the German lines ; and, he added, " if in the course of such work the cloud of noxious vapours could be rolled back and the Germans dosed with their own poisonous gases justice would be amply satisfied."

This brings me to the famous Ayrton fan about which there was a good deal of acrimonious controversy, which resulted eventually in a two-column letter to the ' Times ' from the inventor, as well as a leading article. Mrs Ayrton was the wife of a distinguished physicist, and her fan consisted of a light covered framework, about eighteen inches square, hinged on a stick handle in such a manner that by flapping it in a certain way air currents could be produced in one direction only. Its chief object was to drive back a gas cloud, or at any rate to keep it out of our trenches : a secondary object was to clear gas from trenches and dug-outs with it.

The fan was offered to Sir John French, who, for his own protection, had found it necessary to appoint an " Inventions Committee " at G.H.Q. (referred to in Chapter III., p. 41) to deal with such matters, and to relieve him of much personal correspondence, as well, perhaps, as of a certain amount of abuse. This Committee rejected the fan, but pressure was brought on Mr Lloyd George, Dr Addison, Mr Zangwill, Sir Douglas Haig and others, and eventually a trial of the fan was arranged at Helfaut, a number of my men having been trained first in its correct use by Mr Greenslade, Mrs Ayrton's lecture assistant. When the trial took place the men were lined up in a trench, each with a fan, and a gas cylinder was turned on to them from a little distance off, up-wind. They were, of course, provided with gas helmets, and it was suggested in fun to Mr Greenslade, who was also in the trench, that he would probably be able to use his fan more freely if he took his helmet off. Mr Greenslade and his party were quite unable to prevent the gas from entering the trench ; and, after all, King Canute was no more successful when a similar task was imposed on him. The fan was found to have no appreciable effect whatever on the gas cloud : in fact, it was actually worse than useless, as with the type of helmet then worn (as with all others) any exertion on the part of the man wearing it reduces the degree of protection it affords owing to the more rapid rate of breathing. For clearing dug-outs, too, the well-established system (which requires no physical exertion) of lighting a fire to create a draught of air was considered to be better ; but such was the influence that had been enlisted that five thousand of the fans were ordered at once, two hundred for each mile of front, and eventually more than a hundred thousand were supplied to the army in France.

The Americans, too, finding the fans part of the British trench equipment, and very naturally adopting British methods while evolving their own, ordered fifty thousand more.

Late in the war I inquired from more than sixty Divisional Gas officers (there was one in each division who was responsible for all matters of gas defence) whether there was any advantage in retaining the fans, and they were unanimous in stating that they served no useful purpose whatever for protection against gas—though it was suggested that the handle, being made of wood, provided at times a valuable emergency fuel. I ought to add that Mrs Ayrton gave the fan to the army and refused to accept any reward for it.

Among the offensive devices proposed was a series of rockets which, when fired in the direction of the enemy, carried with them lengths of light canvas hose for attachment to our cylinders, enabling gas to be liberated close to the German parapets, and therefore in higher concentrations. The ' push-pipe ' had the same object, and it was actually tried out in March 1917 (see Chapter XII., p. 196) at the request of an army commander, though the labour involved was very considerable in comparison with the advantage to be gained. Throughout the war I found officers of high rank almost too receptive of novel proposals, especially when they were based on anything mysterious or scientific.

The Maggiora ' Vortex gun,' used in wine districts abroad to break up heavy clouds and disperse destructive hail-storms, was also given a trial for projecting concentrated gusts of gas, it having been first proposed for bringing down hostile aircraft !

Among the experiments that were made by General Jackson was one to scatter powdered calcium arsenide (Ca_3As_2) in shells with the idea that when it came in contact with moisture in the air, or with rain, the poisonous gas (arseniuretted hydrogen) would be formed : it was thought, too, that in the absence of rain the dry powder would be taken up into the system in the form of dust and would act upon the acids of the stomach and so cause arsenic poisoning ; but the experiments were disappointing and were abandoned.

Quantities of fine coal dust were also fired over an area which would, it was hoped, when ignited, cause an explosion such as occurs in mine disasters; and a trial was made with volatile oils with the same object; but it was found that these effects could only be produced successfully in a confined space, such as a closed chamber.

Another experiment which seemed promising at first was made with fine carborundum dust : it was hoped that when scattered over artillery and machine-gun positions it would destroy the moving parts of their mechanisms; and with certain chemicals for combining with and clogging the lubricating oils ; but the results were poor.

One ingenious idea which occurred, apparently, both to Dr Shakespear and Lieutenant Hemens (of the Special Companies) was put forward to enable warning to be given of the approach of a gas cloud by means of a ' detector,' a delicate instrument to be installed in No Man's Land which, when exposed to chlorine gas, would ring a bell automatically or light a fire : this result depended on the ' resistance ' of a length of bare wire which formed part of an accurately balanced electric circuit being affected by exposure to the gas.

Another suggestion made by Dr Pring, a Special Company officer, was not adopted, though it was similar in principle to one actually employed both by the Germans and ourselves (I refer to the use of chloropicrin by us and to the enemy's ' Blue Cross ' shells) : this was to discharge first of all a gas called silicon tetrachloride which formed a gelatinous colloidal film on the surface of a respirator and so prevented breathing ; after the enemy had been compelled to remove his respirator to avoid suffocation, a second discharge of a lethal gas would be made which would, of course, find him in an unprotected state.

Some of the suggestions made were more amusing than useful. One was that German divisions should be shelled with distinctive scents which are difficult to expurgate, such as musk, oil of skunk, &c., so that when they appeared subsequently in different parts of the line they could be identified by their smell !

Another that was meant quite seriously was made to General Gough after the battle of Loos, which was intended to guide him in the conduct of future offensive operations carried out in conjunction with discharges of gas. The writer suggested that as the artillery bombardment disclosed an intention to attack it might be dispensed with altogether, except for wire-cutting a week or ten days beforehand. Then, " after a few days quiet, select a moonlight night in winter with a gentle breeze in the right direction, after a severe frost, when the ground is hard." When a gas discharge of one hour's duration had taken place, massed troops along a fifteen-mile front would advance in absolute silence : every man was to rush forward, the supports following, as fast as possible, without firing a shot, till 4 A.M., at which hour he would dig himself in before daylight ; and he concluded by saying, " I am confident that this is *the* way to use gas."

This scheme was sent to me, together with some additional suggestions which it was thought might be helpful, by one of the younger officers of General Gough's staff, who pointed out the improbability of experiencing a severe frost with a westerly breeze ; but, in order not to forgo the opportunity of making the ' marathon attack ' a real success, he advised " damning the frost and having a go in the mud."

As the artillery was obsolete it should be converted into additional gas units : an extra cheese ration was to be issued to sustain the flagging energies of the runners who would be kept to their task by the supports, if necessary, with the bayonet. Any man firing a shot would have his name taken.

We discovered this paper after the armistice, and my office draughtsman, Corporal Barrett, attempted to illustrate the course that such an attack might take. I reproduce his effort, in which it will be seen that the artist supplies additional hints of his own, notably in regard to a costume considered suitable for infantry subalterns, and various suggestions for foiling German machine-gunners.

A great many other proposals were examined by the Ministry of Munitions, some of which must have put them to considerable trouble and expense.

Some unexpected results, too, were obtained on investigating the action of certain gases which before the war had the reputation of being highly toxic, but which were found on close examination to be much less so than was supposed. Among these were prussic acid gas (HCN), phosphine (PH_3), nickel carbonyl ($NiCO_4$) and arseniuretted hydrogen (AsH_3) : as regards the last I seem to remember

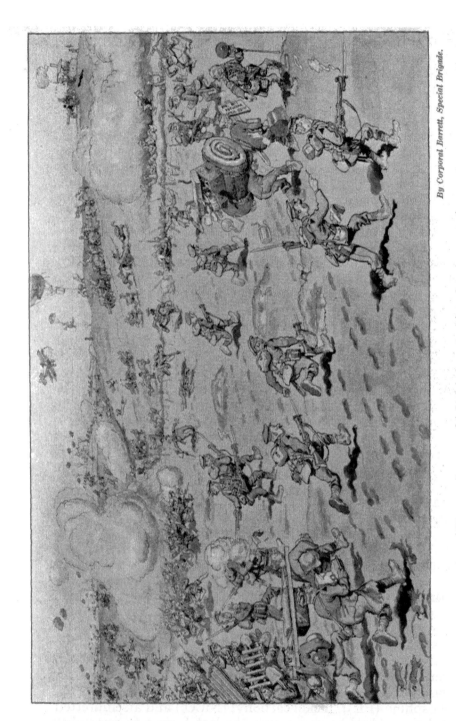

By Corporal Barrett, Special Brigade.

Humorous pen and ink drawing of an imaginary gas attack.

reading in my school chemistry book that it was so dangerous that a single bubble of the gas would, if inhaled, cause instantaneous death; but in an experiment made in England, a pig which was placed in a trench and exposed to a strong concentration of the gas was apparently unaffected by it; and Commander Brock (who was reported missing later on, after the affair at Zeebrugge) and I both entered the trench, and while the smell of garlic was very strong the gas had no effect on me, though I believe that Brock suffered some ill-effects from it afterwards.

Sulphuretted hydrogen (H_2S), on the other hand, well known to most schoolboys who have employed it surreptitiously in many an escapade in class, was found to be surprisingly toxic. Sir John Cadman was responsible for the earliest experiments with this gas, and, as all the substances which were made use of were referred to under some cipher, he called it NG in the hope of annoying his close friend, the late Sir John Norton-Griffiths ("Empire Jack"), who was present at one of the demonstrations at Cannock Chase. Livens, who was also present with me on this occasion, entered the path of the cloud as the gas emerged in high concentration from a cylinder: he was testing the protection afforded by a service gas helmet, but the latter was penetrated almost at once and Livens fell unconscious, though he recovered quickly when dragged out of the cloud. Sulphuretted hydrogen has a very strong characteristic odour which, however, is not perceptible when the gas is in high concentration, and it can only be liquefied under great pressure (three times that required for chlorine), so that the noise of discharge as it issues from a cylinder is considerable: the fall in temperature, however, is so great that the cloud keeps low in spite of the fact that the gas is but little heavier than air (17 as against 14.4); and as it is highly inflammable and small leakages in the trenches disclose its presence very easily to the enemy, it is by no means an ideal battle gas. In spite of these disadvantages, owing to the output of phosgene being very slow for a time, H_2S was accepted for use in France, and it was actually employed on two occasions in 1916, but mixed with carbon disulphide (10 per cent) to increase the density. This mixture was still more inflammable than H_2S alone, and it was known as NG_2, or '2-Red Star': it was used against the Germans in somewhat remarkable circumstances, as will be related in the next chapter.

The ban against prussic acid gas was lifted in 1916, and although much had been expected of it, the experimental results, when examined, did not appear to me to warrant its substitution for phosgene in any form of gas attack. I expressed this opinion in a memorandum as early as 3rd March 1916, and pointed out that it was much less stable than phosgene, and was, in addition, considerably lighter. Experiments and manufacture were, however, allowed to continue in view of the large demands that were being made for phosgene and the disappointments that were being constantly experienced at home in its production.

We employed prussic acid gas in artillery shells from 1917 onwards, but although, as soon as I succeeded General Thuillier as Director of Gas Services in June of that year, Sir Douglas Haig requested the War Office to discontinue the supply of this shell filling altogether, unexpended stocks of it were actually being used up at the time of the Armistice, nearly eighteen months afterwards. This is a good example of the 'lag' which is bound to occur, in the case of a country so little prepared for war as ours was, between a decision arrived at in the field and its accomplishment. Another instance of this lag may be quoted in the case of the supply of chloropicrin : this gas (which will be referred to again later on) was made in the laboratory, developed in a small-scale plant and finally produced in bulk in the factory after many technical difficulties had been overcome, eight months after it had been first suggested. Similarly, the process which was eventually adopted for the manufacture of 'mustard gas' proved extraordinarily difficult to develop, and the first British shells with this filling were fired in the last days of September 1918, fourteen months after the gas had been asked for. (German mustard gas shells were fired by British gunners from composite batteries of captured guns some weeks earlier ; and the French were able to employ mustard gas of their own manufacture as early as in June 1918.)

These delays are not at all surprising when it is remembered that prior to April 1915 most of the known gases were regarded merely as chemical curiosities : methods of making them had to be discovered and the necessary plant constructed from the beginning, the strictest safety precautions being enforced all the time. Nor was this experience confined to ourselves : the French had similar difficulties, and the Americans, although they had the benefit of our failures and successes, seem to have added to theirs by the stupendous scale on which all their production was planned. Even the Germans, who alone had a completely equipped and flexible chemical industry at their command, were slow in introducing some of the substances which they employed, as their value must have been known to them long before they appeared on the battlefield.

Prussic acid gas produces a reaction on the nervous system, and it has a more rapid lethal action than any other when present in sufficiently high concentration, such, however, as can seldom be established in the field. At lower concentrations its casualty-producing value is nil, and the effects of inhaling it soon pass off, recovery being rapid and complete.

The French believed in it firmly as a shell filling, and considered that they had definite evidence of its mortal effect on the enemy : they employed enormous quantities of it, and persevered with it till the end of the war in spite of our own experimental results. Some of their artillery field trials which I witnessed were certainly impressive, and in one of them all the dogs placed in a system of trenches at Satory were killed by the gas after a brief bombardment. Our physiologists, however, established the fact that dogs are far more susceptible to this substance than human beings, and to substantiate this theory finally Professor Barcroft (of Cambridge University) entered a closed chamber while quite unprotected, together with a dog, and exposed himself to a measured quantity (1/2000) of the gas : he remained in the chamber for ten minutes, writing notes of his sensations the whole time, though the dog had convulsions and died thirty-three seconds after the experiment commenced.

Of all the gases used as shell fillings prussic acid was considered by our own artillery officers as the least effective, judging from the results of their bombardments in silencing the German batteries. " VN [1] is a bad last," it was reported.

The Germans seem to have had the same contempt for prussic acid gas that we had, and they never used it in

[1] Named after the French factory at Vincennes.

France, though it was reported to have been employed on a large scale in an Austrian artillery bombardment in Italy on the Trentino in September 1915. They circulated reports more than once of its manufacture in vast quantities : this may have been designed to compel interference on the part of the Red Cross with a view to initiate steps in the interests of humanity for the abandonment of gas warfare ; or perhaps it was hoped to influence the allied morale, or even to encourage the French to continue with its use. But the rumours were recognised as attempts to mislead us, and they were correctly interpreted as foreshadowing the arrival of a new gas, to the nature of which there was as yet no clue.

In some notes taken at a German anti-gas lecture which were found on a prisoner the toxic values of our gases were tabulated thus :—[1]

> Phosgene . . 320 (apparently the product of the number of minutes' exposure and the number of cubic centimetres of the gas required to kill a man).
> Chloropicrin . 2000
> Prussic acid . 2500
> Chlorine . . 6000 ;

and the following words were added : " Prussic acid is harmless compared with the others." And in the notebook of another prisoner, a German regimental gas officer, HCN was marked as " not so dangerous," while phosgene was shown as " very dangerous."

Finally, General Schwarte says in his book : " Of the twenty-five gases used by the enemy the only effective ones were phosgene and dichlorethyl sulphide (mustard gas) " ; and Dr Hanslian writes : "Actually these shells were very much overrated by the French. So far the Germans are not aware of one case of death through vincennite (prussic acid) poisoning during the war."

While I am dealing with this subject it might be of interest to state that all the animals experimented with had peculiarities of susceptibility to various gases, and allowance had to be made for these variations when checking results : for instance, it was found that goats and men are equally resistant to prussic acid gas, while

[1] Dr Hanslian quotes Dr Haber's opinion of the comparative lethal values of some of these gases :—
Phosgene, 450 ; Di-phosgene, 500 ; Xylyl bromide, 6000 ; Chlorine, 7500.

mice have been shown to be ten times as susceptible as men are to carbon monoxide, for which reason miners use them (as well as canaries) as detectors of the presence of this gas. A man's eyes are by far the most sensitive of his organs, and he is ten times as susceptible to lachrimators, compared with a dog, and a thousand times, compared with a horse.

In the same connection a writer in the 'Frankfurter Zeitung' (August 1916) made some interesting remarks on the effects of our gas clouds during the Somme battle on other living creatures: "All the pets in the trenches suffer from the gas attacks. The guinea-pigs are the first to scent the gas, and the cats also complain at once. Many dead rats and mice are found in the trenches after gas attacks. Owls are greatly excited. Behind the front, fowls and ducks are said to have become restless a quarter of an hour before the gas clouds approached; and the gas kills ants and caterpillars, beetles and butterflies. I found a hedgehog and an adder both killed by gas. The only birds that seem indifferent to gas are the sparrows."

Pigeons, too, seem to have been found to be susceptible, because the Germans kept their carrier birds in gas-tight boxes which had ordinary respirator drums screwed into one side.

Before taking my readers to the Somme battlefield where we were soon to carry out more than fifty cloud gas attacks in aid of the infantry operations in the course of the first eighteen days, and over a hundred by the end of the year, I must touch briefly on three matters on which our activities were to depend.

The 4-inch Stokes Mortar.—I have described the principle of the Stokes mortar in Chapter IV. (p. 50): various improvements, both in the mortar and the bomb, were introduced from time to time, until by the end of the war the Stokes was a marvellous weapon for use either with gas or high explosive bombs. (Only the 4-inch was used for gas, the 3-inch remaining an infantry weapon.) It was possible for a well-trained crew to load the bombs into one mortar so rapidly that fifteen of them could be counted in the air before the first one projected struck the target; and, as each contained two litres of liquid gas (nearly three times as much as in a 6-inch howitzer shell), the concentration of gas that could be established on a target by means of rapid fire from a number of mortars may well be imagined.

The first improvement was a device to obviate the danger supposed to be inherent in the automatic ignition of the time fuze from the flash of the explosion of the cartridge fixed in the base of the bomb. This danger was removed by resting the bomb on an iron pin passed through the mortar, near the muzzle, while the time fuze was being ignited with a port-fire: on withdrawing the pin the bomb was released (with the fuze alight), and it dropped into the mortar as originally planned. But when the head of the bomb was fitted with the spring release device employed in the Mills hand-grenade, the ignition of the fuze became automatic. Later still, the "Allways" fuze replaced the Mills device, and the bombs exploded on striking the ground instead of after an interval, by means of a time fuze. The Allways was an ingenious arrangement which caused the bursting charge carried in the bomb to operate however the bomb fell—on its nose, on its base, or sideways: the percussion method is a much more satisfactory one when surprise is such an important factor in a gas bombardment.

As regards the bomb itself, the projection in its base, which originally contained the 12-bore Ballistite blank cartridge, was replaced by a perforated 'cage' in which 'biscuits' of E.C. powder were placed, their number varying with the range required. Later on, towards the end of the war, cordite 'propellant rings' were substituted for the biscuits, and ranges up to sixteen hundred yards resulted; but the rings were found to cause overheating of the mortars as well as a very noticeable noise and flash which helped to disclose the mortar positions and to guide German retaliation. The final improvement adopted was the introduction of a series of radial cordite sachets into the 'cage,' with a central bag of black powder to facilitate their ignition. It was found also that the pin in the base of the mortar became blunt from constant wear, so that it was eventually attached on a disc to the 'cage' itself, and then came in contact with a flat anvil when the bomb dropped into the bottom of the mortar.

During the early stages of the Somme battle only smoke bombs (with a range of three hundred and fifty

The 4" Stokes mortar.

Flame Projector in action.

yards) were available for the use of the mortar companies, for the formation of smoke screens to cover infantry assaulting parties. In September 1916 the first supplies of ' SK ' (lachrymator) bombs arrived and were used, but lethal gas bombs for the 4-inch Stokes only appeared in the spring of 1917, although I had asked for both lethal and lachrymator bombs in July 1915.[1]

The Flame Projector.—Reference was made in Chapter IV. (p. 49) to the German use of portable flammenwerfer in the middle of 1915. Our Ministry of Munitions had now designed three different types of flame projector : the first was a portable apparatus, a one-man load, with a range of twenty to thirty yards ; the second a two-men load with a range of fifty yards ; and the third a heavy machine for fixed installation in a trench, with a range of over seventy yards. I did not consider the first two to be of any value in an assault, because if an infantry attacking party ever succeeded in carrying such a dangerous and cumbersome machine to within close range of a German trench, it would be only for the reason that there was little or no opposition to be overcome ; while for clearing trenches and dug-outs, hand-grenades would be equally effective, and would require no specially trained troops or special apparatus for their use. The largest flame projector had, however, better prospects if it could be set up within range of a German trench ; and the intense heat from it, and the roar of the flame as it issued, accompanied by dense volumes of black smoke, had a terrifying effect. But the model shown (it can now be seen in the Imperial War Museum), designed by Captain Vincent [2] of the Ministry of Munitions, had certain undesirable features : some of the parts were much too heavy (the four oil-containers each weighed 212 lbs. when full), and the compressed air used for propelling the oil seemed to constitute a source of danger owing to its oxygen content.[3]

Livens, who was with me, thought that he could

[1] " The ammunition for the Stokes gun is infinitely more difficult to produce than the guns themselves." Dr Addison in ' Four and a half years.'

[2] " Vincent has invented the most diabolical flame apparatus, calculated to clear any trench within 150 yards of it." Dr Addison in ' Four and a half years.'

[3] In the demonstration of the portable flame projector on the same occasion it transpired later that the inventor (not Captain Vincent) had employed compressed oxygen ! I was standing near him when the apparatus exploded and set him on fire, and I put out the flames with his overcoat.

design a better apparatus than Vincent's, with more portable parts and longer range ; and he occupied himself with this problem for several months, the Ministry of Munitions giving him all the assistance he required. Eventually two of his machines arrived in time for employment on the opening day of the battle of the Somme (1st July 1916), and they were fired successfully immediately before the infantry assault took place. The oil found most suitable was a mixture of one part light and two parts heavy, and de-oxygenated compressed air was employed as an inert propellant. The company which he trained at Hatfield was capable of using twenty-four of these large machines at a time ; but on the whole they were a disappointment and only a few of them were ever manufactured.

'White Star' Cloud Gas.—I have mentioned in Chapter IV. (p. 53) the steps taken by the Ministry of Munitions for the manufacture of large quantities of phosgene. Many difficulties were met with at first in the new factory of the United Alkali Company at Lancaster, but fortunately the output of the Calais factory, in which, by arrangement with the French Government, we now had a part interest, developed far more rapidly than had been expected from the original 3 cwt. a day.[1]

As phosgene was to prove to be our main battle gas for the remainder of the war, I ought to explain here why it held such a high place in our estimation. It is, perhaps, ten times as toxic as chlorine (the German estimate was twenty times), but as a battle gas it is still more valuable as it possesses other dangerous properties. It is, besides, a specific poison : it can be breathed in fatal doses without undue discomfort or coughing, which, in the case of chlorine, limits the intake ; and it has a remarkable 'delayed action' of which we were unaware at this time, and which I, of course, did not realise when I exposed myself to the gas frequently while it was in the experi-

---

[1] At first a number of civilian workmen were sent over from England to help in this factory, under an expert chemist, Dr De Moulpied ; but they proved to be troublesome and of poor physique. They had to be replaced by two officers and two hundred men from the Special Brigade, who worked in three shifts, night and day, and remained there for the rest of the war, being exchanged from time to time. This detachment was known as " the Special Factory Section," and their withdrawal from the Brigade on whose strength they were borne of course handicapped our activities in the field.

mental stage. Both chlorine and phosgene act as lung
irritants, and cause inflammation of the lung tissues and
the exudation of moisture, which leads to asphyxia;
in other words, the victims in severe cases are drowned.
But with phosgene even a small intake of the gas, varying
in amount with the idiosyncrasies of individuals, is liable
to cause alarming symptoms as long as twenty-four and
even forty-eight hours after exposure, and cases constantly
occurred of men who declared positively that they had not
breathed the gas at all collapsing and dying after some
such interval. In fact it was due to ignorance of this
peculiarity of the gas that most of the casualties among
men of the Special Brigade occurred in June and July
1916: the training at Helfaut had been carried out with
chlorine cylinders, and the men knew to what extent they
could breathe small quantities of chlorine without harmful
results. With phosgene, however, death sometimes occurred after only a whiff or two of it had been inhaled,
an insufficient dose even to cause coughing, and the men
affected felt little inconvenience at the time and made no
complaint of indisposition. In one instance a sergeant
got a slight dose of gas the day after an attack had been
made, while disconnecting pipes from the empty cylinders:
he paid no attention to it, did not even mention it at the
time and carried on with his duties. He slept and break-
fasted well on the following day, but an hour later he
became very ill and died twenty-four hours after inhaling
the gas.

A similar case was described by a German prisoner
of a man who died suddenly two days after one of our
gas attacks while writing a letter to his family; and a
remarkable instance was often quoted of a German prisoner
who was captured in a raid after a gas attack. When
questioned about the effects of the gas, he ridiculed it
and expressed supreme confidence in his mask; but
after passing before various Intelligence officers he died
from gas poisoning twenty-four hours after his last interrogation.

I can perhaps give my non-technical readers some
idea of what is meant by the toxicity of the gases used in
the war by comparing phosgene with carbon monoxide,
the gas with which they are probably most familiar and
which is often mentioned in the case of accidents in mines

and in tragedies resulting from escapes of ordinary domestic gas, of which it is a constituent. Strictly speaking, of course, one gas cannot be compared with another owing to the different effects produced on the human system, as well as for other reasons. Carbon monoxide would seem at first sight an ideal gas for use in war, because it is easily made and it is colourless, odourless and penetrates every known means of protection excepting the oxygen breathing set; but it cannot be liquefied at ordinary temperatures, however great the pressure applied. Its action is indirect, as it unites with and so impairs the normal function of the red pigment in the blood, which is to carry oxygen from the air to the various parts of the body; so that when this process fails asphyxia ensues. Exercise, of course, increases this harmful action to a marked degree (as in the case of phosgene) on account of the extra demand of the body for oxygen. It has been established that one part of phosgene by volume in fifty thousand of air is a concentration which proves fatal to an unprotected man in ten minutes; whereas a concrete instance is known of a man breathing a measured volume of one part of carbon monoxide in one hundred and fifty of air for the same period without a fatal result. So that in this rough-and-ready way it may be estimated that phosgene is more than three hundred times as toxic as carbon monoxide.

Phosgene cannot be used by itself from cylinders: its boiling point is 46° Fahr., so that in winter-time, and often at night in the summer, its vapour pressure is insufficient to force it out without help; and some propelling agent is required, as in the case of the liquid in an ordinary soda-water syphon. If, therefore, a propelling gas were employed which was in itself toxic, so much the better; and chlorine naturally suggested itself at once for the purpose, though it was obviously advantageous to use as little of it as possible, provided that there was sufficient to enable it to fulfil its function properly at all ordinary temperatures. The probable factory output of phosgene had also to be considered, and eventually, after many experiments, a compromise was adopted and a mixture of half phosgene, half chlorine was decided on: this mixture went by the name of ' white star ' gas, and we used vast quantities of it until the end of the war.

It was so satisfactory, not only in its behaviour but also in its effect on the enemy, that when phosgene became more plentiful the more toxic mixture of 75 per cent phosgene, 25 per cent chlorine was never employed, though it was considered.

I have seen it stated recently by a distinguished public man that " phosgene is to-day as antiquated in modern warfare as the blunderbuss " ; but that is not my opinion, and I think that it will be found equally valuable in the future, if gas is retained as a weapon, provided, of course, that its tactical employment is adapted to whatever new set of conditions are met with. I doubt whether any more formidable lethal gas has been discovered since the war.

When using ' white star ' gas some device is necessary in cold weather to atomise the liquid completely as it emerges, and $\frac{3}{16}$ths inch ' nozzles ' screwed into the ends of the parapet pipes were found to serve this purpose admirably, though they caused a certain amount of hissing noise which it was sometimes found necessary to disguise by means of artillery or rifle fire at the beginning of an attack. Without the ' nozzles ' the discharge was almost absolutely silent, but a small quantity of the phosgene separated itself in cold weather and dripped on to the ground from the end of the pipe which took a little while to vaporise ; so that ' nozzles ' were never used except when it was the intention to send out infantry raiding parties from trenches from which cylinders had been discharged.

I have already pointed out that phosgene easily penetrated the early types of respirator which had been designed for protection against chlorine alone, and at first we hoped that when we came to use it the German masks would be found to give inadequate protection. In order not to give the enemy warning of its coming I had induced G.H.Q. to request the French General Staff to refrain from using phosgene shells, which I knew that they were preparing to do, in view of the far more important results which both armies might achieve if it were employed in clouds, especially if its disclosure were deferred until large supplies of the gas had been accumulated. The French loyally agreed to this proposal, though they were compelled to use phosgene shells in the defence of Verdun, after all.

Late in 1915, however, an Intelligence agent reported that the enemy were preparing to use phosgene themselves, the gas having been manufactured in Germany before the war, and it was identified in a cloud attack made against the British front on 19th December 1915. It is surprising that its value was not recognised by them earlier, and that it was not used in their first cloud gas experiments.

They had forestalled us, but not before every man in the British Expeditionary Force had been provided with the necessary form of protection. Even if the German troops were found to be similarly protected (but see p. 137 and footnote) we could still hope to take them unawares, especially if our cylinder installations were carried out with the same secrecy as at the battle of Loos and the gas was liberated silently and at night. We could expect that some, at any rate, of the German units would prove to be deficient in gas discipline, and that if the clouds were not recognised promptly the sounding of the gas alarms would be delayed. We could be certain of finding the same human weaknesses present among the Germans which were evident in our own men, and were the cause of nearly all the gas casualties that we suffered—namely, over-exertion on the part of officers and N.C.O.'s, over-confidence, carelessness, disobedience of instructions, ignorance, stupidity, excitement and fatigue.[1] And, finally, we knew from the systematic examination which was made of a proportion of all the German respirators that came into our possession, and from the periodical standard tests to which the respirators carried by our own men were put, that a large number of them, amounting to at least 10 per cent, would always be found defective in some way or other after they had been carried in the trenches for a week or more, exposed continuously to bombardment, rain, mud and barbed wire. Full confirmation of all these suppositions was obtained

[1] Mr Robert Graves, in ' Good-bye to all that,' has written of the period of the Somme battle : " The standing order with regard to gas shells was not to put on one's respirator, but hurry on. Up to that week there had been no gas shells except lachrymatory ones ; these were the first of the real kind, so we lost about half a dozen men."

The standing order referred to in this passage was, of course, if ever issued, in direct disobedience of the instructions given by G.H.Q. If these could be so misinterpreted by an officer or by his superiors, and in such an important respect, what follies might not the ordinary soldier be capable of ?

on numerous occasions in the next few months, the following being some of the reasons given by German prisoners to account for their losses :—

90th Fusilier Regiment, on 8/10/16. " South of the river (Scarpe) there were about twenty-five casualties in the left company. Most of these men died as they did not know whether it was gas or not, and would not put on their masks."

" While the old soldiers found the gas masks good protection, the younger men were careless in their use. In their excitement small gaps between the face and mask allowed the gas to enter."

" Men were slow in adjusting their masks, and often put them on badly : others had difficulty in breathing and took them off. As for damaged masks, in spite of inspection there were always some men who neglected to report defects, and who would therefore be gassed in the event of an attack."

The 85th German Regiment at Ficheux, on 13/11/16, suffered very heavy casualties : prisoners put the deaths in the regiment at 20 per cent of the strength, this being due to the screw-in portion of the drums being old and defective.

" Twenty men (of the 169th Regiment at Hebuterne on 26/6/16) when on patrol were all killed because they had not taken their masks with them."

Similar reasons were advanced by our own men and by our Allies ; for instance, on the night of 5th June 1917 the Germans discharged what was believed to have been a chlorine gas cloud against the French at Nieuport under unfavourable conditions—*i.e.*, in bright moonlight and a high wind. Colonel Cummins found 120 of the men who were gassed in one hospital, and on being questioned they attributed their incapacitation to the following causes :—

39 ' surprise effect ' or carelessness ;
15 raising the mask too soon ;
32 bad fitting of mask ;
30 displacement of mask ;
 2 inadequacy of mask ;
 2 obsolete type of mask ;
———
120

so that only four of this number claimed that the degree of protection afforded by the mask had been insufficient.

Again, a gas defence under-officer of the 120th German

Regiment who was captured at Bullecourt on 17th May 1917, stated that "on an average in a company 40 per cent of the masks were found to be defective in the gas chamber after a unit had been six days in the line"; and an N.C.O. prisoner of the 2nd Battalion of the 86th Reserve Regiment, captured on 10/9/17, said that at his anti-gas course at Cambrai (for N.C.O.'s) at the end of 1916, the gas officer instructor told them that in a cloud gas attack mean total losses of 15 per cent of the units exposed must be reckoned with.

Again, the gas N.C.O. of the Ersatz Battalion of the 162nd Regiment, captured on 12th October 1917, said that it was found that in a platoon of fifty men, fifteen to twenty of the (leather) masks would be found defective when tested.

These statements may seem exaggerations, but they were fully borne out by our own as well as by German experiences; for instance, the enemy discharged a gas cloud against the British at Hulluch on 29th April 1916, and although we suffered a large number of casualties it appears that the cloud blew back into the German lines during part of the discharge. (For the German account of this accident see pp. 180-181.) The diary was captured later of an N.C.O. of the 4th Bavarian Division in which there was an entry that this unit itself had sixteen hundred gas casualties owing to a change in the wind; and the report was confirmed quite independently by a prisoner of the 1st Machine-gun Company of the 3rd Bavarian Reserve Regiment, who was gassed himself on this occasion. "He said that the drift back of the gas caused six hundred deaths and more than a thousand gas cases: he saw trenches full of men lying gassed." A copy of the record of the official German investigation of this accident also fell into our hands; in this it was stated: "By the most careful estimation, even after excluding all defects which might have occurred subsequently, there remained 30 per cent of cases in which the men who were in the accident had been equipped with gas protection which should have been recognised on inspection as needing to be exchanged. Defects due to fitting could not, of course, be detected at all. A further examination of 839 masks obtained from reserves all along the western front showed that $11\frac{1}{2}$ per cent were not gas-proof against chlorine."

As a final example of the wear and tear of respirators

in the rough life of the trenches I may add that during 1918, when the British respirators were at their best (and certainly better though not so comfortable as the German), on an average 26 per cent of those withdrawn from units in the line for periodical test were found to have unsatisfactory lives—though it must be admitted that the standard aimed at in the tests was very high.

CHAPTER VIII.

THE BATTLE OF THE SOMME.

THE battle of the Somme brought the great German attack on Verdun (which began on 21st February 1916) to an abrupt close : it also fulfilled the purpose of General Joffre in another respect, which was to wear down the enemy's man-power ; and it certainly succeeded in this, though perhaps at undue cost of life to the Allies. It had, further, a very definite influence on the final result of the war, as for the first time there was unmistakable evidence of weakening of morale among the German troops and of their confidence being shaken.

The front of the British attack and the day on which it was to open were once again determined by the French G.Q.G. The main assault was to be made by the Fourth British Army, and it was to be supported by subsidiary attacks carried out by the French Sixth Army on our right, and by the Third British Army on the left, while demonstrations were to be staged all along the rest of the front of the B.E.F.

To this general plan the Special Brigade was to conform : its distribution to the four British armies had been arranged by G.H.Q. several weeks beforehand, and I had made all the preliminary arrangements with the staffs of the larger formations concerned in the gas operations, while my battalion and company commanders had completed the reconnaissances of the front line in their respective sectors before the various moves of men and cylinders took place. The greater part of the brigade was naturally allotted to the Fourth Army, but the use which it was proposed to make of the gas was not the best possible. A cloud discharge was planned to take place at the commencement of the preliminary artillery bombardment as part of the preparation for the assault, whereas the ideal method would have been to time it for the end of this bombardment, immediately before the infantry advanced, so that the latter might benefit to the maximum extent from the certain loss that would be inflicted on the enemy—small or great—and from the demoralisation and confusion that would result from it.

As will be seen from the meteorological chart opposite page 124, there was a strong probability at this season of the year of a favourable wind at all times ; so that dependence on the weather was only likely to necessitate the prolongation of the bombardment for a day or two, if at all. However, as General Joffre had fixed not only the day but the hour for the commencement of the battle, the circumstances were such that it was impossible to press for any alteration in the programme.

On 10th June we were still 524 men short of our establishment, besides the 200 who were employed by the Ministry of Munitions at the phosgene factory in Calais ; and during the previous month 300 trained men had been engaged continuously in making up nearly ten thousand pipe connections from odd material and in remedying certain shortcomings in the cylinders, nearly all of which had arrived from England with the handles wrongly attached, or without any at all.

Of the 35,000 'white star' cylinders demanded only 16,600 had been supplied ; and of the 26,600 pipe fittings, only 6300. Fortunately we still had 10,000 'red star' cylinders in France (including 3000 which had gone to Egypt and had now been returned), as well as 780 'blue star' ; and 2100 '2-red star' (H_2S) cylinders were due to arrive shortly.

Owing to the scattered distribution of the brigade (along a front of seventy-five miles) the movement of the twenty companies from Helfaut ("Z" Company was still in England) and of the cylinders from Les Attaques (our new central cylinder store near Calais), all of which took place between 13th-16th June, was much more difficult to arrange than in the smaller preparation for the battle of Loos, thirteen separate Army Corps having now to be provided for and eleven different railheads used : nor was it possible to keep the battalions intact, a fifth composite one (4A) having to be created from units withdrawn temporarily from the other four. Thus the First, Second and Third Armies each had three cylinder companies allotted to them, while the Fourth Army had seven, divided into a left and right group. Of the four Stokes mortar companies, one went to the Third Army and three to the Fourth; while "Z" Company was earmarked for the Fourth Army if it could be ready in time.

All these moves took place without a hitch, and on 24th June there were more than 20,000 cylinders in position along a (broken) front of about 30,000 yards, as well as 192 4-inch Stokes mortars, grouped in their own emplacements, with covered bomb-stores alongside. I had also visited personally the whole front of the Fourth Army in which my detachments were located. A précis of the staff arrangements which had been made in September 1915 for the installation of cylinders had been circulated to all concerned, for guidance, but Divisional Commanders were, of course, given a free hand as to the arrangements they would make in each case. A few managed to carry up all their cylinders (variously described, for the sake of caution, as 'accessories,' 'bottles,' 'rogers,' 'rats' and 'mice,' 'jackets,' &c.) in a single night (there were to be twenty in each emplacement) : some preferred to build wooden frames under the fire-step for their reception, so as to increase freedom of movement along the trench and facilitate subsequent discharges of gas from the same sector ; others employed thin reinforced concrete slabs to cover the cylinders, instead of sand-bags, thus saving space and providing extra protection against accidental injury ; while the arrangements made for rapid communication with the front line were improved to such an extent that in one case a message sent from the headquarters of the division (the 24th) reached the gas officer in charge of the emplacements only two minutes after its despatch.

The first gas operation in the series I am now about to describe took place on the front of the 20th Division in the Ypres Salient on the 13th June. It was not intended to precede the others, but it had to be carried out at short notice owing to the infantry action from which it was designed to attract attention having been accelerated. Only four and a quarter hours' notice was given to the officer in charge of it, and in this time 300 cylinders were carried into the front line and installed in groups of twenty, pipes were connected up and, after an exchange of wind messages and orders, the whole of them were discharged

Photo. by C. R. Alderson.

Cylinder " emplacement " in the front line.

Photo. by C. R. Alderson.

Smoke apparatus used in North Russia.

successfully at the appointed time without any kind of mishap. Chlorine gas was used on this occasion : the protection given by the German mask against phosgene was still none too good, and it was intended to lull the enemy into a sense of false security.

This was only a small operation, but it showed that the officers and men had benefited from their training, and it gave me great confidence in their technique and in the apparatus we now had at our disposal.

On the main battle front (Fourth Army) the gas discharge was first fixed for 20th June, but it was postponed till 10 P.M. on the 24th, the day on which the preliminary artillery bombardment commenced. At that hour there was a dead calm, except on the front of the 4th Division, where the gas was successfully liberated, attracting heavy retaliation. On the following day the Army Commander, much to my disappointment, left the arrangements for the discharge of the remainder of the gas to his five Corps Commanders, who, in turn, delegated them to the thirteen Division Commanders in the front line, the result being that the one big operation that had been planned was broken up into a number of smaller attacks, thus putting the enemy on the alert after the first had taken place, and enabling him to concentrate the inevitable artillery retaliation on each one in turn.

Worse still, the Division Commanders, few of whom had had any previous experience of gas, disliked the novel responsibility imposed on them, and there was a distinct tendency to ' get the stuff off ' as soon as possible owing to the serious risk to which, it was imagined, the troops continued to be exposed while the cylinders remained full in the trenches, though they were accustomed to accept similar risks from the presence of stores of trench-mortar bombs and hand-grenades, and were reconciled to occasional accidents from their own artillery.[1] Further

[1] The fact of the matter was that this new danger was an unfamiliar one, and for that reason it impressed the senses unduly. For example, the horror with which most people regard poisonous snakes almost disappears after residence in a country in which these reptiles abound, when it is found that although the danger exists it has been mentally exaggerated. Similarly there are as many deaths from motor accidents in this country every year as were caused by the Boers to our troops during the whole of the South African War, though, through familiarity with the facts, they cause hardly any public comment ; and yet, the British Government of the time was so shocked at the extent of the losses in South Africa that they issued instructions to our commanders which resulted in seriously limiting their freedom of action.

experience proved (as I will show later) that these fears were much exaggerated ; but the result of this attitude was that many of the gas attacks on the Fourth Army front were ordered to take place by daylight, so that there was a deplorable sacrifice of the surprise effect which might otherwise have been gained.

Nevertheless, all the gas discharges went off well, and infantrymen in the front line who had grumbled at the carrying in became enthusiastic as they watched the dense low clouds floating over towards the enemy. The absence of all leakage of gas, except from an occasional direct hit by the enemy's artillery, did much to restore their confidence, and there was a marked change in the attitude of the troops by the end of the year.

Elsewhere than on the main battle front, where, of course, the artillery activity on both sides was most intense, much better use was made of the gas, and nearly all the discharges took place at night. It will be seen from the wind chart (p. 125), which was compiled from records of the previous ten years, that in this part of France the wind was, especially at this time of year, far more favourable to us than to the Germans. Actually, all through the summer and autumn of 1916 we were remark-ably fortunate in the moments chosen for our cloud gas attacks, the velocity and direction of the wind being almost ideal on every occasion ; in fact, in only one instance was there any sort of a mishap, and this will be mentioned later. A great deal of variety was introduced in the pro-grammes arranged for the gas discharges, the chief feature in all being a very high concentration of gas aimed at at the commencement of the emission ; and in many parts of the front all the cylinders (there were never less than twenty per emplacement) were opened simultaneously. A few long programmes, commencing and ending with high concentrations of gas, were adopted, but these were dis-couraged owing to the prolonged exposure of the men in the trenches to the enemy's artillery and trench-mortar retaliation, as well as to avoid the risk, always present in these delicate operations, of a change or fall of wind during some part of the night.

Every sort of tactical device was resorted to with the object of making the surprise more complete : artillery co-operation was usually dispensed with until some minutes

WIND ROSES based on Synoptic Charts for 10 Years, 1905-1914.

In the following diagrams the lengths of the radii in various directions represent the relative frequencies of surface winds of between 4 and 15 m.p.h. *from* these directions in the British Army area.

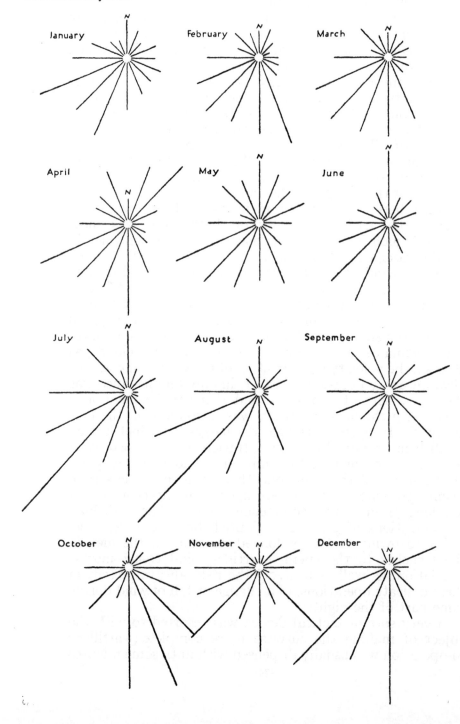

after the gas had started, though it was sometimes arranged to blind the enemy's sentries by obliging them to take cover ; while occasionally the discharge was preceded by rifle and machine-gun fire in order to compel the enemy to leave the partial protection of his dug-outs and man the parapets in the expectation of a surprise assault. Smoke, too, was frequently used, both by itself and in combination with the gas ; and when, for example, the disturbance which its appearance created had died down and everything was quiet again, a gas discharge would follow some hours later, and perhaps a second, and even a third, with irregular intervals between them during which infantry raids would be carried out. The reason for this was that it was known that in some German units the enemy had orders to man the parapet after the gas cloud had dispersed, in anticipation of a raid ; while for the sake of variety the gas was sometimes liberated after a raid had been carried out. Once or twice gas was discharged in a wind blowing at ten to fifteen miles an hour : such a high velocity was ordinarily considered unsuitable, so that a gas discharge in it would not be expected ; but, provided that enough gas was liberated, the comparative loss of density would be more than compensated for by the speed at which the cloud would travel and by the prospect of taking even alert sentries unawares.

Although it was usually some months before any reliable information was obtained of the casualties inflicted by these gas attacks, there was little doubt at the time that they affected the enemy's morale. The special correspondent of the ' Vossische Zeitung ' wrote at this period : " I devote a special chapter to this plague of our Somme warriors—the horrid nuisance of poison gases to which they are perpetually exposed. The English and French have fallen so deeply in love with this atmospheric weapon that they incessantly claim its help. The plague is steadily getting worse. In the trenches themselves it is particularly unpleasant, because here it settles down and cannot be easily dissipated by the wind. But even in the open country it pursues its course and tortures human beings." And under the date 30th June the following entry appeared in a diary found on a prisoner of the 76th Regiment : " Every moment the English are letting off gas, we get no rest at all. And every moment there is an alarm. 8.30

gas alarm. Left and right of us intense artillery fire and gas attacks."

On one occasion in daylight a German shell burst an unexploded smoke bomb which was lying in front of our parapet; the gas alarm was given immediately, and gongs and bells were sounded continuously in the enemy's lines for more than five minutes. And on another a German trench-mortar bomb punctured one of our cylinders, and the gas from it drifted towards the enemy's front line. Some of their infantry thereupon left the trench and ran across the open towards the support line, several being shot down by our Lewis gunners. One German prisoner stated, "After a gas attack large numbers went sick and they were granted fourteen days 'no duty'"; while, in a letter written in shorthand by a German soldier, there was the following: "Since the beginning of July an unparalleled slaughter has been going on. Not a day passes but the English let off their gas waves over our trenches at one place or another. I'll give you only one instance of the effects of the gas: people 7-8 kilometres behind the front have become unconscious from the tail of the gas cloud; its effects are felt even 12 kilometres behind the front. One has only to look at the rifles after a gas attack to see what deadly stuff it is. They are red with rust, as if they had been for weeks in the mud."

Many references appeared in the English papers about this time, supplied by correspondents at the front, as well as other accounts inspired by interviews with wounded men in hospital, of the numbers of gassed Germans found in trenches entered by raiding parties; and French journals, too, expressed lively satisfaction at the results that were being obtained with gas on the British front. Thus, the 'Daily Chronicle' of 1/7/16 had this: "British wounded brought back from the German trenches by their comrades relate that the effects of the new gases experimented with are terrible. One soldier of the H.L.I., who took part in one of the principal incursions into the enemy trenches, declares that all the Germans occupying that particular sector were dead. Two hundred and fifty corpses were counted lying huddled together." And the 'Figaro' of the 2nd July: "The English are giving them tit-for-tat, and hundreds of German soldiers before dying yesterday a terrible death and so expiating a collective crime learned that there is something in human justice."

I have explained in a previous chapter why information concerning the effects of a gas attack can seldom be expected from a raiding party, even when one is sent out specially to obtain it : the men only enter a few bays in the front line, and there is little time for investigation before a counter-attack is delivered or the recall signal is given, while little can be seen in the dark. Nevertheless, many successful raids were planned and carried out, in which men of the Special Companies sometimes took part. For example, after the gas discharge on the 47th Division front opposite Liévin on 27th June, a number of raids were organised. On their return all the parties agreed that only dead Germans remained in the front line, and of these a large number were seen. One report said : " Many dead Germans were in the dug-outs, apparently caught asleep and covered with blankets which had been damped with some chemical solution " ; and another : " Forty Germans were found in one dug-out either unconscious or dead : they were not wearing smoke helmets. At least eighty dead bodies were lying in the trench." [1]

After the gas attack on the front of the 37th Division (Third Army) opposite Monchy on 27th June (which was a continuous one, lasting two hours) a very successful raid was made, and an officer of the Loyal North Lancashire Regiment reported that the German trenches were full of dead. " An immense number of corpses were observed, and in one communication trench an entire barrier had been formed with them, while some of the enemy were found gasping." On the following morning the whole of Monchy wood was seen to be discoloured, most of the leaves having fallen from the trees. This raid met with only two casualties out of the two hundred men who took part in it. Another raiding party of one hundred and fifty men went over after a gas discharge at Hulluch on 5th July : they remained out for an hour

---

[1] A reference to this gas attack was found in the diary of a prisoner of the 18th German Division : " June 28th. I went to look for a pump, and so came past the 31st Regiment Aid Post. Inside it lay a whole heap of men who had been poisoned with gas during the night. They looked pale as corpses and gasped for air." Later entries in the same diary showed that the men were very demoralised, and became frantic whenever the word ' gas ' was called out. " Gas ! Gas ! was the cry, and all dashed away in panic."

and a half, and, although they failed to penetrate the enemy wire, they reported that complete silence reigned in the German lines.

It will be realised, I hope, that the desire to investigate the results of these gas attacks was not inspired by ghoulish curiosity: it was of the utmost importance to ascertain the effects of the gases we used, as well as the success of the tactics employed. We were really carrying out experiments on a gigantic scale, and were in the same position as a chemist in a laboratory who, unless he can observe the reactions taking place in his test-tubes, is wasting his time; or a doctor who can only judge the success of a certain line of treatment by watching closely the progress made by a patient. In the case of our cloud attacks surprise was what was aimed at above everything else, and the degree of success achieved in this respect could always be estimated by noting the enemy's behaviour when the gas reached his lines: thus on one occasion his alarm signals were observed only eighteen seconds after zero; in others, flares or rockets were sent up, and horns, gongs, bugles, bells or hooters were sounded as much as twelve minutes after the discharge commenced, an interval which would allow a cloud travelling at the rate of five miles an hour to penetrate more than a mile into the enemy's trench system; while on some occasions no alarm of any kind was given, there was no artillery or rifle fire, but only an ominous silence during and after the emission.

In his report of a gas attack near Arras the Commander of the 42nd Brigade wrote: " All firing from the German trenches ceased at zero plus five minutes in the area covered by the gas, except from one point where there was a gap in the cloud "; and on another night, when gas was discharged on the 8th Division front near the River Ancre on 27th June, the enemy's artillery fire, which had been particularly active, ceased altogether shortly after the gas attack commenced, and rifle and trench-mortar fire died away entirely. It was reported that for thirty-six hours afterwards no shelling at all was experienced from field-guns or mortars, but only from heavy artillery, the battery positions of which are, of course, usually much farther to the rear. At 7.30 A.M. on the following morning it was possible for infantry working parties on this front to stand on the fire-step for an hour and a half, exposed to view from the waist up, without being shot at ; and men were heard to say, " It's not that it quietens the blighters, but it sort of silences them altogether ! "

Apart from what raiders themselves are able to tell, the statements of prisoners taken on these expeditions are of little value, as events in a few bays on either side of them are the only ones that come within their knowledge. But when prisoners are captured a few weeks after they have experienced a gas attack, the accounts that they give of it, if they can be induced to communicate them, are of much greater interest, as in the interval they will have heard all the regimental gossip.

Deserters are of a type who are more likely to volunteer information than men who have submitted through force ; but still more reliable information is to be obtained from captured diaries, the entries in which are generally made with deliberation and with no intention of disclosing details which the enemy might consider of value. The best of all evidence (apart from that contained in books published after the war, which are sometimes suspect) is contained in the orders and official memoranda issued by the Commanders of German formations, bearing in mind that the worst of the news is generally withheld in these documents to avoid causing unnecessary alarm ; and if such evidence is confirmed independently from several of the other sources mentioned it ought surely to carry conviction to the most incredulous critics of the gas weapon, of which there were many at this period of the war.[1]

I cannot, of course, enter into much detail in regard to this series of cloud attacks, but a brief description of a few of them may be of interest.

On the right and centre of the Fourth Army front, where, as at Loos, the greatest infantry advance was made

---

[1] Information was also sometimes obtained by the use of listening sets—e.g., a telephone conversation in German, picked up after a projector attack at Bullecourt on 9th September 1917 : " The battalion requires a report regarding the affair this morning. Yes, a catastrophe. Now the main thing in question is how could such an incident take place. Yes, the whole 3rd Company must be relieved " ; and even by intercepting wireless messages—e.g., one after a projector attack at Oppy on 11th October 1917, which, when decoded, read : " From O.B. to B.1 Regiment " (this was either the 358th or the 50th), " Bei gas ehrebliche Verlust " —" considerable losses from gas."

at the commencement of the battle, fluctuations of the line and congested communications prevented any installation of cylinders after 1st July, though it was attempted in one or two places ; but on the left, opposite Beaumont Hamel and Hebuterne, and on the Third Army front, opposite Gommecourt and Monchy, as well as in a number of sectors occupied by the First and Second Armies, farther to the north, frequent gas attacks were made, sometimes repeatedly on the same front, though the German regiments were not necessarily the same on each of these occasions.

Beaurains.—Nine hundred and seventy cylinders were discharged on the front of the 14th Division (Third Army) at 3 P.M. on 27th June, in a west wind blowing at 6 m.p.h. All the cylinders were opened simultaneously so that the concentration of gas in the cloud was very high. An aeroplane observer reported that the village of Beaurains was completely hidden by the cloud, and that the latter was still very thick at Monchy-le-Preux, five miles back. Reports from all along our line were to the effect that noises denoting panic were heard from the enemy's trenches six to eight minutes after zero ; but as it was daylight no raiding party was sent out, and it was not till some months later that the French at Maurepas took prisoners belonging to the regiments affected (the 10th and 12th Bavarian Reserve Regiments), and sent us extracts from their examination of them.

A man of the 10th Bavarian Reserve Regiment stated (to the French) that one of the English gas attacks was effective ten kilometres back, where numerous men were taken ill and evacuated : there were twenty to thirty casualties to his own knowledge. Some were made ill after several days, and one died two days later while writing a letter to his family. (This incident was mentioned on p. 113.)

Two diaries, written by men in this regiment, were translated. One said : " On June 27th the English made three gas attacks against us, but they did not come out of their trenches. In the 7th Company, which occupied our position, there were 25 deaths and 30 others ill from gas. July 1st. We had 1 death, 3 or 4 severely wounded and more than 20 poisoned by gas." And the other : " 27th June. Gas attack in the course of the afternoon. We had

12 deaths and 15 ill." (The number of the company was not mentioned.) "The attack lasted from 4 till 7 o'clock."

A prisoner from the 12th Bavarian Reserve Regiment said : "There were many deaths in the 5th Company from the English gas attack. The men were thrown into disorder and raised their masks because they were suffocating. Many fell in running to the rear, and a number did not become ill until the next day. Vegetation was burnt up to a depth of 8 kilometres." And another man of the 10th Company of the same regiment said "that a working party of 12 men had 8 gas casualties, of whom 5 never returned." [1]

Reference was frequently made to the injury sustained by troops situated far behind the front : thus, in a document issued by the headquarters of the Second German Army (the one opposite our Fourth Army) and captured by the French, it was said : "From the 25th June to the 22nd July there were 59 gas attacks on the north of the Somme [2] and 11 on the south, making a total of 70. The (precautionary) wearing of masks is not necessary after 3 or 4 kilometres back, but sometimes the area is affected to a depth of 10 kilometres. On June 26th gas emitted on the Boisselle-Fricourt sector (1043 cylinders discharged) caused much inconvenience to troops in Bapaume, 16 kilometres away. The greatest depth reached by the cloud appears to have been 24 kilometres, but beyond 10 kilometres no ill-effects need be feared. The present danger zone should be increased from 4 to 10 kilometres."

And in a memorandum written by the headquarters of the 1st Guard Reserve Division on 29th June 1916, referring to the gas attack at Hulluch the previous day, it was stated : "On the front of the 5th Bavarian Reserve Division the enemy liberated gas three times at intervals of a quarter of an hour. All rats and mice were killed and the birds dropped dead from the trees. The gas was particularly effective in villages behind the lines. The

---

[1] Apparently the 9th Bavarian Regiment was also present on this occasion, as in its History it is stated that on the night of the 27th-28th June 1916 there was a cloud attack between 2 and 3 A.M. (*sic*), accompanied by heavy artillery fire: the regiment lost two men killed, nine wounded and twenty-three gassed. It was this unit which suffered from its own gas attack at Hulluch in April 1916 (see p. 180).

[2] Probably the Ancre was intended, as the French Sixth Army was south of the Somme and they made no attacks with gas clouds.

English frequently preface their gas attacks by artillery fire, so that the emission of the gas is difficult to recognise. The machine-guns are much damaged by rust. Stables had to be evacuated and the horses became ill : they must be taken to the nearest hill. The alarm was frequently not given quickly enough in the villages. The approach of the gas, especially at night, is difficult to recognise."

Again, an officer of the 458th Regiment, taken prisoner at Villers Plouich on 25th April 1917, " admitted that some of our gas attacks had been very successful, especially on the Somme. During his officers' course he was told that the English gas had penetrated behind the lines from 20-26-30 kilometres, the average depth being 20 kilometres. The farthest depth reached was 34 kilometres, and during this attack all the horses, in fact every living thing except dogs, which were not affected, was killed."

Carnoy.—On this front, held by our 18th Division, owing to shortage of labour only 237 cylinders were carried in, and they were arranged in three separate small sectors and were discharged at 2.30 A.M. (107), 3.30 A.M. (79), and 6 A.M. (51), on 30th June, twenty-four hours before the infantry assault, the wind being south, 4 m.p.h. in each case. This attack, although a small one, seems to have been particularly effective, as on 1st December two prisoners of the 62nd German Regiment were examined and said " that they had very heavy losses from gas on July 1st on the Somme. In the 1st Battalion half the men were gassed, killed or sent to hospital. The 2nd Battalion also had severe losses. The attack took place early in the morning about 5.30 A.M. and was a complete surprise. In the 2nd Company (to which one of the prisoners belonged) there were over 100 gassed cases." This information was confirmed by a British medical officer who made an examination of the German trenches captured by the 18th Division on the same day : he reported that after the assault " he found the bodies of many dead German soldiers that had no wounds : as they were lying on their backs, the clothing round the neck and chest loosened, and there being marked signs of cyanosis in each case, there could be no doubt that their deaths were caused by gas poisoning. In some of the cases respirators were hung round the neck and they appeared to have been worn." And in a letter written to his brother in the

Special Brigade an officer in the 7th Buffs (18th Division) said : " We found a large number of Bosches (of the 62nd Regiment) dead in their dug-outs—some with their gas helmets on, others who had not even had time to put them on. They had no wounds and the dug-outs in question had not been blown in. So you may certainly count a number of Bosches to your credit : how many I do not know, as the dug-outs have been filled in instead of the men being taken out and buried."

Monchy.—At 10 P.M. on the night of 30th August 1250 cylinders were double-banked with the object of attaining as high a concentration of gas as possible, one emplacement having no fewer than 88 cylinders in it ; two others, 80 ; three, 64 ; and two, 56 ; the average number in each emplacement being 36. The attack took place in a very favourable wind, and the resulting concentration of gas was higher than in any other gas discharge up to this time, though it was considerably exceeded in some of the great cylinder attacks in 1918. The British Divisional (46th) summary contained the following reference to this operation : " On the discharge of gas from our trenches the enemy north of the Bienvillers-Monchy road remained inactive, except for rockets. South of the road shouts, screams, gongs, whistles, bugles and bells were heard." We learnt quite a lot from the enemy's side of what happened, as, only five days afterwards, a deserter from one of the regiments (the 63rd) exposed to the gas, said : " Since the date of going into the trenches the 6th Company had lost 20 men killed in the gas attack, 1 killed, 4 wounded and 4 prisoners in the raid, but it had no casualties from artillery fire or snipers."

A prisoner of the 7th Company of this regiment said : " The 7th Company lost seven men and several were evacuated to Germany." Another was behind the line at the time of the attack, and spoke of a fatigue party of ten men who had all become casualties because they had forgotten their masks : he added, " The effect of the gas was appalling."

Three prisoners of the 23rd Regiment were examined at G.H.Q. on 12th December 1916. A. said : " The gas came over very suddenly in the late evening : it was terribly strong, and they had very heavy casualties as no one was expecting gas, so that half the company were killed." B. said: "Over sixty men were killed." C. (in the 4th Company) said: "One company of the 1st Battalion was on parade at Douchy-les-Ayette (7 kilometres). Very few men were carrying their gas masks. The gas came over so suddenly that they thought it was from artillery fire. No warning was given and about sixty men were killed here." (*Note*—7 kilometres from the front!) "After this occurrence more stringent orders were issued about always carrying masks in villages behind the lines. Many of the men who suffered were orderlies, servants, &c., who found it difficult always to carry gas masks."

An officer-'stellvertreter' (deputy) of this unit admitted that thirty-eight men were killed in this attack, but he refused to say whether the casualties occurred in his own company or in the whole battalion.

The 62nd Regiment, too, seems to have suffered. Prisoners in the 2nd and 9th Companies said: "In the 1st Battalion nearly half the battalion was gassed, killed, or sent to hospital. The 3rd Battalion also had very heavy losses." "In the 2nd Company there was a total of over one hundred gassed cases."

Two captured German documents also mentioned this affair. One, issued by the headquarters of the XIVth Reserve Corps, and dated 6/9/16, stated that men working behind the lines were surprised by the gas without their masks, and added, "even the towns of Gomiecourt" (not Gommecourt) "and Courcelles" (9 and 11 kilometres respectively) "were endangered"; while the other, written on 1st September 1916 by the headquarters of the 12th German Division and signed 'Fouque,' said: "Although the men were all awake and the alarm was spread very rapidly, the gas cloud came on so quickly in the strong wind that some men were too late in getting their masks on. The cloud attack caused heavy losses. The following casualties have been reported so far: 63rd Regiment, 13 dead (8 of these only died after a few hours), 20 severe and 31 medium and slight. The cases were mostly severe and the large majority require hospital treatment. The losses are to be ascribed to two chief causes. After their casualties in the Somme battle the 63rd Regiment was half composed of new reserves and recruits whose training was not sufficiently good. The alarm arrangements in the position they took over were insufficient. Some men were taken by surprise and put on their masks too late, others ran too quickly and tore off their masks because of the difficulty of breathing. Others, again, tumbled about during the alarm and either had their masks torn or displaced."

Hulluch.—On the night of 5th October 2527 cylinders were discharged in three separate waves, each of very high concentration. (Other British cloud attacks on this front took place on 28th June, 7th July and 20th August.) The first wave (917 cylinders) was liberated at 8 P.M., the second (555) at 8.45 P.M., and the third (1055) at 10.30 P.M. Smoke candles were lighted six to eight minutes after the gas discharge commenced on each occasion. Altogether about eighty tons of 'white star' gas were liberated, this being the largest cloud attack, up to date, carried out by a single company ("C"). The usual German alarms were observed, but it was noticed that they only came from the German reserve line on the second and third occasions. A large raiding party, consisting of one hundred men of the 2nd Devons and six N.C.O.'s and men from "C" Special Company, went over to the German lines after the last discharge, but although they got through the German wire they failed to enter the enemy's trench owing to our own artillery shells falling short and killing a number of the men, including the captain in command, and disorganising the remainder, who fell back, so that no prisoners were captured. Nevertheless there were a number of indications that the gas had taken effect : at nine o'clock the following morning the silence in the enemy's trenches was described as 'uncanny,' and the usual artillery and trench-mortar fire failed to provoke any kind of retaliation during the next forty-eight hours. In fact, so unusual did the situation seem that a lance-corporal (Wilson) of the 2nd Devons walked over to the German position in broad daylight, and spoke (in German) to a solitary machine-gunner there, the rest of the trench being empty, except for two German officers who came up during the conversation. He asked permission to remove the dead and wounded raiders, and was ordered to place the former in a shell-hole near the German parapet without removing any of the equipment. With the help of a private in his own regiment he then carried the wounded back to our own lines, covered all the while by the machine-gun and the revolvers of the officers. These two men observed numbers of the enemy leaving the German back area without equipment or arms and appearing feeble and sick, and during the day many stretchers were seen at work and forty ambulances were counted in the distance. The German troops opposite were relieved the next day, and the 8th Division Intelligence summary of 6th October contained the words : " The discharge of gas appeared very successful. It is thought that it is responsible for the lack of retaliation."

Two months afterwards an undespatched letter of a prisoner of the 248th Reserve Regiment came into our possession, from which the following extracts are taken : " 13/10/16. I am sorry to say that my friend was killed by gas poison after being back a few hours from leave. The hostile gas attack lasted about three hours on the night of October 5th. It really amounted to three gas attacks each lasting an hour. The 9th Company especially suffered considerable losses, for the attack was strongest in our sector." " 9/11/16. You ask whether Stark had no gas mask. He had one near him, but he put it on too late. We also had the old gas masks and found it difficult to breathe. If we had had new masks we certainly would not have had these losses. Now it is too late."

A Saxon prisoner in this same regiment, examined in April 1917, said that " his regiment was in a very big attack on October 5th, 1916, which had caused moral effects a long way back from the line. He had heard that there were 1000 casualties—that is, men evacuated from the line. Besides these there were many deaths : the trenches were spoken of as blocked with dead. Such was the moral effect of this attack that for some while afterwards he admitted himself that they used to try to run back whenever there was an alarm—even when no gas came. The gas was felt as far back as Pont Maudit and Estevelles (8 kilometres). His regiment then had only the old type of mask with the nose-clip which had to be damped before use with solution from a box. Prisoner was quite definite about this. They did not get the masks with the drum till later." [1]

[1] This was certainly exceptional, but even some of the later German masks, with drums, gave no protection against phosgene. On the 6th June 1916 two prisoners of the 231st Reserve Regiment (50th Reserve Division) were captured

Another prisoner of the 153rd Regiment, captured in April 1917, said : " About the end of September his regiment relieved a division which suffered very heavily from a gas attack and lost in killed the equivalent of two battalions. The gas made people sick at Harnes, 8 kilometres behind the front. At Courrières, 10 kilometres behind, the troops suffered from gas sickness. The gas affected the 54th Reserve Division, which had only been in the line for a week or two. His company commander told him of the extent of the losses mentioned and attributed them to the surprise effected."

I felt convinced that this was one of the most successful cloud discharges that we carried out throughout the war, but at the time the disinclination of our commanders to believe in the success of this method of attack was illustrated in the following reports :—

8th Division to Ist Corps, dated 9/10/16.

" No very direct evidence was gained as to the effect produced on the enemy by our gas attack, but I am inclined to think that the comparatively feeble retaliation directed against our lines was due to the casualties and confusion caused."

Ist Corps to First Army, dated 21/10/16.

" There is unfortunately no evidence of the effect of the gas on the enemy. The assumption that the relief was due to heavy casualties from gas, and not to other reasons, is, I think, far-fetched. The gas may doubtless have caused heavy losses to the enemy, but we have no facts on which to base an opinion. The management of the gas attack left nothing to be desired, and reflects great credit on all ranks of the Special Brigade concerned in it."

First Army to G.H.Q., dated 31/10/16.

" I consider the attack was well organised and successful."

It seems that the 54th Reserve Division (which consisted of the 245th, 246th, 247th and 248th Reserve Regiments) was the one chiefly affected by this attack. It had suffered heavily in the Somme battle, and was sent to

during a raid just east of Armentières, and were found to be equipped with the old mask fitted with the ' one-layer ' drum, which gave no protection against phosgene : one of these had a washer missing, so that it was useless in any case. It is evident, therefore, that in the middle of 1916 the issue of the new ' three-layer ' drum was not general in all the German formations.

Hulluch on 26th September for rest and reinforcement, as this was supposed to be a quiet front. The fact that it was despatched only ten days later to the Vosges suggests some very strong reason for this second relief. In the History of the 246th Reserve Regiment the gas attack is mentioned, but no particulars are given. The History of the 248th Reserve Regiment admits that the gas attack had produced a great effect, and records the loss in the regiment of three dead and sixty-nine others gassed. And the History of the 245th Reserve Regiment, which also appears to have been present, says that the watches were badly tarnished, the sand-bags turned chrome yellow and the rats swarmed out of their holes and died. "On the 5th October, after a heavy bombardment, the enemy discharged a cloud in the late evening which produced an asphyxiating gas. The strength of the companies, with all available personnel, was reduced to thirty men. New reinforcements, inexperienced in the use of gas masks, swallow gas. There are a number of gas casualties." This last extract affords a good example of the strict reserve which is maintained in all German post-war histories in regard to their losses from gas. I am commenting on this subject in a later chapter.

A reference to the map at the end of this chapter will show that from certain sectors of the British front gas attacks were made more frequently than from others, and the same deduction may be drawn from the maps at the end of Chapters XIII. and XVI., which illustrate our gas operations in 1917 and 1918 respectively. This was partly due to the fact that these sectors favoured the prevailing wind, which was rather south of west ; and partly, in the case of the Hulluch sector, because it was occupied for long periods by " C " Company, the Commander of which (Captain Davies), like myself, was a firm believer in the cylinder method of attack.

On one occasion a division whose commander was notorious throughout the brigade, and was known to disapprove of the use of gas and to disbelieve in its efficacy, came to occupy the Hulluch sector. "Who are you ? " he asked Davies, who replied, " I've come to arrange a gas attack with you." "Take your bloody gas away," he stormed, " I'll have nothing to do with it." " Just as you say, sir," said Davies, who was already primed for this encounter. " All the same, it isn't as bloody as you seem to think." " How do you mean, not bloody ? " asked the General. " Well, haven't you read last week's Army Intelligence summary ? " he said, as he produced from his pocket a copy of the document, which happened to contain a particularly encouraging report of a German prisoner's gas experiences. The report was studied, and the end of it was that arrangements were made for the cylinders to be carried in. As regards this attitude towards gas on the part of some of the British commanders, it is interesting to read in an American book of which General Fries, the chief of the gas service in the American Expeditionary Force, is joint author,[1] that American gas officers, when they first came into action in the early summer of 1918, had the greatest difficulty in persuading the commanders of their formations to make use of their services. " Chemical Warfare Service officers," it was said, " have to go out and sell gas to the army " ; and he relates one instance in which the General Staff of an American formation insisted on a written certificate being signed to the effect that if gas was used it could not possibly result in a single American soldier becoming a casualty !

Davies' justification came in June 1918 when a number of French repatriés from the area behind Hulluch volunteered information of their experiences in the German lines. One, a Dr Colle, said that " he had been invited on a certain occasion to visit the German military hospital at Dourges (14 kilometres in rear of Hulluch) in 1916 and he had seen fifty gas casualties there : in most of the cases there were little signs of anything being the matter when the men were admitted, but they subsequently became blue, and in nine-tenths of the cases they died on the second or third day.

" Vegetation and garden produce was affected by the gas as far back as Henin Liétard, which was 14 kilometres from the front line. The Germans feared our gas very much, and frequently stated that their masks did not give them adequate protection. They suffered heavy casualties, for when gas cases came in the two hospitals in Henin Liétard, each containing 100 beds, were several times emptied and refilled on one and the same occasion. The same occurred at other hospitals in the vicinity of

[1] ' Chemical Warfare '—Fries and West.

Drocourt and Dourges. Large numbers of the men died as the result of having walked, often as far as 14 kilometres, to billets after having breathed gas. In November 1917 there were 3500 Germans who had died of gas poisoning buried at Dourges cemetery." (See also the extract from the History of the 10th Bavarian Regiment in footnote, pp. 231-232.) "The danger of exertion after exposure to gas did not appear to have been generally known by the enemy at that time."

Another repatrié, M. Prudhomme, the Director of Mines at Dourges, collected some very definite information from his employés, some of whom had worked for the Germans, and he confirmed Dr Colle's statements.[1] He added that in Dourges cemetery alone, up till June 1917, 2500 men who had died from gas poisoning had been buried; and by November 1917 this number had risen to between 3000 and 4000. (Between April and November 1917, five cylinder operations and six projector and 4-in. Stokes mortar gas shoots took place on this front.)

I must not devote too much space to this period of the Somme battle, though there is much more to tell: even some of the small gas discharges, in which only 200 or 300 cylinders were emptied, seem to have had remarkable results. I cannot refrain, however, from describing two more gas attacks which are specially interesting: one because it was the only time in the war that sulphuretted hydrogen was liberated, and the other because we undertook it in a sector occupied by French troops.

Monchy.—The experiments at home with H_2S have already been mentioned: this gas was used on the front of the 46th Division at Monchy on the night of 13th July 1916, by which date 1670 '2-red star' cylinders were in position, in addition to 240 'white star.'

Only a fortnight previously (27th June) 2000 'white star' had been discharged on this same front (other gas attacks took place on this sector on 30th August and on 13th November), so that the enemy was known to be on the alert: besides, several of the H_2S cylinders were injured by a German shell before the night of the attack, and we were reconciled to expect that no surprise was

---

[1] According to the French Intelligence report: "L'un de mes employés qui était resté à Dourges et qui m'a rejoint par la suite à Fresnes (Nord), un homme absolument digne de foi, m'a raconté . . ."

likely to be effected, though we hoped that the new gas would penetrate the enemy's masks.[1]

At 1 A.M. the '2-red star' cylinders were turned on simultaneously, with the result that a cloud of very high concentration was created. In view of the high pressure of this gas special precautions had been taken to fasten down the parapet pipes to the ground with staples and to weight them, in addition, with sand-bags in anticipation of the 'kick,' and each cylinder had a separate pipe to itself. Three minutes after the discharge commenced a very violent and accurate bombardment by the German artillery started which did a great deal of damage to the pipes, resulting in leakages of gas in the trench. None of the infantry suffered, as they had been cleared out of the bays, but the Special Company concerned (Pelling, "N" Company) had one officer and seven men killed, and one officer and fifteen men wounded or gassed. Further, the gas issuing from a number of the jets all along the line was ignited by what was thought at the time to be phosphorus bombs fired deliberately with that object, but which proved later to be a new pattern of Verey light : this did no harm except that some of the gas was wasted, and the greater part of it, amidst the roar from the ignited jets and the inferno of the bombardment, floated well over to the enemy in an ideal wind and hung about the village of Monchy for some time. Two hours later (at 3 A.M.) the 'white star' cylinders were discharged, with some smoke, and this second cloud, too, went over perfectly. The Commander of the division, on hearing of the casualties and of the ignition of the jets, reported that he considered that the gas was too dangerous to use, but he was so impressed with the effect it had had on my men, regarding it as "very poisonous indeed," that he was instructed by the Corps Commander, after the latter had consulted me, to carry out a second attack with the cylinders which remained over in two sectors of his line for which the wind on the 14th was unfavourable. This took place at 10 P.M. on the 17th, and no more favourable opportunity of testing this battle gas could possibly have occurred.

[1] The leakage from some of the cylinders was such that the trail of gas from the convoy which brought them forward had been so marked and disagreeable that the inhabitants of the French villages were seen to hold up their aprons to their faces as the lorries passed.

On this occasion none of the gas was set alight, and it went over well to the German lines in a heavy thick cloud ; the enemy's rifle fire was noticed to diminish perceptibly and we had no casualties.

At this period the British Army was still using the helmet type of respirator (the ' PH '), but as an experimental measure the men of the Special Brigade had been equipped with the first pattern of ' box respirator,' which gave better protection against all the usual war gases and the issue of which became general a little later. In spite of this it was evident that the protection even of the new mask against H_2S in high concentrations was insufficient, and as this gas is never likely to be used again in war, and few cases of poisoning from it have been known to occur (with the exception of the instance given on p. 105 when Livens was affected [1]), it will be of scientific interest to record what some of its observed effects were, especially as the occasion was the only one throughout the war of an officer of the Special Brigade being killed by our own gas.

One or two of the men appeared to have been killed instantaneously when in close proximity to severed pipes : their faces were calm and showed no trace of suffering, and their bodies, when examined later by a medical officer, were found to be deeply cyanosed all over. The officer who died was unconscious for three hours, when he succumbed. Another officer was not cyanosed at all, but he became delirious and had to be held down, as his one desire seemed to be to jump over the parapet and ' go for ' the enemy. One man underwent the most remarkable muscular contortions, and when he recovered consciousness he was paralysed and was unable to move for some hours. Two others who were also rendered unconscious came to half an hour later, remembered nothing and only felt a general weakness. One or two struggled violently, bit the men attending to them and appeared to be temporarily insane : their revolvers had to be taken away from them and they became hysterical, but they soon recovered completely. The Divisional Commander himself complained bitterly that he suffered from diarrhœa after every visit

[1] In 1901 some sensation was caused in the West Indies when an Englishman was overcome with ' gas ' and died in the volcanic crater in Dominica in which the ' Boiling Lake' is situated. His body was recovered, and I was the first person to visit the scene a year later, when I found his camera, &c., lying where it had fallen. There were strong fumes present which were undoubtedly H_2S.

to that part of his line in which the cylinders were awaiting discharge.

This attack appeared at the time to have been a fiasco, but this was by no means the case. Two prisoners of the 73rd Fusilier Regiment, Alsatians who were quite willing to give information, were interrogated on 7th December 1916. Both were in a machine-gun company, and one of them had the following entry in his diary: " On July 13th " (it was I A.M. on the 14th) " there was a gas attack accompanied by artillery drum-fire. We had 73 men and 6 officers dead." He said that they had been warned that a gas attack was probable and they saw the cloud. They considered our gas very powerful. It was necessary to adjust the mask correctly : once gas entered the mask it was no use adjusting it. They had seen several cases of men who dropped down and died of gas poisoning before they had time to adjust their masks. Froth appeared at the mouth and their faces assumed a bluish hue. One of their officers had arranged for cloth covers to protect the glass eye-pieces when masks were not in use. These pieces of cloth slipped over the mouthpiece while the mask was being adjusted, and consequently gas entered through the edges of the mask. They knew of eleven deaths caused in this way. Sometimes the rubber washer was lost, which caused the masks to leak. There were many cases of delayed action, five in their machine-gun section. Some came back after two or three weeks, others never returned.

Another prisoner of the 73rd Fusilier Regiment, questioned on a subsequent occasion, said that his company had 30 men killed by cloud gas near Monchy in July 1916. The 2nd Battalion was practically annihilated, suffering losses in dead alone amounting to 300, besides the majority of the remainder gassed. Prisoner was gassed himself and was away from his regiment for two months. Their masks were not so good then as now.

Nieuport.—The other gas attack to which I want to draw attention also had certain special features : it took place in October 1916 on the front of the 29th French Division (XXXVIth French Army Corps) which was holding the sector on the extreme left of the Allied line on the English Channel.

My attention had been attracted to statements repeatedly made by prisoners of the German Marine Corps and published in the Intelligence Summaries, to the effect that the employment of gas on this sector was considered by their own officers to be impossible on account of the variability of the sea breezes. We were careful as to what German divisions we selected as targets for our gas operations, Landwehr troops, for example, not being considered worth the effort; and from time to time I was supplied by our Intelligence Division with lists of units which had either arrived recently from the Russian front, and which, in their ignorance of gas warfare, might offer particularly favourable marks, or which were expected to be transferred to the main battle fronts on the Somme, Ypres, &c., in relief of exhausted divisions, and which it would be advantageous to weaken beforehand.[1]

A gas attack was therefore proposed to the French XXXVIth Corps Commander, and he at once gave his consent.

On 17th September 2050 'White star' cylinders were despatched in great secrecy to Oost Dunkerque, and two companies of the Special Brigade arrived there at the same time.

Although he was the junior of the two company commanders I put Captain Lefebure in charge of the operation, because he was the better linguist and it was essential that no misunderstandings should occur in making the arrangements with the French Staff. (Later on Lefebure became liaison officer in Paris for our Ministry of Munitions, and he has written several books on gas warfare since the war—e.g., 'The Riddle of the Rhine' and 'Scientific Disarmament.')

On the same day a very careful study was commenced of the land and sea breezes: a special meteorologist was detached for this duty, and eight observation stations were established behind the line at each of which wind readings were recorded every hour, both by day and night, during the whole period before the discharge took place.

The arrangements made by the French Staff—they had never before undertaken such an operation—for carrying in the cylinders were excellent, and the installation was complete on the 22nd. We of course realised a

---

[1] Sometimes we even postponed an attack, the preparations for which had already been made, in order to wait for a particular division whose arrival on that front was known to be imminent.

special responsibility towards our Allies, and the most careful arrangements were made throughout, communication to the front line being duplicated and all messages being sent by code, for which the following diagrammatic system was adopted :—

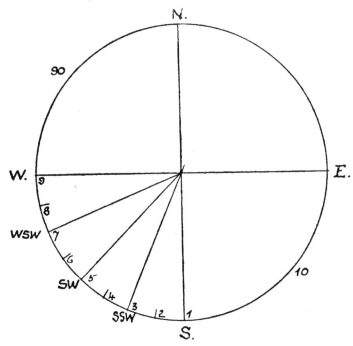

The figure in the message dealing with the 'direction' preceded that showing the 'velocity' of the wind: thus, '78' meant "Wind W.S.W.—8 m.p.h."; and '904' meant "Wind between W. and N. (and therefore unsuitable)—4 m.p.h."

Arrangements were also made for weather forecasts to be received independently from the Meteorological Office at G.H.Q., from the headquarters of the Second British Army and from the French Poste Météorologique d'Aviation.

When the plan for the attack was being discussed it was the intention of the XXXVIth Corps Commander to follow up the gas discharge with an infantry assault, and I found myself in the unusual position of urging caution, and even had difficulty in dissuading him from ordering the infantry to advance while the gas discharge was still in progress !

From 23rd September to 5th October there was a spell of unfavourable weather : small parties of French troops were in the habit of entering No Man's Land every night, where they sometimes met Germans who were similarly engaged on reconnaissance duty. To avoid any possibility of prisoners being taken through whom the presence of gas cylinders might be made known to the enemy, the order was given to cancel all patrols for the time being. This change of procedure apparently aroused suspicion, and the Germans raided the French trenches one night in great strength ; and although they did not remain long enough in the front line to discover our cylinders, twenty prisoners were taken, and in consequence the French Commander abandoned all hope of bringing off a surprise. However, after all the labour that had been expended he decided that the gas should be discharged at the first favourable opportunity, but the infantry operation was cancelled. At 11 P.M. on the night of 5th October (about the same time that the gas attack at Hulluch was proceeding—see p. 136 *et seq.*—and also a third at Armentières) the discharge took place, the wind being just what was required—*i.e.*, S.W., 5 m.p.h. All the cylinders (twenty per emplacement) were turned on simultaneously, and the cloud of gas travelled towards the German trenches, keeping low. As anticipated, the enemy was well prepared, the gas was recognised within a few seconds, alarm signals were sent up, intense rifle and machine-gun fire was opened (the Germans expected an infantry attack to follow), and a fierce artillery battle ensued which lasted for two and a half hours, and in which a large number of trench-mortars on both sides participated. Two of our semi-portable flame-projectors were also fired successfully from a salient in the line, which was only thirty yards distant from the German trench opposite.

From a technical point of view this gas attack was a complete success, and our organisation and methods seemed to have impressed the French Commanders very favourably ; so much so, in fact, that the 45th French Division which was due to relieve the 29th wanted us to stay on and stage a second operation for them, it being considered that a surprise attack was still possible.

Only two Frenchmen were gassed in this engagement, both very slightly, while we lost two men killed, eight wounded and eight others slightly gassed.

The following appreciation was sent to me from the French Corps Commander through Prince Alexander of Teck (the Chief of the British Mission with the Belgian Army) :—

"36 Corps d'Armée.   Au Q.G. le 7 Octobre 1916.
      Mon cher Général,—

Le détachement de la Brigade Spéciale Brittanique commandé par le Capitaine Lefebure a exécuté une émission de gaz sur le front du secteur de Nieuport dans la nuit du 5 au 6 Octobre.

Il a préparé cette opération en faisant preuve de la plus grande compétence technique et de plus bel entrain : il l'a exécutée dans des conditions parfaites, malgré le bombardement intense déclanché par l'ennemi peu de temps après le commencement de l'émission.

Je suis heureux de vous exprimer toute la satisfaction que m'a causée la collaboration du détachement du Capitaine Lefebure, et j'ai l'honneur de vous demander de vouloir bien en transmettre l'expression aux autorités militaires Brittaniques dont relève ce détachement.

Veuilliez agréer . . .   (se) M. Balfourier."

In my report to G.H.Q. on this operation, I wrote : "Although, for reasons previously stated, the element of surprise was lacking from this attack, it is reasonable to suppose that a certain number of casualties were inflicted on the enemy by the gas : at any rate an excellent target was offered to the superior French artillery, of which full advantage was taken."

It will be seen from the foregoing that we had no reason to suppose that this attack had met with any particular success, and it was not till six months later that we heard to the contrary. Early in March 1917 the Intelligence Department of the War Office obtained and sent to France the following interesting account which had been given by a deserter from the 1st Matrosen Regiment (of the Marine Corps), who escaped into Holland and volunteered the information to an agent there :—

"On the evening of October 2nd, 1916, the raiding party of the 2nd Battalion of the 1st Matrosen Regiment reported that preparations were being made in the French line for a gas attack, and it was learned from the French prisoners who were captured that British Engineers were engaged in the operation. Prior to this date there were no special gas alarm orders, as no one thought a gas attack possible as the coast winds changed so frequently; but after the raid a gas attack was expected daily, except on the 5th when the battalion gas officer reported that the wind was too strong. Later on this officer said that he had been taught that gas would be ineffective in any wind more than half as strong as that on October 5th.

" The gas affected the 1st and 4th Matrosen Regiments in particular. At 11 P.M. the deserter with a platoon of 37 men was on fatigue duty, pushing a truck, and they heard the gas alarm sounded. All put on their masks. The gas came on them quickly, but some had insufficient time, the masks of others did not fit, many others tore their mask where the respirator is attached to the material. Seventeen of the above 37 were gassed, of whom 10 died on the ground and the remainder have never returned. Deserter attributed his safety and that of others to finding an adjoining dressing-station protected by a gas-proof curtain, where all stayed till 2 A.M., when the attack stopped. The remainder of that night, and all the following day and next night, hundreds of dead and gassed were being carried out of all parts of the line. Deserter's 7th Company was 180 strong, and lost 68 gassed, of whom the majority are known to have died : he believes all eight companies of his regiment suffered similarly, as did also the reserve battalion of the 5th Regiment ; and the 4th Matrosen Regiment and 1st Marine Pioneer Company suffered still more heavily. No one actually believed in the possibility of a gas attack before October 2nd, and the men had not been adequately trained, nor had their masks been properly fitted and tested. The masks, too, were of inferior quality, and were so bad that men with weak lungs were forced to remove them. The fatigue battalion of the 4th Matrosen Regiment had left their masks on their rifles and packs, and the 1st Pioneer Company had left theirs in Middelkerke.

" Deserter heard the Division Chaplain say at church parade on the 8th at Ostend that the Division had to deplore the loss of 700 men dead after the recent gas attack who had been buried in the Division sector. This was apart from gassed cases sent to Ostend and Bruges, of whom many died *en route* and in hospitals owing to the lack of adequate appliances for treating such large numbers sufficiently quickly. It was commonly estimated in the 1st Matrosen Regiment that there had been 1500 gas casualties in the Division, counting the five battalions principally affected and the Divisional units, of whom the great majority ultimately died. Even before October 2nd, French deserters had said that preparations for a gas attack were in progress. The gas was so strong that after the attack deserter's company could not unlock the bolts of their rifles, and all metal arms and equipment of his battalion were rendered unserviceable and handed into store. The rifles and side-arms were described as if they had been for weeks in salt water. The gas seemed to come in six separate waves, and the effects were felt as far back as Raversyde (9 kilometres). Several transport horses of the Pioneers were killed in Middelkerke (6 kilometres)."

Both the French and Belgian Intelligence Departments were able to confirm parts of the above story. On 23rd April 1917 the French forwarded a report in which it was stated : " But there appears to have been some carelessness which, although the German Command had some knowledge of our intention, caused many casualties, for our attack surprised the majority of men and they had no masks with them." And just a year later (19th April 1918) the Belgians interrogated some prisoners of the 1st Matrosen Regiment, who said: " The 12th Company, 1st Matrosen Regiment, was in support at the moment of the gas discharge and only had slight losses—about two killed and six gassed. The 1st Battalion of the 1st Matrosen Regiment which was in the front line would have lost about four men, but the 4th Matrosen Regiment on the left had much higher losses. In the rear zones there were also casualties."

On 1st May 1917 another deserter, this time from the 4th Matrosen Regiment, was examined at G.H.Q. : he confirmed fully the whole story as previously related, and added that of the party of 36 with whom he was working 10 were killed either by gas or shell fire. Several men had left their masks behind as a gas attack was not expected.

In September 1917 a man of the Marine Pioneer Company was examined at G.H.Q. : he said " he had been with a depot unit in Ostend for over two years. He remembered the English gas attack in October of last year. He saw between Middelkerke and Westende Bains 30 to 40 dead horses about two days after the gas attack which had been killed by the gas : he had heard that a much larger number had been killed in the same way. Civilians in Middelkerke suffered slightly and were much annoyed because gas had been let off. Civilians were afraid to talk about the gas attack, as in these cases they were very severely punished.

" While the 2nd Battalion was in rest prisoner had the

opportunity of conversing with medical N.C.O.'s, and he was definitely informed that the 2nd Battalion had 80 to 90 men killed by gas and 150 to 160 gassed besides. He was perfectly certain of these figures and saw no reason to consider them over-estimated, as the medical N.C.O.'s would know more accurately than the average man what casualties had been caused. He heard that the total casualties had been very severe, but could give no definite figures. Men had no masks with them and gas discipline was very relaxed."

Finally, yet another prisoner of the 1st Matrosen Regiment, also captured in September 1917, repeated the same story. He said that the 1st Battalion of his regiment was in the line and the 3rd in close reserve. He himself was a member of a regimental patrol of 40 men who raided the French trenches and brought back 22 or 23 prisoners. The latter gave them no information about preparations for a gas attack, nor did they see any cylinders, but parapet pipes were found in dug-outs—he himself saw these. He had heard that an officer in the 4th Matrosen Regiment was without his mask in the front line at Lombartzyde when the cloud came, and offered a man 25 marks if he would lend him his, which the man refused to do. Many of the Pioneers used to leave their masks behind, and used the boxes for carrying cigars. In spite of the rumours that a gas attack was imminent anti-gas discipline was very bad. He heard that there were 40 to 60 deaths in his regiment, as well as 80 evacuated to hospital. He added that a day or two after the attack he went to see a wounded friend of his in hospital at Ostend. About 80 gassed men were there from various units, several of whom died afterwards. The majority of cases went to Oudenburg, which is where all gas cases are now sent. Shortly after the attack their gas officer told them in a lecture that through carelessness their regiment had had 300 casualties from the gas. He also heard that 70 horses were killed near the Steinstrasse.

During the war, especially in its later stages, hundreds of statements made by prisoners and deserters were forwarded to me from various sources, but no other account so complete and so fully supported was ever received as in regard to this attack at Nieuport. It is not reasonable to assume that because of this the success was isolated;

and it is interesting to note that it was achieved in the course of a few minutes and at very small cost in men and materials, while the personnel employed were about equivalent in strength to that of one battery of field artillery. It is very doubtful if the enemy lost as many men as on this occasion in the whole of the preliminary bombardment at the battle of Messines eight months later, in which 2571 guns and howitzers of all calibres were engaged continuously during a period of eight days and nights, and more than three and a quarter million rounds of ammunition, weighing nearly fifty thousand tons, were expended ; though it must, of course, be remembered that the sole object of this bombardment was not, as in the case of the gas attack, the destruction of the enemy's personnel. (See also footnote to p. 312.)

General Schwarte has written in his book : " In 1915 and 1916 the gas alarm played a great part against cloud attacks. The English and French carried out frequent cloud attacks, but the strict orders given succeeded in soon eliminating losses almost completely." Other equally untrue statements have been made in this connection, and I am dealing in a later chapter with the attitude adopted by German writers, the object of which has been to conceal their gas losses during the war : this attitude seems to have been prompted by the desire to cover up the grave error of judgment of which the Supreme Command was guilty in introducing a weapon without full considera-tion of the consequences to themselves—a decision which it should have been realised from the first would react eventually to their own disadvantage, at any rate on the Western front.

That their losses were inconsiderable was certainly not a belief held by the German troops in the field : prisoners frequently remarked that the British had made gas the chief weapon of modern war, and that in this respect everyone knew that the Germans ' had come off worst.' Among some lecture notes found on a prisoner the anti-gas officer of his regiment was quoted as saying : " Regard your masks as sacred, for gas causes as many casualties as artillery "—a belief which was often expressed, as in a letter written by a man of the 64th Reserve Regiment (1st Guard Reserve Division), in which he said : " The worst thing here (Lens) is gas : we have had most losses through it."

An under-officer of the 15th Reserve Regiment stated in the course of his interrogation : " The Germans are very sorry that they ever started gas warfare and believe it to be, as far as morale is concerned at any rate, the most dreadful weapon used in modern warfare. After an hour it became difficult to breathe through the German drum, and he himself would not be able to use it any longer, even if he kept still. If a gas cloud lasted five hours every man would be killed. If an offensive were conducted with gas shells only, half the Germans would be put out of action and the other half would malinger."

Lack of confidence in the efficiency of their masks was often apparent ; for instance, in a letter written by a man of the 55th Reserve Regiment (2nd Guard Reserve Division) there was this sentence : " He sent us over gas, too, and that is the most frightful thing, *for everyone knows* that if the gas continues for long we are done for." That this want of faith was very prevalent and caused the German Commanders considerable concern was shown in many of the captured orders in which the attempt was made to reassure the troops on the point.

There was never any misapprehension as to the quality of our cloud gas. In a letter written by a man of the 24th Light Ammunition Column after one of our cylinder attacks at Hulluch, he said : " About a week ago the English suddenly liberated gas : 42 men in the unit were poisoned because the sentry had gone to sleep. If once you get your nose full of it you are done for." And again, after the cloud attack at Frelinghien on 30th June 1916, prisoners of the 133rd Regiment said : " The right bat-talion lost 20 men killed, and the left about 32. There were practically no cases of slight gas poisoning. If men put on their masks quickly enough and in the right way they were unharmed. If a mistake was made it cost a man his life." Over and over again, too, reference was made to men who had only been slightly gassed at first, but who had died subsequently.

That the enemy's troops were given special instructions to hush up their gas casualties there can be no doubt whatever, in illustration of which statement I give a few extracts from British Intelligence summaries :—

"All the prisoners (of the 1st Bavarian Reserve Division) showed the greatest reticence concerning gas, and appeared to have received special instructions not to mention gas casualties." [1]

"Generally speaking, although prisoners were quite willing to talk about ordinary matters, they were very reticent indeed on the subject of the effects of British gas. One officer in particular, who spoke quite freely about other matters, went so far as to ask permission not to discuss the effects of British gas."

"A group of officers were questioned about the gas attack, and an artillery officer said with emphasis that it was ' sehr schlimm ' (very bad). They then became suspicious and refused to answer any more questions. The officer referred to was severely censured afterwards by the others for giving away information about gas."

On another occasion a feld-webel (sergeant-major) of the 10th Reserve Regiment, a very intelligent man, a Pole and a bank director, expressed the opinion that gas had caused the Germans more casualties than they would ever care to confess. He commented on the extreme secrecy maintained on the subject which had aroused his suspicions before. The prisoner added that he never read the German communiqués as he had become disgusted at their entire untrustworthiness.

Finally, it was reported more than once that burial parties were cautioned individually not to talk to anyone of the deaths from gas poisoning.

Echoes of their gas disasters on the Somme seem to have even reached the battle fronts in the Eastern theatres of the war, for Austrian prisoners referred to these reports and said that they had been told that British gas was much more to be feared than that of other countries ; while prisoners of a German gas unit, captured in August 1918, said that when they were employed on the Russian front they had heard on several occasions of the heavy gas casualties suffered by their troops during this battle ; and they added that the only reason for their not employing cloud gas on the Western front was the lack of favourable winds.

---

[1] On one occasion a prisoner, who was something of a humorist, carried this attitude too far : when asked, after one of our biggest gas attacks, if he had experienced anything unusual he replied : "Well, yes, now that you mention it I did notice a peculiar smell, but I thought it was my mate ! "

One prisoner, taken in France in June 1918, who had passed the whole of his previous service in Russia, was specially warned by his regimental gas officer of the danger of cloud gas, which, he told him, had been the cause of the severest losses : on one occasion during the Somme battle in 1916 over one thousand men had been killed by gas owing to the neglect of ordinary precautions. (In regard to this statement I should remark here that we collected no information at all of the effects of a large number of the gas attacks that we carried out. For example, a cylinder discharge took place at Angres (south of Lens) on 27th June 1916, to which the 31st, the 84th and 86th Reserve Regiments were exposed. Prisoners of the last-named regiment were taken who gave an account of their own severe losses on this occasion, but they said they were nothing compared with those suffered by the 84th, which, in consequence, became a byword in the division. When men referred to the subject among themselves they exclaimed, " 84th Reserve—Gas ! " and yet we never obtained any details of this disaster apart from the reports made by raiders (see page 128, at Liévin) which may have referred to this unit.)

Even as late as October 1918, when so many German documents fell into our hands that it was impossible to examine more than a few, references were found to the Somme gas attacks which belied the post-war German pretence. One written by the gas officer of the Sixth German Army summarised our cylinder operations in the Armentières sector and was dated November 1916 :—

" Considerable losses were caused by the gas attacks which have taken place lately. The casualties were mainly due to the men being surprised in dug-outs, to the neglect of gas discipline, masks not being to hand, to faulty masks and to the use of old-pattern drums which could not afford protection against the type of gas used by the enemy."

Another was a report of the " Staff Officer for Gas " of the same German Army, and it referred to the period August-September 1916 :—

" These gas attacks were executed on a small front, dense waves of gas being produced. No infantry action followed. In one attack 15 men were killed and 80 to 100 gassed."

And yet another referred to a cloud attack in July 1916 :—

" There were 525 gas cases and 16 deaths. The greater number of these cases were slight and the majority of the severely affected will recover. The reason for the casualties is that the drafts from home arriving latterly are entirely without experience of gas attacks, and casualties were caused, as a rule, through carelessness or unusually unfortunate circumstances. Some men were surprised asleep : others tried to run from the gas, became breathless and took off their masks."

In view of the great mass of evidence that was collected during the war, much of it documentary and from German official sources, it is absurd for our late enemies to pretend that these gas attacks produced but little effect on their troops ; and in estimating their losses our own experience of the German cloud attacks cannot be disregarded. Omitting the earliest of these—that is those which took place in April and May 1915, when our losses were naturally extremely heavy on account of our troops being without respirators or only inadequately protected —there were only five further cloud attacks on the British front during the remainder of the war, and these took place between December 1915 and August 1916. Although none of them succeeded in taking our men by surprise (see p. 179 *et seq*.), we suffered on an average a loss of 876 men in each attack, the percentage of mortality being 24 per cent. In only one of these attacks was the presence of phosgene in the cloud positively identified, but it was assumed in the remaining four on account of the high rate of mortality experienced, which in one case amounted to 46 per cent. American troops were never subjected to a cloud gas attack, nor, I believe, were the Belgians ; but the average losses of the French in eight of the last attacks made against them were 1236 per attack, while the percentage of mortality was somewhat similar to our own— namely, 20 per cent.

With these comparisons available, together with all the additional evidence to which I have referred, it is impossible to resist the conclusion that the German losses from gas were exceedingly heavy during the summer and autumn of 1916 (as indeed they continued to be in the two following years), especially in view of the number of attacks which took place (110), the heavy concentrations of gas liberated, the deadly nature of the gas employed, the silence of its emission (it was hardly audible on our own firestep) and the frequency with which a complete surprise was effected.

And it is equally certain that their percentage of mortality was very high.

I cannot close this chapter without paying a tribute to the skill and gallantry displayed at all times by the officers and men of the Special Companies. The majority came under fire in June 1916 for the first time, but their behaviour under the intense artillery bombardment which the gas discharges invariably invoked, sooner or later, was beyond praise. They often accompanied infantry raiding parties, and in one instance several officers and twenty men asked for special permission to carry out a raid of their own. An infantry officer of the 55th British Division wrote on one occasion : " The wonderful way in which the R.E.'s, under Mr Sullivan (of ' P ' Coy.), stuck to their job under very trying circumstances was the talk of the trench. They were magnificent." And in forwarding this report to the headquarters of the Third Army on 4th July 1916, Sir John Keir (commanding our VIth Corps), added : " I think this expresses better than any words of mine the feelings of all ranks towards the Special Brigade."

It must be remembered, too, that the responsibility of some of the junior officers—and even of the N.C.O.'s —was often heavy. Generally the order from a higher command to discharge gas was permissive rather than compulsory, and the actual responsibility for opening the cylinders rested with the gas officer in the line. On one occasion when a sergeant took charge of a section in the absence of his officer who had been wounded, he refrained from discharging his gas, when given a zero hour, on no less than six occasions, but complied on the seventh, when the conditions seemed to him to be favourable.

The casualties in the brigade, too, were at times high : during the first month of the battle of the Somme these amounted to 28 officers and 712 men, of whom 6 officers and 76 men were killed and 57 men died of gas poisoning. This was the period of our heaviest losses during the war (see chart at the end of Chapter XVIII.), and the figures quoted represented 14 per cent of the strength of the brigade, about the same total percentage as in September and October 1915, though the deaths from gas were now fifteen times as numerous. Many of these gas cases were very slight at first, and some of them occurred when removing the pipes from the cylinders after the gas attack was over, the ' after effects ' of phosgene poisoning not being known during the first few days of its use.

Phosphorus smoke cloud, formed by artillery.

CHAPTER IX.

SMOKE CLOUDS, THERMIT AND FLAMMENWERFER.
THE LIVENS PROJECTOR.

MEANWHILE the four Stokes mortar companies had been very actively employed on 1st July : they were in action all along the front, from north of Gommecourt to beyond Mametz, and were engaged in putting up smoke screens to protect the various infantry columns from view as they advanced to the assault of the German line. (Sixty-four infantry battalions took part in this assault.)

The bombs in use at this period weighed 13 lb., contained red phosphorus and their range was only 350 yards.

All the 192 mortars were in action, and they were distributed in detachments of from four to twenty-four, each with a definite prearranged task. The men had been engaged for days in constructing their own mortar emplacements in or near the front line, and in bringing up supplies of bombs, which were stored in protected shelters alongside the emplacements.

Smoke screens, unlike gas discharges, can be employed in any kind of wind, though they are, of course, more effective when the velocity of the latter is low : even when the direction of the wind is from the enemy, bombs fired on to strong-points and machine-gun nests are useful in blotting out the view and reducing the accuracy of fire, though in such circumstances there is always a danger of infantry advancing *through* a fog losing its direction.

In some of these smoke operations screens were established by the mortar detachments to obscure the view of the enemy on whom *a frontal attack* was being made, and they were often reinforced (the wind being favourable on the day of the battle) with phosphorus hand-grenades and smoke candles manipulated by the infantry themselves before zero hour. For example, in the attack of the 56th Division on Gommecourt the smoke created in this manner was so dense that line after line of infantry moved forward in orderly fashion and disappeared in the haze without haste or confusion, the fire directed on them being wild and high. According to the German official account the smoke so completely hid the start of the attack that the enemy were unable to get out of their dug-outs in time and were overrun.[1]

Another type of smoke screen was one established to conceal assaulting columns from view *from the flank*. Such a screen was arranged by the 36th Division for their advance between Thiepval village and the River Ancre. I had an excellent close-up view of this operation from the high ground known as ' Jacob's ladder,'[2] and it seemed to me, watching through glasses, that this division advanced for a long way, out of sight and over the horizon, without a single casualty, the movement being entirely hidden by the smoke barrages which drifted along the northern edge of Thiepval village and which flooded the Ancre valley.

A third type of smoke screen was arranged *as a feint* on a front on which no advance was contemplated, to draw the enemy's fire from assaulting columns elsewhere. In one such case, on the front of the 48th Division, a smoke screen was kept up by twenty-four mortars for a period of four hours, and it attracted a concentrated artillery bombardment from German guns which would have been much more usefully employed elsewhere.

A fourth use to which the mortar battalion was put was the *provision of mobile detachments* which accompanied the infantry in their advance with the object of creating

[1] In the History of the 91st Reserve Regiment it is stated : " It was due to the smoke that the English, in spite of heavy infantry fire, were able to break into our position X3 with 25 men."

[2] The spy mania, of which there were many amusing experiences at home, also existed in France. Shortly after 1st July I found myself at dinner one night at the long table in a restaurant in St Omer sitting—of course, in uniform—next to a temporary Major of Artillery whose observation post had been in about the same spot in 'Jacob's ladder' as my own. Impressed by the interest I showed in this remarkable vantage-point he slipped away presently and reported to the Provost-Marshal that I was quite obviously a German spy in disguise ; and his suspicions seemed to receive confirmation when he returned to the restaurant a little later with this official and found me in conversation with the late Colonel Sir Alexander Sprot, M.P. for East Fife and the local Area Commandant. The latter vouched for my identity, as he had known me intimately and continuously for the previous twenty years, and I escaped arrest ; but even then the gunner major was unconvinced, and he subsequently renewed his accusation in an official letter !

smoke screens in aid of various moves in the subsequent phases of the battle. For example, Lieutenant Rathbone took up eight mortars with the 21st Brigade from Maricourt to Glatz Redoubt, and, establishing them in shellholes, he succeeded in forming a screen to one flank to cover the advance of the 90th Brigade from view from the Germans holding the Briqueterie, and kept it up for sixty-five minutes.[1]

This screen was commenced with rapid fire from all the mortars, and it was kept effective by watching the gaps in the cloud as they occurred and directing the subsequent fire of the mortars accordingly.

And, finally, smoke screens were established in a number of places *to conceal various minor operations,* such as raids and the cutting of wire and the digging of communication trenches.

Altogether forty-six separate smoke operations were undertaken on 1st July in which 5000 smoke bombs were expended : 2000 more were discharged in the following week, during which many of the smoke operations were extemporised at very short notice : in one instance an officer (May) was asked by an infantry commander to establish a screen from a forward position which had just been captured, and although he had sent all his men back to bring up a fresh supply of bombs he succeeded in firing the twenty which remained with him with his own hands from a single mortar.

Nearly all these operations were very successful while they lasted, but their duration proved to be too short : the reason for this was the fear of impeding the view of our own artillery observers ; but the result was that while the first lines of advancing infantry often reached their objectives with little loss, succeeding waves suffered severely from machine-gun fire.

The men of the mortar companies behaved with great gallantry during this trying period ; most of them—like the rest of the Special Brigade—now came under fire for the first time, and their losses in the first week of the battle were four officers and ten other ranks killed, and three officers and ninety-two other ranks wounded. They

---

[1] According to the Diary of the 21st Field Artillery Regiment " the smoke was so thick in Montauban and Caterpillar Valley that one could only see two or three yards ahead."

L

continued to be actively associated with the infantry battle until it died down towards the end of the year, and it was a matter of regret that no gas bombs were available as many opportunities presented themselves of employing them with great effect.

Supplies of ' SK ' (lachrymator) bombs began to arrive in September—they were first fired into Thiepval on the 24th—and they were used for neutralising areas from which flanking fire was expected but which there was no intention of occupying for the time being : they were most effective for this purpose (the new bombs weighed 25 lb. and their range had now been improved to 600 yards), and they caused the enemy great inconvenience on many occasions, prisoners often stating that they had been compelled to put on their masks at frequent intervals and to wear them for long periods, while they were unable to occupy their dug-outs for days together.

A portion of " Z " Company arrived in France only just in time to participate in the opening of the battle, four large flame-projectors and sixteen portable machines being detrained at Corbie on 26th June, together with sufficient trained men to handle them. The attempt was made to set up three of the large machines on the front of the 18th Division, branches from existing underground mine galleries being utilised for the purpose.[1]

The opposing trench systems were about 200 yards apart in this sector, but the galleries enabled the erection to be carried out only 60 yards from the enemy's front line : one gallery ran out towards Casino Point and the other two were astride the Carnoy-Montauban road and were 160 and 175 yards long.

---

[1] The range of any flame-thrower is limited by the distance it is possible to project a jet of oil before it is all burnt or broken up into spray or droplets which do not carry except with a following wind. To obtain ranges of 100 yards with jets it is necessary to discharge large quantities of oil through nozzles an inch or more in diameter, using a pressure of hundreds of pounds per square inch. The Livens apparatus had the greatest range of any used by the German or Allied Armies (in the design Mr F. H. Livens, M.I.C.E., M.I.M.E., collaborated with his son), and a ton of oil was required for each shot. The apparatus was therefore necessarily heavy, and as each part had to be limited in weight to what two men could carry, many parts were required.

In the comparatively rare cases in which enemy positions were reported to be within flame-thrower range from our trenches, investigation generally proved that they were merely sentry or listening posts, sparsely or intermittently held, and therefore useless as targets for flame-throwers. It was for this reason that Livens designed his apparatus for erection in, and discharge from, mine galleries.

On 28th June one of the galleries was blown in by a heavy shell, and all the men employed in putting the projector together were entombed ; but the 183rd Tunnelling Company came to the rescue, the men were dug out and they resumed work three hours later. By mid-day on the 28th the three machines were nearly complete, but in the afternoon all the galleries were blown in by artillery fire, though they were quickly reopened by the same tunnelling company.

On the 29th the gallery opposite Casino Point was once again destroyed, and this time the projector in it was so badly damaged by the explosion that it was abandoned and parts of it were carried away to replace damaged portions of the other two, which were ready to fire on the 30th.

The floor of one of the galleries was 10 feet below the surface of the ground and that of the other 17 feet 6 inches, but these differences of level had been provided for in designing the machines, as the heads of the latter which carried the jet and the automatic lighting device were capable, through the addition of extension tubes, of rising to a height of 20 feet above floor level. The pressure gas used for propelling the oil was utilised to raise the head of the machine vertically upwards, and the steel cutter which covered the jet was in this manner forced through the last remaining crust of earth, just before the signal to fire was given.

At zero hour on 1st July the two jets appeared out of the ground to a height of two or three feet above the surface, opposite the German trench and well within the range of the machines : the automatic lighters functioned perfectly, and with a roar the streams of oil became ignited and shot forward towards the enemy, being traversed slowly from side to side, while dense clouds of black smoke, flecked with flame, rose a hundred feet into the air. No living thing could possibly survive under this visitation, and, as a machine-gun detachment emerged from another mine gallery on one side and sprayed the enemy's trenches with bullets while our infantry were crossing No Man's Land and a mine was blown under the German line on the other, it was not surprising that our infantry met with no opposition at this point. The ranges obtained by the projectors, as measured along the burnt ground, were 94 and 87 yards. Only a few charred German bodies were found in the trench when it was entered, but the latter had been partly filled in by the débris from the mine and nobody was anxious to investigate what lay beneath.

The Commanders of the 1st Brigade and of the 18th Division both expressed the opinion that the flame-projectors had been of material assistance in enabling the division to accomplish its task.

Several detachments equipped with portable machines accompanied the infantry in their advance on 1st July, but they found no opportunity of coming into action, though they were kept in readiness for several days. Five of them were detailed to assist the 36th Brigade in their attack on 'White Trench' on the 10th July, but they were unable to fire ; and two others were taken into Pommiers Redoubt on the same day, but were destroyed by the German artillery while waiting for the moment of the assault.

The large projectors each weighed two tons and required two or three hundred 'men-journeys' to carry them to their destination : it had not been intended to use them in the semi-open warfare which had now developed, but in spite of this a number of attempts were made to bring them into action. Two were fitted together in open saps leading off the infantry position for the attack on High Wood and were ready to fire at 7 A.M. on 18th August, but both were buried in the bombardment and were put out of action. Two days later one machine was erected in Leipzig Salient, and it could have been fired on the 21st, but, as it was considered that the infantry would have no difficulty in reaching their objective which was known to be lightly held, the order was given not to use it. On the 28th a large projector was taken up into Arrowhead Copse, south-west of Guillemont, and it was fired on the 3rd September, on which day four others (including one of the Vincent type) came into action in the attack on High Wood. At this spot the Germans were offering a stubborn resistance, and three of these four machines were re-fuelled and fired again on 8th September. This was the last occasion but one (see Chapter XIII., p. 225) on which the large flame-projectors were used during the war.

Both the Vincent and the Livens types of machine proved to be disappointing. The latter was a horizontal structure consisting mainly of a $9\frac{1}{2}$-inch steel tube, 12 feet long and made up in short portable lengths which were bolted together in the emplacement. The Vincent, on the other hand, was of the vertical type, its four separate steel containers being connected up in a group, so that the whole machine took up less room. The containers, however, were 4 feet 6 inches high and 14 inches in diameter, and each one weighed over 200 lb., so that they could only be moved at night across the open. The machine could be put together more quickly than the Livens (in five hours as against six) : its range was much the same, but the jet was only capable of a traverse of 45 degrees against 90 degrees. The Livens had the further advantage that three shots could be fired from the reservoir as against one from the Vincent.

Two of the semi-portable machines were used in the attack of the 48th Division on 17th July, and two came into action in the French trenches at Nieuport on 5th October (see p. 147, Chapter VIII.) ; but, as I had anticipated, these apparatus were found to be totally unsuitable for the open fighting that was taking place on the Somme, and their use was abandoned by us.[1]

It had become equally evident that the local effect produced by the large projectors did not justify the great expenditure of labour and effort involved in bringing them into action, and still less the construction of special saps in which to install them in order to bring them within range of their objectives. Livens, who by this time had his whole company under canvas at Toutencourt, thereupon set out to meet this difficulty. It was necessary to get a longer range for the burning oil, and he did this by throwing it out of extemporised mortars which consisted of the ordinary steel containers in which his oil was received, other oil-drums of slightly less diameter and

---

[1] I believe, however, that the French persevered with their use, and the Germans often employed them up till the end of the war. In September 1918 they frequently brought them into action in small numbers when making counter-attacks and in raids, but never with any marked success. In one raid, on 21st September 1918, German bombers advanced behind a screen of flammenwerfer, but the latter were only capable of emitting smoke and flame to a distance of about ten feet, and the party was wiped out by our Lewis gunners. Similar tactics were adopted at Havrincourt on 18th September 1918.

A German document issued by the Corps of Engineers and Pioneers from G.H.Q. on 21st April 1918 stated : " Flammenwerfer must be engaged in great numbers and must fight in close liaison with the infantry, which helps them with the fire of its machine-guns and its grenades."

wrapped in sand-bags being employed as projectiles. The mortars were buried in the ground in rows, almost touching each other and with only the muzzles visible above the surface, and in this manner they were set in the required direction, while pieces of metal from any that happened to burst—of which there were quite a number!—were prevented from flying about. The drums were filled with oil and cotton-waste, and they were opened up and their contents were lighted and scattered by charges of gun-cotton fixed to the surface and detonated through lengths of time fuze which were lighted by the flash from the black powder propellant charge. The mortars were fired in groups of half a dozen or more by fuze, a 'junction box' being used to ensure a simultaneous shoot, a method which soon gave way to electric discharge by means of the service exploder.

Such was the origin of the 'Livens projector'[1] which was destined to play havoc with the German troops during the last two years of the war, and which was even to acquire a certain popularity among our own Commanders. Twenty of these primitive oil-projectors were dug in on the parados of a trench, and were used for the first time against the enemy to help an attack of the 48th Division to the west of Pozières early on the morning of 23rd July 1916, and they appeared to have been of assistance to the infantry (the 4th Gloucesters), although the effect produced was probably only moral: the range obtained on this occasion was only 200 yards. Thirty more were fired successfully at the eastern corner of High Wood on 18th August, and an encouraging report of the damage done was made by the 2nd Argyll and Sutherland Highlanders, who said that they met with no opposition from the sector on which the drums fell.

On 3rd September at High Wood two batteries of oil-mortars were dug in close to the flame-projectors previously referred to (p. 164), and in describing this operation the Commander of the 1st Brigade said: "From the infantry point of view the flame-projectors were successful. The left battery of mortars was practically wiped out by our own Stokes guns" (the 3-inch, firing high explosive and handled by the infantry), "but the right worked well and I am sure assisted the infantry attack." The range had by this time been increased to 280 yards.

[1] This is not to be confused with the flame-projector.

In all these operations, and in the experiments which led to them, Strange of " Z " Company assisted Livens, and proved himself an able and gallant lieutenant. Accidents, however, were too frequent on the experimental ground, and the original oil-can mortars were gradually replaced by lengths of welded steel tube of various diameters, with one end closed, which were procured either locally or from home : even sections of the steel body of the flame-projector were adapted and pressed into service.

Gas bombs, too, were experimented with, the earliest consisting of complete ordinary ' red star ' cylinders which were shot out of mortars and burst by means of charges of ammonal attached to their surface ; and cans filled with 30 lb. of high explosive were also tried for destroying wire entanglements. At one demonstration which Livens arranged at Toutencourt on 19th August, at which General Gough (whose headquarters were in the same village) and a number of senior officers were present, besides shots from both types of flame-projector (and from a ' fougasse ' charged with $2\frac{1}{2}$ tons of oil in petrol cans), drums filled with oil and others with ammonal were fired, the latter in the direction of a specially constructed wire entanglement. Not much damage was done to the wire owing to the inaccuracy of the projectiles, and as some of these did not appear to have detonated, Livens waited for a quarter of an hour before he approached the entanglement with the Army Commander to investigate the result. Just before they reached the spot one of the bombs exploded with a terrific roar, but fortunately no one was sufficiently near to be hurt.[1] As a result of this and several previous mishaps it was a joke in the Special Brigade to threaten a man guilty of some minor offence with the prospect of duty in " Z " Company.[2]

" F " Company (Thomas) took a hand in these early developments, and after one of their shoots in October the Commander of the New Zealand Division wrote : " Brigadier reports co-operation of ' F ' Company most satis-

[1] Livens claimed that this was the only occasion on which he ever ordered a General to run. He was promptly obeyed !

[2] When my field company took over (in May 1915) a very untidy billet just vacated by another Engineer unit newly arrived in France and not yet acclimatised, among the papers left in the litter an order was found which contained a threat that if a certain type of misdemeanour continued to be prevalent in the unit, the guilty parties would render themselves liable to transfer to the 11th Field Company R.E. !

factory on October 1st. Liquid fire bombs were fired into German trenches at zero, causing heavy casualties. Two groups of dead Germans, 15 and 20 bodies respectively, were found badly burned and hardly recognisable. Services rendered by ' F ' Company were of the greatest value." On this occasion thirty-six oil-drums were projected into the German trench one minute before zero, and the infantry advanced on an objective blazing all along its extent and blotted out by a dense cloud of black smoke.

Meanwhile " G " Company (Slade) was developing the gas bomb principle, and was assisting the 2-inch trench-mortar batteries by emptying the bombs of their high-explosive contents and refilling them with ' white star ' gas taken from our standard cylinders. The 2-inch proved to be a very suitable mortar for use with gas (see my proposal to Sir John French in June 1915, p. 46, Chapter III.—this had never been acted on), and a number of most successful shoots were carried out into Thiepval, Beaumont Hamel, &c., and excellent accounts of the casualties inflicted by the ' gas mines ' were obtained from prisoners from time to time. The 52nd German Division wrote (in a captured order) : " The unexpected use of large trench-mortar bombs on the front of the division caused the death of 6 men and the gas poisoning of 24 others. A strong gas cloud was rapidly developed and masks could not be put on quickly enough. Brigades are asked to report what protective measures they can suggest."

On 28th October the most successful shoot of this series took place, 135 40-lb. gas bombs (referred to as ' judgments ') being fired from $9\frac{1}{2}$-inch steel tubes into the Y Ravine and the village of Serre, as well as thirty rounds of the 60-lb. 2-inch trench-mortar bomb, each of which contained 15 lb. of gas.

Several interested officers examined these targets a few days later, and numbers of dead Germans who had obviously been killed by gas were discovered lying about and in the dug-outs.[1] Based on this experience Livens,

[1] In one of these dug-outs in which sixteen dead Germans were found the enemy's gas drill could be followed exactly : the men nearest the entrance had succumbed before they had time even to attempt to make use of their masks ; farther in they had opened the mask container ; still farther the masks were out, and in some cases half adjusted ; while the men lying farthest from the entrance were seen to have been killed in spite of the fact that their masks were properly in position.

A Projector emplacement (not yet camouflaged).

in writing his report on the operation, calculated from the data at his disposal that if the use of projectors were developed on a large scale, the cost of killing Germans would be reduced to only sixteen shillings apiece ; and he was sent to England soon afterwards to co-operate with the Ministry of Munitions in developing a standard projector and drum which would possess a reasonable margin of safety.[1]

Several thousands were manufactured during the winter months, and suitable propellant charges were calculated and range-tables were made out at Porton ; and the projectors were used for the first time on a large scale at the opening of the battle of Arras on 4th April 1917. During the remainder of the war they were gradually improved and they were fired literally by the hundred thousand. The drum fillings were normally pure phosgene ; but at one time or another drums were used for special purposes containing high explosive, oil and cotton-waste pellets, thermit, white phosphorus and ' stinks,' the last consisting of malodorous harmless substances, such as bone oil and balloon dope (amyl acetate) to simulate gas on occasions when the latter could not be employed safely and to compel the enemy to meet our infantry assault with their masks adjusted, and therefore on unequal terms.

The Livens projector in its final form consisted of an 8-inch solid-drawn steel tube 2 feet 9 inches or 4 feet long, only $\frac{1}{4}$ inch in thickness and closed and rounded at one end. It was buried up to the muzzle in a trench cut at an angle of 45 degrees, and the force of its recoil when fired was taken by a steel base-plate shaped something like a Mexican sombrero, in much the same manner as a stepped concrete foundation takes the weight of a building and distributes it over a wider area of soil. The projectors were packed as near together in the trench as the base-plates would permit in batteries of twenty-five, each normally in charge of a corporal, the number in a battery

[1] Livens, who had a strong personal feeling in the war connected, I believe, with the sinking of the *Lusitania*, was most anxious to get his projectors into action as quickly as possible, using the welded tubes and any others that could be extemporised. I had, however, to resist this policy, as owing to the number of prematures and bursts which were occurring on the experimental ground there would have been a good deal of waste of effort as well as considerable danger to our own infantry which would have increased their prejudice against the use of gas. There were practical difficulties at first in obtaining the solid-drawn steel tubes that we wanted, owing to the requirements of the Admiralty, but these were gradually overcome.

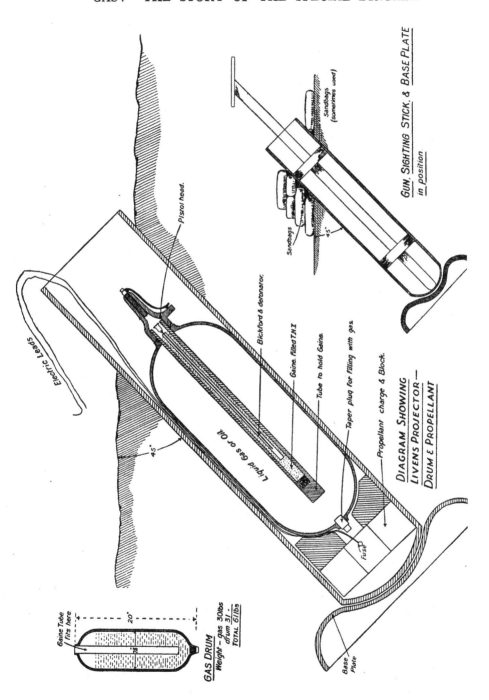

Gun. Sighting Stick, & Base Plate
in position

Sandbags (sometimes used)

Sandbags

45°

Pistol head.

Electric Leads

Bickford & detonator.

Gaine. filled T.N.I

Tube to hold Gaine.

Taper plug for filling with gas

Propellant charge & Block.

Liquid Gas or Oil

45°

Fuse

Diagram Showing
Livens Projector—
Drum & Propellant

Gaine Tube fits here

20°

Gas Drum
Weight — gas 30lbs
drum 31.—
Total 61lbs

Base Plate

being limited by the capacity of the service exploder to fire them all off simultaneously and the electric leads being arranged ' in series.' Nearly four thousand were fired in a single operation on one occasion, and the signal for discharge was usually given by a special coloured Verey light, a burst of machine-gun fire, or some other easily recognisable means. A clinometer was used for setting them at the correct angle in the trench and a sighting-stick for aiming them in the required direction, in conjunction with a luminous compass when the targets were invisible, as when working at night : the projectors were then kept in position by ramming the earth all round them back into the trench.

Variations in range (which were measured off the trench map) were obtained by altering the size of the cordite propellant charge. The latter was contained in a tin box, and a wooden block, shaped on one side to take the rounded end of the drum, acted as a wad.[1] The drums were filled with 30 lb. of phosgene, and were fitted with a central ' gaine-tube,' which held the T.N.T. bursting charge, a detonator and a length of Bickford fuze : this last was ignited automatically by a ' pistol head ' of the Mills hand-grenade type, but it was replaced eventually by the ' Allways ' percussion fuze. The drums fitted sufficiently loosely into the projectors to allow the electric leads to pass down their sides into the boxes containing the propellant charges, and just before firing, the continuity of the electric circuit was tested by means of a galvanometer.

Projector positions were usually sited out in the open, a few hundred yards from the front line : special care was taken to camouflage them, and the companies became so expert in this art of concealment that the sites were seldom recognisable when the enemy scrutinised their air photographs.

I have described the Livens projector in some detail because, although the cloud method of gas attack was not abandoned—in fact, we were hoping for decisive results from it in 1919 if hostilities had continued a little longer —the Special Brigade was now about to carry out hundreds of operations with this weapon during the two remaining years of the war. Ranges up to a mile were obtained with

[1] Later on a steel ' gas check ' was substituted.

it, but such was its inaccuracy that the targets selected had always to be *areas*, like villages and valleys honey-combed with dug-outs, rather than definite objects which were more suitable for attack by artillery.   Nevertheless it proved to be a most effective means of making a gas attack, and the concentrations of gas which could be established with it in a target were such that the German respirators, even when adjusted in plenty of time, were useless against them, and they were far superior to those obtainable by any other means, with the exception, perhaps, of the 4-inch Stokes mortar.

The Germans were seriously alarmed at the casualties they suffered from it, and they were compelled to imitate us in retaliation, though with the weapon they adopted—their ordinary 18-cm. minenwerfer—they failed to obtain the best effect, as the number of bombs they fired at a time was far too small, while the gas content of each was only 16½ lb., compared with our 30 lb.[1]

The 18-cm. German smooth-bore minenwerfer fired 17.5 cm. high-explosive bombs known to our troops as 'rum-jars,' and these were converted to a gas filling, the range being found to be 1400 metres : the time fuzes fitted to them emitted a stream of sparks, so that their flight through the air at night could be easily followed. Some of these projectors were captured by us in position in August 1918 at Boiry Becquerelle and Neuville St Vitasse, and they were found to be installed precisely like ours, grouped in series of twenty-five and provided with base-plates, but with the electric leads passing through holes in the base of the tubes.

Towards the end of the war the Germans introduced a *rifled* projector of 15.8 cm. diameter which was capable of firing to a distance of 2½ kilometres ; but with this development the enemy fell still further into error, because, although the capacity of this bomb was greater than that of the smooth-bore projectile, the quantity of *free* phosgene contained in it was only one-fifth, the remainder being absorbed in pumice granules which were introduced to

[1] The first German projector attack against the British took place on the La Bassée canal on the night of the 10th December 1917, and against the French at Rechicourt on the night of 5th December ; according to Dr Hanslian, the weapon was employed against the Italians still earlier " in the great attack which broke through on the Isonzo on October 24th, 1917," although on this occasion " the attack seems to have been imperfectly executed."

give persistence, so that gas continued to be released for some time after the bomb burst. In this way the main principle on which our successful use of the projector was based was almost entirely sacrificed, as the ' mass effect ' of the sudden release of a large volume of gas was lost. The rifled projector was first used on 21st August 1918 (Dr Hanslian), and the Americans and French captured a few specimens : it appears that their range was varied by setting the tubes at different angles, from 30 degrees to 45 degrees, instead of by the method we followed of varying the propellant charge. Some of them were supported on a wooden framework, only the base-plate being buried in the ground.

It is interesting to note that even after the enemy had taken the projector into use, " Leaders and troops often preferred high-explosive bombs from the projectors, as the effect of the loud explosion seemed to indicate greater success than gas whose effect did not impress the senses so strongly and could rarely be proved " (General Schwarte).

And the same author, in ' Die Technik Im Weltkriege,' describes how the development of the use of projectors " was continually hampered by lack of understanding on the part of the troops which was difficult to overcome."

Dr Hanslian claims that the projector principle of gas attack was considered by the Germans in the year 1915. If this was so, it is difficult to understand why their decision to retaliate with this weapon, arrived at in April 1917, was not put into effect much more quickly.

CHAPTER X.

DURING the period with which I have been dealing (24th June 1916-19th March 1917) 110 separate cloud attacks were carried out by the Special Brigade, in the course of which nearly 50,000 cylinders containing 1500 tons of gas, mostly ' white star,' were emptied.

On 2nd August 1916 General Thuillier, in forwarding one of my summaries of these operations to the C.G.S., paid us a generous tribute, and a few days later General Kiggell wrote : " The Commander-in-Chief has read with much interest the report on the operations of the Special Brigade and your remarks thereon. He has noted and fully concurs in your commendation of the work done by Colonel Foulkes, and the officers, N.C.O.'s and men under him. Great energy, gallantry and ability were displayed, and the success achieved was of very considerable value in the operations."

This letter was followed by a circular instruction to the Army Commanders in which the Commander-in-Chief requested them to give their earnest attention to the advantages to be gained by the discharge of gas on every available opportunity along some portion of the defensive front. It was pointed out that these gas attacks materially assisted the main operations by incapacitating enemy troops who were potential reserves for the battle. " Troops who have suffered heavily from an effective gas attack have to be withdrawn from the front line to refit, and their places are taken by troops who might otherwise have been employed in resisting our advance. Evidence from prisoners and from our own raiding parties who have followed up gas attacks shows that casualties which sometimes amount to a large proportion are suffered by the enemy from our gas discharges. From a recent examination of a prisoner it was found that on a front where only

190 cylinders had been discharged, his battalion had suffered approximately 18 per cent of casualties, of which half were fatal. While fully realising the extra work imposed on troops by the installation of cylinders on portions of the front where the line is lightly held, the Commander-in-Chief feels certain that all ranks will realise that these attacks are of very real assistance in wearing down the enemy's reserves and lowering the moral of his troops. He trusts, therefore, that Army Commanders will seize every possible opportunity for the installation of cylinders. As soon as a discharge of gas has taken place, the recesses should be filled again in readiness to repeat the attack at the first favourable opportunity."

This instruction was succeeded by another a month later, and by a third on 18th October which was rather more peremptory in tone. " Ample resources of gas are available," it stated, " for armies on demand, and in view of weather prospects which are likely to prove suitable, armies will take immediate steps to give effect to the Commander-in-Chief's instructions as already notified."

It may be thought that one gas attack carried out on an average every other day somewhere along the front was sufficient response to the pressure exerted by G.H.Q., but this was by no means the case, as many opportunities of gas installation were neglected ; while on more than one occasion, for one reason or another, cylinders which were all ready awaiting discharge were actually carried out of the trenches again by order of a commander newly taking over the front. At one period (see previous chapter) I had even to put companies into French trenches in order to find employment for them. One Divisional Commander would perhaps be unwilling to carry out a gas attack because he was due to vacate the sector in a few days' time ; another because he had just arrived and wished to familiarise himself with the front before undertaking any aggressive action ; and a third because his defences consisted of breastworks which he considered unsuitable for accommodating cylinders.

G.H.Q. was never in doubt, during the whole war, about the value of our gas attacks, but about this time they invited the opinions of the commanders of formations who were not engaged on the Somme, especially in regard to the prospect of success of an infantry advance immediately after a gas discharge. The replies to this invitation are very interesting as they represent the general attitude of the B.E.F. towards gas at a time when, it must be remembered, very little information had yet been collected of the effects on the enemy of our operations.[1]

The First Army considered that the losses inflicted on the enemy and the demoralisation resulting therefrom were uncertain and varying quantities and were merely a matter of conjecture, while the chances of taking the enemy unawares were slight. The value of gas discharged from cylinders was questionable, while the disadvantages —the labour involved, the danger to our own troops, &c. —out-weighed the advantages. For an infantry operation in which infantry action was contemplated gas shells would be preferable. (*Note*—No gas shells were in use by the British artillery at this period, so that the benefits to be gained by employing them in such circumstances were, of course, conjectural too.)

The Commanders of the Ist and IVth Corps, however, both of which were in the First Army area, dissented from this view. The Ist Corps referred to two of the attacks carried out by " C " Company at Hulluch, " which were most successfully and efficiently prepared," but the tactical results of which were very disappointing, as on each occasion the raids which followed the gas cloud met with strong opposition. It was thought, however, that " the occasional liberation of gas cannot fail to have an ill-effect on the morale of the enemy's troops."

The IVth Corps quoted a report on the subject made by the Commander of the 47th Division. (It will be remembered that this division had benefited more than any of the others from the gas attack at Loos, though its commander was doubtful whether the effect produced on that occasion was chiefly moral or material.) He referred to two gas attacks which had been recently carried out in his sector, and thought it probable that the casualties inflicted on the enemy by the gas and the artillery bom-

---

[1] During the third battle of Ypres, in 1917, the soft ground in the Salient had proved to be unsuitable for the action of our tanks, and the Commander of our Fifth Army reported adversely on them, in which opinion he obtained a good deal of support. It was said that they could not negotiate bad ground : that the ground on a battlefield was always bad ; so that consequently they were no use on a battle-field.

bardment which accompanied it were very considerable—and certainly the moral effect was very great, as the very successful raids which followed could not have been made without it. Apparently all the men originally holding the German front line had either taken to flight, had been removed as casualties or had taken refuge in dug-outs. Even the German artillery did not come into action until nearly an hour after the discharge. " On the whole, the use of gas when the attendant circumstances are favourable is of great advantage, if only for the reason that the losses to our attacking troops are much reduced through its agency."

In forwarding this statement the IVth Corps Commander (Sir Henry Wilson) wrote : " In connection with the raid made on the 27th June gas was distinctly favourable to our raid—we crossed No Man's Land and entered the enemy's trenches without being met by either machine-gun or rifle fire, and the enemy's artillery were very slow in coming into action and were wild in their shooting when they did fire. After changing my mind several times I have now come to the conclusion that gas was distinctly favourable to our raid, and I propose to try the gas again."

The Commander of the 61st Division contributed a useful experience in showing that the presence of gas in the trenches was not so dangerous as was generally supposed. He said : " 1800 cylinders have been in the front line for nearly two months " (this was on the Fauquissart sector, and a (rather infrequent) north-west wind was being awaited), " during which the breastworks have been repeatedly hit by 5.9-inch and 4.2-inch shells, especially during a six hours' bombardment on July 19th. On only one occasion has a cylinder been damaged by an enemy shell and no one was gassed. On another occasion two cylinders were hit by one of our own shells from the rear, resulting in five deaths from gas poisoning."

On the other hand, the Commanders of the Second, Third and Reserve Armies were all doubtful of the value of the gas attacks. (The Fourth Army engaged on the Somme does not appear to have been consulted ; or perhaps its opinion was already known.) The Second Army said : " There is little direct evidence of the effects on the enemy of the nine separate gas attacks between

June 28th and July 14th. As a general rule the enemy's rifle and machine-gun fire on the front attacked has ceased within two or three minutes from the commencement of the discharge, and it is a fair assumption that at any rate a certain number of the enemy were affected. There can be little doubt, from the effects on our men, of the virulence of our gas. The Special Brigade carried out admirably all the technical work connected with the gas attacks."

The Third Army said that little evidence had been obtained from the raids—the best was after the H_2S attack at Monchy—so that normally not much was to be gained from following a gas discharge with a raid. Gas shells would be best if an infantry attack was to follow, except when the object was only to kill with gas.

And the Reserve Army thought that gas was useful because the artillery bombardment was drawn away from an infantry attack elsewhere!

It will be seen from the foregoing that while the labour involved in gas installations on fronts which were very often held by units which had been withdrawn exhausted from the Somme battlefield, and the (largely) imaginary danger from the presence of gas cylinders in the trenches, contributed towards the unpopularity of our gas operations, the main objection to them was caused by the fact that evidence of their effect was not apparent at the time. If only the evidence which came into our possession eventually had been available immediately, I feel confident that all commanders would have realised that in the war of attrition to which the Allied Armies were committed the risk of the presence of gas cylinders was not too great, and that the labour which they were called upon to supply could not have been more profitably employed in any other way for reducing the enemy's man-power, especially as the cost in material and the losses involved were negligible and were far less than in any other form of warlike activity.

However, it now rested with me to apply myself energetically to remove as far as possible all the objections which had been raised, and I will explain in the next chapter how I set about this task. It is interesting at this point to note that the Germans themselves, in spite of the fact that we, as well as the French, suffered heavy casualties from every one of their cloud attacks, also disbelieved in the efficacy of this method.[1]   Incidentally, support will be found in the five examples I am about to quote for my statement (see p. 86, Chapter VI.) that heavy losses always result from cloud attacks, no matter what the circumstances are in which they are delivered.[2]

1. In the German gas attack north-east of the Ypres Salient at 5 A.M. on 19th December 1915 we had 1069 casualties, including 120 dead.   Ample warning had been received of this attack.   On 4th December an N.C.O. prisoner of the XXVIth German Reserve Corps had given information of the installation of cylinders, and confirmation of his statement was received from another source.   Full precautions were therefore taken, and sentries were posted in the front trenches at all the alarm horns and gongs and at the entrances to all the dug-outs, and they gave warning immediately the gas was liberated.

The German official account of this attack contained the following remarks: " At the end of the discharge twenty patrols went forward against the British positions.   They were to discover the effects of the discharge and also bring in prisoners and make booty.   But only two of the patrols reached the British trenches.   The rest could not advance under the heavy fire and some suffered severe losses.   The general impression was that in spite of the relatively very favourable conditions the gas had not the expected effect, and that a break through of the enemy position solely as the result of the gas discharge would not be possible." (*Note*—This was the first time that the enemy used phosgene in their clouds, and they apparently based their hopes on the surprise effect of this new and powerful element.)

2. Another German gas attack took place at Hulluch on the 27th and 29th April 1916.

The 27th.—A deserter gave information on the 23rd of a raid which was to be preceded by a gas attack.   There was also noticed an exodus of rats from the German to

[1] General Ludendorff writes of what appears to have been the first *cloud* gas attack launched against the Russians : " The gas attack took place on May 2nd (1915) and was not a success.   The wind was favourable, but the troops had not been properly instructed.   The gas was emitted as intended, but the troops imagined that the enemy ought not to be able to move at all.   As the latter was still firing in places and our own artillery did not co-operate as it should have done, the infantry did not attack.   They assumed that the gas had had no effect."

And General Schwarte, too, says : " Our own front troops did not like cloud attacks and did not believe in their success."

[2] These were the last five cloud gas attacks of the war against British troops.

the British lines which was attributed by us to the presence of leaky cylinders in the former. 'Gas alerts' were therefore practised daily. At 5.10 A.M. gas clouds were seen, and everyone was ready for them. The flow lasted for half an hour, and the gas was so thick that it was noticed fifteen miles behind the lines. German patrols of twenty to thirty men advanced, but they were driven back. At 5.55 A.M. another gas cloud was released and further raids were made, three of which succeeded in entering the British trenches, eighty dead Germans being left in or near the latter when the raiders were expelled.

The 29th.—At 3.45 A.M. the Germans again discharged gas. At 4.10 A.M. the gas blew back over the enemy, who were seen to leave their trenches in panic on a front of half a mile and run back with the cloud. Here again our troops had full warning and were prepared, but in spite of this, and the fact that it was light when the gas clouds were released, there were in the two attacks (which were treated as one in summarising the casualties) 1260 men poisoned, of whom 338 died. (Two of the battalions exposed to the gas cloud lost 634 men—*i.e.*, 48 per cent of their trench strength.)

In the history of the 9th Bavarian Regiment it appears that these attacks were carried out by the 5th Bavarian Reserve Regiment and the 5th and 9th Bavarian Regiments of the 4th Bavarian Division; by the two former on the 27th and by the last-named on the 29th, who discharged their gas 'by higher order,' though the wind was not so favourable as when they refrained from doing so on the 27th. "In places at times there was a calm and the direction of the wind frequently veered. The gas crept over the enemy's positions, but then returned and flooded the trenches of the 9th Bavarian Regiment and partly those of the 5th. The unexpected change had the result that the gas masks were not put on in time or with the necessary calm and care, and the 9th Regiment had heavy losses to bewail: dead, 1 officer and 132 men; gas sick, 6 officers and 280 men, of whom 30 subsequently died. The losses of the other two regiments of the 4th Bavarian Division are not available, but the 17th Bavarian Regiment, the left of the 3rd Bavarian Division on our right, records in its history that in its No.2 Company there were 4 dead and 30 sick from the German gas blowing back. The losses of the gas troops and other non-infantry units are not at present available." (*Note*—Other accounts of this disaster, obtained during the war, were described on p. 118, Chapter VII. ; and in the American Intelligence compilation, ' Histories of 251 Divisions of the Germany Army,' this entry appears opposite the 4th Bavarian Division : "About the end of April 1916 it lost 1100 men while attempting a gas attack.")

3. The Germans discharged gas at Wulverghem on 30th April 1916, and on this occasion it was thought that only chlorine was employed. On the 21st, 22nd and 23rd British shells had exploded gas cylinders in the German line from which gas clouds were observed to drift. The ' gas alert ' was in force from 22nd April onwards. On 26th April two deserters came over and gave warning that a gas attack was imminent ; and on the 29th two more stated that the attack was to take place the same night. Full preparations were therefore made, and men were even sent over to wait in No Man's Land and to keep a look-out and listen for the gas.

At 12.35 A.M. the gas was launched along a two-mile front, there being some gaps in the continuity of the cloud.

Although everyone was ready for the gas, the Verey lights revealed the cloud to view, the wind velocity was high (12-15 m.p.h.) and our artillery came into action only a few minutes later, we had 512 gas casualties, of whom 89 died.

The German raiding parties were again driven off with heavy losses.

4. On the same front and against the same troops another gas attack was launched on the night of the 16th June. At 12.40 A.M. when the ' gas alert ' was in force, our sentries saw the gas in the bright moonlight as it left the German trenches a quarter of a mile away, and they gave the alarm. There was ample time for our men to adjust their helmets. The flow continued for fifty or sixty minutes, and towards the end of it the gas began to float back on the enemy. Once more the German raiders were driven back.

In the History of the 209th Reserve Regiment it appears that 80 per cent of 2000 large and 3000 small cylinders were opened on this occasion. After the discharge officer patrols were sent forward, only to report "the enemy perfectly intact and undisturbed by the gas attack. Thus the enterprise could not be carried out." All the same, we had 559 gas casualties, including 59 deaths.

(*Note*—In all the four German gas attacks which have been described (in some of which only chlorine was used, and in the remainder probably only a small percentage of phosgene) our casualties were incorrectly attributed to the insufficient protection afforded by the British helmet. In December 1915 the ' P ' type, which had been introduced in anticipation of the use of phosgene by the enemy, was in use, and in the other three attacks the ' PH,' which gave a still higher degree of protection against this gas. In reality both types gave absolute protection against much higher concentrations of gas than could be experienced from a gas cloud, provided that they were in good condition and properly adjusted in time.[1])

5. Only one other cloud gas attack was made by the Germans against the British during the rest of the war : this took place at Wieltje, in the Ypres Salient, on 8th August 1916, on a front of only 1000 yards, and this was the only occasion on which the presence of phosgene in the cloud was definitely established by professional chemists. In the four battalions which were mainly affected there were 804 gas casualties, including 370 deaths (46 per cent), and in addition the 1st Canadian Division lost 174 men from the gas, although their area was hardly invaded by the cloud.

General Thuillier himself was not very enthusiastic about the future utility of the cylinder companies at this time, and in commenting on their unpopularity he suggested that the scope of the 4-inch Stokes mortar companies would be greater as soon as gas ammunition became available for them, as with the bombs gas could be deposited *in* the target instead of being allowed to drift over it. He pointed out at the same time that within its range the Stokes bomb was much more effective than the 4.5-inch howitzer shell, as it contained 8 lb. of gas as against only 3, while the mortar itself was capable of a far greater rate of fire than the howitzer.

In December 1916 General Thuillier again reviewed the situation and definitely recommended an increase in the

[1] In the standard tests the ' PH ' helmet kept out a concentration of one part in one thousand of phosgene for one hour.

British " PH " smoke helmets.
Note : one of them is incorrectly adjusted.

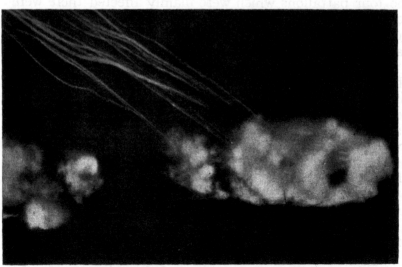

Projector discharge by night on the Arras-Lens front.
The streaks in the air are due to fragments of the silk bags which contain the
propellant charges (early black powder type).

number of Stokes mortar companies at the expense of the cylinder units, and that the former be transferred to the Royal Artillery. He also asked for a reduction in the rate of supply of cylinder gas, the development of the ' projector ' method of gas attack and the retention of the flame-projecting machines for occasional use.

The headquarters of the battalions of the Special Brigade had by this time become attached permanently, through circumstances, to the headquarters of armies, so that their abolition and substitution by similar organisations which were to form part of each army headquarters and to control the gas operations of all the special companies which happened to be acting in that army area did not involve much alteration in procedure. (The companies ceased to be formed in battalions: eleven of them were operating with the Fourth Army in July 1916 ; and at one time, in 1917, during the preparations for the attack on the Messines Ridge, ten of the special companies—*i.e.*, nearly half of the brigade—were working in the Second Army area.)

On the defensive side, at this period, each Army Commander had a ' Chemical Adviser,' and each Divisional Commander had a ' Divisional Gas Officer.' It was now proposed to appoint, in addition, a ' Chemical Adviser ' to each Corps Commander, with a suitable staff, to provide which the strength of the Special Brigade was reduced by about a sixth, the number of sections in each of the sixteen cylinder companies falling from six to five. A little later, in February 1917, General Thuillier proposed the merging of the two appointments of Director of Gas Services, which he held, with that of the Commander of the Special Brigade (myself), and he recommended me for the new post ; and, although the proposals in regard to the reduction in the number of cylinder companies and the transfer of the 4-inch Stokes mortar companies to the Royal Artillery were never acted on, the remaining ones were approved, and I became ' D.G.S. and G.O.C. Special Brigade ' on 17th June 1917 and was promoted to Brigadier-General. General Thuillier returned to an infantry command, and was appointed to the 15th Division with, of course, the rank of Major-General.

CHAPTER XI.

IN December 1916 and January 1917 those companies which had gas operations on hand were left to complete them, while the remainder were withdrawn into ' G.H.Q. Reserve ' at Helfaut, where they were trained in the use and tactics of the new Livens ' projectors.' The four Stokes mortar companies were beginning to get supplies of lethal gas bombs, and they had sufficient occupation in studying the best tactics to employ and in working out new range tables, &c.: in the later stages of the war they were trained in handling projectors as well, and one of them even undertook a cylinder operation in 1918.

It was, of course, realised that the existence of pro-jector installations must not be revealed to the enemy through aerial photographs, and great care was taken in training the brigade to camouflage these positions, an expert being borrowed from the camouflage school for the purpose, the success obtained being checked from photographs taken by arrangement with our own Flying Corps.[1]

I had now to occupy myself with the apparently hope-less task of popularising the use of gas with the army staffs and with the troops. The first step was a simple one—namely, to remove the impression that the presence of gas cylinders in a trench was a source of great danger. Careful records had been kept of every instance of damage being done to cylinders while awaiting discharge, and from them a table was prepared and given a wide circulation, which showed that during the whole period of eight months, between 20th June 1916 and 8th February 1917, cylinders had been burst by shells and trench-mortars on twenty-five occasions : on fourteen of these no casualties whatever

---

[1] It was found in the course of these experiments that the ordinary camouflage netting in use did not conceal newly turned earth so well as ' scrim,' coloured to suit the particular locality.

had occurred from gas leakage, and in the remaining eleven accidents thirty-one men of the Special Brigade and Infantry had been killed by gas poisoning ; that is, only four per month out of the whole strength of the British Expeditionary Force—this, too, during a period of intense artillery activity and when more than 20,000 cylinders had been in the front line at one time.

What was still more striking was the fact that half these deaths occurred from our own artillery shells falling short : five of them were referred to by the 61st Division Commander (see p. 177, Chapter X.) : this was the most serious accident of all, and it was caused by one of our 4.5-inch shells striking a cylinder emplacement on the 61st Division front on 8th July, as the result of which five men lost their lives from gas poisoning. There were no complaints of infantry suffering from the effects of our own gas at the actual time of the discharges, because there was no longer leakage from the pipes except when cut by the bombardment ; and the system was adopted of keeping men away from the cylinder bays, and, very often, of isolating the latter from the rest of the trench by means of impregnated curtains hung across them.

In only one of the 110 cloud attacks carried out was there any loss incurred through the cloud drifting back : this accident happened on the front of the 36th Division opposite Messines on 1st September. Only 118 cylinders were discharged on this occasion—a remnant from a previous attack—and for some curious reason there was a temporary check in the movement of the wind, which had been blowing at 4 m.p.h., and the cloud drifted into one section of the front trench (but not beyond the parados), and no less than nineteen infantrymen lost their lives.

This was the worst accident we had in the whole course of the war, and it was the more regrettable because special orders had been given to clear the trench of all troops except a few Lewis gunners and sentries. It was said that the men who suffered were a working party who had come up without being informed of the order ; but however that might be, they became excited and lost their heads, although none of the men of the Special Brigade who were in the same drift suffered at all. Curiously, too, the Special Brigade officer in charge of the operation was particularly expert in judging wind movements : he was a meteorologist by profession and had served for nine months under Major Gold in the G.H.Q. weather bureau, and he was absolved from all blame for the accident in the inquiry that followed.

There still remained the problem of relieving the infantry of part, at any rate, of the labour involved in a gas installation, and of convincing them that this labour, when undertaken, was productive. An appeal to the Ministry of Munitions resulted in the Leeming aerial ropeway being brought to my notice : this was a most promising system of transport, and it consisted of a series of frail steel trestles standing about fifty yards apart, connected together by a wire and supporting a light running steel cable which was operated on a revolving drum by an electric motor. The current was supplied by leads from a petrol-engine which could be placed at any distance to the rear. The ropeway might be of any length up to 1000 yards, and for concealment in the daytime all the trestles could be lowered simultaneously (and raised again when required) by means of the connecting wire. Cylinders could be hung every few yards by means of hooks on carriers which gripped the running cable, so that it was only necessary to load the cylinders at one end and to lift them off at the other at some central point for subsequent distribution.

This ropeway took a very long time to perfect. We had one at Helfaut in March 1918, but by September only two others had arrived ; these were sent to Savy, where a school was established, at which all the Special Companies were trained in its use in turn, the intention being that each company should have one set as part of its normal equipment. The war ended, however, before the ropeway could be used in aid of any gas operation.

The introduction of projectors partly solved the difficulty of infantry labour, because, although in a projector operation the total weight to be transported for a given quantity of gas discharged was actually four times as much as in the case of a cylinder attack, the carry was usually to the neighbourhood of the support, instead of to the front-line trench. A projector installation, too, was much more gradual, it being practicable to take up and set a few tubes each night, often without any infantry assistance at all.

Trench tramways were also developed as the war

progressed, and they saved the infantry a great deal of labour in the transport of every kind of material to the front line.

Finally, by the introduction of the ' retired ' method of cloud attack, cylinders were discharged from the support trenches and from lines even farther to the rear, while on a number of occasions in 1918 they were taken up by tram and train and were discharged on the trucks, without even removing them from the latter.

To bring to the notice of the army in general the effects produced on the enemy by our gas operations, it was now necessary to abandon the policy of secrecy which had been observed hitherto and enter on a vigorous propaganda campaign. This was done by means of publications and by delivering series of lectures and arranging demonstrations. Adams, a schoolmaster by profession and an excellent linguist, was transferred to my headquarters as Intelligence Officer, and he established contact with the various Intelligence departments at the headquarters of armies and corps, supplied them systematically with the names of the German regiments that had been gassed and arranged for the interrogation of prisoners, whom he often examined himself in the ' cages.' Their statements, as well as extracts from captured German official and private documents, were published and distributed in a ' Monthly Summary of Gas Intelligence,' care being taken to bring copies in which particular operations were mentioned to the notice of the commanders of the formations that had carried them out. These summaries were printed at G.H.Q. from July 1917 onwards. Besides the result of our own gas attacks, any innovations by the enemy in tactics or new chemicals or shells were fully described, and warnings were issued in regard to the circumstances which experience showed to be the cause of most of the casualties which our own troops suffered from time to time.

Numerous demonstrations were given at Helfaut which the Commander-in-Chief and all the Army Commanders attended in turn, together with the whole of their Corps, Division and Brigade Commanders and their principal staff officers. On several occasions there were more than 100 Generals present at a time, and 300 or 400 officers altogether. These demonstrations were very popular, as we displayed every form of ' frightfulness ' (by which name the Special Brigade was known in the army) which we were capable of undertaking in a spectacular manner, so that later on, when no major operations were taking place at the front, they were attended every Thursday by hundreds of regimental officers who arrived by motor-bus in relays, each formation sending its quota in turn.

On these occasions I gave a short lecture in the village school, after which everyone moved out on to the common where cylinders were discharged from trenches, projector drums were fired containing gas or burning oil (' liquid flame '), expert Stokes mortar detachments set up smoke barrages and fired gas bombs into a system of trenches, and thermit (molten metal) and white phosphorus incendiary bombs which were timed to burst in the air just overhead. Shots were also fired from the fixed and portable types of flame-projector.

Many distinguished visitors came to our demonstrations at one time or another, among whom were MM. Painlevé and Thomas from Paris, Mr Winston Churchill, the Duke of Westminster, Mr Bernard Shaw, Sir Keith Price (who was responsible for the manufacture of the whole of the explosives and gases in the Ministry of Munitions), the Military Attachés and Missions of all the Allied nations, and General Jackson and most of the distinguished scientific men who were working on gas at home, including Dr Haldane, Sir Richard Threlfall, Sir John Cadman, and Professors Baker, Thorpe, Pope, Frankland, Crossley, Barcroft, Donnan, Starling and Leonard Hill, and a number of French and Belgians as well. A few of them were conducted into the front-line trenches to see a projector or cylinder installation *in situ*, and even to watch an actual gas attack on the enemy.

Parties of manufacturers from England were also invited to attend some of these demonstrations, so that they might visualise how the products of their own labours were being utilised in the field ; and amongst these were members of the Association of British Chemical Manufacturers, including Mr R. L. Mond and Mr Roscoe Brunner.

Periodical visits were arranged from the officer students at the various schools—the army schools, the R.E. school at Blendecques, the staff officers' schools at Hesdin and Clare College, Cambridge—and from the Chemical Advisers of the Home Commands ; and I embarked on a series of lectures throughout the B.E.F., visiting the bases and corps areas in turn—on one occasion three on the same day —where audiences several hundreds strong were assembled for the purpose in some public hall. I also lectured once a fortnight at the R.E. school and once every six weeks at Cambridge ; and one day I met 200 officers from the War Office, the Home Commands and the Ministry of Munitions in the lecture hall at Millbank.

I was asked once to entertain a number of military attachés from neutral countries, and as one never knew which of the latter would be drawn into the war next— or on which side !—the demonstration had to be arranged with some discrimination. While it was in progress some of the more irresponsible of my young officers amused themselves by hinting in whispered asides at our latest gas discoveries and their devastating effects. One of these, it was said, would penetrate the skin without injuring it, and in spite of all known treatments continued its action till it rotted away the bones ; another converted strong men into confirmed epileptics ; while a third we hesitated to use from motives of humanity, as it induced sterility in its victims eventually.[1] As regards the last I believe that some gases which have been used as vermicides, such as prussic acid, have actually the opposite effect, as under their action vermin have been observed to multiply at an exceptional rate before succumbing. Perhaps this is in accordance with Nature's dispensation when her creatures feel themselves instinctively to be on the brink of extinc- tion : probably the ' war babies ' were another illustration of the same law, and it may also explain why the wives of Lieutenant-Commanders in the Navy figure so frequently at the top of the front page of the ' Times ' !

We had an amusing experience when a party of fifteen Russian officers who were making a tour of the war area were sent to me : they were fresh from the revolution in St Petersburg, so we imagined that they were more in need of entertainment than instruction. I lectured to them in French on gas : they listened to this quite politely,

[1] Mr H. G. Wells makes use of the same idea in his ' History of the next 100 Years,' when a Chinese Vindication Society carries out an air raid in 1935 with a " Sterilising Inhalation " : all the inhabitants of Osaka and Tokyo, together with their cats and dogs, are involved in this disaster.

and after the usual demonstration we invited them all to dinner in the evening.

One of my officers, Lawford, had lived in the country and spoke Russian fluently, and as he seemed to realise the formidable nature of the undertaking he was left to make all the arrangements for the dinner in a local hotel, and only the more stalwart of my officers were allowed to be present.

The dinner was a huge success and wine flowed freely : when coffee had been served the French waitress brought round a tray on which about twenty filled liqueur glasses had been set out, and the senior colonel who was sitting beside me took up the nearest glass and swallowed the contents at a gulp. To the astonishment of the maid he then proceeded to empty eight or ten more, quite impartially and with equal gusto, regardless of colour or flavour, before he allowed her to pass on ; and all the other Russians signified their appreciation in a similar manner.

About ten o'clock I made my excuses and left the other officers to see the evening through. Next day, on inquiry, I was disappointed to find that they had failed to stand the test ; but Lawford, who was the last on the scene, had a distinct recollection of seeing a bald-headed senior officer with a wooden leg stumping up the stairs to his room about 4 A.M., with a bottle of champagne under one arm and a tin of lobster under the other, and of hearing him muttering apologetically something about having to keep body and soul together.

CHAPTER XII.

1917.

THE year 1917 was one of exceptional activity for the
Special Brigade, the projector being the weapon employed
in the majority of the gas attacks. Altogether nearly
100,000 drums, filled for the most part with pure phosgene,
were fired, while 12,000 cylinders of ' white star ' gas were
also emptied ; in addition nearly 120,000 4-inch Stokes
mortar bombs, filled with gas, smoke and thermit, were
expended, and there were four shots from flame-projectors,
these being the last of the war. The total weight of gas
liberated amounted to 2050 tons.

The operations undertaken between the 4th April
and the 15th December were so numerous that any detailed
account of them would be tiresome ; but the scale on which
the brigade was engaged may be judged from the fact that
gas was discharged on 141 nights out of the 257, no less
than 348 separate attacks having been carried out in this
period. The maximum weight of gas discharged on any
one night was 106 tons on the 4th-5th October 1917,
when a simultaneous combined attack with cylinders,
projectors and Stokes mortars took place on the front
Festubert–Hulluch.

That the Germans suffered very substantial losses as
the result of these operations is beyond question, it being
admitted by nearly every prisoner who fell into our hands,
as well as in many of the official German documents which
came into our possession ; while their harassing effect
was also very marked. On 23rd June our First Army
published the following extract from a captured German
diary : " The last few days we have again had many
casualties through gas poisoning. I can't think of anything worse ; wherever one goes one must take one's gas
mask with one, and it will soon be more necessary than a
rifle. Things are dreadful here ; one can't talk about

them." In a letter written by a man of the 2nd German Division at Wytschaete and dated 6/6/17, he said : " From a shell-hole in hell. All night long we lie ready for action with our gas masks on. The wounded and gas cases are carried off in batches. There are many killed by gas. We are quite powerless against the English." And in another letter, written by a man of the 156th Regiment at Lens and dated 26/7/17, this sentence appeared : " An intense bombardment was opened on our front trench. Then all at once gas projectors were discharged and every-one swallowed gas. When we were relieved two days later our company was twenty-four strong. On account of our heavy losses we went straight from the front line to rest." (Prisoners from this unit stated that the 1st Battalion had fifty killed and many gassed. The 3rd Battalion had seventy-six casualties evacuated to hospital, thirty of whom died, besides men killed on the spot in the trenches.) A German captain of Landsturm, captured at Hill 60 on the 4th June, after describing the gas losses of his unit, expressed the opinion that the Germans had made a great mistake when they first began the use of gas, as it had caused them constant and serious casualties.

The Special Companies participated in the preparations for all the major tactical operations of the year ; and in addition to numerous other efforts they carried out a series of attacks during a period of a fortnight on the Belgian front opposite Dixmude in October and November, in which cylinders, projectors, Stokes mortars and flame-projectors were employed. There were no operations from French trenches, though we provided our Allies with a number of projectors, which they employed for the first time in a successful attack at Soissons on 23rd November, after which they counted fifty of the enemy dead.

It was found possible on many occasions to use the Special Companies in the moving battle. For instance, on the night 19th-20th October 156 projectors and 15 Stokes mortars were placed in position under very difficult con-ditions in Poelcappelle at a time when the enemy held part of the village. On this occasion 136 drums were fired among the enemy occupying Meunier House and 285 4-inch bombs into the buildings of the Poelcappelle Brewery.

Apart from a number of tactical novelties introduced, two new substances appeared on the scene—namely, chloropicrin gas and thermit : both had been the subject of experiment at home for some months, and they were to find a wide use in the field in addition to phosgene which was also now available for the first time in bombs and shells.

Chloropicrin was a gas which had a number of desirable offensive properties : it was a lethal compound causing inflammation of the respiratory organs, like chlorine and phosgene, but with a degree of toxicity somewhere between the two. It was also a strong lachrymator, though not so intense in its effect as the true lachrymatory substances such as SK ; while it had the additional advantage of being capable of penetrating the German masks which were in use at the beginning of 1917. It was given the cipher name of PS as it was first investigated by Lever Brothers at Port Sunlight.

The main tactical idea in using PS—apart from the surprise effect to be expected from the sudden release of a lethal gas—consisted in the fact that on penetrating the mask it produced an intolerable irritation of the eyes, as well as coughing and vomiting ; so that even when the masks were in position the enemy would be compelled to remove them and expose himself to the full toxic property of the gas, as well as to the phosgene which it was intended to discharge at the same time, it being our normal practice to fire PS and CG bombs alternately from each 4-inch mortar. For use in clouds chloropicrin was mixed with chlorine (70 per cent) and was then called ' yellow star ' ; and also with sulphuretted hydrogen (35 per cent), when it was called ' green star.' This last mixture was never actually used. It had been found previously that stannic tetrachloride ($SnCl_4$), although a comparatively harmless substance in itself, had remarkable penetrative properties (see p. 249), so that in order to increase still further the most valuable property of chloropicrin—namely, as a penetrant gas—a small percentage (20 per cent) of stannic chloride was mixed with it in all the projectiles, artillery and trench-mortar, used by the British Army. This mixture was known as NC and it gradually replaced PS altogether. It had the further advantage of being heavier and more stable on detonation than pure PS, so that on the explosion of the projectile more unaltered chloropicrin was actually released. Another chloropicrin mixture that was used later on in 4-inch bombs and artillery shells was PG, so-called because it contained PS (75 per cent), and CG (25 per cent). Its obvious advantage was that when the projectiles burst, chloropicrin and phosgene were released at the target simultaneously, instead of as formerly from shells and bombs fired alternately.

Thermit is the well-known metallic mixture of powdered aluminium and iron oxide, which, when suitably ignited, undergoes a peculiar chemical reaction which is accompanied by an astonishing rise of temperature amounting, it is said, to 5000 degrees centigrade. As a result the metals become molten, and they were observed on one occasion, in the course of the experiments, to set fire to grass which was wet from a recent shower of rain. In the preliminary investigation of thermit it was found very difficult to procure complete ignition of the compound with the bursting charges employed, and of reconciling the best scattering effect with the most effective size of the fragments of molten material. This difficulty was overcome when Professor Thorpe discovered that the new explosive ophorite (which he himself had invented) served this purpose admirably owing to its rate of detonation being remarkably slow.[1] It was realised that little tactical use could be made of the incendiary effect of thermit against trenches, but by fitting artillery time fuzes to the 4-inch bombs it was found possible to burst the latter very accurately in the air 50 or 100 feet over the heads of the German infantry manning a parapet, and it was often so used preparatory to an assault, and even while our infantry were crossing No Man's Land. The cascades of molten metal descending on the heads of the enemy at these stirring moments provided a magnificent spectacle, and the effect on our opponents must also have been terrifying. For instance, our Third Army Intelligence Summary contained a statement made by a prisoner of the 176th Regiment who was captured east of Villeret on 11th September 1917. He said : " Not many casualties were inflicted by our ordinary gas shells, but they had dreaded much more

[1] Ophorite itself was so called as a chemical pun on the O_4 content of the potassium perchlorate ($KClO_4$) used, with magnesium powder, in its manufacture. This explosive was one of great scientific interest, partly because it could be set off by time fuze, and required no detonator, as in the case of ammonal, gun-cotton, &c., and partly because the products of decomposition were found to be solids, whereas all other explosives yield gases on detonation.

Thermit bombardment with 4″ Stokes mortars.

the effect of our thermit bombs." And again, a prisoner of another regiment, captured two days earlier north-east of Hargicourt, said: " The moral effect of the thermit was very great and it caused considerable casualties. It set fire to dug-outs and to wood lying at the bottom of the trench." In regard to this operation the G.O.C. of the 34th British Division reported: " The operation required of the 4-inch Stokes mortar companies was successfully carried out, and there is no doubt the work of the assaulting party was greatly facilitated by their co-operation. Judging from prisoners' reports the thermit had a great moral effect. The duck-boards in the captured trenches were smouldering on the entry of our troops and one dugout with its entrance beneath a flying traverse was set on fire."

On another occasion, on 7th June 1917, 300 thermit bombs were fired into German trenches in the attack on the Messines Ridge, and nine hours later, when the targets were examined, many bomb fragments were found in the trench itself. One dug-out was burning fiercely, as well as a heap of clothing, and a number of dead Germans were found covered with burns. The dug-out was still alight twenty-four hours later, and although it was largely built of concrete all the wooden ribs, frames and linings were still aglow.

The difficulty of employing thermit in artillery shells was never overcome, but it was used occasionally as a filling for the 2-inch trench-mortar bombs, as well as in our projector drums.

During the whole of 1917 a good deal of variety was practised in our methods of gas attack. In the cylinder operations, besides the normal ' white star ' gas, chlorine (' red star '), as well as the chlorine-chloropicrin mixture (' yellow star '), were used, the latter notably on the La Bassée front by " C " Company on the night of the 6th November 1917. On this occasion 700 cylinders were emptied, and there was a certain amount of leakage of the gas in one of our bays which established the fact beyond question that, contrary to expectation, it penetrated even the British box respirator to some extent, causing uncontrollable coughing and vomiting; so that it undoubtedly penetrated the German masks as well.

This cloud went over extremely well in a south-westerly

breeze blowing at 3 m.p.h. Machine-gun fire died away absolutely on the gas front and none of the usual light signals were sent up. The German artillery and trench-mortars also ceased fire and remained extremely quiet for the next two and a half hours. (For an account of this attack from the German Commander see p. 231.)

On a previous occasion, on 1st September, at Hulluch, all our three gases—white, red and yellow stars—were discharged in the same cloud. (See sketch, p. 92.)

In December 1916, Captain Reid Kellett interested G.H.Q. in the idea of liberating cloud gas close to the enemy's front line by utilising ' push-pipes,' and the Third Army was requested to give the method a trial. A large dug-out was therefore specially constructed for the purpose in the front line opposite Arras, and seven 1-inch pipes were pushed out from it underground, the longest one emerging ninety yards from the dug-out. The process proved to be a very slow and laborious one, and to make things worse the weather was so cold at the time that the water used for the drill sometimes froze. Forty gas cylinders were connected to each pipe, as well as another filled with compressed air with which it was intended to blow out any liquid gas remaining in the pipes at the end of the discharge. Reid Kellett went out himself at night to examine the nozzles as they came out on to the surface and to make sure that the ends were clear of earth. The discharge took place eventually on 18th March 1917, but we never gained any information as to its effect on the enemy.

The method was obviously an unsuitable one, as, although it increased the concentration of gas reaching the German front line, the additional labour entailed was the one thing above all others that we wished to avoid.

Another novelty was the discharge of cloud gas by the ' mobile cylinder ' method which I proposed in May in a circular to all the Special Companies. The idea was the one which I had originally in mind in June 1915 : it was to make no installation until a favourable wind forecast was received, but to carry up the cylinders to the front line at the latest moment, using wheeled transport as far forward as the roads would permit, and to empty them the same night at a prearranged zero hour, thus avoiding any risk of having our project disclosed prematurely to the enemy or of damage to the apparatus while awaiting suitable weather conditions. Five hundred small cylinders, each weighing 50 lb. gross and therefore capable of being carried by one man, were specially made for this purpose and filled with ' white star ' gas. They were thought to be particularly suitable for making local attacks during a temporary check to the troops in the course of a battle, and they were so employed a number of times, the gas being discharged from our outpost line. One small operation of this kind was carried out very successfully on 17th April by " C " Company, each man making two journeys along a 600 yards carry and installing 405 ' mice ' in the front line without any infantry assistance. Another example of the ' mobile cylinder ' discharge occurred at Dixmude in October, when 1000 large cylinders were used ; but this operation will be described in its proper place. The method was not a popular one in the brigade, as it entailed too much labour on the part of the men of the Special Company concerned on the actual night of the attack ; and when infantry labour was not available it was only suitable for a small operation which involved a short carry.

The tactics to be employed with the Stokes mortars and the projectors had been carefully studied during the winter months, and memoranda embodying them were written in March and distributed to the staffs of all the larger infantry formations. These tactics were taken as a model by our own artillery as soon as they were supplied with gas shells, and they were adopted a good deal later by the Germans, whose artillery gas tactics had previously been faulty and ineffective.

For the 4-inch Stokes mortars we now had for the first time an abundance of bombs which contained smoke and thermit, and lethal as well as lachrymatory gases.

There were three means of inflicting casualties on the enemy with gas : (a) by *surprise*. This was our normal method, and it aimed at the establishment of the highest possible initial concentration of gas *in* the target by a lavish expenditure of ammunition fired by massed mortars at the most rapid rate possible on a succession of targets in turn, the duration of fire directed on each one being only one minute—or two at the most. After this period had elapsed we considered that individuals who had been caught unprotected would have been already incapacitated, while those others who were not carrying their respirators on their persons would have had time, if still capable of such action, of laying their hands on them and putting them on ; so that any prolongation of the bombardment would not only be uneconomical, but it would enable the enemy to identify the emplacement positions by the flashes from the mortars and would facilitate his retaliation against them. (b) By the *exhaustion* of the enemy's protection. This could be realised only by carrying on desultory fire over a period of many hours, and ordinarily it was not worth attempting. (c) By the *penetration* of the enemy's masks. This could be effected at this period of the war by using a gas such as chloropicrin ; or by setting up extremely high concentrations of gas, phosgene for preference ; or as the result of defects existing in a proportion of the masks ; or by all three circumstances combined.

The use of the powerful lachrymator SK for neutralising localities which we had no intention of occupying has been previously mentioned, as well as the simultaneous employment of PS and CG bombs. As regards smoke, we now had a much improved bomb containing white phosphorus —the best smoke-producing substance discovered in the war—with which magnificent smoke screens were established. In addition, these smoke bombs were sometimes burst overhead for incendiary effect in the same manner as the thermit bombs.[1]

It will be seen that the commander of a Stokes mortar company had a great variety of means at his disposal, not only for inflicting casualties on the enemy's troops, but also for giving material assistance to our own infantry at the critical moment of the assault.

A good example of the use of the 4-inch mortars was furnished by No. 1 Company on 1st December, during a bombardment along a one-mile front opposite Monchy-le-Preux. Forty-four mortars were engaged, and they opened with a half-minute bombardment with thermit, which brought the Germans hurrying out of their dug-outs to man the parapet in anticipation of the infantry raid

---

[1] The American gas troops also used our 4-inch thermit and white phosphorus bombs, and have referred to the catastrophic effects obtained with them, in particular on one occasion in July 1918.

Livens gas drums exploding.

which they thought to be imminent. Then came one and a half minutes rapid fire with CG bombs, followed by twelve minutes with PS and NC for penetrative effect, with a final one and a half minutes with CG. The whole attack lasted for a quarter of an hour, during which 2300 rounds of ammunition were fired.

One more example of the nature of a four-inch operation may be given : this took place in co-operation with an infantry raid carried out by our 40th Division on 28th September. After the operation was completed, the Commander of the 120th Brigade wrote : " The results were eminently satisfactory. (a) The smoke barrage " (six mortars) " assisted by the P bombs " (infantry smoke grenades) " completely blotted out Pine Copse, and it caused the enemy to put on his respirators. (b) The thermit " (six mortars) " successfully silenced enemy machine-gun and trench-mortar fire, and not a shot was fired on the raiding party from the strong-points west of the railway. (c) The feint : the greater part of the enemy's barrage and all his machine-gun fire were drawn on to Highland Ridge, &c., and our raid came as a complete surprise. The work of the Special Company was of the greatest value and contributed materially to the success of the enterprise."

The principle of the projector has been explained in a previous chapter. This weapon was one which, if the installation had been carried out carefully and camouflaged successfully, was capable not only of flooding the enemy's trenches unexpectedly with a deadly gas a few seconds after notice of its approach had been given by the flash of the discharge, but of establishing such a high concentration of poisonous vapour—especially in the neighbourhood where each drum fell—that no respirator, however efficient and however quickly adjusted, could be expected to give adequate protection to its wearer. This supposition was frequently confirmed by prisoners, who stated that it was common knowledge that our projectors produced clouds which easily penetrated their masks. They were told that when this happened they were to put a handkerchief in front of the drum and move to a flank !

This ' mass effect ' had, of course, not been achieved to any marked extent during the Somme battle, when only a dozen or two makeshift drums were discharged at a time; but now that we were proposing to fire several thousands of them simultaneously in a single operation, the effect might well be expected to be—and in fact was—profound. In a captured German document, dated 27/12/17, an English gas projector bombardment was described as follows: "The discharge in sight and sound resembles a violent explosion; volcanic sheets of flame or the simultaneous occurrence of many gun flashes, thick black smoke clouds, powerful concussion, whistling and noise of impact up to 25 seconds after the flash of discharge. The mines, contrary to the manner of discharge, do not all burst exactly simultaneously: the noise resembles that of an exploding dump of hand-grenades. Fragmentation is very slight."

That the introduction of the projector on the British front had created considerable consternation was shown in a Fourth (German) Army Headquarters document, dated 4th June 1917 and signed by "General der Infanterie Sixt von Arnim."

This memorandum was headed, "Not to be taken into the front line," and it mentioned the use of a new English gas mortar in increasing quantities since the beginning of April, and referred to it as a "dangerous weapon," and to its "high degree of effectiveness." It went on: "The exact details of the mortar are unknown, but it is apparent that the gas mines are fired with a shaft attached for steering purposes" (!) "which springs off before the projectile strikes the earth. As the report of the discharge is very weak, often inaudible, it is probable that compressed air or even a catapult is used for the purpose. The range has been observed to be more than 1000 metres. The British use the gas mine very cleverly, and considerable losses have been sometimes experienced. It is impossible to eliminate the possibility of casualties being caused in the immediate neighbourhood of the first salvoes of gas mines, as but a few mouthfuls of the highly concentrated gas suffices to do immense harm to unprotected persons. A distance of at least 10 kilometres behind the front line must be considered a danger zone owing to the drift over the rear positions. Dug-out entrances, N.C.O.'s posts, wiring parties, trench reliefs, &c., are looked upon as specially suitable targets."

And again, in a memorandum of the 111th German

Division dated 8th July and signed " von Busse," the range of the projectors was referred to as being 1500 metres. It went on to say : " The projector is placed in an underground shelter " (this is a compliment on our skill in camouflaging the positions). " The enemy has combined in this new process the advantages of gas clouds and gas shells. The density is equal to that of gas clouds, and the surprise effect of shell-fire is also obtained. The enemy aims essentially at surprise. Our losses have been serious up to now, as he has succeeded in the majority of cases in surprising us, and masks have been put on far too late." Then, after certain instructions about giving the gas alarm : " It does not matter if several false alarms are given. Men affected, even if apparently only slightly, must be treated as serious cases, laid flat, kept still and taken back as soon as possible for medical treatment."

In another document captured in the same month it was stated that, " We cannot hope to prevent gas casualties owing to the surprise effected and to the heavy concentrations of gas obtained ; but we can only attempt to reduce our losses to a minimum by the strictest gas discipline."

The nature of the steps taken by some German units to cope with the difficulty is indicated in the following extract from an order issued by the IIIrd Bavarian Corps, dated 23/6/17 : " To be handed over on relief. Danger zone of hostile gas is fixed at 10 kilometres from the enemy's front line. In the trenches exposed to hostile fire from minenwerfer men are on no condition allowed to sleep at night."

That the fall of the projector drums sometimes caused a panic appeared from the statement of a prisoner of the 93rd Regiment (of the 4th Guard Division) when describing an attack on 29th August : " The 6th Company had eleven men killed at once and thirty gassed ; the 8th Company, thirteen killed and twenty-three gassed ; an assault unit was practically wiped out, having ten killed .and seventeen gassed ; while the 5th and 7th Companies had two killed and nine gassed. Men were asleep at the time, and in the confusion that arose it was impossible to find masks which had been laid aside. A large part of the battalion " (the 2nd) " ran back from the gas towards Regimental Headquarters in Cité St Auguste. The battalion commandant, a captain, gave the order for a ' sauve qui peut ' from the gas-infested area." Prisoner was the batman of the captain referred to, and he heard the officers mention the figures quoted. He also heard the order given for the burial of a batch of twenty-three dead.

As a rule, the projectors were sited out in the open some little way behind the front line, so that digging, aiming—either by direct sighting or by compass—and wiring up the electric leads were easier. When camou-flaged skilfully the positions were not known to the enemy beforehand, so that although he was able to recognise the *direction* from which the flash of discharge came he was uncertain of the *range*, so that his artillery retaliation was ineffective. Of course, these installations could only be

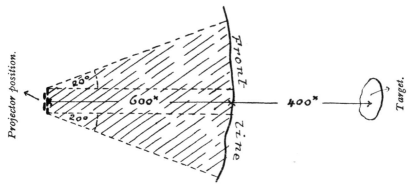

Shaded area to be cleared of troops.

carried out at night. The digging of the narrow trenches did not involve much labour, and later in the war the pro-jectors were only buried to a depth of about a foot, instead of up to their muzzles. It was found that this did not affect the accuracy of fire, especially as the rule was observed of siting rows of projectors not less than five yards apart, so that in case the discharge was not quite simultaneous the setting of one row was not disturbed by the concussion from the next.

In order to safeguard our own men from ' shorts,' an area was marked on the map, as a preliminary to every operation, from which all troops had to be withdrawn before zero hour. (See sketch above.)

This area allowed for the possibility of drums reaching only 60 per cent of the estimated range, and of their being diverted laterally 20 degrees from the central line of fire by the wind or from some other cause.

It was distinctly laid down as a principle that, owing to the inaccuracy of the weapon, the most suitable targets were *areas* which were either strongly held or which contained underground shelters in which the occupants were safe against artillery fire. Sometimes, when projectors were to be fired immediately before an advance by infantry, the latter preferred the employment of oil-drums instead of gas, so that the operation could take place with certainty at the appointed moment, independently of weather conditions. In such cases the artillery co-operated with shrapnel fire so as to catch the enemy when in flight from the burning positions.

Various ruses were made use of to deceive the enemy. For example, the projector positions were sometimes scattered over a considerable area, although the drums were all directed on one target ; in other instances they were dug in away to a flank, the drums travelling obliquely towards the enemy, who, in the absence of any flash immediately opposite to them, failed to realise in time that they were the objects of the attack. On one occasion rows of powder charges were set alight in the open to simulate a projector discharge, but twenty drums filled only with a smoke composition were fired. As a result the raiding party which went across shortly afterwards took the Germans at a serious disadvantage, as they found them all with their masks on although there was no gas present. In another raid, carried out in daylight, a similar feint was employed when 120 drums filled with bone-oil—a strong-smelling but harmless substance—were fired. This time, too, the enemy were found wearing their masks, and, as they refused to leave the shelter of their dug-outs, the latter were blown in by the raiders.

On another occasion, by way of a ruse, a dummy projector position was camouflaged with studied carelessness, so that it was discovered by the enemy's airmen and subjected to repeated bombardments ; while from the actual projector position 300 yards away drums were fired again and again without disturbance or annoyance from enemy retaliation. As a result of these practices during this nine months' period of the war, in spite of continuous activity all along the front, the casualties suffered by the Special Brigade were remarkably few.

On the other hand, judging from hundreds of statements made by prisoners and from the information contained in captured documents, the enemy found themselves quite unable to guard against this new method of gas attack. General Schwarte writes : " The projector method owes its first successful application to the English, who, with it, took up a useful idea very cleverly from a technical and tactical point of view. When, in the summer of 1917, the projector form of attack appeared for the first time in Flanders, troops unaccustomed to gas warfare suffered very heavily. On the whole, one might say that it represented the most important success of the gas war, and that this importance hardly diminished towards the end of the war ; but in far-reaching effect the gas projectors did not reach the importance of artillery." (The reference here, apparently, is to the enemy's use of mustard gas shells.)

I will mention two instances of the kind of evidence that was obtained almost daily of the German losses from gas at this period. Five hundred and seventy gas drums were fired by " F " Company into the ' Electric Station ' (which was captured three days later) near Lens on the night of the 31st May 1917, and the First Army Intelligence Summary of the 12th June contained the following : " It is clear from the statements of reliable prisoners that the Germans have lately suffered heavy casualties from our gas. A stretcher-bearer of the 11th Company, 88th Regiment, states that his battalion had nearly 40 killed and about 60 sick as the result of our gas projection on 31st May-1st June. A N.C.O. of the 156th Regiment states that on the same night the 10th Reserve Regiment " (which was in the same, the 11th Reserve Division) " lost 120 dead from gas." Confirmation of these figures was obtained repeatedly in the following months. In July many prisoners were taken who were present in the gas attack, and they said that the 10th Reserve Regiment which was in the sector suffered total casualties of 400, of which 130 were fatal ; and other prisoners taken in November mentioned the same numbers. Even as late as August 1918 an account was given of this attack in one of our Intelligence Summaries : " A battalion relief was taking place and the drums fell in and around the crowded trenches. In one battalion alone 60 deaths occurred in the line or at the dressing station, and the other battalion had a still larger number of dead, the total casualties amounting to at least 400.''

The accuracy of this report is confirmed in the History of the 10th Reserve Infantry Regiment, in which the following account appears. (*Note*—This is one of the very few instances of gas casualties being mentioned in German Regimental Histories. For my remarks on these books see pp. 340, 341.)

'' On the night 31st May-1st June 1917 the 1st Battalion relieved the 3rd Battalion in the usual rotation. Just as the relief was in full swing the enemy made a very big gas attack. The mines struck our trenches so accurately that many men, though they had practised a good deal, put on their masks too late. Also, owing to the relief and the transport of material and kits, many men did not have their masks at hand as they should have done. A number of them died instantaneously ; others were so weakened that they could not walk back by themselves to the rear, and when their comrades who were not quite so feeble took them back, they in turn became sick and died soon afterwards. Probably they had swallowed gas themselves, even if in small quantities. The old rule was justified that gassed men must remain at rest after inhaling gas. The losses unfortunately mounted up in an appalling manner. There were 100 casualties in the 1st and 3rd Battalions, 60 of which proved fatal. Above all others the 4th and 9th Companies were the most severely affected.''

At 2.52 A.M. on 14th June '' J '' Company fired 372 projector drums against Fontaine, and the VIIth Corps Daily Intelligence Summary of the same date said : '' Gas was successfully liberated this morning against Fontaine. Following on this operation observers reported 200 stretcher cases, and men being assisted, moving away from this area.'' And on the 17th : '' A prisoner of the 8th Company, 190th Regiment, captured yesterday said that in the projector attack on Fontaine the 3rd Battalion of his regiment in Rotten Row had severe casualties. The 10th Company lost its commander and 57 men killed, and the 11th Company had 18 men killed ; and these were not full figures. The sick-rooms in Sandemont and Ecourt were full of men suffering from gas sickness. In one case a gas mine fell just outside a dug-out in Rotten Row containing 25 men, every one of whom was killed. His battalion was sent up to reinforce the 3rd, and all the resting battalions of the 220th Division were brought forward in support." (This division consisted of the 190th and of the 55th and 99th Reserve Regiments.) Here again confirmation of the casualties inflicted was forthcoming, and eight months later the following appeared in one of our Intelligence reports : " Evidence of the casualties in the 99th Reserve Regiment has already been obtained, while the 55th Reserve Regiment was stated to have suffered much more severe losses." (I can now find no trace of either of these reports.) " Prisoners of the 190th Regiment were told by a sergeant-major in the Recruit Depot that in June last year their regiment had 400 men fatally gassed. The 3rd Battalion was stated to have been reduced to 17 men, and the 1st and 2nd Companies of the 1st Battalion had 48 killed."

It might be asked why we continued to discharge cloud gas when such good results were being obtained with the projectors, practically without loss to ourselves. The answer is that the two methods differed in material respects and had rather different objects. There is no doubt that our projector operations were far more popular with our own infantry for several reasons, in spite of the fact that it was realised that they were less ambitious in scope. For instance, the provision of labour was much more gradual, and the installation could proceed slowly and, if necessary, with Special Company labour alone ; while it could be interrupted at any time for an indefinite period without anxiety in regard to the presence of gas in the trench system, as the drums which contained the gas were usually only loaded into the projector tubes at the last moment. Hitherto, moreover, cylinders had always been discharged from the front line, so that although the latter was evacuated by its normal infantry garrison during the gas attack, the enemy's artillery retaliation on a definite line, the range of which was known, usually necessitated a certain amount of restoration to make good the damage done. The commanders of the Special Companies, too, were compelled to expose their men to this bombardment for a short while when they were handling the cylinders, whereas when they were at work on the electric exploders used in firing the drums they could choose positions away from the projectors and could even operate them in protected dug-outs.

Projectors, nevertheless, possessed certain definite advantages. They could be used between rather wider limits of wind direction and velocity, and even, if suitable precautions were taken, in a dead calm. Less warning —amounting to only twenty to twenty-five seconds—was given to the enemy, though the nature of this warning was, of course, unmistakable; and higher concentrations of gas were established in the target, so high in fact that in the neighbourhood of direct hits no mask was capable of keeping the gas out. On the other hand, the projectors were very inaccurate, so much so that in 1917 and 1918 almost the only casualties suffered by our infantry from our own gas occurred when, in spite of the clearance of a wide area of the trench system, isolated drums fell short or wide. The wind, too, affected the flight of the drums considerably, and its effect could not, of course, be estimated at the time when the projectors were ' set.' [1]

Actually four times as much labour was required for a projector discharge as when the same weight of gas was liberated from cylinders, though it is true that until the ' retired ' cylinder method was adopted the projector material did not have to be carried so far forward. The tubes weighed as much as a filled cylinder (120 lb.), the drums were a one-man load (65 lb.), and the base-plate and propellant charge another (40 lb.); whereas the drums contained only 30 lb. of gas, compared with 65 lb. in the cylinders. Even in evacuating the material after the operation twice as much weight of metal had to be removed.

The cloud attack was far more formidable in its effect on the enemy. Our own experience of the German attacks by the two methods bears this out, and it was surprising to find that even the percentage of mortality was higher in the case of cloud gas. Projectors were directed on

---

[1] As regards this inaccuracy of the projectors, I was once demonstrating their action to the French Minister, M. Thomas, when he asked me if the drums always fell where they were intended to. I replied: " No, but there are always Bosches," a remark which caused him the greatest amusement. I think he had in mind the weekly estimates which were published in the early days of the war by well-known journalists of the tremendous wastage of the enemy's manpower, and their confident calculations of the rapidly approaching date when the German Army would become extinct.

limited areas, such as villages and other special localities, and the duration of exposure to the gas freed from the bursting drums was only momentary; whereas in the case of the attack with cylinders the discharge took place on a continuous front, and it lasted for ten minutes or more. Instead of a series of localities which might not happen to be occupied at the moment chosen for the discharge, and which, even if occupied, might not be reached by the drums owing to their inherent inaccuracy, the whole area opposite is flooded with gas from a cloud: the latter, instead of passing over in one dense gust, has time to circulate and to penetrate into every nook and cranny of the enemy's trench system. Not a man escapes contact with the gas wherever he is and whatever his occupation: gas curtains fail, in time, to afford protection to men sheltering in dug-outs, and defective masks give out. Finally, penetration in great depth can only be attained by cloud gas, because lateral dispersion of gas is almost eliminated, as it is compensated for by the gas-cones spreading from both sides, while the cloud is also being reinforced continuously from behind. It will be evident that many more of the enemy's troops are exposed to cylinder than to projector gas, while the former reaches the back areas where the situation is much more favourable for surprise. (In a cloud gas attack in April 1917 the French had a casualty 40 kilometres behind the front.)

Some may have thought me conservative in continuing to press for the employment of cylinders whenever the circumstances admitted of their use, in view of the recognised success of our projectors; but I may mention here that our main hope for the 1919 gas campaign was based on the liberation of a cloud—I refer to the contemplated employment of the ' particulate cloud ' of which Mr Winston Churchill has written in his ' Thoughts and Adventures ': " Poison gases of incredible malignity, against which only a secret mask (which the Germans could not obtain in time) was proof, would have stifled all resistance and paralysed all life in the hostile front subjected to attack."

American writers agree with me in considering cloud gas as by far the most effective method of attack (Farrow); and General Fries (' Chemical Warfare ') was of the same opinion, though he preferred a more portable cylinder than ours—one having a gross weight of 65 lb., which he ordered in large numbers. I think, however, that with practical experience of the ' mobile ' method of cloud attack which they contemplated adopting as the normal one, the Americans would have abandoned it in favour of the fixed installation, for reasons I have already given.

As regards German opinion, a sergeant-major of the 75th German Regiment, when questioned by our First Army on 29th April 1917, said that whenever we had sent cloud gas over, the Germans had always suffered severe casualties. He feared cloud gas far more than gas mines. And General Schwarte writes : " The German gas pioneer troops thought that no other fighting method could harm the enemy so much with so little effort as the cloud attack, though our front-line troops disliked it and did not believe in its success."

I have pointed out in Chapter VIII. (p. 139) how the Hulluch front favoured the use of gas by the Special Brigade ; but the sector just north of Armentières was even more advantageous owing to the conformation of the ground occupied by the enemy. The writer of the following letter, which was captured in February 1918, failed to do us justice in supposing that we had not recognised this circumstance (see also map at the end of the next chapter) : " Gas circulates here " (the Lys valley) " and takes a long time to dissipate. After a cylinder attack in March 1917 and on succeeding occasions we were obliged to evacuate temporarily this sector of the line owing to the time taken by the gas to disperse. If the English knew this they would surely take advantage of it ! All men fear British gas very much. At the end of September 1917 the gas arrived before the alarm could be given, the consequence being that about 200 men were severely affected." (On the 27th September " L " Company fired 130 drums at Warneton and 165 near Pont Rouge.) A remarkably exact and quite independent corroboration of this story was furnished by a French lady, Madame M., who had been living in Turcoing and had had German officers billeted on her. After her repatriation she gave the French authorities in Paris much valuable information ; and the following part of her statement on the subject of gas was forwarded to me on 29th January 1918 : " Lieutenant —— of the —— Bavarian Infantry Regiment " (I purposely refrain from filling in the blanks) " was the Director of Gas Services. He told me that at the end of September 1917 the British gas attack at Warneton had been 'very murderous,' the consequence being that 200 men were seriously affected and were carried to a factory at Croix. These men were burnt inside and were suffering so much that people outside heard them screaming very loudly. In that neighbourhood gas does not dissipate : it seems to circulate round about. German troops are bound to evacuate the trenches. This was first noticed in March 1917, and the officers said if the English and French knew that they would certainly take advantage of it. Everyone said that the new leather masks (introduced owing to the shortage of rubber in Germany) were no good at all. When in billets all the men grumble individually over the inefficiency of their masks. They all fear British gas very much. Only the officers have rubber masks. About the same time another gas attack made them suffer about 100 casualties, but that one was not so bad and some of the men were only evacuated for a few days."

As regards the March cloud attack referred to in both these statements, a captured order of the 40th German Division, dated 31/5/17, said : " The 4th Bavarian Division recently lost 100 men in a gas attack. The greatest precautions against hostile gas attacks are to be taken." And a medical N.C.O. prisoner of the 9th Bavarian Regiment said that forty serious gas cases had passed through his battalion dug-out on this occasion. Men were forbidden to discuss casualties arising from gas ; while yet another prisoner from the same regiment admitted that his company alone had twenty-three gas cases, all of whom went to hospital.

CHAPTER XIII.

1917 (CONTINUED).

THE chief incidents in the war on the British front during the year 1917 were the battle of Arras, which commenced on 9th April; the capture of the Vimy and Messines Ridges; the battle of Ypres, which began on 31st July; and the great tank attack at Cambrai on 20th November. Sir Douglas Haig made an extensive use of the Special Brigade during the preparation for all these operations.

Arras.—This battle, which was remarkably successful in its opening stages, was notable for the fact that projectors and artillery gas shells were used by the British on a large scale for the first time. The former were dug in along the whole battle front, targets having been selected after consultation with the Intelligence branch of the Third Army. There were 31 of these, and they extended from Tilloy village, south of Arras, to the German trenches opposite Thélus, under the Vimy Ridge, 25 to 100 being allotted to each according to its estimated importance, and the ranges varying from 500 to 1500 yards. " H," " J," " O," " Q " and " Z " Companies carried out these shoots.

At the same time forty-eight 4-inch Stokes mortars belonging to Nos. 1 and 3 Companies were distributed along the same frontage, and they fired CG, PS (both for the first time) and smoke bombs on other targets at ranges up to 600 yards.

The digging in of the projectors commenced on 31st March, and by 4th April they were all in position. 6.15 A.M. on the 4th was fixed for zero hour of the gas attack, and, as may be imagined, I watched the discharge with a good deal of interest from a central position (Mont St Éloi) just behind the line. The wind was not very favourable, as it was blowing at about ten miles an hour, but the direction was good, being almost south with just sufficient west in it for the cloud to drift right along the German positions without there being any danger of its coming in contact with the British line.

The discharge took place practically simultaneously: a dull red flash seemed to flicker all along the front as far as the eye could reach, and there was a slight ground tremor, followed a little later by a muffled roar, as 2340 of these sinister projectiles hurtled through space, turning clumsily over and over, and some of them, no doubt, colliding with each other in their flight. About twenty seconds later they landed in masses in the German positions, and after a brief pause the steel cases were burst open by the explosive charges inside, and nearly fifty tons of liquid phosgene were liberated which vaporised instantaneously and formed a cloud so dense that Livens, who watched the discharge from an aeroplane, noticed it to be still so thick as to be visible as it floated over Vimy and Bailleul villages.

There was a noticeable absence of alarm signals from the German trenches, and, indeed, the enemy could hardly have realised the nature of the new terror which had appeared amongst them and which was to add to the insecurity of their lives. At the same moment the Stokes mortars were pumping out bombs as fast as they could fire, the new combination of chloropicrin and phosgene gases being now tried for the first time. They persevered with these shoots on the succeeding nights, and at 5.30 A.M. on April the 9th they set up thermit and smoke barrages while the infantry advanced to their successful assault. During the 9th and the following days a large number of prisoners and papers were captured. The 14th Bavarian Division, consisting of the 4th, 8th and 25th Bavarian Regiments, and the 11th Division were principally affected by the projector discharge, and a captured order issued by the former and dated 6th April, said: "The bombardment of our front line by trench-mortar gas bombs has caused considerable losses." The nature of these losses was indicated by many prisoners of the Bavarian units, one of whom put the total gas casualties of the division at 450. A soldier of the 11th Company (4th Bavarian Regiment) said that fifteen men were seriously gassed in his company: he was in a trench near a dug-out where a bomb dropped, and the eight men inside were all gassed and died within half an hour. A corporal of the 12th

Company of the same regiment was on the western apex of the 'Railway triangle' in which fifteen men from minenwerfer detachments were gassed : all died before they could be removed from the trenches. Sixty gas cases came into the village of Athies during the 4th April, principally from the 10th Grenadier and 51st Regiments (both of the 11th Division). In the 8th Bavarian Regiment, which had at least 200 gas casualties, the 5th Company had 30 and the 6th Company 20 : the Major in command was gassed, as well as some of the other officers. All the prisoners admitted that the morale of the division was shattered—they surrendered *en masse* on the 9th—and the men were only awaiting the approach of our troops in order to give themselves up. General Ludendorff writes of this incident : "The situation was extremely critical. . . . A division had failed here which had previously enjoyed a high reputation. . . . A day like April 9th threw all calculations to the winds." The 14th Bavarian Division was withdrawn soon afterwards and transferred to the Eastern front.[1]

Dr Hanslian has written : "The first attack of this kind on a large scale was made by the English by the so-called 'Livens projectors' against German trenches near Arras on April 4th, 1917. The result was so striking that this method was immediately adopted by the Germans."

A little later the French Intelligence Department sent us a résumé of the interrogation of prisoners taken by them from the 11th German Division : "The large gas projectors caused very heavy casualties on the 1st and 2nd line trenches. About 17 per cent of the total strength of the 51st Regiment was put out of action by the gas, and it was only 600 strong when it was relieved after April 9th. The 12th Company had only 6 men left. A prisoner of a Grenadier regiment said that it was generally known in Douai that in the gas operation before the infantry assault on the 9th the 14th Bavarian Division lost 200 killed by gas and had a total of 500 to 600 gas casualties."

The day after the battle of Arras commenced we

[1] The 14th Bavarian Division lost 2800 prisoners on 9th April. In the American compilation, ' Histories of 251 Divisions of the German Army,' these entries appear : " It has always been a good Division " and " The morale of the 14th Bavarian Division appears to be high," so that its spirit seems to have been broken by the gas attack on the 4th and the British assault on the 9th.

The 11th German Division lost 2200 prisoners on the 9th.

carried out a projector and Stokes mortar attack against the strongly fortified village of Bullecourt: this was just on the right flank of the Arras battle front, it formed part of the famous Hindenburg Line, and it was the scene of tremendous fighting and was captured three weeks later. Prisoners taken from the 120th Regiment, who were holding the line, gave various accounts of the losses of the regiment on this occasion. The 1st Battalion had 70 to 80 dead and 150 gas cases besides; and the 11th and 12th companies alone of the 3rd Battalion had 20 dead and 54 gassed. The effect of the gas was very deadly and few who inhaled it recovered. In many cases death took place after three or four days, though some of the men were killed instantaneously: others who had apparently recovered after twenty-four hours' treatment fell dead on attempting to walk. A corporal said that the 1st Company (of the 1st Battalion) had only 25 men left after the gas attack, the company strength having been 170-180 men. Another man of this regiment said that his company had severe casualties, of whom 60 subsequently died. The regiment had to be prematurely withdrawn before its relief was due.

On 3rd May an interesting incident took place: 320 thermit bombs had been fired into Roeux Wood, and a little later, when German troops were assembling out in the open to deliver a counter-attack, a few more rounds of thermit were fired among them and over their heads. The effect was magical, the enemy scattering immediately and running back to their trenches.

On the 12th May seventy projector drums filled with ammonal were fired into a strong-point west of Bullecourt, the effect of the explosion of a ton of high-explosive being appalling.

Vimy.—At the same hour on the same day as the assault at Arras the four divisions of the Canadian Corps captured the Vimy Ridge. Five projector companies and the two remaining mortar units were detailed to assist in this operation. The same tactics were employed here, our object being to inflict casualties during the preparatory period and to assist the infantry assault with smoke and thermit at the commencement of the battle. None of the 600 projectors which were installed were actually fired, however, as the decision to employ them was only reached on 3rd April, and the programme of infantry activity did not allow of gas discharges on the nights on which the weather conditions made them possible. The Stokes mortars, however, came into action on a number of occasions between the 4th and the 9th April, and the final smoke and thermit barrages screened the infantry attacks on the 9th and were much appreciated. One of these, in which ten mortars of No. 4 Company kept up a flank barrage with 1000 rounds of smoke bombs for one and a half hours on 'the Pimple' (which was captured three days later) on the extreme left of the battle front, undoubtedly saved the 4th Canadian Division many casualties.

The German facilities for observation were much superior to our own on this sector, and as their artillery was very active the Special Brigade suffered an unusual number of casualties during this battle from its fire, twenty-five men being killed and two officers and ninety-nine men wounded : fifty-eight of these casualties occurred from shell-fire in one billet some distance in rear of the line.

Messines.—For the attack on the Messines-Wytschaete Ridge in June it was proposed to make an extensive use of gas. Six companies were to operate as frequently as possible in the time available with projectors and 4-inch mortars along the actual battle front, there being many suitable targets consisting of dug-outs, nests of machine-guns and strong-points ; while four more companies were to prepare a cloud attack on a frontage of six miles with 5000 cylinders on the right flank, astride the River Lys. In addition, by way of a demonstration, " Z " Company was detailed to install a line of flame-projectors along the Ypres canal in the neighbourhood of Boesinghe, particularly at the road and railway bridges, each of which was strongly defended by machine-guns. In preparation for the last-mentioned enterprise, trenches were specially dug at Helfaut to reproduce on a full scale the defences on both sides of the canal, and the flame-projectors were fired to enable the Corps Commander concerned to judge personally the probable effect they would have. But for one reason or another this operation never took place, so that only ten companies with a strength of 103 officers and 2400 other ranks participated in the preparations for the attack on the Ridge.

From the 24th May till 3.10 A.M. on 7th June, when the assault was delivered, the German troops had an unhappy time ; for, besides a continuous artillery bombardment planned on a more stupendous scale than any other in the war, gas attacks were made by " A," " L," " Q," " N " and Nos. 2 and 3 Companies nearly every night. Besides minor discharges on intermediate occasions, 700 projector drums filled with phosgene were fired on 29th May, as well as 1000 4-inch bombs ; on 1st June, 900 drums ; on the 2nd, 100 ; on the 3rd, 1500 oil-drums into the Bois de Wytschaete, Grand Bois and Unnamed Wood, in co-operation with 1000 bombs from the Stokes mortars ; while at the moment of the assault on the 7th there was a magnificent display over the German trenches with air - bursts from 750 white phosphorus and thermit bombs during the infantry advance across No Man's Land.

This movement provided the grandest and most thrilling spectacle of the whole war. For eight days there had been an incessant bombardment of the strong German positions with over 2500 guns and howitzers of all calibres, ranging from the field-gun to the 15-inch howitzer. Half an hour before zero hour this fire ceased entirely and there was an ominous silence all over the battlefield : it was as if the conductor of a gigantic orchestra had tapped his music-stand and with baton uplifted was pausing momentarily while the sounds from the tuning of the instruments died away. Precisely at the hour fixed for the final artillery bombardment the baton seemed to descend for the opening crash of the music, and pandemonium broke loose : every piece of artillery commenced to fire at the maximum rate of which it was capable, the sound resembling the continuous reverberation of a dozen kettledrums and the volume such that no single explosion could be distinguished from the rest ; while everywhere, as far as one could see, bright flashes of flame stabbed the half light and attracted the eye momentarily, and in rapid succession, like the tiny electric sparks in a motor-show exhibit, when the sparking plugs of a multi-cylinder engine are in operation. Nineteen immense mines were fired almost simultaneously under the German trenches, the ground rocked backwards and forwards, and, after the mushroom-like excrescences thrown up by the explosions had subsided, the dull red glow of incandescent gases could be plainly distinguished flickering over the newly formed craters.[1]

For the enemy the long-expected fateful moment had arrived : light signals of every kind shot up from their trenches, red lights, white lights and rockets breaking out into stars—frantic calls for artillery support. And as the smoke and dust rose higher and higher from the bombarded area, even these signals, as well as the white puffs from our shrapnel bursts, were obliterated, and, at the appointed hour, the assaulting columns swept towards the doomed battalions into a position overhung with a thick pall, like a low-lying thundercloud, and disappeared from view.

The discharge of oil-drums by " O " and " K " Companies on the night of the 3rd was the biggest operation of the kind that we undertook during the war (on 19th July 1918 " E " Company fired 425 oil-drums in the attack and capture of Meteren by our 9th Division) ; and although the drums exploded well and ignited the undergrowth, and the targets were seen to be a mass of smoke and flames and to be burning for an hour, few traces of the projectiles were to be found when the positions were visited on the 8th. The artillery bombardment had been so destructive that the German trenches themselves had disappeared, and even the woods had been practically obliterated.

A prisoner of the 33rd German Regiment (which had occupied the area on which the oil-drums fell) stated that they had caused the utmost confusion and panic in the lines : word was passed that the English were breaking through, and a general stampede ensued. He himself ran away and finally wandered into No Man's Land, where he surrendered to a patrol of the 2nd Royal Irish Regiment. The Germans were then expecting a mass attack at every moment.

It was a great disappointment that many of the gas attacks which had been prepared at Messines could not be

---

[1] The preparations for the attack on the Messines Ridge had begun in April 1916, and this action would probably have been substituted for the Somme battle in July of the same year if the British Commander-in-Chief had been free to decide. The mines had been completed in June 1916.

The largest of them, the one at St Eloi, was excavated at the end of a gallery more than a quarter of a mile long, and it was charged at a depth of 125 feet below the surface with 43 tons of high-explosive. The actual crater formed measured 176 feet in diameter, though, of course, the area over which trenches and dug-outs were destroyed was far greater.

carried out even when the weather was favourable, as here again these operations had to be co-ordinated with various phases of the preliminary preparations for zero day, and even with the events of zero day itself. The cylinder attack on the right flank had to be abandoned for fear of jeopardising the infantry in the new positions which they were now consolidating; and altogether 4700 cylinders, 4800 projector drums and 4250 4-inch bombs, all of which were ready in position and which contained nearly 300 tons of gas, remained undischarged.

On 18th June General Plumer, in a letter to the Commander-in-Chief, expressed his " thanks and appreciation for the excellent work performed by the Special Companies both before and during the recent operations, and to their untiring energy and help "; and on the 23rd Sir Douglas Haig requested the Army Commander " to inform the Special Brigade of his satisfaction with their good work which had helped appreciably in gaining the last as well as previous successes." [1]

Ypres.—A similar use was made of the Special Brigade in the preparations for this battle, seven companies being engaged. Between the 15th and 21st July 1917, 5100 projector drums and 14,000 Stokes bombs were fired, representing 100 tons of gas; and at zero hour (3.50 A.M. on the 31st July) 330 oil-drums and 1300 thermit bombs were fired over the heads of the infantry as they advanced to the assault. The operations continued under the most difficult possible conditions until the battle died down in November. During the whole of this period a continuous stream of reliable reports reached our Intelligence Department of the heavy losses suffered by the German units engaged in the terrible struggle for the Passchendaele Ridge, of which the following are typical.

From a company order of a unit in the 80th Reserve Division: " Latterly we have suffered numerous losses through bombardment with gas trench-mortar projectiles. They are always fired in conjunction with bursts of artillery fire and are therefore not recognised. They produce a

---

[1] It was on 4th June that the War Office asked Sir Douglas Haig to send one Special Company and 2000 gas cylinders to Egypt; but his reply was that none of the companies could be spared, and that even more of them could be profitably employed in France.

very strong effect by intense concentration of gas. *The chief danger is the element of surprise.*"

Hooge, 20-21/6/17.—Prisoners of the 46th German Regiment said that No. 1 Company had 45 men killed on the spot and a large number gassed. A private of No. 7 Company said that they had only 2 killed and 5 gassed, but he formed part of a burial party on the 16th which buried 41 men of No. 1 Company : the men were warned individually that gas losses were not to be discussed. Various statements were obtained in confirmation in April 1918. No. 2 Company of the 46th Regiment had 80 gas casualties, and No. 1 Company a still larger number, about 50 per cent being fatal. A Pioneer company 250 strong had come to work in the front line without their gas masks and only one man came out unharmed. The 46th Regiment had 100 men killed by gas in June 1917 and a further 100 in July. A N.C.O. of the 3rd Company said his company had 35 men killed outright and a large number gassed—about 100 ; and another of the 4th Company said that in a dug-out where he was standing two men were killed and five others evacuated to hospital. Sixteen N.C.O.'s and men, examined independently, all agreed that it was common knowledge that the 1st Battalion had 200 men killed in all in addition to those poisoned, who were evacuated. The 119th Division (46th, 58th and the 46th Reserve Regiments) was known to have suffered 400 fatal gas casualties on the Ypres front in 1917. This was confirmed by an officer of the 7th German Division.

Lombartzyde.—The casualties in the 237th Reserve Regiment from one of our operations in July 1917 were 330 to 340, including 200 dead. Prisoners stated that these losses were due to the presence in the regiment of a large number of 1918 recruits who were inexpert in using their masks.

18/7/17.—From a battalion order of the 90th Fusilier Regiment : "During the last relief" (on 15/7/17, near Bellewarde Lake) "the enemy made a gas attack on our trenches and communication trenches, causing considerable casualties in dead and sick. All ranks are again warned that, at the slightest indication of gas, masks are to be put on immediately."

21/7/17.—Pilckem and Boesinghe. The 102nd Reserve Regiment lost 150 dead in a few days from gas, 80 men being killed in one company. " All men are very much afraid of the gas mines." " The heavy losses of the regiment were a matter of common talk : it had lost one-third of its effectives in recent gas attacks."

18/9/17.—Captured message from the O.C. 1st Battalion, 395th Regiment, to the Commander of his 4th Company : " I regret inability to send two sections as supports. As the fighting strength of all companies is so weak I have pushed the 3rd Company into the front line. All companies except the 3rd have suffered heavily from gas."

A prisoner of the 15th Reserve Regiment was in hospital in the Exhibition Building in Ghent between 31st July and 20th August 1917 : this was one of the largest special hospitals for slightly wounded and gas cases, and held at that time 2000 patients, of whom half were suffering from gas poisoning.

Cambrai.—On the 19-20th November 1917, the night before the great tank raid on Bourlon Wood, seven Special Companies fired 4200 projector drums and 3100 4-inch bombs on the front of the attack. As a result of one of these operations prisoners of the 73rd Fusilier Regiment (at Cherisy) said that it had been given out officially to their company as a warning that the regiment had 40 killed and 170 severely gassed.

An examination of the Hindenburg Line in the Gonnelieu sector showed that the Germans were very much on the alert against gas. Numerous printed notices were found posted up at the entrances to dug-outs and in battery and machine-gun positions, such as " Gas mask on the chest in the special alert position—the English gas ! " and " Gasmaske nicht vergessen ! "

In spite of some expressions of contrary opinion, I constantly urged the maximum employment of the Special Companies throughout the war on *active* battle fronts rather than elsewhere ; because, although the conditions there were far more difficult for gas discharges, the effects of the latter were certain to be much greater owing to the activity of our artillery which by this time had developed extraordinary power. In the confusion which was certain to exist in the enemy's trench system while these bombardments were in progress, not only were the routine arrangements for giving the *collective* gas alarm by means of gongs, telephones, &c., bound to become disorganised, but the *individual* protection on which each soldier could only rely if his mask was in perfect condition was sure to be diminished in such distracting circumstances.

Apart from this important consideration, owing to the stupendous preparations which were required before the commencement of a battle, it was impossible to deceive the enemy as to where the blow was about to fall : only the exact moment was uncertain, so that an attack being known to be imminent the German trenches were more strongly held, and therefore offered us the most favourable targets. Further, by weakening the resistance they were about to encounter we could render our own infantry the maximum amount of assistance at the supreme moment of the assault.

Hulluch.—Nevertheless, owing to the ease with which they could be moved about, the Special Companies were constantly transferred from one part of the line to another, and gas attacks were carried out almost continuously all along the front of the British Expeditionary Force (see map at end of chapter). In fact, the brigade was beginning to win a popularity in the Army which resulted in a demand for its co-operation which could not be met fully without increasing its strength. A good example of an attack in which use was made of nearly all the weapons at their disposal occurred when five companies took part in a combined gas operation on the night of 4th October on the comparatively quiet front Festubert-Lens. The carrying and other preparations for this commenced on 25th September, much of the work being done without any infantry assistance ; and on the night of 4th October " C " Company discharged 1250 cylinders opposite Hulluch all in one wave, there being practically no retaliation till one hour and ten minutes after zero. At the same moment " N " Company discharged 1180 cylinders opposite Auchy : here the cylinders were packed very close together, so that the resulting concentration of gas in the cloud must have been extraordinarily high. These two clouds were given three minutes start, and then " D " Company fired 980 projector drums north of the canal in front of Givenchy; " B " Company fired 900 more into the Cité St Auguste ; and No. 4 Company, with thirty-four mortars in action, bombarded the Cité

St Elie, the Quarries and the Corons de Maroc—all familiar features on the old Loos battlefield—with 1500 CG, PS and NC bombs. The last-mentioned operation lasted for seven minutes : the CG bombs were discharged in a preliminary concentrated burst at the maximum rate of fire ; the PS and NC followed more slowly for penetrative effect ; and then came a final rapid bombardment with CG, in order to exploit the situation which it was hoped had been created by the enforced removal of the enemy's masks.

On this one night a total amount of 106 tons of gas were discharged, and the Army Commander (General Horne), in commenting on the operation to G.H.Q., wrote on 11th October : " I consider great credit is due to all concerned, both as regards the amount of gas installed in the limited time available and the large percentage which was successfully discharged. Owing to the shortage of labour the Special Companies had in places to reclaim derelict trenches in order that the gas cylinders might be installed." And Sir Douglas Haig, in his reply two days later, said : " These gas operations seem to have been well planned and admirably carried out. Much hard work was entailed on all ranks of the Special Companies. Please convey my best thanks to all concerned in the operations. Everything seems to have gone well."

About this time " E " Company alone had no fewer than six separate projector operations in hand in the neighbourhood of Oppy at the same time, all ready for execution as soon as they were required : these consisted of 250 drums in one place and 120, 280 and 200 in others, as well as 120 and 100 ' dummy ' drums which were to be used in conjunction with infantry raids.

Dixmude.—One other series of gas operations in 1917 is worth mentioning ; partly because it was the only occasion during the whole war on which every one of the Brigade's means of offence was brought into use at the same time—namely, cylinders, projectors, 4-inch mortars and flame-projectors ; partly, too, because it provided the best example of the ' mobile cylinder ' method of cloud discharge ; and partly because it was carried out in trenches occupied by Belgian troops.

In October 1917 the German trenches defending Dixmude were held by a Landwehr division, this front being

known as a 'quiet' one. In order to compel the enemy
to call upon his fighting reserves elsewhere by withdrawing
the Landwehr division from the line and replacing it by
an active one, it was decided to threaten the Dixmude
defences by means of gas operations and by a general
display of activity on the part of the Belgian infantry and
artillery. An advance from this sector might not be
regarded by the enemy as improbable in view of the
progress which had been made by British and French
troops towards Passchendaele, a few miles farther to the
south, where the allied attack, in conjunction with a
projected landing of British troops at Ostend, was delivered with the intention of advancing the left flank of
the British Expeditionary Force to the Dutch frontier
and resting it there instead of on the sea.

I visited the Belgian Commander and made all the
preliminary arrangements with him, and suggested a
detailed programme of gas attacks. Our General Staff
wished the Belgian Army to co-operate with the movements in the Ypres Salient by counter-battery work with
their heavy artillery commencing on 26th October, and
by gas discharges on the 26th and 28th, accompanied by
infantry raids in force. The position held by the Belgians
was a rather unusual one, as only the width of the canal
separated their breastworks from those of the enemy.
The canal was twenty-five yards wide and was almost
dry at this time, so that the parapets on both sides rose
ten or fifteen feet above the muddy bottom. The centre
of the position was dominated on the German side by the
massive ruins of a factory building known as the 'Minoterie,'
in which nests of machine-guns were concealed and from
which the enemy's look-outs had a clear view of everybody
approaching the Belgian front line along the shallow communication trench only fifty yards distant. Warned of
this peculiar situation, I wore an old trench coat and a
Belgian steel helmet when making my examination of the
position, and I arranged an issue of these helmets to all
the British troops which took part in the gas operations.
The men were also instructed as to the various badges of
rank in the different grades of the Belgian Army, and
they were provided with copies of Belgian Standing Orders ;
so that with the willing and friendly co-operation of the
Belgian Staff the best relations were maintained between

our Allies and ourselves throughout the month that we worked by their side. Our men, of course, as was their habit, maintained the strictest reserve in regard to their special business, all the work in connection with which was done at night. We brought Fullerphones, too, with us, so that none of our telephone conversations could be 'tapped.' As a result of these precautions our first gas discharge took the enemy completely by surprise, as until that moment, in spite of the facilities of observation which they enjoyed, they had no idea that British Engineers had appeared on their front.

On 9th October "M" and "N" Companies arrived in the area, and Captain Pelling, who commanded the latter, was put in executive charge. The digging in of the projectors began on the 14th, and proved to be very arduous work, owing to the marshy nature of the ground. To avoid calling on the Belgian troops for labour "P" Company was brought up to assist, and a section of "Z" Company set about installing a large flame-projector opposite the 'Minoterie,' while a section of No. 2 Company put ten of their mortars in position for the attack of the same strong-point. The cloud attack with which the operations were to commence afforded a very successful example of the 'mobile cylinder' method of discharge: no emplacements were constructed in the front line, nor was any protection afforded for the cylinders during the discharge. The concrete dug-outs along the canal were vacated by the Belgian infantry on the 22nd October, and in four nights 1000 cylinders were carried up and stored in them; so that for the discharge on the 26th they were simply removed from the shelters, distributed along the firestep and emptied in the usual way through the discharge pipes.

I was in some doubt as to how this cloud would behave in the peculiar circumstances, because unless the wind was blowing fairly strongly and at right angles to the general line of the canal there was a danger that the gas might sink into the deep obstacle in front and, failing to mount the high bank on the far side, drift along the canal to a flank. Such a deflection of the cloud might imperil the Franco-British line Merckem-Vyfwegen, which was only five miles distant, so that it was necessary to lay down very definite limits of wind velocity and direction.

However, during the night of the 26th these conditions were fulfilled, and the order was given for the discharge to take place at midnight.

The cloud carried over extremely satisfactorily. It was observed to dip in crossing the canal, but it surmounted the German breastwork and created such havoc that no alarm signals or calls for artillery retaliation were noticed with the exception of a single bell in the 'Minoterie,' and all rifle, machine-gun and artillery fire were silenced for a period of two hours. "P" and "N" Companies released this gas, while No. 2 bombarded the 'Minoterie' with 200 CG bombs, as, owing to its commanding position, it was considered that the cloud would swirl round it and fail to surmount the obstacle and penetrate the recesses of its ruined masonry.

Two hours and forty minutes later the flame projector came into play and fired two shots into the 'Minoterie,' enveloping it in smoke and flame. At the same instant the Stokes mortars put over 150 rounds of thermit into the same target to cover the passage of the canal, and several raiding parties, accompanied by officers and men of "P" Company, waded across and entered the German trenches without difficulty, only to find that they had been abandoned by the enemy in panic.

The 20th Landwehr Division, which was holding this front, was withdrawn shortly after this attack, and two new divisions were crowded into it, one of which—probably the 54th Reserve—was subjected to the subsequent projector operations.

Just a month later twenty prisoners of the 386th Landwehr Regiment were captured at Cambrai, having been overrun by our tank attack, and on examination they stated that the gas attack at Dixmude had come to them as a complete surprise. In the 1st Company of No. 1 Battalion there were 2 killed and 41 severely gassed; in the 2nd Company 2 killed and 47 gassed; in the 3rd Company 3 killed and 25 gassed; and in the 4th, 10 men gassed—a total of 7 killed and 123 gassed in the battalion. All the prisoners were in approximate agreement as to the figures, and a medical corporal confirmed them, saying that the 1st Battalion had 7 men killed on the spot, while 130 to 140 severe gas cases were passed through the dressing station in the course of the night, of whom 11 died soon after they were carried in ; the remaining cases were severe. There were also many casualties in the back area, including 80 in Dixmude. Only about one and a half battalions were exposed to the gas in the front line, otherwise the losses would have been far heavier had the trenches been held in greater strength. Two Alsatian prisoners who joined the regiment after the attack in a draft of 100 men said that following this experience all the units in the regiment appeared to be extremely afraid of gas, and that their morale was lowered to such an extent that they were withdrawn on the following day. The flame projector had caused no casualties in the ' Minoterie,' as the garrison had fled in terror.

On the night of 29th October 1480 projector drums were fired at ranges up to 1750 yards into a series of targets stretching from Dixmude to a strong-point about half a mile to the south of the town. On 2nd November No. 2 Company fired 400 SK bombs into Dixmude, where a troublesome heavy trench-mortar battery was silenced for six or seven hours ; on the 6th 960 projector drums were discharged ; and on the 9th No. 2 Company, who now had 40 mortars in action, fired 1530 bombs into Dixmude, the whole of the ruined town being blanketed by the resulting cloud.

All these operations were carried out without a hitch and with practically no loss to the Belgians or ourselves. They served admirably the strategic purpose for which they were intended, and the happy relations established between the Belgian troops and our own were shown by the following letter (written in English on 11th November) from Lieutenant-General Drubbel, the Commander of the 2nd Belgian Division :—

" MY DEAR GENERAL FOULKES,—I take the opportunity of my departure from Alveringham in asking you to accept my best thanks for the valuable help you and your troops gave to us during the operations we have undertaken against Dixmude.

I much appreciate your kind earnestness in preparing your skilful co-operation, and I beg you to transmit my warm congratulations to Captain Pelling and to the officers and the troops of his detachment for their good works and their splendid spirit. Believe me, &c. . . ."

I might add that the Belgian authorities were extremely generous in their awards of decorations to our officers and men.

As the result of the steps taken to interest our Intelligence Service in the interrogation of German prisoners with regard to their gas losses, a vast amount of evidence reached us at this period of the war. In order to save space I will refrain as far as possible from quoting any further from the statements made, but in some of the German documents, which also reached us in increasing numbers (and which are still on record), there are to be found vivid word-pictures which are of special interest, as they not only illustrate the opinions held by the German commanders in the field of our gas campaign, but they also serve to show beyond the possibility of dispute how futile is the pretence affected by some German writers that their losses from gas were negligible.

An order of the 10th Ersatz Division, dated 7/8/17, showed the concern felt on the subject by the Supreme Command. (This division seems to have been in Lorraine at this date, but it was about to appear at Langemarck, in the Ypres Salient.)

" General Headquarters telegraphs as follows : ' The English have recently achieved not inconsiderable successes by using gas mines in bursts of fire on one point from a considerable number of projectors. Casualties have occurred because the gas arrived without warning, and because its density was so great that a single inhalation caused illness. The successes of the British suggest that we should, on our side, employ the same procedure with gas shell fired from the medium minenwerfer.' "

That the enemy fully realised the great danger arising from the bursting of the phosgene drums is also shown in the following extracts :—

" Corps Headquarters, St Quentin Group, 18/7/17. Warning concerning gas mines. The enemy by means of these gas mines can envelop our trenches in a minimum of time, and even with a contrary wind, with a heavy, dangerous gas cloud which remains for a long while in our position. Masks are to be put on as soon as a loud explosion is heard in the enemy's lines. Anyone who has breathed gas while unprotected, even if the case appears to be light, is to be regarded as a severe case. Such a case will be placed in a position of rest and will be carried back as soon as possible for medical treatment. (sd) Albrecht, G.O.C."

"Headquarters, 9th Reserve Division, 4/11/17. A gas operation against Sector V₂ South" (600 drums were fired on 27/10/17 at Honnecourt, south of Cambrai) "caused considerable losses. Every gas case, whether slight or severe, is to be taken by *stretcher* to the nearest medical officer. It is better to remain lying, with the mask on, in the vicinity of the gas cloud and wait for the arrival of stretcher-bearers than to increase the activity of the lungs by walking back : otherwise slight cases may become severe and death may supervene. (sd) Hildemann."

"Sector order (of the 470th Regiment, 240th German Division), 1/11/17. Report on hostile gas attacks on the nights of the 2-3rd and 6-7th November 1917. As a result of the first operation" ("J" Company fired 800 drums at Fontaine) "a large number of casualties are regretted, dead, severely and slightly gassed. The high number of losses was due to the unfortunate fact that at both points struck a large number of men happened to be collected at the time. The second operation" (4-inch bombs fired by No. 3 Company) "caused a smaller number of casualties. The casualties occurred chiefly because the gas mines fell directly into the trench and the men there had to breathe once or twice before putting on their gas masks. Several men were gassed because they took off their masks too soon in dug-outs where the gas still remained. Men who have in the first place inhaled but little gas, who initially feel few ill-effects, may show the worst symptoms of poisoning a few hours later and die. Every man who admits he has breathed gas should be *carried* to the dressing station.
(sd) Brandt, Major, O.C. 470th Inf. Regt."

"Headquarters, 54th Division, 13/10/17. On the evening of the 5th instant the gas mines struck points occupied by listening-posts, a working party and part of the supports in dug-outs. One mine burst at the entrance of a dug-out, affecting all the occupants, whose first warning was the presence of the gas. The gas alarm prevented surprise in and behind Havrincourt. At the points struck by the mines masks were at once adjusted, but officers and men had already breathed gas. Casualties were mainly due to surprise. In some cases masks had been laid aside in dug-outs and by the working party and could not be found in the confusion. Most of the men apparently slightly affected walked to the aid post in the churchyard at Havrincourt, a distance of more than a kilometre. On the succeeding night and the following day the majority died although the necessary treatment was applied. The serious effect produced and the large number of fatal cases make it urgent to ensure that more energetic measures are taken for protection. Even greater emphasis than before must be laid upon the fact that in apparently slight gas cases every movement is attended by the utmost danger. An increase in the medical personnel will be arranged by the regiment holding the affected sector. If a unit or part of a unit has been subjected to gas, the Regimental Commander will see that a relief takes place and fresh troops are brought up. The danger is so great that an immediate examination will be instituted by the commander concerned regarding the necessary protective measures and officers and men will receive detailed instruction. The English have punished this disobedience with death. In future the least punishment I shall give for similar neglect will be arrest." (!)

(*Note*—The 84th Regiment was the one affected by this attack, 596 drums having been fired by " G " Company and 500 4-inch bombs by No. 3 Company. The following accounts were given by prisoners at various dates of what happened : a regimental order was read out on parade, in which it was said : " Owing to the culpable negligence of the men in failing to adjust masks in time the regiment has suffered 100 fatal gas casualties, and there were many gassed besides " ; 20 men were gassed in two dug-outs in the third Battalion sector ; the 1st and 3rd Companies had 17 men killed and 120 gassed ; 100 men were killed by gas on this occasion ; and in a captured medical report dated 19/10/17 the number of men passed through an aid post during a period which included the night of the attack were given as—

" Casualties from artillery . 17 ⎫
   ,,   ,, trench-mortars 18 ⎬ —deaths, 7
   ,,   ,, rifle fire . 8 ⎭
   ,,   ,, hand-grenades 3
   ,,   ,, gas . . 32—deaths, 21, plus the majority of the remainder by delayed action."

This regiment was unlucky about this period, as only a fortnight previously it experienced another projector attack, in referring to which a 54th Division order said : " Men were killed by gas although it was stated that their masks had been adjusted. Alarming rumours were set on foot that the English were using a new gas against which the German mask gave no protection.")

Similar rumours apparently spread elsewhere :

"Corps Headquarters, Dixmude Group, 21/9/17. Not to be taken further forward than Regimental Battle Headquarters. Extract from a divisional report on a sudden English gas mine attack" (apparently the 1st Guard Reserve Division, as this was the unit concerned) : "'During the night 12-13th September 1917 the English made several attacks in the divisional sector with the 22-cm. phosgene gas projectors long known to us.' ("B" Company fired 875 drums at 11.20 P.M. and 290 more at 3.35 A.M.) 'They proceeded in the usual manner by suddenly firing a great number of these projectiles simultaneously. Unfortunately a large number of casualties resulted. One of the regiments had 105 cases, of which within 5 to 15 minutes 15 proved fatal. One company had 11 dead and almost the whole of the remainder ill. These heavy losses are due to the fact that the projectiles appeared in large numbers and were mostly direct hits on the trenches. A test will be made of a "dud" from which it will be established whether a stronger gas than usual has been employed.
(sd) Humser, Major (for G.O.C. Corps).'"

(*Note*—This attack took place at Lens where the 1st Guard Reserve Regiment had experienced another pro-jector attack only nine days previously ; and it was again attacked on 15th October. Various prisoners of this unit said : One of the battalions had over 50 men killed and many sick, the heavy losses in this sector being the cause of frequent comment among the men ; the division suffered 600 gas casualties, including 200 dead in the first part of September ; in the 3rd Battalion the 12th Company had 7 dead and 30 gassed, the 11th Company 12 dead and 35 gassed, while the 9th and 10th Companies also suffered severely ; in the hospital at Oignies 200 gas casualties were brought in on the 15th October, of whom 28 died in one day.

In the History of the 1st Guard Reserve Regiment the following appears : "On the 13th September, at midnight, gas mine and H.E. attacks took place in rapid succession on the whole sector, which were repeated at 4 A.M. In the confusion among the sleeping men heavy casualties were caused, 20 men being killed and 71 gassed" ; but although this regiment was subjected to twelve gas attacks by the Special Brigade in six months in 1917 alone, there is hardly any other mention of gas in the whole book. In the

American Intelligence compilation, ' Histories of 251 Divisions of the German Army,' the 1st Guard Reserve Division is referred to as follows : " Gas attacks caused it to suffer equally heavy losses in September and December 1917.")

" Corps Headquarters " (apparently the IVth), " 10/11/17. In this cloud attack " (at Auchy on the 6th November against the 453rd and the 10th Bavarian Regiments) " the British caused us considerable losses in slight gas cases. They discharged chlorine gas, which is much less effective than the phosgene contained in the British gas mines and gas shells. It has not yet been clearly shown whether another gas was mixed with the chlorine [1]—*i.e.*, a lachrymator which penetrated the drum or even the mask itself." (*Note* —This was ' yellow star ' gas, chlorine plus chloropicrin, see pp. 193 and 195-196.) " It was only some hours after the gas attack that our artillery opened fire on that sector of the enemy's trench whence the gas was discharged. This shows that effective communication between the infantry and the artillery broke down. A thorough training in anti-gas measures and an iron gas discipline are particularly essential in this sector where hostile gas operations of all kinds have continually to be faced." [2]

---

[1] Dr Hanslian, however, in describing one of the last cloud attacks made by the Germans on the Western front (against the French in Champagne on 31/1/17), says that a mixture of chlorine and chloropicrin was used, and that according to French reports this was " the strongest and most terrible of the whole war " : there were deaths 15 kilometres behind the front and heavy casualties 20 kilometres away : even at 40 kilometres gas was definitely noticeable. It was claimed that the French casualties were 2062 (20 per cent of the strength of the troops exposed), of whom 531 died, half of them having been killed instantly.

[2] The 10th Bavarian Regiment was subjected to ten gas attacks by the Special Brigade in five months of 1917, but the only references to them in its History are as follows : " Gas mine attack. On August 17th, 1917, the enemy employed gas tactics hitherto unknown to us, with electrically projected gas mines. In the vicinity of the first English position a great number of these projectors were installed in chess-board formation. A yellowish-red flash appeared, a dull explosion was heard, a short intense whirring through the air and the gas mines of 19.5 calibre landed in our trenches. The effect of the gas was based on surprise and on the development of a high concentration of gas. Probably phosgene was used. Our gas masks proved to be sufficient protection. It was only necessary to put them on in time. This had to be done at the first sight of the flash in the enemy's position, otherwise it was mostly too late.

30th August.—A particularly heavy gas attack took place The enemy began at 1.25 A.M. Heavy artillery and machine-gun fire compelled the sentries to take cover. All at once the enemy's fire ceased. An English infantry attack seemed imminent. Everyone came out of the dug-outs at once and manned the parapet, chest high. Suddenly the English gas mines arrived in the trenches which were densely occupied by our men. Many were thrown down by the pressure of air from the incoming mines : others were sprinkled with the liquid on their faces and hands. The mines fell with surprising accuracy. The gas alarms carried the warning to the

The constant insistence on stricter gas discipline was a regular feature in all these orders, though it was evident that through carelessness and the distracting conditions of trench warfare it was difficult to enforce. For example, the death from gas poisoning of Generalarzt Dr Reinhardt (the Assistant Director of Medical Services in the XIIIth German Corps) was reported in the enemy Press in September 1917 : apparently even he carelessly forgot to take his gas mask with him when on a visit to the trenches near Caudry. An order of the 226th Reserve Regiment, dated 16/7/17, had the following passage : " In the enemy gas attack to-day (at Langemarck) several men did not put on their masks rapidly enough. Although a stringent gas alert had been ordered, one man at the commencement of the hostile gas attack could not find his mask, and another had no drum attached to his face-piece. Some gas cases unfortunately occurred through this criminal stupidity. All possible measures must be undertaken to forestall impending gas losses." And after an attack on the 392nd Regiment (on 21/7/17, also at Langemarck), Dr Dennert, the Medical Officer of this unit, reported : " 21/7/17, noon. At 2 A.M. the enemy made a gas attack with gas projectors. Up to now sixty-two casualties have arrived at the regimental dressing station. Two of these died half an hour after their arrival, and all show symptoms of acute suppuration of the lungs. Six cases appear to be serious. A number of men attribute the cause to the surprise of the attack : the majority, however, assert that the gas penetrated their masks. I have convinced myself, from samples taken at random, that the masks were too large for the men owing to the marked emaciation of their faces and the long period during which the testing of the masks in the gas chamber have been discontinued."

That we were successful in reducing the fitness for battle of the German regiments selected for attack was illustrated in a captured warning order, dated 5/8/17, of the 165th Regiment of the 7th Division (which relieved the 8th Division near Lens at the beginning of August 1917) :

rest billets. The sight of the numerous gas casualties in the trenches was appalling. Their moaning and cries may have reached the English positions. Many died on the way to the dressing station. The 5th and 6th Companies in Fresnoy Park were particularly affected. During the next few days the 2nd Battalion paid the last tribute to numerous comrades interred in common graves in the military cemetery of Henin Liétard."

" In spite of the abnormal artillery fire lasting several weeks the 8th Division suffered relatively small casualties from shell fire. On the other hand, considerable casualties were caused by gas, owing to masks not being to hand and to lack of caution." And in a similar warning order of the 208th Division, dated 21/9/17 : " The infantry of the 36th Division " (the next one to it, on the south) " had suffered considerably during the preceding days from hostile artillery fire, and particularly from gas, which had weakened its fighting powers." (*Note*—All three regiments of the 36th Division—namely, the 5th Grenadier and the 128th and 175th Regiments, seem to have suffered from a projector attack on the 18th September at Langemarck, as prisoners stated : one company had 49 men killed, and all the remainder went back to report themselves gassed ; the report of the sergeant-major of the company showed that there were only 6 men left. In the 128th Regiment : 20 out of 50 men in his company were gassed, as well as a large proportion of men in other companies, many of whom died. The whole fighting efficiency of the regiment was destroyed. From other prisoners (gassed, in a British hospital) : 45 men in the 4th Company were affected, half of whom were serious cases, and the losses in the 2nd Company were also serious. Four officers of the 36th Field Artillery Regiment confirmed the heavy casualties suffered by the 128th Regiment : the projectors were very effective and caused extraordinary losses. 175th Regiment : the 3rd Battalion had, on an average, 25 gas casualties in each company.)

Finally, it seems that the enemy resigned themselves to these losses in despair. Memorandum issued by the " Staff Officer for Gas at (Fourth) Army Headquarters (Ypres sector), entitled ' Experiences regarding gas warfare in Flanders, 30/8/17.' Hostile gas tactics : (1) the familiar phosgene mine : sudden bursts of fire up to 100 rounds simultaneously—effect produced by surprise—one shoot produces 100 to 200 gas cases, mortality about 10 per cent " (*i.e.*, one to two casualties per drum). " (2) ' Cylinder ' or ' roll bombs ' : cylindrical bombs about 8 cm. calibre, 35 cm. long " (our 4-inch Stokes mortar bombs)—" contents probably a new strongly lachrymatory gas " (chloropicrin is here referred to)—" effect running at the nose, severe irritation ; fatal in considerable quantity."

In his despatch of 23rd December 1917, Sir Douglas Haig referred to the work done by the Special Brigade during the year, and he also took the opportunity of acknowledging the debt owed by his troops to the scientists at home :—

" Great fertility of invention has been observed and very great credit is due to the special personnel employed for the rapidity and success with which these new arms (gas and liquid flame) have been developed and perfected, and for the very great devotion to duty they have displayed in a difficult and dangerous service. The army owes its thanks to the chemists, physiologists and physicists of the highest rank who devoted their energies to enable us to surpass the enemy in the use of a means of warfare which took the civilised world by surprise. It is satisfactory to be able to record, on the evidence of prisoners, of documents captured and of our own observation, that the enemy has suffered heavy casualties from our gas attacks."

CHAPTER XIV.

THE GAS DIRECTORATE. *A.* OFFENCE.

FOR the period of the battle of the Somme I joined General Thuillier in his office in Beauquesne where he was established with the " B " (defensive) branch of the Gas Directorate, in close touch with Advanced G.H.Q. : later on we all moved to Montreuil (G.H.Q.), and still later to Wailly. However, I found this too far back for visiting the Special Companies and for controlling their operations, and in May 1917 I obtained permission to set up the head-quarters of the brigade in St Omer, which, although frequently bombed by German airmen, was a very con-venient road centre and was also within easy reach of Helfaut. We remained here till nearly the end of the war.

When in June 1917 General Thuillier assumed command of the 15th Division and I became Director of Gas Services, I moved the defensive branch to St Omer also, and we occupied a large house in one of the main streets, where we established our mess, the various officers being billeted in different parts of the town. We were not far from the camp of the F.A.N.Y.'s, that wonderfully efficient and gallant corps of women ambulance drivers, and my own billet was the room which Lord Roberts had occupied when on his last visit to the army in France, and in which he died.[1]

The ' Fannies ' were not above playing a practical joke, and I always considered them answerable for a telephone call which reached us one night complaining that the gas had gone wrong in one of the messes—would we please send someone to put it right.[2]

[1] There is a brass plate to Lord Roberts on the wall of this house to-day. Its owner, Madame Eloi, was the soul of patriotic hospitality and refused any payment for rent from the British authorities. When I left her in 1918 she insisted on my taking away the key of her front door, which I was to use at any future time and make free of the house, whether she was in residence or not.

A refugee nun (from Ypres, I believe) helped in the housework and brought early morning tea to my room before I was up—an experience in her own gentle life as strange, I imagine, as the war itself.

[2] The idea of this jest probably originated in the drawing in ' Punch,' about this time, of an old lady who is represented as saying : "What a poor supply of gas there is ! Ah, well, I mustn't grumble. Perhaps we are attacking with gas at the front to-day."

Colonel Cummins now rejoined his corps, and Major Hartley, the Chemical Adviser of the Third Army, took his place as Assistant Director for " B " duties. Eddis became Assistant Director for " A " duties (operations) and Rivers, the Brigade Artillery Officer, was promoted to Brigade Major.

Rivers conducted our mess, and when on one occasion, after examining his accounts, he complained of the cost of eggs and suggested that we might keep our own fowls in the backyard, the proposal was agreed to. He said he knew of an outlying farm where young birds could be purchased, and he set off one day after being reminded that French peasants were very hard business women. " You can leave that to me," he said, " I haven't lived five years in Mexico for nothing. Besides, there isn't much about poultry-keeping that I don't know."

So eighteen very young chicks appeared in due course and were comfortably and rather expensively installed in the yard. The price paid for them seemed to us very high, but Rivers explained that the woman had refused to allow him to pick out the pullets, but that when he insisted on doing this he was charged extra accordingly.

The chicks thrived and were the centre of interest in the mess : special delicacies were even put aside for them in a dish at table so that they might reach maturity the sooner and prove more prolific.

Occasionally, however, as time went on, a suspicious crowing began to be heard from the back of the house, and when we glanced at Rivers inquiringly he tried to appear unconcerned and affected not to have heard it. But the truth was finally disclosed. After months of deception sixteen of the chicks turned out to be cockerels, after all ; and I was told that the two remaining ones were ducks ! — though this may have been an exaggeration.

The control of the Special Brigade operations became more and more arduous as the extent of front held by the British Expeditionary Force increased. In order to retain the confidence of infantry commanders it was most important that conflicting opinions should not be expressed by different officers when dealing with the various staffs, so that unity of doctrine throughout the brigade was insisted on from the very first. The officers commanding special companies at the headquarters of armies and the company commanders constantly met me in conference, and as many of them were able chemists it was not difficult, after discussing controversial subjects, to arrive at a policy which they upheld loyally thereafter. Nevertheless, they were allowed a good deal of liberty of action in experimenting with variations in tactics, &c., and when any such action by a company commander appeared to have been attended with successful results a full description of it was circulated for the benefit of the others : this happened, for example, when various devices were adopted for the electrical discharge of gas from cylinders. Every encouragement, too, was given for the submission of novel proposals, and if any of these promised to be of value the officer concerned was sent to General Jackson (and later on to General Thuillier when he went to the Ministry of Munitions) in London, who gave every facility for working it out. Thus Livens, who was always full of ideas, gave up the command of " Z " Company to Bansall after a time and became liaison officer between ourselves and the Ministry, and he was finally employed entirely by the latter during the last year or two of the war.

Whenever a gas operation was suggested by G.H.Q., or proposed by an army commander, the Special Company detailed to carry it out, after making a reconnaissance of the ground, sent me a descriptive report and a sketch plan. I sometimes commented on this or suggested some variation ; and every day subsequently a brief message reached me of the progress made with the preparations for the operation, so that at any moment I was able to show the General Staff at G.H.Q. how each company was employed, what operations were in hand, and when and where they were due to take place. And after the gas had been discharged a full report of the attack was sent to me giving details of its apparent effect on the enemy, and mentioning any failures of apparatus, &c. Summaries of the operations were sent to the C.G.S. weekly.

All these results were tabulated by Adams, my Intelligence officer, who kept a record of the German regiments affected on each occasion and circulated lists to the Intelligence sections of armies and army corps, and in turn received from them reports of the statements made by prisoners (whom he sometimes examined personally) as well as copies of German diaries and official documents that had been captured.

From time to time the Intelligence Branch at G.H.Q., who knew the exact location of every German division opposed to us—and very often, too, their intended movements from one part of the line to another, or to another theatre—provided me with lists of units which for one reason or another it was specially wished to weaken. For instance, we gassed the 1st Bavarian Reserve Regiment fifteen times and the 1st Guard Reserve Regiment twelve times in six months in 1917, and the 10th Bavarian Regiment ten times in five months.

The 9th Bavarian Regiment was gassed fourteen times between 28th June 1916 and 1st August 1917, and the 161st Regiment fourteen times between April 1916 and September 1917, and the 156th Regiment ten times in the year September 1916 to October 1917.

In exercising my control over the operations of the brigade, Eddis, who was the only Regular officer I had with me during the whole war, was invaluable, and his presence at my headquarters enabled me to make frequent visits to the companies in the line, as well as to England, and, at one time or another, to the Belgian, French, American, Portuguese and Italian fronts.

I tried to make a practice of spending at least one day in every week in the trenches. On these occasions I would examine some gas operation which was in course of preparation, and take with me the local division gas officer and inspect at the same time the condition of the gas-proofed dug-outs, the Strombos horns and other gas alarms, and perhaps the gas school in rear. At the Special Company billets I had to present decorations on parade and interview N.C.O. candidates recommended for commissions in the brigade—perhaps twenty or thirty at a time. In one instance I visited six of the companies, and travelled 400 kilometres by car in one day.

All the while there were visitors from London, &c., to be met, conferences to attend, trials of new materials to be carried out and demonstrations and lectures to be given; and as an example of the number and variety of the matters that occupied my attention I recall that on the night preceding the most important of all our demonstrations at Helfaut (7/7/17) no less than eight gas operations took place at different parts of the front—one with cylinders, five with projectors and two with Stokes mortars.

H.M. the King at the Front (attended by the Author).

There were also pamphlets to be written from time to time on such subjects as the tactical employment of smoke, projectors, 4-inch Stokes mortars and lethal and lachrymatory gas shells, as well as on the defensive measures to be taken against gas. One pamphlet, which was printed and issued monthly, was entitled 'Gas Warfare' (SS 184) : in it was summarised everything of importance connected with the gas war that had taken place in the period, such as the Special Brigade operations, with a brief résumé of the effects obtained, according to prisoners and documents ; and, on the defensive side, any novelty introduced by the enemy—for example, mustard gas—with a full description of the tactics employed, the nature and markings of the shells used, the effects on our troops and the precautions to be adopted to avoid casualties : changes in the enemy's protection—for example, the introduction of leather face-pieces, due to the shortage of rubber in Germany ; while from time to time summaries were compiled pointing out the tendencies in German gas tactics and in their gas training and discipline.

As 'Gas Adviser,' before and after General Thuillier's occupation of that post, I had also to make suggestions at various times to the C.G.S. One of these was the proposal to use phosgene shells when the wind was favourable in the moving artillery barrage. Insufficient gas would be released to do any harm to our own troops or to the enemy, but the latter would be induced to adjust their masks, and experience showed that this put them to a serious disadvantage when opposing our advance.

Another suggestion was to carry out an attack over an area on which we had used mustard gas, but after a much shorter interval than the six days which the Germans usually allowed to elapse before such an advance was permitted. If certain specified precautions were taken by our troops the risk run by them would be more than compensated for by the unexpectedness of the movement. Actually this suggestion was followed with excellent results on the very first occasion that our artillery used mustard gas, in the attack on Bellenglise on 29th September 1918, only two days after 10,000 of these shells had been fired in the course of the preliminary bombardment.

One of the most interesting duties was attendance at the conferences held by the Commander-in-Chief about once a month, at which all the army commanders, accompanied by their chief staff officers, as well as the principal staff officers and the various Directors at G.H.Q. were present. The proceedings began with an explanation of the position, condition and movements of all the German divisions on the Western front. This occupied nearly half an hour, and was made by the head of the Intelligence Branch (Brigadier-General Cox during the period with which I was concerned, until he was drowned while bathing at Paris Plage in 1918), who stood in front of a blackboard on which a large map had been pinned. His remarkably lucid and fluent summaries were in marked contrast to the situation reports which the army commanders next made when called on in turn, and they were only rivalled by the clear explanation of his plan of battle which I heard Sir John French deliver at the conference at St Omer (p. 63) just before the battle of Loos.

The Minister of Munitions himself, Mr Winston Churchill, took the keenest interest in the gas war and paid us a number of visits, and I was able to take him to advanced observation posts to witness some of our daylight operations.

A number of more or less fanciful schemes came up for examination, some of which took me to the Admiralty. One of these was to attack with barges filled with gas the Germans in occupation of important points on the Belgian coast; but this operation was deemed inexpedient owing to the obvious danger to the civil population and the risk of infringing Dutch neutrality by the drift of gas over the frontier. Another was to prepare the way for a landing on Heligoland by means of gas clouds released from specially fitted submarines; and a third to gas the Turks in the Dardanelles from twenty gas ships. Naturally none of these schemes survived expert examination.

Another suggestion, which seemed more promising at first, was to stage a cloud attack which should last for twelve hours, preparatory to an infantry advance. This was the result of the knowledge that the German troops, if subjected to a prolonged attack, would be unable to wear their masks continuously for such a long period. It will be recalled that the exhaustion of the enemy's masks had once previously been aimed at on the occasion of our first cloud attack at Loos, the oxygen sets with which their officers and machine-gunners were provided at that time, and which were known to have a maximum life of only half an hour, being considered to be the chief obstacle to our success. Experience had shown, however, that for a gas attack to be practicable over a period of twelve hours it would be necessary to give complete protection against artillery bombardment to the cylinders and to the men handling them. The installation of cylinders in mine gallery on the Hulluch front offered a solution to this difficulty. This was a continuous gallery, some 6000 yards long and 20 to 30 feet below ground, which extended from Givenchy to Hulluch, and it had listening galleries every 20 yards along its length running out a similar distance towards the enemy. The idea was to install 120,000 cylinders at the ends of the listening galleries, and to connect them, 200 together, to main pipes which would be pushed through the roof, to emerge above the surface. There were doubts as to whether these main pipes would not, owing to their length, become frozen during a gas discharge, and also as to whether extra pressure would not be necessary to force the gas out of the containers to such a height ; and experiments were initiated at home to examine these problems. Eventually the proposal was abandoned, partly because such a small frontage of attack was now recognised as futile, from a tactical point of view ; partly because, owing to the impossibility of mobilising such a large number of cylinders in a short time, the construction of special tank containers which would be useless elsewhere, owing to their immobility, would be necessary ; and partly because a much more practical scheme now came under review.

Every army staff was, of course, concerned in finding some solution for the stalemate which existed in the western theatre of war ; some new tactical principle was required which would enable an advance to be made on a wide front without advertising the intention by the usual preliminary destructive artillery bombardment. The latter had not proved too successful so far : it did not always destroy the enemy's wire ; it failed to reach their machine-gunners in the deep dug-outs from which they only emerged at the last moment ; it cut up the ground to such an extent that movement over it became difficult ;

and it only left the enemy in doubt as to the exact moment when the assault would be delivered.

To ensure success it was necessary for the way to be cleared to enable infantry to reach the enemy's artillery positions, at least, at the first rush, and I felt certain that this could be done if gas was used in the proper way. Hitherto it had been discharged with the general object of reducing the enemy's man-power: this was undoubtedly useful in influencing the result of the war, but it had only an indirect effect on the course of each of the great battles. My idea was to time the gas attack in such a way that it would achieve both objects simultaneously. It was not intended to dispense with the action of tanks (which, it will be remembered (see p. 176), were rather under a cloud at this period, owing to the unsuitability of the ground over which they had been operating during the third battle of Ypres), or with the artillery bombardment, but it was important for the latter not to be concentrated only on the front chosen for attack, in such a way as to give the enemy a sure indication of the plan. Above all, gas must be made the primary factor, and all other considerations must be sacrificed to it if the scheme was to be a success.

On 26th October 1917 I circulated my proposal for study among the Special Companies, and it became known as the 'retired cylinder' method of cloud attack.

Reference had been frequently made by German prisoners to the depths to which our gas clouds had penetrated, and to distances as great as 10, 20 and even 30 kilometres behind the front at which they had suffered casualties; and both French and our own experience confirmed the truth of these statements. It seemed therefore that there would be no great disadvantage if a cloud were liberated half a kilometre or even more behind our own front line. The loss of gas concentration in the enemy's trench system could be compensated for by the installation of a greater number of cylinders than ever before, while the normal practice of opening all the cylinders simultaneously would be followed.

It would, of course, be necessary to withdraw all our infantry from the front of the discharge before the latter commenced, but this would only occupy half an hour, and while the front trench was empty it would require no defence other than the gas cloud. Such a withdrawal would not have been considered by our commanders for a moment in 1915 and 1916, but they were accustomed by this time to sanction it on narrow fronts when projector attacks were being made.

On the other hand, the advantages of the proposed method of discharge were very great. As regards the transport of cylinders, the worst part of the journey along narrow trenches would be avoided, and the length of the carry reduced, while much of it could be arranged across the open. Further, from the experience gained in each particular sector, a cylinder line could be chosen which was normally comparatively free from hostile bombardment and which was easily accessible by road or by the existing trench tramway system, so that manhandling the cylinders might be dispensed with altogether. Where necessary ' spurs ' from the main tramway system could be constructed along the general line of the installation at the rate of a quarter mile per company each night, in which case the saving of labour would be enormous. The cylinders would be off-loaded and laid flat on the ground in the open in irregular-shaped dumps of 1000 or so, and camouflaged in such a way as to defy detection from aerial observation ; or narrow, shallow trenches might be dug in which they would stand, buried up to the neck, with only the outlet valves exposed. Wherever suitable roads and tramlines existed, roughly parallel to the front, the cylinders might even be taken up on the night of the discharge in horsed waggons, motor lorries and trucks, halted at intervals along the line, discharged without off-loading them and removed to the rear when empty. No discharge pipes would be required, as in the normal attack from trenches.

This method of cloud attack was obviously not applicable to a front on which active operations were actually taking place, because under such circumstances traffic along the roads near the front line would usually be impossible owing to the many shell-holes, tram-lines would have been rendered useless, hostile artillery fire would be intense and the difficulty of organising the withdrawal of infantry insuperable.

All the Special Companies were set to work to study this proposal, and it was considered to be perfectly feasible technically. Alternative methods of establishing dumps of cylinders and of protecting and camouflaging them were experimented with, and Wilson, one of the subalterns, put forward what seemed to be the best of the methods of opening the cylinder valves electrically, which obviated the necessity of handling them and which ensured the liberation of gas simultaneously all along the line. This device consisted of a spigot which was screwed into the valve outlet : the latter was then fully opened, but the gas was prevented from escaping by a soft lead disc which had only to be perforated to allow it to escape. The destruction of the disc was arranged by fitting a blank rifle cartridge against it, which was fired by exploder in the same manner as the projector charges, with which everyone was by this time familiar.

So promising did this method of attack appear after only a brief examination, that on 10th November I wrote a memorandum to the C.G.S. in which I explained it and urged that any offensive undertaken by the B.E.F. in the spring of 1918 should be preceded by a cloud attack carried out on a colossal scale by the whole personnel of the Special Brigade.

The main idea was that our infantry should benefit for once by the discharge of gas, not only from the confusion and the disorganisation and loss of morale that it would cause among the enemy's troops, but from the certain losses, estimated at from a minimum of 10 per cent up to 50 per cent, which would occur not merely in the front system of trenches, but in the supporting battalions, the artillery personnel and the reserves in the billeting areas far behind the line.

The principle was the same as the one it had been intended to apply at the commencement of the battle of Loos ; but whereas on that occasion the assault had to be delivered at a fixed date and hour, with or without the gas, the chances of success were now so promising that there would be justification for postponing the infantry advance by prolonging the artillery preparation until the weather conditions were favourable.

It had been found possible at G.H.Q. to forecast the weather correctly for the next twenty-four hours in ninety cases out of one hundred ; and according to the wind chart (see p. 125) there was an almost even chance of a favourable wind along our whole front on every day in the year except in September and October (and in April, between Armentières and the La Bassée canal).

Moreover, an attack would now be carried out by highly skilled and experienced men, and with a gas in regard to the deadly quality of which no one was any longer in doubt.

I emphasised the advantages of a gas attack immediately preceding the assault, and explained the necessity for using cylinders rather than projectors, as well as the extreme simplicity of the ' retired ' method. The latter removed nearly all the difficulties that had been previously encountered, especially in regard to dispensing with infantry labour, the avoidance of hostile artillery retaliation, and the elimination of the nervous fear engendered by the presence of cylinders in the front line.

The attack could be staged on any selected part of the front, though some sectors naturally offered better facilities than others : these were compared in detail.

As regards the number of cylinders, we had at the time 56,000, filled, in France : the French, with whom I had been in communication, could put 10,000 more at our disposal, which were 50 per cent larger than ours and contained pure phosgene and compressed air : there were 50,000 others at home or in transit, and 1000 tanks, each with a capacity of 30 cylinders ; and as many more could be manufactured in the time available, the total required number of cylinders—namely, 200,000, would be forthcoming, especially as the Russians now no longer required our gas and there were enough filled projector drums in France to last us several months.

As regards the gas attack itself, a tremendous concentration of gas—much higher than any that had ever been attempted before—would be liberated in the first wave, soon after dark on the selected day. This would be followed by smaller intermittent discharges at short intervals throughout the night, alternating, if the supply of gas proved insufficient, with smoke which would compel the enemy to wear his respirators continuously ; and finally, an hour before the assault at dawn, there would be another discharge in extremely high concentration.

Up till now we had depended for the success of our gas attacks almost entirely on the element of *surprise* : this time it was proposed, in addition, to *exhaust* not only the

enemy's troops by compelling them to wear their respirators all night, but also the respirators themselves, as
by reason of the prolonged discharge the degree of gas
absorption of which they were capable would be diminished.
There was also every prospect of the respirators being
penetrated, not only because it was certain that many
would prove to be defective through wear and tear, but
also by the very heavy concentrations of gas that would
be liberated, and by the fact that we would bring into
use for the first time our 'green star' gas, of which there
were already 14,000 cylinders in France and 10,000 more
awaiting despatch at Widnes.

('Green star' gas consisted of chloropicrin (65 per cent)
and H_2S (35 per cent). It was under high pressure, which
made it undesirable for use in trenches owing to the
risk of leakage: it was not inflammable, in spite of its
H_2S content, but even if it were, this, and the other draw-
back mentioned, would not have been of importance if
the cylinders were used from a 'retired' position.)

I proposed that the troops detailed for the assault
should be held back a few miles, out of shell-fire. On the
receipt of a favourable wind forecast they would be warned
to hold themselves in readiness, and they would eventually
be set in motion so as to reach an assembly position just
in rear of the cylinder line shortly before the final gas
discharge; and they would occupy the front line (but
would not enter dug-outs) from five minutes to an hour
later, according to the advice of the experts on the spot.

Meanwhile the enemy's back areas would have been
shelled for days previously at extreme ranges in order
to force back the civil population; and during the gas
discharge and at zero hour the hostile artillery would be
silenced by a concentrated bombardment with gas shells
accumulated for the purpose and employed on a scale
never previously attempted. Recent incidents on our
Second and Fifth Army fronts had proved that the complete temporary neutralisation of batteries could be effected
in this way. (See footnote, p. 343.)

These proposals were accepted by G.H.Q. in principle,
and on 9th October I was instructed to make all the
necessary arrangements for the collection of material, and
the Ministry of Munitions was notified accordingly.

The whole thirty miles of the Third Army front, from

Gavrelle to Gouzeaucourt, was selected provisionally for the gas attack, and it was divided up into sections among my officers, who carried out a complete reconnaissance of it, particularly in regard to the existing tramway systems. A special telephone circuit was projected which would have enabled me to control the attack and vary it if necessary, at very short notice, during its actual progress. The installation of a huge cylinder store at Mondicourt was also started.

The front selected offered many technical advantages : it was almost straight, it favoured the probable direction of the wind (south-west), the tramway system was the best on the British front, and the country opposite, in German occupation, was fairly flat, so that no ' gas islands ' were likely to be formed. Moreover, the numerous river valleys, the Scarpe, Cojeul and the Sensée, in which the majority of ruined villages were situated which served as enemy billets, would conserve the concentration of the clouds.

However, with the cessation of fighting on the Russian front the initiative in the war had passed to the Germans before the proposal could be carried out, and our Third Army (as well as the Fifth) was attacked on 21st March 1918. Ten days later I was sent to consult the First Army Commander as to transferring the front of the gas attack to the line Festubert-Bailleul (north-east of Arras), divided, as shown in the sketch (see next page), into three sections (*a*), (*b*) and (*c*) ; and another complete reconnaissance was made, the tramway systems here, too, being found to be excellent or capable of being made so.

The whole of the brigade was ordered to this new front. But the army commander vetoed section (*c*) on account of the known prejudice of the Canadian Corps, which held it, against the cloud method of attack. (In March 1917 the 4th Canadian Division planned a raid which was to follow the second of two gas discharges. Owing to a fall in the velocity of the wind this second discharge was cancelled, and as the raid was carried out without it and the raiding party met with serious opposition, the gas was considered to have been a failure.)

Eventually, on 2nd April, G.H.Q. issued instructions for the attack to be launched between Hill 70 and the La Bassée canal, and nine of the companies were detailed for it.

A movement which was considered in co-operation with this attack was an infantry advance from Sallaumines Hill to Cité St Auguste, with a tank raid farther to the right from Mericourt southwards, all with the object of the capture of Lens.

However, as the First Army itself now became involved in the German offensive, the bigger scheme was abandoned and orders were given for the discharge of the few thousands

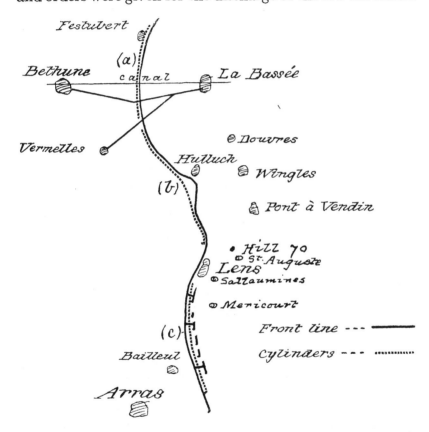

of cylinders which had been put into section (*b*). This attack took place on 12th May.

But I was to have one more opportunity of presenting my favourite plan for execution—that is, for the discharge of gas on a stupendous scale immediately before a major tactical movement.

The Germans had introduced their Blue Cross shells about the same time as they made their first mustard-gas bombardment : these contained a substance called diphenyl chlorarsine.[1] It was mixed with phosgene and di-phosgene in the Green Cross shells for certain calibres of artillery, and in others it was embedded in the high-explosive as a colourless solid contained in a glass bottle.

This compound (which we called DA) was a lachry-mator, a sternutator (causing sneezing) and a respiratory irritant, but it had no vesicant (blistering) action like mustard gas. According to the German chemist, Meyer, DA in large doses—which, however, we never experienced from their shells—causes motor disturbances, numbness, fainting and unconsciousness. We found that when present in minute quantities in the air, in such low concentrations as one in a million, it produced an intolerable irritation of the nose and throat, running of the eyes, prolonged sneezing and a burning sensation in the chest, followed by a severe pain in the head and giddiness, as well as mental depression and general misery ; and one part in fifty millions of air was found to be the average of human endurance during five minutes exposure. Curiously enough, these symptoms passed off in course of time and there were no serious after-effects. Chloroform put up for the purpose in small glass ampoules also gave immediate relief.

We discovered all this for ourselves in the course of investigations at home, as DA, used as it was in the German shells, was comparatively innocuous, in spite of the fact that the British respirator was not at first completely proof against it. The enemy's object in using it was, as in the case of our introduction of chloropicrin, the causation of such irritation as to compel our men to remove their masks and expose themselves to other lethal gases which were present at the same time.

The Germans put the greatest faith in their Blue Cross shells, and fired millions of them up till the end of the war, but actually they grossly over-estimated their value ; the casualties resulting from their use were insignificant, and, although they had some harassing effect, no fatal cases from the gas were known to have occurred. Of course, the high-explosive effect of the Blue Cross shells was

---

[1] This was not the first arsenious compound used in the war, as the French ' VN ' and our own ' JBR ' and ' CBR ' shells all contained arsenious chloride, together with other substances.

proportionally reduced by the space occupied by the bottle.

When the DA was scattered by the high-explosive it was liberated not in the form of a gas, but in fine particles : these were not sufficiently minute to penetrate the box-respirator completely, and absolute protection was very soon obtained by adding an extension to the box which contained a cheese-cloth filter.[1]

Colonel Watson, who was the head of the Central Laboratory at Hesdin, had suggested in September 1917 the study of particulate clouds ; and one of my officers, Sisson, in a spirit of investigation, put a pinch of DA which had been extracted from a German shell on the hot plate of a stove in his room at my headquarters. The result was so remarkable that everyone was driven out of the house immediately, and it was found that the latest pattern of German mask, even when fitted with the extension that had been supplied to give protection against Blue Cross shells, gave no protection whatever against the DA cloud produced in this way.[2]

This was the germ of a new and very valuable idea, and steps were taken immediately to investigate how DA could be best volatilised in the most highly effective and penetrant form by bringing it in contact with the heat evolved from the combination of a suitable mixture of chemicals ; and a ' thermo-generator ' was soon designed, which consisted of a tin containing the DA and the heating mixture in separate compartments and which weighed two or three pounds.[3]

[1] If cigarette smoke, which is also a ' particulate cloud,' is blown through the fold of a tightly stretched handkerchief, the greater part of it will be seen to have been deposited on the fabric. The explanation of the success of the mechanical filter and the failure of the chemical apparatus is that particles, such as we are considering, consist of aggregations of molecules and only possess slight ' Brownian movement ' : this enables them to penetrate between the interstices of the granular contents of the respirator container. True gases, owing to their violent molecular motion, have a greatly increased chance of collision with the active chemicals in the container and of being absorbed by them. This was also the reason why our NC shells and bombs succeeded in penetrating the German masks, as the stannic chloride element of NC, being also in the form of particles, carried the chloropicrin gas with it.

[2] Mr Churchill, who, with the Duke of Westminster, was dining at our mess one night about this time, was invited to test this discovery for himself, but he excused himself and added, " But I have a very vivid imagination ! "

[3] Dr Hanslian says in his book that the French reported finding, in August 1917, in German trenches which they had raided, apparatus designed on this principle which, it was supposed, were intended for employment in combination with a

By permission of the War Office.

The " M " device in action.   (Taken from the air).

Unfortunately great difficulty was experienced at first in finding a practical method for the manufacture of DA itself, until our chemists evolved a process which was superior to the one known to have been employed by the Germans and was much less costly.

In chamber experiments with DA in a concentration of one part in a million of air it was proved that effective penetration of all types of German drums, including the best and most recent patterns issued, was complete in fifteen seconds, and experienced observers equipped with these masks suffered severe discomfort after one minute and were compelled to retire after only two or three minutes' exposure, suffering acutely in the nose and throat. It was also proved in field trials that under favourable weather conditions the German mask was easily penetrated at a distance of several miles.

In the course of these investigations at home a still better substance for our purpose than DA was discovered which had not been previously known. This was the analagous compound diphenylamine chlorarsine, which was labelled DM. It was equal to DA in its physical action, was actually superior to it as a penetrant and was found to be effective in concentrations of one in 25 millions. The DM cloud also travelled better and farther.

It was now my business, as expert adviser to the Commander-in-Chief, to suggest to the General Staff how these arsenic particulate clouds could be put to the best use in the special tactical situation of the moment; and in another memorandum addressed to the C.G.S. in May 1918 I explained the new discovery and once more pressed for the employment of a cloud attack on a vast scale to precede an infantry advance.

The plan of attack was similar to the one previously put forward for gas; but as the particulate cloud was effective in one-hundredth the concentration of the gas cloud, and the German protection against it was non-existent, complete success was absolutely certain if only the secret could be kept.

The proposed assembly of the infantry assaulting columns would be simpler than in the former proposal,

chlorine-phosgene cloud. The installation was destroyed by artillery fire and never came into use. The design cannot have been satisfactory, or it would have been persevered with.

because there was no longer any need to use a retired line for the discharge. In fact, it was not even desirable, because the discharge would now be a much shorter one, and the 'M' device (as the thermo-generators came to be called) would have to be used on a grand scale—hundreds of thousands being set alight with a simple friction lighter, as in the case of the familiar smoke candles—so that the infantry themselves would be called upon to assist the Special Brigade in handling the tins. The latter were not dangerous under artillery bombardment, like gas cylinders, and in any case the hostile fire would be silenced in the course of a few minutes by the cloud and by our own intensive gas bombardment.

Tanks would be employed, as before, to exploit the success gained.

Another new tactical consideration arose in the circumstance that although DM or DA could be depended upon to incapacitate the enemy completely by causing almost intolerable pain and discomfort its effect was not lethal and it was only temporary ; so that it was essential for the cloud to be followed up as soon and as far as possible. Moreover, the device would only be useful for a period of a few weeks at the most, as, except for the shortage of rubber, it was easy to modify the design of the German mask with a view to providing protection against it.[1]

It will be noticed that the intention, with the 'M' device, was not merely—as in the case of the German employment of this same arsenic compound in their shells and our own use of chloropicrin—to cause the enemy to remove his mask and so expose himself to lethal gas discharged at the same time, but actually to disable the enemy completely, if only temporarily, in spite of the use of the masks, through the penetration of the latter resulting from the far more effective method adopted of dispersing the 'smoke.'

The 'M' device would open the road for our infantry in the minimum of time, without any warning and practically without loss ; and trench warfare would be converted into open warfare in a day. Its possibilities were such that even at the risk of the war ending without the opportunity arising of using it, it must be kept in the background until

---

[1] Mr Beverley Nichols is misinformed when he says, in 'Cry Havoc,' that up till now no efficient respirator has been invented to protect against the various arsenical smokes.

vast quantities had been accumulated in France. This was the most effective chemical weapon ever devised and we must make the maximum use of it, in contrast with the waste of opportunity which was the result of the first use of gas by the Germans and of our premature employment of a few tanks in the battle of the Somme.

These proposals were accepted by the C.G.S., and the Ministry of Munitions was requested to arrange for a very large output of the 'M' device. Stokes mortar bombs and Livens drums were also to be adapted for DM filling.

A large-scale trial was made by the French at Cahors, in the South of France, in July 1918, with 1000 cylinders containing a harmless smoke-producing substance, at which some of the Special Brigade officers and I were present, the object being to study closely and on a really large scale the effect of ground features and irregularities on the progress of the cloud. And later, in September, in a field trial in which only forty-eight 'M' generators were lighted at intervals over a period of ten minutes it was found that in a wind of five to six m.p.h. the latest patterns of German mask were penetrated effectively in three or four minutes at a distance of 2000 yards, a sample of the cloud being taken to show a concentration as low as one in 2,700,000. In another experiment carried out still later at Entressen, on the Mediterranean coast, near the mouth of the Rhone, in a wind of seven to ten m.p.h., new German respirators of the latest pattern (11. c. 11., some fitted with the extensions intended to give protection against the Blue Cross shells) were all penetrated at 3000 metres in three to five minutes, and at 5000 metres in five to seven minutes.

Steps were taken at the same time to design a new British respirator to give our own troops protection against the arsenic cloud, and the 'Green Band' container was the result. This not only served the purpose mentioned (by the inclusion of a few layers of cheese-cloth), but by the substitution of more active charcoal and chemical granules it gave better protection against high concentrations of all the other gases than any other mask previously issued, while at the same time there was less resistance to breathing. It was being secretly made in large numbers at the time of the Armistice, but strict orders were given that it was not to be issued until the last moment, as an examination of its construction by the enemy would have given a clue to the purpose of its introduction.

The ' M ' device was never used in France ; but if its secret had been kept there is not the slightest doubt that its effect on the enemy, both moral and physical, would have been overwhelming ; and if it had been properly and fully exploited it would have had a more important bearing on the course of the war than any other measure that was put to a practical trial on the battlefield or that was even considered.

It is, of course, no longer a secret, and it was actually used at Archangel, after the Armistice, but not in the way originally intended, as, owing to the extent of the forests there, containers had to be dropped from aeroplanes. Lord Rawlinson wrote of it that North Russian experience had shown that, used in the proper way, " the generator is a most formidable weapon, and the effects of the gas were exactly what was expected."

Exaggerated rumours of its annihilating effects naturally spread after hostilities ceased ; and since that date writers of great distinction, enthusiasts in a cause but ill-informed, have made sensational forecasts of the fate awaiting the civil populations of great cities in the next war from gas bombs of this and other types, dropped from aeroplanes.

Here are some of the opinions I have seen expressed by these well-intentioned terrorists :—

" The collapse of civilisation under circumstances of unimaginable horror—that, and nothing else—is what a future war on the grand scale has in store for us and ours. So far as there can be any certainty in human affairs, this thing is certain."

" Millions of human lives would be lost in a few hours by a gas bombing attack."

" It was no fairy-tale to state that London could, within twenty minutes, be reduced to a collection of smouldering ruins over which hung a cloud of poisonous vapour."

" One single bomb filled with modern asphyxiant gas dropped, say, on Piccadilly Circus would kill everybody in an area from Regent's Park to the Thames."

" Science was able to put a whole nation to sleep for twenty-four hours by gases given off from aeroplanes controlled from a distance."

" With the aid of ' Lewisite,' the most deadly poison gas yet produced, London's population could be choked to death in three hours."

It is not my purpose to enter into controversy with these writers in this book, but I would like to say in passing that in my opinion all these statements are very wide of the truth, and that they are likely, if taken seriously, to foster, through fear of the unknown, the panic which would be the main object of hostile aircraft despatched on a gas-bombing mission—a panic which would, of course, result in additional air squadrons being withdrawn from the theatre of war for home defence.[1]

While fully admitting the grave danger to cities of attacks from the air I do not believe that gas in bombs or in the form of a spray would inflict anything like as much loss of life as H.E. I cannot go into any detail here, but I might point out that the conditions in a town are very different from those on the battlefield: houses, for instance, if their occupants are taught to use them properly, can be made tolerably safe places of refuge against gas, whereas they increase the effect of H.E. owing to the danger of falling masonry and outbreaks of fire.

I know that in expressing this opinion I expose myself to the accusation (made by a Swiss lady enthusiast in the cause of no more war) of being " one of the people of the old school who close their eyes to these dangers with an incredulous smile"; and I must content myself by quoting Mr Lloyd George, who writes: " The conscience of a devotee is an eccentric thing and argument never converts but only exasperates a true believer! " ('War Memoirs').

The almost accidental discovery of the valuable use to which DA could be put in particulate clouds was one result of the habit of keeping at our headquarters a small museum of interesting exhibits which consisted of samples of the gases obtained from German shells and various other components. On another occasion, however, a private investigation of a bottle of mustard gas had a less fortunate result, when through some mischance a trace of this substance found its way one day to the seat of the chair occupied by one of the members of my staff. When

[1] Note this entry in Dr Addison's ' Four and a half years': " The people are very angry because the German aeroplanes got to London " (on July 7th, 1917) " and sailed over it practically unmolested. The raid provides a striking example either of coincidence or of well organised espionage, seeing that the two fighting squadrons which have hitherto been kept over here to combat raiders returned to France on Friday evening " (July 6th).

he reached hospital, in due course, he inquired of the doctor what treatment for the burn it was proposed to employ; and when told he expressed strong disapproval. Instead of the bicarbonate of soda dressing he insisted on the carbonate being used, and in view of the position he was known to occupy in the Gas Directorate the doctor good-naturedly let him have his own way. He thereupon made up a thick paste which he applied himself to the affected surface, adjusted the bandage and retired to bed. Next morning, however, he realised his mistake when it was found, much to his chagrin as well as the embarrassment of the nurse, that the paste had set hard and had reproduced an exact model of part of his person. The treatment subsequently followed orthodox lines.

I have referred in a previous chapter to the ruse which was adopted from time to time by the enemy of deliberately spreading rumours of the manufacture by them of new and powerful battle gases. Such rumours became very insistent early in 1918. The reports were numerous and they came from many different sources, but they deceived nobody, as it was obvious that they were purposely disseminated, which would not have been the case if the intention of using a new gas really existed.

But the enemy's object in spreading these reports gave rise to some speculation. One suggestion was that the Germans had obtained information of the vast scale on which the Allies were preparing to employ mustard gas against them; and that they had even heard of the ' M ' device and realised the difficulty which faced them, through the shortage of rubber, of providing themselves with protection against it. It would be to their advantage, therefore, if the Council of the International Red Cross could be induced (as actually happened) to make an appeal to all the belligerents, even at this late hour, to abandon the use of gas on humanitarian grounds. By the time such an appeal could have any practical result the enemy would have already launched their March offensive, for the success of which they relied very largely on their artillery gas bombardment.

I do not think, however, that this was the correct explanation. It was true that by this time the Allied production of mustard gas was well advanced, but the ' M ' device was still in the embryo stage. It was

known to very few people, and the difficulty of manufacturing DA itself had not yet been satisfactorily
overcome.

In my opinion the rumours were circulated in the
mistaken hope that they would create a feeling of alarm
in the Allied armies. The new artillery gas tactics which
the enemy were intending to employ had proved so remarkably successful in Russia, and so much depended on
similar results being obtained on the Western front, that
every effort was made by the German Supreme Command,
relying on the important psychological consideration, to
increase to the utmost the moral effect of the coming gas
bombardments through the feeling of uncertainty and fear
of the unknown.

I am explaining in a later chapter how these efforts
failed.

CHAPTER XV.

ON the defensive side of my staff Hartley was of the greatest assistance to me, as he had had long experience in the gas schools and was familiar with the difficulties of enforcing gas discipline among the troops. General Thuillier, before resuming his infantry command, had already introduced the small box respirator into the army, but modifications of it—*e.g.*, the substitution of triplex for plain glass eye-pieces—were constantly under trial by selected personnel at the front, and other improvements were introduced from time to time.

The accompanying diagram shows how the whole of the Gas Directorate was organised at the end of the war. The first duty on the defensive side was, of course, the protection of the British troops against hostile gas attacks, but the department was so constituted that it carried out automatically an almost equally important rôle as a complete and most efficient chemical intelligence service. Each of the sixty-four divisions, the eighteen army corps and the five armies had a 'Chemical Adviser' (in the division he was called the 'Division Gas Officer'), whose duty it was to advise the commander to whom he was responsible on all matters of protection against gas, as well as to instruct the troops in the use of their respirators and to ensure that the latter, as well as all the arrangements for the 'collective' gas alarm, were always in good condition and understood.

The division commanders, of course, supported their efforts energetically, and an amusing story was told of one of them who was determined to tighten up the gas discipline of his troops. On some occasion he was paying a visit to the front trench system, accompanied by a staff officer, but when they reached the communication trench they realised for the first time that they had for-

ORGANISATION OF GAS SERVICES, B.E.F., FRANCE.

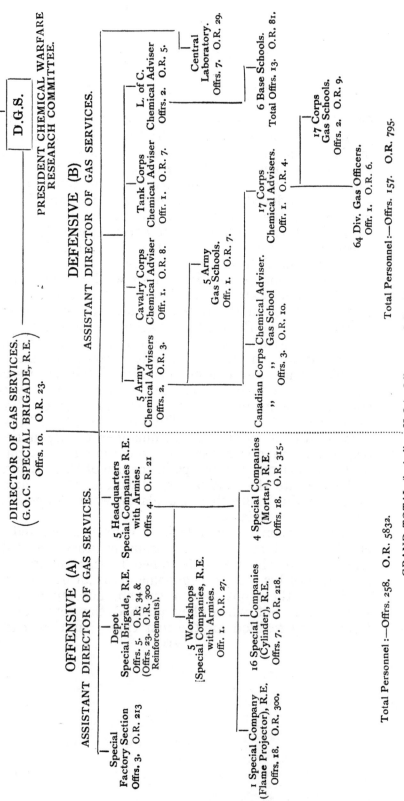

MINISTER OF MUNITIONS.

D.G.S.

PRESIDENT CHEMICAL WARFARE
RESEARCH COMMITTEE.

(DIRECTOR OF GAS SERVICES.)
(G.O.C. SPECIAL BRIGADE, R.E.)
Offrs. 10.   O.R. 23.

OFFENSIVE (A)
ASSISTANT DIRECTOR OF GAS SERVICES.

Special Factory Section
Offrs. 3.   O.R. 213

Depot Special Brigade, R.E.
Offrs. 5.   O.R. 34 &
(Offrs. 23.   O.R. 300
Reinforcements).

5 Headquarters Special Companies R.E. with Armies.
Offrs. 4.   O.R. 21.

5 Workshops Special Companies, R.E. with Armies.
Offr. 1.   O.R. 27.

1 Special Company (Flame Projector), R.E.
Offrs. 18.   O.R. 300.

16 Special Companies (Cylinder), R.E.
Offrs. 7.   O.R. 218.

4 Special Companies (Mortar), R.E.
Offrs. 18.   O.R. 315.

Total Personnel :—Offrs. 258.   O.R. 5832.

DEFENSIVE (B)
ASSISTANT DIRECTOR OF GAS SERVICES.

5 Army Chemical Advisers
Offrs. 2.   O.R. 3.

Cavalry Corps Chemical Adviser
Offr. 1.   O.R. 8.

Tank Corps Chemical Adviser
Offr. 1.   O.R. 7.

L. of C. Chemical Adviser
Offrs. 2.   O.R. 5.

Central Laboratory.
Offrs. 7.   O.R. 29.

5 Army Gas Schools.
Offr. 1.   O.R. 7.

Canadian Corps Chemical Adviser,
,,   Offrs. 3.   O.R. 10.

Gas School
Offrs. 3.   O.R. 10.

17 Corps Chemical Advisers.
Offr. 1.   O.R. 4.

6 Base Schools.
Total Offrs. 13.   O.R. 81.

17 Corps Gas Schools.
Offrs. 2.   O.R. 9.

64 Div. Gas Officers.
Offr. 1.   O.R. 6.

Total Personnel :—Offrs. 157.   O.R. 795.

GRAND TOTAL (including H.Q.), Offrs. 425, O.R. 6650 = 7075.

gotten to bring their own gas masks with them! Rather than return some distance to the car they stopped two men who were leaving the line, took over their masks, strapped them in the regulation position and proceeded on their way. On reaching the front line the General found a platoon sergeant, and collected a number of men around him and put them through the drill, himself timing the period occupied by them in removing the masks from the satchels and in the completion of the adjustment.

"Very bad," he growled. "Just as I thought : the gas discipline here is very poor. And your masks look none too good."

"Now watch me," he continued, as he handed the watch to the A.D.C. ; and men gathered round to learn how the thing should be done.

On the signal being given he plunged his hand into the satchel, but to his great discomfiture and the delight of his audience all that he withdrew from it and exposed to view were a packet of ' fags ' and a pair of old socks !

There was a strong desire in many of the formations to appoint Brigade Gas Officers in addition to the ones in divisions, but this policy was discouraged by G.H.Q. as it was thought that specialisation was being carried too far throughout the army, thus absolving regimental officers from their full share of responsibility. Such appointments were, nevertheless, frequently made un-officially, and in at least one case this led to disastrous results, when, through an error of judgment on the part of one of these unauthorised officers, 178 casualties, which included the whole of a Brigade Staff, occurred after a German mustard gas bombardment. Other unofficial appointments were made to Divisional artillery, Corps heavy artillery and Corps troops.

In November 1917 the anti-gas schools in divisions were abolished and Corps schools were substituted to free the Division Gas Officers for other work and with the idea of centralising training ; and it was the intention, towards the close of the war, to extend this policy still further and form five central gas schools as anti-gas wings of the General Central Schools.

Throughout the war anti-gas training followed a definite

scheme, which was laid down in a book called 'Defence against Gas.'

The commanders of the Cavalry Corps, the Tank Corps and the 'Lines of Communication' had additional Chemical Advisers, who were directly under the Director at G.H.Q. The last-named Chemical Adviser had the important duty of seeing that all reinforcements arriving in the theatre of war were familiar with the steps to be taken for their own protection before they joined their units. In October 1917 there were two anti-gas schools each at Havre, Rouen and Etaples, and one each at Abbeville, Boulogne and Calais, all under Captain Lambert; but these were reduced later to a total of six. The importance of the routine duties of the 'C.A., L. of C." may be judged from the fact that during 1918 alone 1,557,809 of all ranks were dealt with at these base schools.

In the later stages of the war these three C.A.'s, together with the five army C.A.'s and the head of the Central Laboratory, met regularly under the presidency of the Director to discuss all matters connected with respirators, gas training and schools ; so that on the defensive side, too, unity of doctrine was ensured. They also took it in turns to attend the meetings of the various scientific committees at home, in order to maintain liaison with them ; and one of them, Barley, went to England for two months from May 1917 to co-ordinate the anti-gas training of the Home Forces.

The Central Laboratory was established originally as an emergency chemical laboratory for classifying and opening up German gas shells, and for making analyses of their fillings and of gas-contaminated earth, water and clothing. But gradually miscellaneous work was undertaken for other departments (such as in connection with carbon monoxide poisoning resulting from firing machine-guns in confined spaces) and for the Flying Corps, which might perhaps have been more conveniently carried out at home.

Periodical routine examinations were also made of captured German masks and of British respirators which were withdrawn from units for the purpose.

It will be seen that the offensive and defensive branches of the Directorate (outside G.H.Q.) were entirely separated. It would have been more convenient if the duties of the officers commanding Special Companies could have been combined with those of the Army Chemical Advisers, but it must be remembered that the latter were appointed for their scientific attainments and had no first-hand knowledge of Special Brigade operations. Later in the war the principle was adopted of filling all appointments on the defensive side from officers who had served in the Special Brigade, and in the course of time the officers and men in the two branches would have become interchangeable. Monier-Williams was one instance in point. He joined me originally at Helfaut as a personal scientific adviser. He was appointed later to command one of the four battalions of the Special Brigade on the formation of the latter, and then became in turn O.C. Special Companies at Fifth Army Headquarters and Chemical Adviser to the Fifth Army. Edwardes-Ker, too, gave up the command of " L " Company to take Hartley's place as Chemical Adviser to the Third Army, and he finally succeeded Hartley again at my headquarters as Assistant Director (B.).

Attached to the headquarters of the Special Companies in each army there was a medical officer who was present at as many as possible of the gas operations and attended men accidentally gassed, so that they became experts in gas treatment. In addition, Lieutenant-Colonel Douglas (now Lecturer in Physiology, St John's College, Oxford), who had served previously as one of these medical officers, was attached to my own headquarters as ' Physiological Adviser,' and he not only kept in touch with the medical officers, but also with all the large British hospitals in the theatre of war in which gas cases were treated, and with the distinguished medical consultants in France who were employed by the War Office. When any unusual gas symptoms were reported from any part of the front he made special journeys of investigation and sometimes stayed for days watching the progress of the patients, it being important to recognise the appearance of any new enemy chemical substance as soon as possible. It is not surprising that with the amount and variety of the experience he gained in this manner, Douglas is now recognised as the chief living authority on gas sickness.

It will be remembered that owing to shortage of ordinary ammunition our artillery was late in taking gas ammunition into use. When gas shells came to be employed, from the spring of 1917 onwards, it became the practice for the Corps Chemical Advisers to be consulted by artillery commanders as to the most suitable gas ammunition to use for particular purposes and the most favourable weather conditions in which to carry out their bombardments.

Particulars of all these shoots were sent to me monthly, and I summarised them for circulation under the title 'Employment of lethal and lachrymatory shell' (S.S. 134), instances being quoted for general information and guidance of any particular successes achieved, such as the neutralisation of hostile batteries and the tactics that had been employed for the purpose.

German gas activity was also watched very carefully, and similar monthly summaries were issued of 'hostile gas activity,' in which all the more important gas bombardments were tabulated, and details were given of the nature of the gas used on each occasion, the approximate number of rounds fired, any variations that had been noted in the tactics employed and the casualties which resulted, the last being expressed as a ratio to the number of rounds fired. This ratio proved, ordinarily, a good check on the gas discipline of the units exposed to a bombardment, and it varied from one to one, to one to seventy shells fired, and served as a rough guide as to the necessity for making a special investigation into the cause of the losses.

Soon after the appearance of mustard gas[1] it became obvious that the least carelessness on the part of the troops would result in an increase in the number of casualties, so that I recommended a discontinuance of the wound stripe which had been awarded until then in all gas cases. Later on it became necessary to take sterner measures in special instances when the ratio referred to above appeared unduly high, and Courts of Inquiry were held to investigate the circumstances and to bring home the responsibility to any officers and N.C.O.'s who were guilty of carelessness or neglect of precautions, though it was recognised that owing to the insidious nature of mustard gas

---

[1] Its scientific name was $\beta\beta$ dichlorethyl sulphide, so that when we came to use it ourselves in shells the latter were labelled BB. The substance itself was referred to as HS (Hun stuff) : the French named it Yperite, because it was first used at Ypres.

the number of casualties could probably only be reduced by about half, even with the strictest discipline. One such Court was ordered to assemble on 21st March 1918 to ascertain the cause of some 3000 or 4000 mustard gas casualties which resulted from the bombardment of the Cambrai Salient between 11th and 15th March, and I was on my way to attend this Court at Ypres, in the Cambrai Salient, on the morning of the 21st when the great battle commenced.

Still further steps were taken to reduce our losses from mustard gas. Skin lesions and inflammation of the eyes were the only symptoms in the majority of cases; but although these injuries were slight, the number of men affected threatened at times, unless the strictest measures were taken, to amount to the equivalent of several divisions and to constitute a serious drain on the strength of the British Army.

An exaggerated view was taken in the first few months of its use of the real invaliding value of mustard gas, partly owing to its novelty and the many and varied symptoms that presented themselves, and partly from ignorance of its possible after-effects; but further experience showed that under skilled medical treatment 80 per cent of the average mustard gas casualties evacuated from army areas could be cured in eight weeks, and a considerable proportion could be made fit for duty in four weeks, whereas inquiry disclosed the fact that 80 per cent of the average cases were sent to England for treatment, where they remained for two or three months, and even longer.

Douglas co-operated with Colonel Elliot of the Army Medical Service in the Boulogne area in an attempt to conserve the strength of the B.E.F. by reducing this period of invalidism, and eventually it was found necessary for only 25 per cent of the cases to be evacuated to England, while about 90 per cent of the remainder were dealt with at convalescent depots in France, from which they returned to duty within twenty-eight days. A great saving in man-power was effected in this way, and just before the war ended steps were taken to apply the valuable experience gained in the Boulogne area to the whole British Army; and there is no doubt that if hostilities had continued the 'hospitalisation' of mustard gas cases would have been prevented in the majority of cases, and that a very definite reduction in the period of invalidism would have resulted.

S.S. 534, 'Defence against Gas,' was a pamphlet which began on a modest scale, but which was revised from time to time and went through several editions. In it were described the precautions to be taken for individual as well as collective protection, and it was profusely illustrated. The enemy apparently thought so highly of it that in a captured order of the Seventeenth German Army, dated 15th July 1918, a flattering reference was made to it, and orders were given for the methods advocated in it for the gas-proofing of dug-outs to be insisted on.

There were many other publications to be prepared besides the ones I have mentioned, and among them were summaries of the gas war, which were prepared from time to time for the use of the commanders of British armies in all the other theatres of war.

Masses of reports had also to be read weekly, relating to the experimental work being carried on at Porton, as well as by American scientists : the latter in particular were very voluminous.

The Division Gas Officers were always very much on the alert for the appearance of any new chemical substances from the German side, and a constant stream of ' dud ' gas shells arrived at the Central Laboratory, where they were opened up and examined, of course at great personal risk.

Thus on the occasion of the first mustard gas bombardment on 12th July 1917, the fact that a new gas had appeared ' smelling slightly of garlic, or mustard,' was, of course, immediately recognised, in spite of the fact that the enemy tried to mask its presence by firing diphosgene shells, shrapnel and H.E. in the same bursts of fire ; and two blind shells were recovered on the first day by Monier-Williams, and their contents were explored, one in the Central Laboratory and the other in London. Hartley, Douglas and I at once visited the scene in order to collect further information. Only two days later, on 14th July, although mustard gas had not yet been positively identified by chemical analysis, its composition was correctly surmised and sufficient information of its nature and effects had been ascertained to enable G.H.Q. to telegraph a warning to the five army commanders, with instructions as to the precautions to be taken to minimise its effects; and in a circular letter dated 16th July the shells and their markings were described, the symptoms and effects were explained very fully and exactly and the chief causes of the casualties were specified, as well as the lessons that had been learnt. In fact, even at the present day there is very little that could be added to the information contained in that paper.

It is interesting to note that it was the men of General Thuillier's 15th Division who were the first victims of the new gas (there were over 2000 altogether, including 50 to 60 dead); and that the medical officers on the spot of the Army concerned (the Fifth) estimated on 15th July that the majority of those affected by ' this mustard oil lachrymator ' should be fit to return to duty in from seven to fourteen days, it being thought at first that two separate gases were responsible for the symptoms that were being treated.

As an example of the vagaries of the human sensation of smell, I may say that although everybody agreed that mustard gas had a distinct and unpleasant odour it was variously described by patients in hospital and others as resembling mustard, rubber, vulcanite, dead horses, diseased vegetables, petrol, garlic and lamp oil!

Information was collected and circulated with the same rapidity after every German innovation in the gas war, such as the introduction of phosgene in the cloud attack of December 1915 and of chloropicrin. Other instances were the employment for the first time towards the end of 1917 of sudden bursts of lethal shells, in imitation of our 4-inch Stokes mortar tactics; the addition of red and purple aniline dyes to the mustard gas fillings, which, though harmless in themselves, enabled the enemy's troops to recognise these particular shell craters from their appearance, and which, of course, afforded the same valuable indication of danger to our own men; and the appearance of Blue Cross and of another ' double purpose ' shell early in 1918, when Yellow Cross ammunition was employed with a greatly increased bursting charge, the object of which was the finer atomisation of the mustard gas on explosion so as to reduce its persistency on the ground

and enable troops to traverse the infected area in a shorter
interval after the bombardment had ceased without incur-
ring risk.

From time to time I addressed special memoranda to
the C.G.S. which summarised recent experience of German
gas tactics, and which even made forecasts of the enemy's
intentions. Examples of this were a warning of the results
of the use of mustard gas in open warfare, in the absence
of gas-proof dug-outs, and of its probable effects on troops
which were arriving in large numbers in the summer of
1918, with insufficient gas training and no previous experience of gas warfare.

Another forecast which received very remarkable veri-
fication was in regard to the probable use of gas by the
enemy in their spring offensive in 1918. On 24th February
1918, G.H.Q. issued this in the form of a printed circular,
in which the following warning appeared: " Owing to
the persistence of Yellow Cross gas if it is fired into our
forward areas the targets would be selected in such a way
that they might be avoided by the attacking infantry,
who would otherwise be affected by the gas. Special
attention should therefore be directed to the gaps which
may be left between gas-infected areas. The enemy will
probably direct his main efforts to the neutralisation of
our artillery in the preparation for the assault, in which
case little registration will be necessary, as areas, rather
than specific targets, will be taken under fire." Instructions followed for the evacuation, wherever possible, of
mustard gas-infected areas and for the selection of alternative positions for headquarters and for reserve troops,
and stress was laid on the necessity for gas-proof dug-outs
for battery personnel.

This warning order disproves the claim made in General
Ludendorff's book: " Uncertainty is of the very nature
of war. The enemy never knew our intentions. We always
surprised him, except on the 15th July 1918, an occasion
when " (in the attack on the French position at Rheims)
" we made things too easy for him."

So far was the British Army from being surprised on
21st March that the exact front of the German assault
was known accurately, as it was actually marked out for
us by the enemy on the map by the preliminary use he
made of mustard gas.

He even gave us an indication of the date of the coming attack when we noted the moment that mustard gas ceased to be used, though, as a matter of fact, more precise information was forthcoming from deserters.

I will explain how this transpired. I have said that the Army Chemical Advisers sent in periodical reports of hostile gas bombardments; but from the date of the G.H.Q. circular referred to, during the critical period before the great battle began, full particulars of all of these were telephoned to me as each one occurred, and they were entered up on a map of the whole front, in different colours to correspond with the gas used, the estimated number of shells fired being indicated by the scale of the entry. This map is reproduced on the opposite page, and it was shown to the General Staff every twenty-four hours.

From the 11th to the 15th March 1918, after three months of comparative inactivity, the enemy bombarded the whole British front heavily with mustard gas, particularly the Ypres Salient and the Cambrai area. In addition, large numbers of Green and Blue Cross shells were used against strong-points and the various headquarters. The most extensive of these bombardments was directed against the Cambrai Salient and consisted entirely of Yellow Cross shells; and on the night of the 10th March and the three following nights some 150,000 rounds must have fallen in this area.

On the 15th the Yellow Cross bombardments continued elsewhere, *but they ceased entirely on the Third and Fifth Army fronts, except opposite Cambrai.* The significance of this was recognised as confirming other indications that had been given that these two armies would bear the brunt of the attack and that the latter would be launched on either side of the Cambrai Salient, 6 days later.

This is exactly what happened; and, although a very large number of gas shells were fired on the 21st (1705 German batteries came into action, the majority without previous registration), these contained nothing but Green and Blue Cross gas. The Cambrai Salient was not attacked at all on the 21st, the enemy's intention having been to penetrate deeply into the British area on either side of it so as to isolate the garrison there.

The green line on the map shows the front of the attack and the extent of the German advance on 21st March, and it bears out exactly the forecast that had been made of the enemy's plan, based on his employment of gas shells.

It is very interesting to compare this map and my forecast, which it was intended to illustrate with the German plan of battle as it has been described by General Ludendorff. The latter describes how his artillery was to carry out a short powerful bombardment, lasting only a few hours, which was expected to paralyse our artillery and keep our infantry sheltering in their dug-outs, in emerging from which they were to be overwhelmed.

" It was decided to strike between Croisille, south of Arras, and Moeuvres, and, omitting the Cambrai re-entrant, between Villers Guislain and the Oise, south of St Quentin," with feints elsewhere and subsidiary attacks on the two flanks.

It will be seen that it was the intention " to cut off the enemy holding the Cambrai re-entrant without entering the gas-inundated area." " This concentration of forty or fifty divisions had not been observed by the enemy, nor had it been reported to him by his highly developed secret service. Nor did the enemy discover anything by other means. I must assume this ; otherwise his defensive measures would have been more effective and his reserves would have arrived more quickly." [1] " On the 18th or 19th March two men deserted from a trench-mortar company. They are alleged to have given information of the impending attack. At noon on the 20th, G.H.Q. had to face the great decision whether the attack was to commence on the 21st or be put off. . . . And yet our artillery relied on gas for its effect, and that was dependent on the direction and strength of the wind. I had to rely on the forecast submitted to me at 11 A.M. by my meteorologist, Lieutenant Dr Schmaus.

" Up till the morning of the 20th the strength and direction were by no means very favourable ; indeed it seemed almost necessary to put off the attack. That would have been very hard to do. At 12 noon the Army Groups were told that the programme would be carried out. Now it could no longer be stopped. Everything must run its

---

[1] Failure to meet this attack with reserves was due to the disagreement between Generals Haig and Pétain, the French Commander-in-Chief, as to where they should be located. The French expected the first German attack to be directed against their front.

course. The rest was in the hands of fate." (Compare
this with the similar situation which Sir Douglas Haig
had to face on the morning of 25th September 1915.)
" On the 21st just before 4 A.M. the battle began with a
tremendous crash on a front of 70 kilometres between
Croisille and La Fère. For about two hours the whole
of our artillery engaged the enemy's batteries, then most
of it switched on to trench bombardment. A little before
9 A.M. most of our fire—only a portion being left on
hostile batteries and special points — was concentrated
to form a barrage. Our infantry advanced to the
assault."

The map which has been referred to achieved some
notoriety, as a few days later a French Staff Officer arrived
at my headquarters from the Grand Quartier-Général,
and Barrett, my draughtsman, sat up all night making a
copy of it. I never heard whether this method of fore-
casting the enemy's plans proved of any value to our
Allies, but it was of the utmost importance to us in the
subsequent German attacks against the British front.
For instance, prior to the German advance on the 9th
April no mustard gas was used (see map on opposite page)
on the front between Armentières and the La Bassée
canal, but only on the flanks, and this was correctly
interpreted as foreshadowing an attack on the sector held
by the Portuguese troops. On the night of 7th April,
Armentières and Houplines were very heavily bombarded,
and 20,000 Yellow Cross shells were estimated to have
been fired into the former town between 8 P.M. on the 7th
and 11 A.M. on the 8th ; but on the front actually attacked
by the German infantry only Green and Blue Cross shells
were used, as was the case in the battle of 21st March.
Armentières itself was not attacked directly on the 9th
or subsequently, and information was received later that
German troops had been forbidden to enter its streets for
a fortnight.

Similar gas tactics were employed for the attacks on
Villers Bretonneux on 24th April, previous to which
20,000 rounds of Yellow Cross shells were calculated to
have been used ; and again between St Jans Cappel and
Wytschaete on 25th April. On each occasion Yellow Cross
shells were fired only on the flanks and on distant targets,
thus indicating not only the fronts of the attacks, but also

the lines beyond which the enemy did not propose to advance.

In the latter battle fighting took place in which both our troops and the Germans wore respirators, and the smell of their Green Cross gas was so strong over Kemmel hill that it was noticed by our low-flying aeroplanes. Men of the 233rd German Division stated that their masks were not proof against their own gas, and many of the men were unable to advance through it.

As an illustration of the scale on which Yellow Cross was used in all this fighting, it may be mentioned that in one bombardment (between Douchy and Ayette on 13th April) the concentration of mustard gas was so great that, although it has only a faint odour, it was recognisable from its smell a mile down-wind. In the bombardment of Armentières so much of it was used that the liquid was observed to be running in the gutters in the streets.

Except for the first cloud attacks at Ypres in 1915, the introduction of mustard gas was the sole event in the gas war from which the Germans derived any substantial advantage. It had also one important effect on our own organisation. Both Sir John French and Sir Douglas Haig had been made aware all along that use was not being made of the whole of the scientific talent that was available at home for research work, and that the latter was paralysed during certain periods as a result of changes in the organisation of the departments in the Ministry of Munitions. But they had declined to interfere in what they considered to be the business of the War Office.

However, on 10th August 1917 the latter wrote indignantly to complain of the Germans having forestalled us in the use of a chemical substance (mustard gas) which had proved to be of such great military value, and he suggested that very energetic action required to be taken by the authority responsible for research work and supply.

The result of this letter was a visit to France by the War Minister, Lord Derby, and Mr Churchill, and at a meeting held to consider the matter it was proposed that the Commander-in-Chief should himself appoint a senior officer from France to reorganise the departments concerned. General Thuillier was thereupon nominated for this duty, much against his personal inclination, and he gave up the command of the 15th Division, which he had only held for four months, and became, on 17th October 1917, President of the Chemical Warfare Committee and Controller of the Chemical Warfare Department in the Ministry of Munitions in London.

The first real step was now taken to enlist the whole of the scientific resources of the country. The new Chemical Warfare Committee became a much larger, more powerful and representative body; and in addition to the staff of the Imperial College of Science on whom the greater part of the burden of research work had fallen hitherto, the services were enlisted of nearly all the eminent chemists, physicists and physiologists who were associated with the various colleges and universities in the country—the majority of whom accepted no remuneration whatever for their work— and qualified members of the Special Brigade were recalled for duty at home; so that at the time of the Armistice thirty-three different laboratories were available for research work into, and the preparation of, possible offensive compounds. At the same time some advance was made towards combining the offensive and defensive sides of chemical warfare in the Ministry (as had been done eighteen months earlier, in France), and a systematic search was begun of the whole of the chemical literature of England, France, Germany, Italy and Russia, in the hope of finding the mention of some new offensive agent that would prove of military value and of forestalling the enemy in its use. This search was completed in a year, in the course of which more than 150,000 known organic and numerous inorganic chemical compounds were examined, many of which had some lethal or toxic properties as well as formidable scientific names. For example, in comparison with

> Iminophenyl-α-naphthylchloroarsine and
> Methylnitrosomethylaminoformate

the German di-phosgene—Trichlormethyl chloroformate— was almost elementary.

The experimental ground at Porton on Salisbury Plain was purchased in January 1916, and on this site complete laboratories were built and trenches and dug-outs constructed for the conduct of field experiments. Much of the work done here was of an unpleasant nature, and some of it was dangerous; but volunteers were always to be found who exposed themselves fearlessly in the chamber tests. In the case of the experiments made with mustard gas, experience showed that a man's skin became more sensitive after one exposure, and the only satisfactory course was to use 'virgin skin.' There was, of course, no scarcity of this commodity in the country, even late in the war, but provision had to be made for a constant supply of new-comers among the experimental staff.

Whenever progress with some new and promising substance had reached a certain experimental stage I arranged to attend the final trials at Porton, and, of course, had to come over from France for the purpose. I tested, personally, the effects of every gas that we took into use—repeatedly, in the case of those for which the penetration of the German mask was claimed.

Unfavourable weather conditions on the Plain sometimes necessitated the postponement of these trials from one day to another, and on the occasion of one such delay a large party of scientists and officials from the War Office and the Ministry of Munitions were assembled in a Salisbury hotel, among whom was one of our best-known chemists, who had established an additional reputation for his appreciation of a good meal and for the justice he did to it. At lunch this day he disposed of several gigantic helpings of beef-steak pudding, which were followed by others of fruit tart and cheese, while waiters ran backwards and forwards replenishing his tankard. The waiting company were impatient to enter the motor-cars for the journey to Porton, but they were loth to interrupt this performance, which they watched with interest and admiration. At last one of them ventured the remark: " You're doing very well, Professor," to which the latter gave a grudging admission. " So so," he replied, " but breakfast's my meal ! "

Colonel Crossley was the Superintendent at Porton, and as his establishment grew, the most valuable and careful scientific work was conducted, and a battery of artillery was stationed there to carry out bombardments of the trench system with gas shells. Animals, for the most part rats and mice (but late in the war the astonishing discovery was made that certain protozoa, paramœcia, served the same purpose as animals in some of the physiological tests), were exposed to the gas clouds, and the concentrations of the latter were measured with the minutest accuracy after being drawn into vacuum flasks by means of an electrical release device. From the results of these experiments deductions and recommendations were made to assist us in selecting the best materials which could be placed at our disposal.

Unfortunately the theoretical results arrived at did not always correspond with the practical experience obtained on the battlefield. For example, it was found at Porton that with a certain rate of artillery fire 100 per cent of mortality resulted in a certain series of experiments among the animals exposed to the gas in the trench, the bombardment having lasted, perhaps, for half an hour. In consequence a rate of fire in excess of this standard was thought to be unnecessary and uneconomical. On the other hand, we, in France, were of the opinion that for surprise effect no rate of fire could be excessive, and that a bombardment continued for more than a minute or two resulted in a waste of ammunition, except for harassing the enemy and causing him inconvenience.

Actually we had in the theatre of war itself a vast experimental ground, which, in its way, was of far greater value than Porton. We could observe the effects of the various gases we adopted and the results of the tactics we employed, as, for example, in the attempts to neutralise hostile batteries ; and we also accumulated a vast amount of information on these points from the statements of prisoners and from German official documents. In addition, owing to the careful watch kept by the chemical advisers, we knew what were the most effective tactics and substances employed by the enemy, while the causes of almost every group of casualties that occurred among our own troops were scrutinised, analysed and tabulated. Human beings provided the material for these experiments on both sides of No Man's Land, and the various weaknesses of human nature—ignorance, fatigue, carelessness, &c.—were vital factors ; while the gas discipline, which varied in the different units, the morale of the troops and even their occupations—for example, if carrying out a trench relief—at the moment of the attack, as well as the weather conditions, had important bearings on the results. None of these considerations could be repro-

duced at home, so that it was essential to estimate the
value of the compounds produced and the methods of
releasing them in strict relation to the conditions of the
battlefield.

Another example of the differences of opinion which
arose referred to the point of impact of an artillery gas
bombardment. At Porton the best results were obtained
by directing fire a little to the windward of a target and
allowing the gas to drift over the latter ; whereas experience in France showed that to produce any appreciable
effect the shells had to fall *in* the target itself. The reason
for this was that the chemical contents of gas shells are
so small (see footnote, p. 320) that *no* dispersion of gas
from drift can be afforded. I am referring here, of course,
to lethal shells of the phosgene type, but the direct hit
was, of course, still more important in the case of mustard
gas, and the chemical advisers were unanimous in regard
to its value in all circumstances.

The employment of prussic acid gas by the French and
the misuse of arsenic compounds by the Germans in their
Blue Cross shells, the results of which must have been
most disappointing in each case, provide further argu-
ments to show the necessity of supplementing the evidence
obtained in the laboratory and on the experimental ground
with that of the battlefield itself.

Apart from these matters of friendly dispute (which
were no doubt common to all the great experimental
departments engaged in war work), there had been throughout the war, especially in its early stages, a lack of close
contact between G.H.Q. and the scientific Committees at
home. There were frequent visits made from both sides,
but for months at a time, during periods of intensive fighting, these interchanges of opinion had been interrupted.
As a result we were sometimes at cross purposes, much
valuable experimental work was negatived, and there
were delays—for example, the provision of a gas bomb
for the 4-inch Stokes mortar was retarded because time
was wasted in designing one for the 3-inch infantry mortar,
which there was no intention of using for gas bombardments.

I do not imagine that the whole responsibility for this
state of affairs rested with the Ministry of Munitions, and
I am only mentioning it as it led to an important development in the last days of the war. After spending a year

in reorganising the research department and putting it on a thoroughly satisfactory basis, General Thuillier became anxious to resume his command in the field ; and to enable him to do so Mr Churchill suggested, in the autumn of 1918, that I should take his place in the Ministry of Munitions. This would have meant promotion to the rank of major-general, but a strong sentimental feeling tied me to the Special Brigade which I had raised and had commanded during the whole period of its existence, and it was eventually arranged that I should become President of the Chemical Warfare Committee and cross over from France to attend its weekly meetings, while the work of the department itself would be carried out by General Thuillier's Deputy Controller, Colonel Harrison. It was thought that by this arrangement G.H.Q., through me, would be able to give a general direction to the experimental work, and so co-ordinate the practical side of gas warfare with the great field of research which was still open at home.

I took over these additional duties in October, and as they reduced my already short week by two days it is impossible to say what would have been the result if the war had continued, especially as I now had a divided responsibility—to the Commander-in-Chief in France and to the Minister of Munitions, who was himself independent of the War Office !

General Thuillier was appointed to the command of the 23rd Division, and took part in the final successful advance of the Italian armies across the Piave River. About the same time Colonel Harrison died—he, like Colonel Watson of the Central Laboratory in France, sacrificed his life, literally, for his work—and Hartley succeeded him in London at Mr Churchill's request.

CHAPTER XVI.

1918.

AFTER a period of rest and training the Special Companies moved out to the front at the end of February 1918 and were distributed fairly evenly over the whole front of 120 miles. All the resources of our factories at home were being utilised for filling cylinders for the big cloud operation referred to in Chapter XIV., but meanwhile there was a sufficient stock of projector drums and 4-inch bombs to keep the brigade usefully employed.

Special attention was devoted to the enemy facing our Third and Fifth Armies, on the front on which it was felt certain that the great German offensive was being prepared, and some very successful operations were carried out, notably at St Quentin, into the outskirts of which 2960 drums were fired on the night of 19th March, and in the neighbourhood of Moeuvres and Quéant, where 1780 drums were projected on the night of 11th March, and 1160 more on the night of the 17th.

As regards the former of these attacks, prisoners stated that 100 men in one regiment, including the whole of the regimental staff, were killed and 200 more seriously gassed —a satisfactory result in view of the fact that the troops assembling here were destined to take part in the German advance only twenty-four hours later.

After the operation at Moeuvres a diary was found belonging to an Alsatian prisoner, an under-officer of the 29th Reserve Regiment (16th Reserve Division), which contained the following entry: " 12/3/18. English barrage accompanied by gas mines. Masks worn for over two hours. Four hundred gas casualties in our regiment." This prisoner (who was captured on 25th May), when questioned, said that no one was aware that gas had been fired, as only high-explosive shells were distinguished. Gas cases continued to occur for several days after the

12th, the majority in the 1st Battalion, and none had returned to duty up to the date of his capture. The strength of most of the companies of this battalion had been reduced to about thirty men. The 30th and 68th Reserve Regiments on his right also had severe losses. The men were told that the British masks afforded no protection against the German Blue and Yellow Cross gases, so that when the advance was made there was no fear of any resistance being encountered. Another prisoner, of the 87th Reserve Regiment (21st Reserve Division), said that in the Cambrai sector his regiment suffered 300 gas casualties on the same occasion, including a percentage of dead, and that only one man had returned from hospital so far. This unit was just south of the 29th Reserve Regiment and seems to have suffered from the *drift* of the cloud.

After the Quéant discharge streams of German ambulances were seen leaving the German sector all the next day, and our own infantry reported that there was a general exodus of rats from the enemy's trenches to ours, many of which died after their arrival. The 15th Reserve Regiment was stated to have had so many gas casualties that it had to be relieved immediately. Forty men of the 14th Bavarian Regiment were said to have been killed and 100 others gassed ; and a British prisoner who made his way back to our lines on 14th April reported that he had been employed in burying the dead after this operation, and that he himself had assisted in disposing of 50 corpses in the sector, and had seen altogether about 200 bodies, the appearance of which was quite different to that of any others. He and all the men employed with him were certain that these were the bodies of men killed by gas.

In view of the imminence of the German attack I had arranged for the whole brigade to be re-armed with rifles and trained in their use ; and on the Fifth Army front, " A," " H " and " E " Companies, which were engaged on the St Quentin front, and No. 1 Company which was preparing an operation at Gonnelieu, all under Major Campbell-Smith, took part in the infantry battle which commenced on the 21st March, and were involved in the British retreat which was only checked on the outskirts of Amiens, nearly forty miles back. The last-named company was put into a section of the Montauban–Mericourt line covering Albert, and joined in the counter-

attack on the enemy on 26th March ; while the other three
held the village of Ham on the 23rd and occupied several
positions subsequently, including Peronne, where they
stemmed the German advance for several hours, and
Liancourt on the 26th.

Owing to the rapidity of the German movement,
the Fifth Army gas dump, containing about 3000 projectors and drums, as well as 4000 Stokes mortar bombs,
had to be abandoned, together with 3000 more projectors
which were still in the ground at St Quentin. All of these
were recovered intact on 31st October. The 36 4-inch
mortars which were in position at Gonnelieu had been
destroyed before the retirement and a large number of
bombs buried. These were the first projector components
which we lost in the war.

On the front of the Third Army, " G," " J," " Q "
and No. 3 Companies were operating at Cherisy, Bullecourt, Quéant and Moeuvres when the storm broke, and
they too were involved in the infantry fighting and were
allotted battle positions in the reserve line. " J " Company, when defending Croisilles, lost its commanding
officer, Captain C. Laycock, who was last seen standing on
the parapet repelling the enemy. He survived the battle,
however, and was repatriated after the Armistice. His
brother, Captain J. Laycock, was also wounded while his
company, " G," was taking part in the gallant defence of
Vaulx, only a few miles away. We lost 122 officers and
men, killed, wounded and missing, during these few days.

A gratifying acknowledgment of the manner in which
the companies performed these unaccustomed duties was
made on 4th April, when General Byng, the Third Army
commander, wrote : " The action of the officers, N.C.O.'s
and men of the Special Companies on the 21st and 22nd
March reflects the greatest credit on their courage and
determination. All ranks seem to have realised that a
great issue was at stake, and took a most enterprising
and successful part in the operations. The report is
most satisfactory, and proves that a most praiseworthy
spirit has been instilled into each Special Company."
Major Bunker, who was in command of these companies,
took prompt measures to evacuate the valuable dump of
gas stores at Courcelles, and he succeeded in removing
the last of them just as the enemy was entering the village.

All the same, the 5000 projectors which were in the front line and some 2000 4-inch bombs had to be abandoned.

The First and Second British Armies were not involved in the first German assault, and the nine companies there carried out about twenty operations with projectors and Stokes mortars during the tense period between the 19th and the end of March, in the course of which 12,000 drums and 7000 4-inch bombs were fired. In the most important of these operations " F," " O," " B " and " M " Companies discharged 3730 drums into Lens and its outskirts on 21st March, this being the largest single projector operation of the whole war ; No. 4 Company fired 1400 CG and NC bombs into the same targets at the same time. This attack was carried out from the fronts of the 1st and 4th Canadian Divisions, the wind velocity at the time being only two miles per hour. The 220th German Division was the one principally affected, and it had 700 casualties on this night, its 55th Reserve Regiment having been caught in a relief and losing 53 men killed and a large number besides in more or less serious cases.

The 2nd Company alone lost 45 men. From the end of March until the beginning of May this division had 1600 gas casualties, other projector attacks having been made against it on 2nd, 7th and 20th April. One of its regiments alone had 120 men killed by gas.

Six of the companies in the First and Second Army areas also took part in the infantry fighting which commenced to the south of Armentières on 9th April, and 10 officers and 200 men were moved into line to reinforce the 74th Infantry Brigade of the 25th British Division.

Our casualties in April were again heavy, and amounted to 357 officers and men.

As soon as this German assault had in its turn expended itself, the Special Companies took up their gas operations once more, and seven of them, including " A," " E " and " H," which had been transferred from the Fifth Army, carried out a large cloud attack on the night of 12th May on the front Hill 70–Auchy (see p. 248). These same companies had executed six different projector operations on the night of 9th May, firing 3250 drums, and on the night after the cloud attack they fired 1750 more drums on about the same targets.

The remaining four companies of the brigade were

engaged on establishing a great cylinder store at Mondi-court for the purpose of the big cloud attack which had been planned on the Arras front, and which I have pre-viously mentioned ; but owing to the course that events were now taking, the preparations had now to be abandoned and the cylinders were withdrawn to safety at Les Attaques.

About this time the situation at the front seemed to be so serious that on 4th April I proposed to the Chief of the General Staff the concentration of the whole of the Special Companies, together with 200 officers and men who were under training at Helfaut, and their conversion into a fighting unit composed like an infantry brigade. I pointed out that although their training as infantry had been sketchy the morale of the men was very high and that of the officers quite exceptional. We only required to complete our complement of Lewis guns, but I asked for a Signal section and a machine-gun company to be attached. This proposal was accepted in principle, and all the staff arrangements were hastily worked out. Each of the four battalions was to have consisted of four ordinary and one Stokes mortar companies, and " Z " Company, which still had an abnormal organisation, was to have acted as pioneers. Our gas equipment was, of course, to have been laid aside temporarily. I, too, sought out several of the commanders of infantry brigades which had recently been withdrawn from the battle, and made myself familiar with the particular problems and diffi-culties with which they had been faced ; but by the time everything was prepared all danger of a German break-through had passed, and it was decided that the brigade would be more profitably employed on its normal duties. Another even distribution of the companies along the front of the British Expeditionary Force then took place, and from that time onwards their activity was continuous.

One of the operations consisted of the discharge, on 23rd May, of 1180 projector drums into the front held by the German 12th Division at Merris. Prisoners stated that over 200 casualties resulted, among which were a large number of dead ; and a captured report of the attack which was issued by the Fourth German Army (but which was taken on the front of the Seventeenth German Army, who apparently considered it sufficiently important for circulation), bearing the date 13/6/18, gave the following interesting, though somewhat querulous, account of it :—

"On the night 23/24 May shortly after midnight the British carried out a heavy surprise bombardment with H.E. ammunition on the position occupied by the 12th Infantry Division west of Merris. *At the same time* a projector attack was made with phosgene drums. The area bombarded included the positions of three regiments on a front of 1500 metres and a depth of 400 metres. The target is thickly scattered with exploded drums, as many as 900 being counted afterwards. The enemy carried out here for the first time a variation of his earlier tactics, as he did *not* carry out separate H.E. and gas bombardments following one another in rapid succession, but projected the gas drums *during* the H.E. bombardment. The recognition of the nature of the projection was made extraordinarily difficult for the troops. The garrison was taking cover and only a few of them noticed the bright flash of the gas discharge, while the report of the exploding drums was lost in the noise of the bursting shells and H.E. bombs. For the same reason the noise of the drums in the air remained unnoticed.

"Even though the British have so often violated the technical laws of gas warfare as regards wind conditions on other occasions, it is still surprising that they should have carried out a gas projector attack on the night in question. There was a very steady south-west wind with a speed of thirteen miles per hour or more" (we estimated it at seven miles per hour) "blowing towards the British line" (this, too, was incorrect). "The gas cloud was certainly very dense immediately after the attack. It was well on the target, as a large part of the trenches received direct hits. However, the cloud was rapidly dispersed by the high wind.

Losses. Eleven men killed (certainly on account of the gas attack) and 121 gassed, including 2 officers, besides 16 men who died later during treatment.

To the credit of the troops it must be emphasised that their good gas discipline and their skill in the use of their masks under adverse conditions enabled them to avoid *even greater losses*.

Reasons for the losses :—

(1) The men who died succumbed to the effect of direct hits : also most of them were struck by splinters.
(2) The novel tactics employed by the enemy in firing gas mines at the same time as H.E.
(3) The impossibility of recognising the projector discharge owing to the noise and the flashes from the H.E. fire.
(4) The unlikelihood of an enemy attack in such a strong wind blowing towards the enemy.
(5) The number of gas mines fired with a weight of about thirteen tons of gas.

Conclusions. The best surprise effect is likely to be obtained when weather conditions appear to be unfavourable for the use of gas. This new method of employment shows the importance of varying the tactical use of gas projectors in order to surprise the enemy."

The effective co-operation arranged between our gunners and ourselves seems to have caused the enemy a good deal of embarrassment, as prisoners often spoke of their inability to remain in their dug-outs because the gas entered them ; while when they were forced out into the trenches they were met with withering and demoralising artillery fire. Men who were unable to withstand this returned to the dug-outs, and it being impossible to keep their masks on continuously they were compelled to remove them, and were later found dead.

Further German references to the success of this co-operation and the variation of our tactics were found in the following extracts from other captured documents :—

Order of the 54th Reserve Division, dated 22/7/18.

" On the 20th and 21st July the division suffered no small losses from hostile gas projector attacks. In both cases the enemy masked his attack by artillery fire. Every H.E. bombardment by the enemy is therefore to be looked upon as a gas alarm and masks are to be adjusted accordingly."

Order of the Second German Army, dated 13/6/18.

" Reports of divisions indicate that a large proportion of the losses suffered in projector attacks are due to the fact that the enemy has latterly installed his projectors for firing from a flank ; also to his masking his use of gas by the employment of H.E. fire which drives the trench garrison to cover. The result is that the flash is not seen and the alarm is given too late."

Intelligence Summary of the 233rd Division, dated 17/7/18.

" Information from the 3rd Naval Division " (1200 drums and 1320 4-inch bombs were fired into Beaumont Hamel on the night of the 13th July). " Very heavy artillery and machine-gun fire was suddenly opened on the 13th July at 12.45 A.M. At 1 A.M. the enemy made a strong surprise projector attack opposite the left flank of the 30th Reserve Infantry Regiment, causing rather heavy losses. This again shows that the enemy is trying to conceal his gas projector attacks in every possible way, and that only extreme alertness can save us from suffering heavy casualties."

Order of the Sixth German Army, dated 30/3/18 and signed ' Lenz.'

" The English in a projector attack used a high percentage of chloropicrin besides the well-known phosgene filling. An irritating effect is apparently expected from the chloropicrin which will make men take off their masks and leave them unprotected against the very poisonous phosgene. Up to now we have practically never had losses from chloropicrin in English artillery shells or from the mixture of the substance in a cloud gas " (but see footnote to p. 231 and p. 285, where this mixture is referred to—" long recognised as exceptionally effective " !) " However, it is possible that in extraordinarily high concentrations of the gas irritation may be expected through the mask. This irritation must be endured and must not be allowed under any circumstances to lead to the removal of the masks."

Intelligence Summary of the 12th Reserve Division.

" It appears that the alarm was given " (at Mericourt, 4-5/5/18) " and masks were adjusted rapidly and correctly. Nevertheless the infantry and the Pioneers working in the area suffered losses in dead and gassed. On account of the H.E. fire men did not hold themselves erect above the edge of the parapet in order to escape from the heaviest concentrations of the gas cloud. Every man must be aware of the necessity of avoiding the highest concentration of gas in spite of the H.E. fire by drawing aside from the point of impact of a projector bomb and attempting to keep his head for a while above the parapet and outside the trench which is filled with a heavy gas cloud."

This recommendation was a counsel of despair, and it can hardly have had a reassuring effect on the German troops as it contained an open admission of the inadequacy of their masks against our projector gas.

On 18th June 975 projector drums were fired into the village of Ablainzeville, which was occupied by the 10th and 12th Reserve Infantry Regiments. An order of the 5th Bavarian Reserve Division described the attack as follows :—

" Only part of the garrison of Ablainzeville saw the flash of discharge which was mistaken for an ammunition dump going up. Only one man heard the whirring noise of the projectiles because this was drowned by the heavy burst of artillery and machine-gun fire which started just before the projectors were discharged and which sent most of the garrison to cover. This ingenious concealment of the surprise gas bombardment resulted in the majority of the garrison taking cover and the first intimation of what they had to deal with was afforded by the bursting of the gas projectiles. At most places the gas alarm was given and masks were put on in time. Direct hits in or close to dug-outs led to the rapid development of such a concentration of gas that the occupants could not put their masks on in time, while the heavy shell-fire hindered rapid withdrawal from the gas cloud. The brunt of the attack fell on the 12th Reserve Infantry Regiment and coincided with a relief of the 3rd Battalion by the 1st. In addition the 10th Reserve Infantry Regiment more to the north was affected by the gas bombardment.

The village of Ablainzeville offers a favourable target for a gas attack, as the ruins and the hedges prevent the dispersion of gas. Dug-out entrances were furnished with gas curtains. The installation of projectors had been suspected, but had not been clearly identified in air photographs. All regiments had been warned about this and stringent precautions had been ordered, so the troops were not taken unawares.

The casualties amounted to—

> 2 officers killed (12th Res. Inf. Regt.),
> 51 men killed,
> 66 men gassed.

One of the officers had four years' war service and had been regimental gas officer for over a year. That so expert an officer should have succumbed shows how difficult it is to recognise a projector attack in time.

Only a few men died on the spot. Many felt so well after the bombardment that they marched back on relief and developed serious symptoms later. The O.C. 3rd Battalion at first reported very few casualties. The mortality in the delayed cases was striking. The gas was assumed to be a mixture of chloropicrin, phosgene and chlorine, long recognised as exceptionally effective, a *single* breath of which may prove fatal.

The casualties were mainly attributed to—

(1) The clever masking of the projector discharge by a burst of artillery and machine-gun fire.

(2) The fact that a relief was in progress, so that many of the gas curtains had been rolled up to make passage in and out easy.

(3) Numerous direct hits in or near the entrance to dug-outs— *e.g.*, Company Commander's dug-out No. 10, 12th Res. Inf. Regt.

The following conclusions were drawn—

(1) Absolutely certain protection cannot be guaranteed with our present defensive measures in the case of direct hits owing to the great concentration of gas. The Army School teaches that direct hits give rise to unavoidable losses.

(2) Dug-outs must be vacated in spite of heavy shelling if thick gas clouds gain entry.

(3) Even men who are apparently not appreciably affected must

avoid every movement when they have got out of the gas cloud.

(4) Gas masks must be put on in the case of every heavy burst of H.E. shelling.

(5) Annihilating fire should be directed on the opposing trenches by way of immediate retaliation." (*Note*—I have already shown that these trenches were always vacated by our own troops prior to each discharge.)

" (6) Every effort must be made to recognise the *discharge* of the projectors and to spread warning.

(7) It is true that in many places the emplacements cannot be identified on aeroplane photographs owing to skilful construction and camouflage ; but any trench-mortar emplacements identified in aeroplane photographs should be destroyed by artillery fire."

My readers can judge for themselves, from this and other documents from which I have quoted, the effect, both moral and material, that our gas operations had produced on the German Army by this time.

The first great German attack on 21st March, made with fifty divisions on our Fifth Army and on part of the Third, had been followed by another blow delivered against the front held by Portuguese troops in the First Army area on 9th April. When these efforts had spent themselves the Germans turned their attention to the French front, and in their attack on 27th May on the Chemin des Dames they penetrated deeply into the area in front of Paris, and were only checked about the middle of June on the line Noyon–Villers Cotteret–Château-Thierry.

But the tide was now about to turn.

The Austrians, by this time reinforced by enormous numbers of prisoners released from Russia, attacked the Italians all along the line on 15th June, and from captured orders it was calculated that 170,000 gas shells were fired in the preliminary bombardment—*i.e.*, about one-third of the total expenditure of artillery ammunition. No Yellow or Blue Cross shells were used, but the Austrians relied largely on gas for their success. However, on 14th January 1918, previously the British Commander-in-Chief on the Italian front had reported that the Italian gas mask did not afford adequate protection, and it was decided, on the recommendation of the Supreme Council at Versailles, to supply the Italian Army with British masks.

300,000 were transferred at once from the reserves held in France, and 1,300,000 were supplied altogether.

The result was that the great Austrian gas attack was a failure, and their offensive produced no result. A number of Austrian divisions were thereupon transferred to reinforce the German armies in France.

On 18th June the French delivered their counter-attack at Soissons, which succeeded in winning back all the ground lost in the previous month, and which finally deprived the Germans of the initiative in the titanic struggle.

On 8th August the British counter-attack was launched from Amiens and Albert, and the successes gained on this day convinced General Ludendorff that the war must be ended. "This was the black day," he says, " of the German Army in the history of the war."

From this time onwards (the Americans attacked the St Mihiel Salient on 12th September) the German armies were pressed back continuously, the speed of their retreat and their demoralisation increasing all the while, until they had reached the positions in which the opposing forces came in contact with each other at the beginning of the war.

The Special Brigade easily adapted itself to the new conditions which had arisen, and although operations on a large scale were planned whenever the line became temporarily stable, their policy now was to carry out small extemporised attacks as frequently as possible and at very short notice, without calling on the infantry to provide any of the labour required. Many disappointments were naturally experienced in such circumstances, and at the moment of the German retreat from Amiens, for example, schemes had to be abandoned for which all the preparations had been made for the discharge of 9000 cylinders, 8000 projector drums and as many 4-inch bombs. Nevertheless, after a projector discharge on Marquion on 20th September, a document of the 12th German Division was captured which referred to 'considerable losses,' and which said : "The casualties in one regiment amounted to 2 killed and 42 gassed."[1] And after 680 drums had

---

[1] In the history of the 23rd Regiment, one of the units of the 12th German Division, the following appears : " On the night of the 19th-20th the enemy fired about 200 gas mines which caused 3 dead and 30 gas casualties. On the 20th they covered our right wing with 300 mines."

been fired into Moyenneville on 13th August, an order signed by the O.C. 12th Company, 80th Reserve Regiment, dated 16/8/18, said :—" After the projector attack there were substantial casualties in the 12th Company of the 88th Reserve Regiment : 4 killed, 2 severely and 23 moderately or slightly affected. The flashes were not identified or were mistaken for an artillery shoot. Men were affected by blinds which continued to emit gas and from taking off their masks too soon. At every burst of shelling and at the slightest irritation of the eyes wake up everyone and put on masks."

Confirmation of the success of this operation was provided in two other captured documents. Order of the 2nd Guard Reserve Division : " The rather heavy losses suffered by the neighbouring division on the right " (the 234th) " renders it necessary again to call attention to the danger of projector attacks " ; and an order of the 453rd Regiment (of the 234th Division) mentioned that " The 452nd Infantry Regiment had suffered somewhat considerable casualties from a gas projector attack."

On a constantly fluctuating line the conditions made gas attacks extremely arduous, and the greatest energy and determination were displayed in preparing for and taking advantage of fleeting opportunities whenever they occurred.

For instance, on the night of 19th April 180 projectors were carried up, dug into position and fired into Merris, which had been captured by the enemy only a few hours previously.[1] On the night of 11th September twelve 4-inch Stokes mortars were set up in the British outpost line twenty-four hours after the recapture of Epehy by the enemy, and 450 bombs were fired into that village. On the night of 6th September 1060 projector drums were fired into Blécourt ; and on the night of 2nd October 700 into Aubencheuf-au-Bac, four Special Companies having carried out both these operations without any infantry assistance whatever.

The keenness displayed by the companies was warmly acknowledged by our troops and many expressions of ap-

---

[1] One thousand one hundred and eight drums were fired into the same place only four days later ; and three days later still—*i.e.*, on the 26th, 200 drums left Helfaut at 5 P.M. by lorry and were rushed up and fired into Merris at 12.30 the same night.

preciation were sent to me, sometimes from commanders with whom it had been found very difficult to work in the earlier days of the war. Throughout the whole year the brigade, like every other British unit, was much under strength, the deficiency varying from 700 on 16th March to double that number (or 25 per cent of the establishment) in September; and, as a result, a far greater strain was put on the remaining personnel, so that the operations were not always on such a large scale as would otherwise have been possible. Another reason for limiting the scope of the operations, especially during the final British advance, was the presence of French civilians in the reoccupied areas and in districts which had been in German occupation during the whole war up till this time. Very firm orders were issued in regard to their safety, and this restricted our activity on many occasions, especially as to the amount of gas released at a time. It is possible that the enemy may have recognised the influence of this factor, as a battalion order was found on our Second Army front, dated 28/10/18, which said: " All movement of civil inhabitants near the front line must be stopped without fail. If necessary rifles may be used for the purpose. The people may not leave the farms."

To enable us to maintain contact with our infantry in their advance a number of mobile detachments were extemporised which consisted of parties of men equipped with gas material who went forward in lorries, prepared to come into action at the shortest notice. But on many parts of the front, especially in portions of the devastated Somme battlefield, communications were so bad that schemes were prepared for using tanks to draw sledges loaded with gas stores so as to reach positions which lorries and horse transport were unable to approach. Eight ' Tadpole ' tanks were put at our disposal on 23rd September, but no operation of this kind was actually carried out, though ' supply ' tanks were successfully utilised for carrying up projectors and drums.

The Stokes mortar companies, owing to their greater mobility, found many opportunities in the last days of the war of facilitating the work of the infantry, and No. 4 Company had the honour of carrying out the last Special Brigade attack which took place at Bossuyt, on the River Escaut, north of Tournai, when 252 thermit bombs were

T

fired on 8th November. (" K " Company fired 50 gas drums into Tournai Wood on 2nd November, and " F " Company 100 at Hergines on the 3rd. On 4th November " Q " and " N " Companies carried out three operations with 550 oil drums at Le Quesnoy and Englefontaine, on the Third Army front ; and on the same day No. 1 Company fired 300 4-inch smoke bombs, No. 3 Company 160 smoke and No. 4 Company 600 gas bombs. This last was the final *gas* attack of the war.)

The following were some of the latest congratulatory messages received on the co-operation of the Special Brigade with infantry units :—

9/5/18. " The Second Army Commander would like to convey to you " (Major Berrisford) " and the companies under your command his appreciation of the excellent work which has been done during the last month."

11/9/18. " The Division Commander (46th) has instructed me to express to you " (No. 4 Company) " his appreciation of the good work done by ' P ' and ' Q ' Sections on the night of September 8th. He realises the work entailed in carrying 1720 bombs in one night. The fact that notwithstanding this operation a smoke barrage and recall signals for the raid were successfully fired reflects great credit on your Sections."

19/9/18. " The Corps Commander (Australian Corps) desires to thank all ranks for their excellent work during yesterday's successful battle. The work of No. 1 Special Company was admirably and gallantly carried out in the face of great difficulties and is very highly appreciated."

The Commander of the 5th Division, on 25th September, after repeating the statements of prisoners as to the heavy casualties they had suffered from a discharge of 400 projector drums, wrote : " The operation was not decided on till 10 P.M. on the 23rd September. The drums were brought forward by lorry to Metz on the 24th and taken by limber to emplacements on the same night. The fact that the operation was carried out within such a short space of time reflects great credit on the initiation and organisation of ' Q ' Special Company and the officers who conducted it."

The Commander of the 1st Division, after writing on 23rd September " The 1st Division through me expresses its thanks and congratulations to No. 1 and ' D ' Special Companies for their skilful, gallant and successful work last night," wrote again on 7th November : " I again have to express to you the thanks of the 1st Division for the very excellent work done by the companies when engaged in operations with this Division. Their help on this occasion was most valuable. They showed much judgment as well as a very fine spirit."

And, finally, the Commander of the VIIIth Corps, when forwarding a report from the 8th Division, said : " The Corps Commander is glad that ' F ' Company under Major Thomas have again shown that they are worthy of the high reputation that they have already gained."

Although circumstances had by this time precluded the execution of the big projected cylinder attack either on the Third or on the First Army front, an increasing use of cylinders was made during the year, the difficulty of carrying them up to the front line being avoided by arranging the installations in rear positions and on lines which were accessible by rail or lorry, all the troops in front being withdrawn immediately before the discharge took place. Ten such cloud attacks were carried out without any serious mischance, in the course of which 27,000 cylinders were emptied. In one case 4000 cylinders were transported in lorries and horse-drawn waggons (the wheels of which were bound round with strips of old motor tyres in order to deaden the sound of movement) and placed in open ditches by the side of a road which ran parallel to the front and about 700 yards behind it, no protection whatever being provided for them except against aerial observation. Although some of these cylinders were hit by chance shells during the eight days that they remained exposed none of our troops were affected by the leakages of gas, the latter seeming to have escaped the enemy's notice owing to the road being concealed from view by hedges and trees.

The cylinders were discharged electrically on 17th June, and as all the gas was released simultaneously the cloud was an exceedingly dense one. " L " Company carried out this very successful operation along a half-mile front opposite to Vieux Berquin, just north of the forest of Nieppe.

As an example of the variety of occupation of the

Special Companies about this period, I may add that after the empty cylinders had been disposed of the same company (" L ") carried out a projector operation shortly afterwards, when they took 300 projectors and drums into a forward position by mule transport. On 6th August " L " Company fired 600 more drums filled with phosgene, and 280 on the 9th ; while on the 21st they discharged 220 drums filled with amyl acetate (balloon dope), an evil-smelling but harmless mixture, in co-operation with an infantry attack on Mural Farm, near Meteren. The British division engaged in this attack suffered very slight loss in their advance and captured 22 prisoners and 2 machine-guns ; and it reported " Mural Farm was held by the 88th Regiment " (56th German Division). " Prisoners captured stated that one company had 20 gas casualties, including six who died five or six hours after the gas attack on the 9th. Three other companies had 10 to 15 casualties each. Such prisoners who were captured " (on the 21st) " were found with their masks on, and there is no doubt that the ease with which the objectives were taken was due in large part to the dummy projector operation."

In the following month " L " Company carried out a large smoke operation in front of Armentières to cover the successful counter-attack of our 31st Division when they recaptured Ploegstreet Wood. Without any infantry assistance 15,000 P bombs and 22 German Nebeltopf (smoke-producing apparatus containing chlor-sulphonic acid and weighing $1\frac{1}{2}$ cwt. each) were distributed along a front of nearly a mile and set alight, and a magnificent smoke cloud was kept up for a period of five hours, in the course of which 20 tons of smoke-producing substances were expended.[1]

[1] " L " Company had made a specialty of smoke clouds, and established a reputation early in 1917 when they co-operated with the 3rd Australian Division in one of the best-planned raids of the whole war. Two thousand smoke candles were used on that occasion, partly to screen the raiding parties, particularly from German search-lights which were a feature of that section of the front, and partly to simulate a gas attack in order to compel the enemy to meet the raiders with their masks on. The raiding parties were most successful, and they penetrated to the third German line and returned with fourteen prisoners, a machine-gun and a searchlight. This was the occasion on which an Australian bomber, failing to induce the occupants of a deep dug-out to come out and surrender when the recall signal had been given, called out, " How many down there ? " " Twelve," was the reply. " Then share that between you," he said, throwing down a bomb among them. The Australian troops were magnificent when in action, and some of their deeds for which Victoria Crosses were awarded were examples of almost incredible recklessness and bravery ;

Photos. by Maj. Salt.

The cloud attack from railway trains.

One more instance of the varied activities of the companies may be given. I have already mentioned that the four mortar units were now capable of carrying out cylinder and projector operations as well as their own 4-inch bombardments. On 23rd June 1918 No. 2 Company fired 480 projector drums as well as 1200 CG and PS 4-inch bombs from 38 mortars near Merris on the Second Army front. On 19th July they fired 850 more drums, and on the 23rd, 240. On 20th September they fired 1000 drums, and 600 more on the 24th. On 27th September they fired 200 smoke drums in connection with an infantry operation, and they had 2000 cylinders installed in position for a cloud attack, though these were not discharged, as the situation had changed before the gas could be released.

I have described one of the 'retired cylinder' operations. The remaining nine were carried out from railway trucks on fronts where the existence of light railway lines and tramways favoured this form of operation, the cylinders being opened electrically without off-loading them, and taken back empty immediately afterwards.

The first of these attacks took place on the First Army front on 24th May 1918, when a considerable number of cylinders were discharged south-west of Lens; and in the largest of them 'white star' gas was discharged from six separate railheads by "B," "C," "F" and "O" Companies between Oppy and Hulluch on the night of 12th July. (Prisoners stated that in their regiment alone there were 200 gas casualties.)

In these novel cloud attacks the line of cylinders was not, of course, continuous, so that the 'beams' of gas from the different railheads sometimes only coalesced some distance within the enemy's lines. Railheads were chosen as near each other as possible so as to avoid too great an interval between 'beams,' and short spur lines were occasionally specially laid for the purpose, and the trains were halted, whenever possible, in positions parallel

so that it was amusing to hear their opinion of the Americans when the latter fought alongside them in one of their earliest battles in 1918: "They're all right," they said, " but they fight a bit rough."

They had the reputation, however, of being difficult to manage when at rest after a battle, and a cockney soldier, when he read the bulletin which announced their capture of Bethlehem on the Palestine front, remarked, "Bet yer the shepherds watched their flocks *that* night."

to the front line and broadside to the direction of the wind.

Both broad and narrow-gauge lines were made use of, and the attack was generally organised as follows: In the course of the afternoon, on receipt of a favourable wind forecast and the message 'Prepare,' the cylinders which had already been tested and were waiting at the railway base were loaded into the trucks, 15 to 100 in each, according to their capacity. About dusk the fully prepared trains were drawn by petrol-electric tractors or light

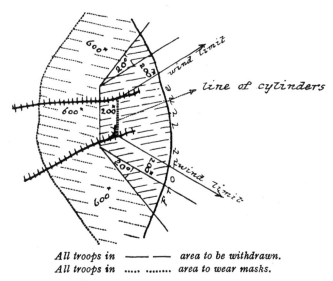

All troops in ——— area to be withdrawn.
All troops in .... area to wear masks.

engines to the 'Power railhead,' where the trains were broken up and the trucks pushed by infantry working parties to their final positions a quarter or half a mile behind the front line. Here the electrical discharge connections were made and final 'All ready,' wind and other messages exchanged by telephone, in code, with the General Staff of the formation concerned.

The area in front of the cylinders was cleared entirely of troops, wide margins of safety being provided on either flank as well as in rear of the line of railheads. This last precaution was found necessary as, owing to the unprecedented concentrations of gas liberated and the consequent fall of temperature in the area immediately in front of the cylinders, back eddies of gas occurred up to

50 or 100 yards behind the points of emission, even, in one case, with a wind blowing at 7 miles an hour. The re-occupation of the front area took place an hour or two after the completion of the attack, on reports received by special personnel sent to investigate whether any gas still remained in it, and the extra precaution was adopted of forbidding entry into dug-outs until each one had been tested for gas by an expert. The noise of the tractors bringing the train-loads of cylinders into position was sometimes drowned by the drone of a special patrolling aeroplane, and a prearranged signal for the discharge was given by two shots fired from a field-gun, or distinctive rockets, and so on, while bursts of Lewis-gun fire masked the sound of the simultaneous explosion of thousands of electric detonators.

These cloud attacks seem to have been very successful, and the Germans appear to have been considerably puzzled as to how and where the clouds originated, as they attempted to solve the problem by means of observation balloons and low-flying aircraft. Accurate indications were, of course, available a few days later from air photographs, as the paths of the clouds could be easily traced from the bleached vegetation up to distances as great as 12,000 yards from the points of emission.

The 'beam' attacks were by no means simple operations to execute. The closest co-operation had to be observed between ourselves and the General Staff of the formation, the infantry supplying the pushing parties, and the signal, meteorological and light railway services, whilst the complete evacuation of the forward area by the infantry garrison was, of course, a matter of careful and anxious organisation. They were becoming increasingly popular in the latter half of 1918, and one scheme was in preparation on the Ypres front in September in which 14,000 cylinders were to have been used on three broad and two narrow-gauge railways covering a frontage of 2000 yards. In other places the construction of lengths of special light line was contemplated, the cylinders on the trains being supplemented with others in intermediate dumps of 1000 between the railheads. These dumps were to have been left camouflaged lying out in the open and were to have been filled by means of wheeled transport or Leeming ropeways, which latter were capable of delivering the cylinders at the dumps at the rate of 200 an hour.

The devastated area around Ypres and the river valleys which ran at right angles to the line farther south were suitable localities for the release of clouds which were capable of travelling great distances, the former because of the absence of any civil population and the latter because they were known to be favourite billeting areas for German troops far behind the front. The depressions formed by the river valleys were particularly favourable for preventing the dispersion of gas, as the dense heavy clouds were observed to be much influenced by ground contours.

"P" Company distinguished itself with 'beam' attacks. It carried out one on the night of 22nd June 1918, from which the 31st German Division was stated by prisoners to have suffered 500 casualties; another on 24th July, from which prisoners of the 9th Uhlanen Regiment, of the 6th Cavalry Division, said that the 1st Landwehr Division had suffered so severely—it was believed from a new gas—that it had to be withdrawn shortly afterwards (it was identified a little later in Alsace); and a third on 26th August. All these took place under very difficult conditions in sectors of the Ypres Salient; and on 11th September the same company carried out a shoot with 580 projector drums.

French civilians in the areas occupied during our advance in the latter half of 1918 all bore witness to the success of our gas operations, and they were unanimous in stating that the enemy made no secret of their fear of British gas. The casualties they suffered were a constant topic of conversation among them. People in some of the larger cities, such as Lille, spoke of the large number of German gas casualties, amounting to a constant stream, which reached the big hospitals, and of the high percentage of mortality among them. The greatest secrecy was always observed by the German authorities, and all burials and evacuations were carried out at night. Vegetation and salads in the gardens at Lille had often been bleached by the gas clouds, and the inhabitants were constantly being warned of their approach by the ringing of bells, when they took refuge in the top rooms of their houses and closed all the windows and doors. They by no means resented the gas attacks, however, and the wife of the mayor of one of the towns, whose house had been used as a German divisional, as well as a brigade headquarters, and who had had German officers always billeted on her, said that the latter feared gas more than anything else. " Give them gas all the time," she said, " and then more gas."

Between 11th March and 7th October gas was discharged on 119 nights out of the 210 in spite of the fact that the work of the companies was interrupted by spells of unfavourable weather and infantry fighting. Altogether in this period 301 separate gas attacks were carried out, while many others were abandoned owing to fluctuations in the line after all the preparations had been made.

This must be considered a very remarkable record when it is remembered that trench warfare conditions had almost ceased to exist, that communications were damaged and that hostile artillery activity was intense throughout the whole period. Besides the 27,000 cylinders already mentioned, 96,000 projector drums and 35,000 4-inch bombs were fired, representing a total discharge of gas amounting to 2245 tons. In addition, over 3000 oil, smoke, thermit, H.E. and ' stink ' (dummy) drums and 6600 4-inch smoke and 1000 rounds of 4-inch thermit bombs were fired.

During the whole year there was practically no loss to the troops from our own gas, owing to the precautions that were adopted and the technical skill that had been acquired. On only two occasions were there any accidents at all, and these occurred, one from a remarkable ' back lash ' from a ' beam ' attack in which three American soldiers lost their lives when they got caught up in barbed wire in the dark while retreating from the cloud, and the other through one or two drums falling wide. Similarly the Special Companies themselves suffered very little from their own gas, though their total casualties in the year were—

Killed—11 officers and 124 other ranks,
Wounded and gassed—60 officers and 1326 other ranks,

the great majority being sustained in the infantry fighting and from artillery fire before and after the gas attacks.

Adding smoke, thermit, H.E. and ' dummy ' discharges

to the gas attacks, the Special Brigade carried out no fewer than 352 separate operations between 11th March and 8th November 1918 : there were 24 in March, including some very large projector discharges ; 40 in April ; 41 in May, chiefly on the First Army front, which remained fairly stable ; 50 in June, including 3 large cylinder attacks ; 66 in July, including 6 cloud attacks ; 38 in August, including 2 cloud attacks ; 63 in September, on 20 nights out of the 30, 20 in October and 10 in November.

The apparent inactivity from October onwards leads me to relate briefly the circumstances which caused the temporary transfer of nearly half the companies for service with the American Expeditionary Force.

Brigadier - General Fries, who became the American Director of Gas Services in August 1917, had visited my headquarters on several occasions to inquire into British methods of gas offence and defence. He has written in a book, of which he is joint author ('Chemical Warfare') : " Investigation showed the British gas organisation to be far superior to the French " ; and again : " The British practically throughout the war were much ahead of the French in all phases of gas warfare." (*Note*—So that my French friends may not take offence at this expression of opinion, I will quote Captain Lefebure, who was the liaison officer in Paris representing the British Ministry of Munitions, who says in 'The Riddle of the Rhine' that the French organisation of the department concerned with chemical warfare was much superior to our own !) However, in view of his opinion, it was not surprising that from 30th September 1917 onwards General Fries sent numbers of American officers to our depot at Helfaut for courses of instruction in our offensive and defensive methods. On 20th January 1918 the first two companies of the 30th United States Engineer Regiment, which later became the First Gas Regiment, arrived for training, under Major Weinberg, and they were put through the same course of lectures and practical work as our own recruits. Early in March this training had been completed, and the two companies were distributed among our own in the front line to gain practical experience, and they assisted us with great skill and gallantry in several of our gas operations on the First, Second and Fourth Army fronts, after which they joined their own Expeditionary Force.

They took with them two of my best officers to act in an advisory capacity, one of whom, Macnamee, was awarded the American Distinguished Service Cross for gallant conduct almost immediately, he being one of the first recipients of this decoration.[1]

In October 1918 General Fries sent his staff officer, Major Richardson, to me to inquire whether it would be possible to spare any of the Special Companies for service on the American front, as his own six companies were badly in need of rest and a new American Army was being formed. And as at this time, owing to the speed with which the British Armies were advancing, gas operations in our own area were becoming more and more difficult, so that some of the Special Companies were being employed on road and railway reconstruction, I arranged with our General Staff to transfer nine of them to General Fries for a while. This arrangement gave me all the greater pleasure because although my first consideration was the engagement of the companies wherever the tactical conditions promised the maximum employment for them the relations which had existed between ourselves and General Fries and his men had been most cordial, and the whole Special Brigade held in the highest regard the purposeful determination and courage which had been shown by the First Gas Regiment during the period that they had shared billets and operations on the British front.

"C," "D," "E," "F," "J," "O," "P," "Z" and No. 3 Companies were therefore moved to the American front on 3rd November, under Lieut.-Colonels Bunker and Campbell-Smith,[2] and they reported to the late Colonel Atkisson (recently Military Attaché at the American Embassy in London), who was now commanding the First Gas Regiment, and they were divided between the First American Army at Verdun, where they came under the orders of General Marchand, of Fashoda fame, and the

---

[1] The Americans requisitioned offensive gas supplies from us, as no cylinders, 4-inch mortars, projectors or gas shells were received from the States until just before the Armistice, although gas in bulk had been shipped both to France and England. Similarly, 100,000 British box respirators were requisitioned in August 1917, and 700,000 were supplied altogether (together with some French masks) before their own began to reach them in July 1918).

[2] The officers commanding Special Companies at the headquarters of each of our armies were raised in status from the rank of Major to Lieut.-Colonel on 6th August 1918, and the company commanders from Captain to Major.

Second American Army which was facing Metz. But the Armistice was signed a few days later, and none of these nine companies came into action in the American area.

I have now brought my readers to the Armistice, which was signed on 11th November, and which alone, in spite of Nazi pretence, enabled the German armies to escape from final military catastrophe [1]; and in the map opposite I have shown all the operations carried out by the Special Brigade during 1918 in which gas was discharged. Smoke, &c., operations were too numerous for inclusion.

It will be noticed that the gas attacks were most frequent in the sector between Bethune and Arras, which was little affected by the great German attacks of the year; while on the remainder of the front held by the B.E.F., although there was time for a few gas attacks to be carried out before the enemy's advance from Cambrai on 21st March and on Armentières on 9th April, most of the subsequent operations took place after these efforts had expended themselves in front of Amiens and Hazebrouck respectively.

In the course of the British counter-attacks no gas attacks were possible during the first few days of the movements, when progress was most rapid, but they can be identified in all the later stages, and, finally, at Le Cateau on the River Oise in front of the town, at Le Quesnoy and Tournai and as far north as the River Escaut, towards Audenarde.

. . . .

I have also included a diagram in which all the operations of the brigade during the whole war are recorded, the quantities of gas, &c., discharged on each date being shown proportionally by the lengths of the columns, and the nature of the discharges, whether by cloud, projectors or Stokes mortars, being indicated in various colours.

[1] " The German higher command, on the other hand, thought that we could no longer face the expected general offensive, and made up its mind on September 28th (1918) to wind up the whole business as quickly as possible " (Professor Banse in ' Germany, Prepare for War ').

It will be seen that except for smoke screens set up by the mortar companies all the operations were cloud attacks up till April 1917. From then onwards, although projector operations predominated, cloud attacks took place continuously both in 1917 and 1918, while in the latter year they were the biggest of the whole war.

With the development of the ' retired cylinder ' method of attack, the provision of a satisfactory design of percussion fuze for the gas bombs and drums, the arrival of the Leeming ropeway and the prospect of large supplies becoming available of the ' M ' device, the brigade had reached its maximum state of efficiency at the time that the Armistice was signed, while its expectation of still greater success in the 1919 campaign was of the brightest.

During the whole war no fewer than 768 separate gas operations were carried out, in addition to many with smoke, thermit, oil, ' stinks ' and high explosive ; 88,000 cylinders were emptied and 197,000 projector drums and 178,000 4-inch Stokes bombs fired, representing a total discharge of 5700 tons of gas ; and there were 16 shots from the flame projectors. The magnitude of the operations varied from the electrical release of 160 tons of gas from 5110 cylinders to the firing of a few score Stokes mortar bombs from the outskirts of a half-captured village. The largest simultaneous discharge of projector drums was the one on 21st March 1918 when 3730 were fired (together with 1400 4-inch bombs) into Lens. On another occasion (19th March 1918) 2960 drums were fired into St Quentin. The largest discharge of oil drums took place on 4th June 1917 when 1500 were fired into the woods on the slopes of the Messines Ridge. Nor do the operations summarised above represent the whole of the work carried out by the brigade, as a great many others were prepared, but had to be abandoned owing to changes in the tactical situation, and for other reasons. Thus 286 tons of gas were ready for liberation on the flank of the Messines Ridge in June 1917, and 400 tons in front of Amiens and Albert in August 1918, when the direction of the British advance in each case necessitated the cancellation of the operations. Finally, the companies were frequently employed, in the intervals of their normal occupation, on corps duties, such as bridging, railway, road and trench construction, and for a few weeks in 1918 as infantry.

The reduction of the enemy's man-power was our main preoccupation, though we attempted on every possible occasion to combine this object with the endeavour to assist our own infantry in the accomplishment of their immediate tasks. Thus the cloud attack at the battle of Loos, without which, probably, little if any ground would have been gained on that occasion, was the first operation undertaken; and the thermit discharge on 8th November 1918, which also covered an infantry attack, was the last.

At only one period of the war, during two months at the end of 1917 and in the beginning of 1918, was the whole brigade ever out of contact with the enemy.

In combination with this diagram I have drawn a curve to scale, which shows the casualties suffered by the brigade from all causes, and their relation to the periods of special activity of the British Armies. It will be seen that these were highest just before the opening of the battle of the Somme, at the end of June 1916, during a period in which many gas clouds were discharged from our front line and the artillery retaliation was intense. At this time, too, we used phosgene for the first time, and its peculiar properties were not fully known.

They were again heavy during the great battles of 1917—Arras, Messines and third Ypres—and they rose to another peak in March and April 1918, when most of the companies took part in the battle as infantrymen. Altogether, in the whole war, we suffered 5384 casualties from all causes, a figure six hundred less than the establishment of the brigade when at full strength.

When it is considered that in the case of our infantry their losses, whether in attack or defence, were comparable with those of the enemy, man for man, and that our own were perhaps only one-fortieth of the number inflicted by our gas attacks, I think I may claim that the Special Brigade played a worthy part in the great struggle, that it fully justified its formation and existence, and that its surviving members can look back on its history with nothing but satisfaction and pride.

Altogether 557 decorations were bestowed, of which 494, including one Victoria Cross, were ' immediate awards.'

.   .   .   .

After the Armistice the Special Brigade was concentrated and began to demobilise. A number of officers and men volunteered for service in North Russia, and I myself was sent to India for a year.

The troops of the Indian Army were not equipped with protection against gas ; and as we had supplied General Denikin with gas shells which, on the collapse of his movement, it was feared might find their way to the Afghan frontier where hostilities had broken out, I was sent by the War Office to advise the Indian Government on the subject and to study the possibilities of gas in frontier fighting. Here, of course, gas would be particularly valuable, as the fighting consists largely of a struggle for hilltops, the evacuation of which can be forced by a very small expenditure of gas ammunition. Besides, gas had by this time been accepted in principle as a weapon by all the late belligerents, and it was considered that it should be included in the training of the Indian Army, if only for the sake of uniformity.

I spent some months with the expeditionary forces in Dacca (Afghanistan) and in Waziristan (the Tochi Valley expedition to Datta Khel), and then enjoyed the probably unique distinction of giving a private lecture to the Viceroy and his full Executive Council in Simla. Before returning home I embarked on an extensive lecture tour on the subject of gas, as it might be used in frontier fighting, in the course of which I visited most of the garrisons throughout British India.

CHAPTER XVII.

SUMMARY.

BEFORE bringing this history to a close, I think it would interest my readers if I attempted a brief review of the gas war and compared the methods adopted by the Germans with our own.

Our late enemies enjoyed at first two very great advantages over us. In their well-established chemical industry they possessed from the beginning a complete technical equipment, and they had during the pre-war years created a practical world monopoly in the manufacture of chemicals. In comparison with this we had no organisation whatever for meeting the emergency we were called upon to face, as practically nothing was known in this country of chemical substances which might be used offensively in warfare, and the manufacturing plant available for their production was almost non-existent. It was only very gradually that this initial disadvantage was overcome; and if the war had lasted a few months longer we would have reaped the full reward of the creative superiority of our chemists and of the development of our own industry, as new chemical weapons of overwhelming potency were in course of production in vast quantities, both by our Allies and ourselves, which would have brought complete disaster to the enemy in the following year.

Secondly—though this proved to be of minor consequence—the Germans, once they commit themselves to war, pursue their aims (quite logically) with a ruthlessness which apparently no other nation dares to imitate, and which, perhaps, is only possible when Army Chiefs are allowed to assume control of the national destiny and are prepared to disregard every consideration likely to interfere with victory in the field.

I have mentioned in a previous chapter how, from humanitarian motives, a ban was placed on our employment of what was thought to be the most dangerous chemical substance in existence (prussic acid gas : this ban was not lifted until July 1916) ; and how Cabinet sanction even to the initiation of any gas reprisals was withheld for several weeks.

The French Government, too, at first banned the use of shells containing phosgene and prussic acid, both of which were in stock at the end of 1915, and only permitted the employment of the former when the situation at Verdun appeared to be critical towards the end of February 1916. The ban on prussic acid was withdrawn later, and it was first used by the French at the opening of the battle of the Somme on 1st July 1916.

German writers whom I have consulted are strangely reticent on the subject, and they even seem to contradict each other ; but it is probable that gas was used on a large scale by the enemy, for the first time in the war, on the Russian front in the form of an artillery gas bombardment at the end of January 1915. Even on the Western front gas shells were used before the first gas cloud, and these contained benzyl bromide and later on xylyl bromide (T-Stoff), both of which are powerful lachrymators and have, in addition, a certain toxic value approximating to that of chlorine. That these shells proved ineffective is not surprising, and ' mass effect ' was then resorted to by the enemy when the cloud method of attack was introduced.

It will be convenient to separate the gas war, as conducted by the Germans against ourselves, into five separate periods. These can be followed on the chart at the end of Chapter XVIII., in which all our gas casualties throughout the war are shown week by week, together with the principal corresponding events. They were partly concurrent and there was no sharp dividing line between them, as the enemy must have had to deal with a certain amount of ' lag,' such as we ourselves experienced to a far more pronounced extent, between policy and production. Still, they are convenient from the point of view of general classification.

These periods were characterised by the use of—

    (a) Gas shells (lachrymators)—April 1915 to July 1916.

    (b) Cloud gas—21st April 1915 to 8th August 1916.

(c) Gas shells (lethal)—15th July 1916 to 12th July 1917.

(d) Gas shells (Yellow Cross, vesicants; Green Cross, lethal; and Blue Cross, sternutators) —12th July 1917 to 11th November 1918.

(e) Projectors—11th December 1917 to 31st May 1918.

Lachrymatory Gas Shell Period.

I have already mentioned these shells. They had, no doubt, a certain harassing effect, but it is difficult to estimate the number of casualties that resulted from their use, as the symptoms they induced were always mild and transitory, while the mortality was probably nil. Lachrymatory gas shells continued to be used throughout the cloud gas period.

Cloud Gas Period.

This should be divided into two stages: (1) when our troops had little or no protection; and (2) when adequate protection was afforded by the P, the PH and the PHG helmets, though none of these was as efficient as the box respirator which was introduced later.

Stage I.

1. 22nd April 1915—Langemarck. The brunt of this attack fell on French troops, and we were hardly affected by the gas cloud.

2. 24th April—Langemarck. The Canadians were affected, and they had, of course, as yet no protection whatsoever against gas.

Some ground was lost and large numbers of dead and badly gassed men were left behind, so that it is impossible to estimate our losses. Only 122 cases were admitted to hospital, of whom 11 died. The Germans (in a captured document) claimed that in these two attacks 5000 men were killed by gas; and Dr Hanslian puts the casualties at 15,000, of whom 5000 died; but both estimates are probably exaggerated, as on the 22nd the French African troops, instinctively and perhaps justifiably, retired too quickly to have lost many men.

3. 1st May—Hill 60. The 1st Dorsets were the chief sufferers in this attack, and altogether 2413 gas cases were

treated in hospital, of which 227 died. Other dead and gassed men fell into the enemy's hands. Here again no respirators were in use apart from the protection afforded by the men's handkerchiefs.

4. 6th May—Hill 60. By this time our men had been supplied with respirators made locally, which consisted of black veiling or layers of flannel dipped in sodium hyposulphite solution, a supply of which was kept in each trench bay. A cotton-wool respirator in a gauze envelope was also extemporised at home and distributed privately, and a million of them were said to have been made up in a single day by the women of England, at the instance of the 'Daily Mail' and the Red Cross Society.

The casualties in this attack amounted to 557, of which 22 died. The last stage of the British retirement to the 'Frezenberg line,' within the Ypres Salient, was completed on the night of 3rd May, and 'collective defence' against gas (by means of gongs, bells, klaxons and other alarms) came into existence for the first time.

5. 10th May—Hill 60. Our losses were only 79, including 2 dead.

6. 24th May—Menin road to Sanctuary Wood. This was a more prolonged attack than the others, and consequently the makeshift official respirators became exhausted and gave out. The unofficial ones (cotton-wool) were found to be useless when dry, and when dipped in the solution they allowed no air (or gas) to pass through them, and they were subsequently withdrawn. A few of the earliest smoke or hypo. helmets were now under trial, and were found to be far superior to any of the respirators. The idea was obtained from seeing a German in one of the earlier attacks moving about in the cloud with a bag over his head.

The hypo. helmet was made of flannel and was dipped in the soda solution and kept moist by treatment with glycerine. It had one large celluloid eye-piece and was chemically proof against chlorine and was easy to adjust, but there was a danger of the celluloid being cracked and of CO_2 gas accumulating inside from the breath. This was overcome by the substitution of glass and the addition of an expiratory tube and valve, and various other improvements were made until the box respirator began to be issued in February 1916.

The casualties resulting from the gas attack of 24th May were heavy, the number of men treated in hospital amounting to 3284, of whom 53 died. Once again numbers of dead and gassed men fell into the enemy's hands.

In these six attacks we have records of 6455 gas casualties treated in hospital, of which 315 died. Probably we had 3000 gassed besides, so that our total gas losses up to this time may have amounted to 10,000 altogether. Owing to the incomplete figures in our possession, I have indicated these losses by a dotted line on the chart. Only chlorine was used in these clouds, but large numbers of H.E. and lachrymatory gas shells were fired in the bombardments which accompanied them.

The casualties were serious, but the circumstances under which they were incurred preclude, of course, any deductions being drawn from the figures for the purpose of comparing the value of the cloud with other methods of gas attack.

Owing to the direction of the prevailing winds no other cloud attack was launched against British troops for seven months, until December 1915, although in October the French were attacked twice and lost heavily on each occasion. In the interval the Germans had carried out a number of cloud attacks on the Russian front which they claim to have been very successful, so that they had gained valuable experience and had improved their technique since the first attacks made at Ypres. Our defensive measures, as well as our gas discipline, had also improved, and it was thought that we had nothing further to fear from gas. In November 1915 an important document fell into our hands in which phosgene appeared in a list of gases which it was stated that the enemy were about to use. With the new gas it was hoped to inflict as many as 10,000 casualties on our troops.

Stage II.

1. 19th December 1915—Wieltje. I have shown in Chapter X. (p. 179 *et seq.*) that in none of the five cloud attacks which come into this second period were our troops taken by surprise, as full warning was given by deserters and otherwise of what was about to occur in each case. On 19th December, in particular, parachute lights of a novel pattern were sent up by the Germans a

quarter of an hour before the gas was released, which were regarded as being intended to test the wind. In spite of this we had 1069 casualties, including 120 dead. One man was actually gassed at Vlamertinghe, 8500 yards behind the line (where 17-inch howitzer shells also fell), and the gas was noticed at Le Cornet Malo, twenty miles from the point of emission.

This attack had two novel features: phosgene was used for the first time in a cloud (we had decided to use it six months previously and were already manufacturing it, but no supplies became available till June 1916), as the 'tobacco reaction' was noticed (after inhaling phosgene tobacco smoke tastes like hay) and 'delayed cases' occurred among men who had apparently not been affected during the passage of the cloud. It was estimated that a mixture of 20 per cent phosgene and 80 per cent chlorine had been employed.

The enemy expected decisive results from the use of the new gas, and its apparent failure came as a great disappointment. This was chiefly due to the fact that our men had been equipped with the P helmet, which was specially designed to give protection against phosgene, and some of them already wore the earliest experimental models of the box respirator. At the same time the cloud shells containing K-Stoff (lethal gas) appeared for the first time in the artillery bombardment, and French observers attributed the delayed symptoms to their action, and were unwilling to accept the view that phosgene was contained in the cloud.

2. 27th and 29th April 1916—Hulluch. After the attack of December the enemy seems to have found no opportunity for further cloud discharges on our front for another four months, until the end of April 1916, though the French, a great part of whose line ran east and west, were attacked at Lihons on 21st February. So far our Second Army had been the object of attention, but it was now the turn of the First. These two discharges (which probably both contained phosgene) were intended as one, and have been so considered in compiling our losses. They were, moreover, disastrous from the enemy's point of view, as though we had 1260 men gassed, of whom 338 died (two of our battalions lost 48 per cent of their trench strength), the cloud on the second occasion blew back

on the German trenches and caused him an equal, and possibly a greater, number of casualties (see Chapter VII., p. 118).

3. 30th April—Wulverghem. On this occasion it appears that chlorine only was used, and our men now had the PH helmet. Our losses, nevertheless, were 512, including 89 dead.

4. 17th June—Wulverghem. The front attacked was practically the same as on 30th April and the gas waves were of short duration, but very dense. They were felt at Estaires, 17,000 yards from the front. We lost 559 men, of whom 95 died.

5. 8th August 1916—Wieltje. This was the last cloud attack of the war on the British front, and it was the only one in this series in which, although it was expected, precautions had been relaxed owing to the shifty wind. It was also the only one in which the presence of phosgene was definitely established by professional chemists familiar with its odour. Their opinion, moreover, was supported by the physiological action of the gas. Only four British battalions were exposed to this attack, and they had 804 casualties, including 370 dead (46 per cent). In addition, the Canadians had 174 casualties, including 2 dead, although a very small portion of the area held by them was invaded by the cloud. The total losses were therefore 978, of whom at least 372 died. Our gas discipline was not good on this occasion as a trench relief was taking place, and some of the men had sent up their helmets on the trench tramway. Besides, one of the two British divisions affected had been recently transferred from the Somme battle, and they contained a large number of officers and men as reinforcements who had received insufficient gas training.

Our total losses in these five attacks amounted to 4378 (average 876), and the mortality was nearly 24 per cent (1014 dead). It is important to bear these figures in mind when it is considered that during the war the Special Brigade carried out nearly 150 cloud attacks against the enemy ; and it is an interesting and significant fact that although through pressure of time and lack of opportunity for experiment our early technique was based on little more than guesswork, it stood the test of time and was found to be almost exactly the same as that practised by the Germans. The latter had two Pioneer regiments, the 35th and 36th (each of two battalions, each of three companies and a Park company). These were increased by the addition of the 37th and 38th (a total of eight battalions) when projectors came into use.

The German cylinders were arranged in batteries about the same distance apart as ours, and they were similarly protected with sand-bags, and had three men detailed to each battery, as with us. The only differences seem to have been that they used lead discharge pipes, while we used rubber; and our cylinders were a little larger—they contained 65 lb. of gas against 45 lb. After the first few discharges of chlorine on both sides phosgene was added to this gas, and while we employed 50 per cent of it in a standard mixture the enemy varied his percentage according to the season of year. Two captured German gas cylinders which were examined at the Central Laboratory were found to contain approximately 25 per cent of phosgene, while another examined by the French had 100 per cent. Probably the average phosgene content varied between 40 per cent and 60 per cent.

In view of these similarities, and the fact that we had undoubted proof that on many occasions we took the enemy completely by surprise (in which circumstances the pattern of respirator with which troops are equipped is of secondary importance), there is no reason to suppose that our cloud attacks against the Germans were any less successful than theirs were against us and the French.

From German accounts their Pioneer regiments undertook twenty-four cloud gas attacks on all fronts between April 1915 and August 1916, and they claim to have caused the death of 35,000 of the Allied troops. It is, of course, impossible to verify these figures, but it is probable that because of their inferior equipment and discipline the losses of the Russians were far higher than those of the British and French.

The latter seem to have suffered at least as heavily as ourselves, and Dr Hanslian quotes figures from French sources which show that in each of four of the attacks which he mentions our Allies suffered an average of 2262 casualties, including 446 dead (mortality, 20 per cent). In one of these, on the night of 19th October 1915, east of Rheims, there were 5096 casualties, including 815 dead;

and it may be deduced from the mortality alone (16 per cent) that phosgene was used in this cloud, in spite of the fact that Dr Hanslian, who is frequently misinformed, says that this gas was first used in the cloud attack against the British on 19th December of that year. In another of these attacks, in the Champagne on 31st January 1917, out of the 10,000 French troops exposed 2062 were gassed, of whom 531 died. (This was a daylight attack, and no surprise was even attempted, the trenches being 1000 metres apart).

The same author gives a few instances of the effects of German cloud attacks against the Russians and Italians, which he claims were extraordinarily effective. On 2nd May 1915, at Bolimow, after cylinders had been in position for three weeks, gas was released.[1] The Russians, who were provided with gas masks, drove off the attacking German infantry, who therefore believed that the gas had failed. Nevertheless it appeared later that the 53rd and 54th Siberian Regiments had been completely destroyed by the gas, and that supporting troops had lost two-thirds of their strength. Altogether there were 9100 gas casualties on this day, of which 6000 were fatal. (For General Ludendorff's remarks on this attack see Chapter II., p. 30.) On 7th September 1916, in another cloud attack, one Russian regiment lost 600 officers and men; and on 17th October 4000 Transbaikal Cossacks were destroyed, together with their horses. On the very next day the Russians lost 1500 men; and in an attack in 1917 they lost 12 officers and 1089 men killed by gas, while 53 officers and 7738 men were poisoned (the total gas casualties on this occasion were 8892).[2]

On 29th June 1916 a somewhat unsatisfactory cloud gas attack was made by Austro-Hungarian troops against

---

[1] General Schwarte, on the other hand, says that the first German cloud attack on the Eastern front took place at Nieborow on 31st April 1915.

[2] Captain Lefebure, in 'The Riddle of the Rhine,' says that between May and July 1915 the Germans made three cloud attacks against the Russians, west of Warsaw. The Russians lost 5000 dead on the field and they had a total of 25,000 gas casualties.

One Siberian regiment which had a ration strength of 40 officers and 4000 men was left, after a twenty minutes' gas discharge, with only 4 officers and 400 men.

He adds: "No other weapon could have reproduced, under the most favourable conditions for its use, in as many days, what gas" (in the form of clouds) "was able to do in as many minutes."

the Italians at Monte San Michele. Only half the cylinders that had been installed were emptied and many of the remainder were damaged by artillery fire, so that much of the Italian front line was missed by the cloud; some of the gas, too, blew back into the Austrian trenches, causing 222 casualties, of whom 3 officers and 33 men died. Yet the Italians were said to have lost 5000 men dead, the majority from gas; and of the 1000 prisoners that were taken a large proportion died from gas poisoning. The 10th Italian Infantry Regiment alone had 1300 gas deaths on this occasion.

From his detailed descriptions of these incidents it is evident that Dr Hanslian has had access to Allied documents of a confidential nature, as he even distinguishes, sometimes, the men who died on the spot from those who succumbed later. However, when he refers to the Allied gas attacks on the Germans he shows marked reticence, though in his Preface he prides himself on his impartiality.

For instance, he says that the French made 20 cloud attacks, the first in February 1916, but "they were not very effective." The effect of the two British gas attacks at Loos are not referred to at all, though he gives the figures of our own losses on those occasions, as detailed in Chapter VI. of this book (p. 93). None of the other 150 British cloud attacks are even mentioned!

In pursuance of the same policy of concealment of the German losses he describes three of the Russian cloud attacks. The first of these took place on 26th January 1917 (the very first Russian cloud attack against the Germans was made on 24th October 1916 at Barano-witschi) and was in two waves, of which the former was very dense. Two thousand phosgene shells were also fired, but "The gas attack was unsuccessful. The Germans had no gas deaths." On 27th March 1917 an attack was made against the Austrians, who had "three slightly poisoned"; and on 15th April 1917, 5 chlorine-phosgene clouds were released against the German 107th Infantry Division, and at the same time 10,000 shells were fired, of which 70 per cent were gas. The gas was smelt 16 kilometres away, but "the German losses were only 5 slightly poisoned"!

I have said that the last German cloud attack on the British front took place in August 1916; and although some were made later against the French—the last one on the night of the 30th June 1917—this method of gas attack was abandoned by the enemy.

The reasons given by German writers for this change of policy are very interesting, but, as I will show, they are obviously untrue. Dr Hanslian says : " Projectors gave the deathblow to the German cloud attacks. Whereas the latter had been very effective on a quiet front and on suitable ground, due to the enormous quantity of gas and to the penetration in depth up to twenty kilometres, it was set aside in favour of the projector, which seemed to be a more effective substitute."

General Schwarte says : " The cloud method often involved weeks of waiting and waste of preparation, and the infantry disliked it. Cylinders were often removed. In the East the poor Russian protection promised greater success. Cloud attacks were therefore abandoned for the time being, especially as the projector method was then introduced."

And General Ludendorff : " The troops were not fond of gas : the installation took too long, and both officers and men disliked waiting with full gas containers in the trenches for the wind. The discharge of gas from cylinders was used less and less, the troops being opposed to it from first to last, and the use of gas shells increased correspondingly. Our men were still apprehensive of damage from our own gas, and it was a long time before things improved in this respect."

It will be seen from the foregoing that, while the cloud gas attack was as unpopular with the German troops as with our own, the writers I have quoted attribute its abandonment to the introduction of projectors and artillery gas shells. This, however, is a mere pretext and is a falsification of history. Except for the small experimental shoots late in 1916 the first British projector discharge at Arras *took place eight months after the last of the German cloud attacks* against the British, and their own first projector discharge *came eight months later still !*

The artillery gas bombardment, as the Germans practised it, was futile, as will be seen in the following pages, and they can have had no reason to think otherwise, until mustard gas appeared on the scene, *eleven months after we experienced their last gas cloud.*

The truth of the matter is that there were two quite different reasons which were far more important in affecting the enemy's decision. The first was that they realised when it was already too late the initial blunder made in introducing the cloud attack on the Western front, as experience showed them that the wind was favourable for the Allies ten times as frequently as for themselves. Seven months elapsed between their attacks of May and December 1915, and four between the latter and that of April 1916. The German General Staff had been carried away by their chemists in the early days of the war and had omitted to consult their meteorologists.

The second reason was that the Germans bungled their cloud attacks, as quite a number of them seem to have brought disaster to their own troops. I have made no special search for these instances, but the following have come to my notice :—

In Chapter VII., p. 118, I referred to the heavy losses, amounting to 1600 men, incurred by the enemy on 29th April 1916 at Hulluch, when their cloud blew back over their own lines. Of this accident we obtained several documentary proofs. (I might point out here, incidentally, that if such a catastrophe could occur to German troops when the presence of gas was actually known and the danger of some leakage must have been recognised, there is all the more reason to suppose that our own gas clouds, which undoubtedly often took the enemy by surprise, were still more successful in producing casualties.)

On another occasion, at St Mihiel, the gas blew back and caused 900 casualties among the German troops, according to the statement of a prisoner of the 73rd Fusilier Regiment, examined on 7th December 1916.

And again, another prisoner, of the 60th Reserve Regiment, captured at Moyenneville on 21st April 1918, described a similar accident which occurred in the Champagne in September 1917. He could not say what the German losses were, but when the cloud came back all the thirty to thirty-five occupants of his own dug-out were gassed, and two of them died.

Dr Hanslian mentions the cloud attack at Bolimow against the Russians on 31st April 1915, when

" another cloud attack was carried out by the Ninth German Army in which the gas blew back and caused heavy losses among the German troops." General Ludendorff refers to the same incident : " The Ninth Army was unlucky with gas. When they repeated the gas attack at the same place " (as at Skierniewice) " later, but not in connection with these operations, the wind veered round. We suffered severe losses by gassing."

The ' Daily Mail,' on 26th October 1915, published a report from its Copenhagen correspondent : " The last 30 Prussians casualty lists issued contained the names of 159,901 officers and men killed, wounded and missing. Among the latest casualties are many killed by poison gas." Hoping to learn something of the German gas casualties at the battle of Loos, I wrote to the editor for further particulars, and he was good enough to forward the following reply from the correspondent mentioned : " 9/12/15. I have learned that the deaths of the German soldiers already reported to have been killed by poison gas were mainly due to German poison gas. In some cases sudden unexpected wind changes led to the fatalities. Even in well-informed circles it seems to be quite unknown that the British have used poison gas. I may add that the Germans have installed poison gas factories in Bulgaria, and especially in Turkey, under the management of German chemists and instructors."

The ' Morning Post,' too, on 2nd October 1916, published a report from its Petrograd correspondent in which reference was made to still another accident on the Russian front : " According to the stories of wounded German prisoners several companies of the German attacking force " (date not stated) " openly mutinied when a change of wind carried their own gas, with disastrous results, back upon themselves."

I have already mentioned the accident on the Italian front on 29th January 1916. German Pioneer regiments were not responsible for this mishap, but it no doubt helped to emphasise the dangers of faulty technique in the minds of the German leaders.

Finally, General Schwarte says : " On other occasions we incurred not inconsiderable losses through misjudging the weather." "In other places minor accidents occurred which were bandied about with great exaggeration and which resulted in loss of confidence ; and clouds were only used to harm the enemy while dispensing with infantry action."

It is clear from the foregoing that although the Germans had definite evidence of the catastrophic effects of some, at least, of their cloud attacks—results which could have been obtained by no other form of gas discharge and by no other weapon—they realised that, at any rate on the Western front, both as regards weather and technique an overwhelming advantage rested with their enemies in this method of warfare.

CHAPTER XVIII.

Lethal Gas Shell Period.

This commenced in about July 1916 and lasted for a year, though the use by the enemy of shells containing substances like phosgene and di-phosgene continued until the end of the war; however, lethal shells played a subordinate part after mustard gas was introduced.

It will be seen from the chart that in comparison with the effort expended, our casualties during this period were insignificant, the total number amounting to only 8806, 532 of which (6 per cent) proved fatal. This number, moreover, included lachrymator casualties which could not be separated from the rest. In some of the German bombardments very large numbers of lethal shells were fired, 10,000 and sometimes 20,000 being counted; but the tactics employed were very faulty, as the fire was continuous and was distributed over large areas which were 'searched' systematically for many hours. In consequence our men were able to avoid entering the bombarded areas, and if they were compelled to remain in them they either entered the dug-outs and drew the gas curtains, or they put on their masks and were only affected by the surprise effect of the first few rounds, if at all. It was remarkable how many of the casualties were the result of ' direct hits,'—*i.e.*, shells which fell so close to groups of men that there was no time to avoid the gas cloud; or which penetrated into dug-outs or cellars in which men were asleep. In these cases, of course, the same results would have been obtained if H.E. ammunition had been employed.

Gas shelling had a certain neutralising and harassing effect, the value of which it is difficult to estimate. It forced men under cover or compelled them to perform their duties under the severe handicap of having to wear respirators. But owing to the sensitiveness of the human eye this result could have been obtained 100 times, possibly 1000 times more economically if lachrymatory instead of lethal gas fillings had been used.

Our own artillery were only able to take up gas shelling seriously at the commencement of the battle of Arras in April 1917, and, in the absence of any experience of their own, they were influenced at first by the instructions contained in a French memorandum which recommended the systematic treatment of targets [1]; but in some units —especially in the Second Army, where Barley was Chemical Adviser—the surprise shoot of one minute duration, as practised by the 4-inch Stokes mortar companies of the Special Brigade, had already been adopted. I had formed a very strong opinion on this subject, and when I became Director in June 1917 and again assumed the rôle of Gas Adviser I wrote a report to the C.G.S. pointing out the almost total absence of results from some of the recent German gas bombardments and emphasising the futility of such tactics as they were employing. Sir Douglas Haig thereupon wrote to the War Office on 19th June and said that the correct principles for the use of gas shells were to be regarded as—

(a) A short burst with lethal shells for inflicting casualties before masks could be adjusted ; and

(b) A slow subsequent rate of fire with lachrymatory shells for neutralisation ; and in pursuance of this policy it was requested that 25 per cent of the gas shells supplied in future might have lethal and 75 per cent lachrymatory fillings.

Of course, when mustard gas appeared on the scene it altered the situation entirely ; and it is now improbable that any lethal or lachrymatory gas shells of the nature that we have been considering will ever again be used in war. Even at the present day I doubt if any more formidable *lethal* gas than phosgene is known, but artillery shells are not the best vehicle for conveying it to an enemy, owing to the small amount of gas contained in each pro-

---

[1] This French instruction seems to have followed the lines laid down in a German document which recommended fire to a depth of 400 metres against infantry positions, the range to be varied by successive increases of 25 metres and each battery to cover a front of 150 metres.

jectile.[1] It was this consideration which influenced Sir John French in June 1915 when he requested research into the most lethal shell fillings procurable (to compensate for the small content), but very soon afterwards an incident occurred which caused him to modify his policy (without consulting me). In July 1915 the Germans made a gas attack against the French in the Argonne on a very large scale, it being estimated that 40,000 shells were fired, some of large calibre; and although it was established that only benzyl and xylyl bromide fillings had been used, the bombardment was a very great success, and all the French soldiers in the gassed area, on a front of 5 kilometres, were said to have been either killed or taken prisoner. The reports of this attack produced such an impression on the mind of the Commander-in-Chief that, in spite of the fact that the success obtained was due chiefly to the lethal value of the two substances mentioned (which was about equal to that of chlorine),[2] he wrote to the War Office on 17th July to say, " I now urge that experiments be made with lachrymatory as well as lethal fillings ; but the output of ordinary shells must not be delayed."

Shortage of ammunition postponed any serious use of gas shells being made by our artillery, though a few experimental SK (lachrymatory) shells were fired during the battle of Loos ; and 10,000 more, of an improved type, were sent to France for trial in April 1916. But it was not until the opening of the battle of Arras, in April 1917, that the difficulties of design had been overcome and the shell situation permitted an extensive use of gas ammunition. Even then, the fillings supplied depended rather on what gas was available than on what was preferred.

The success obtained at Arras was striking, and in a report signed by the G.O.C. of the First German Army, dated 11th April 1917, the following passage appeared :—

" Experiences gained from the Arras battle. It has not yet been established with any certainty whether the enemy employed a new

---

[1] Shells must be designed with very strong (and therefore thick) walls to enable them to withstand the shock of discharge from a gun or howitzer, so that their H.E. or gas content amounts to less than 10 per cent of their total weight. In comparison, bombs are far more effective than shells of the same size, especially when they fit but loosely in the barrel, as in the case of the Stokes mortar and the Livens projector.

For example, the gas content of the Livens drum is about 50 per cent of its total weight. That of aerial bombs might amount to 80 per cent or 90 per cent.

[2] See footnote, p. 108.

gas " (the gas was new : it consisted of prussic acid and arsenious chloride mixtures). "There is no doubt that our own gas masks afforded complete protection, but the fighting power of the men suffered considerably from the wearing of masks for many hours. Horses were greatly affected by the gas. In many cases the failure of the ammunition supply is to be attributed to this. It also appears that the timely withdrawal of batteries was in several cases prevented by the same cause. Artillery activity seems to have been paralysed by the effect of the gas. The bringing up of ammunition by horsed transport columns was unsuccessful owing to the effect of hostile gas because whole teams were put out of action in a few minutes. Preparations must be made for bringing up ammunition by mechanised transport."

Here is an extract from the despatch of a German newspaper correspondent, which gives a vivid account of the conditions at this period :—

"A salvo of gas shells whistles over, bursting 100 metres away with a weak explosion. Gas ! In a trice the masks are on and nosebags filled with moist hay are drawn over the horses' mouths and nostrils. We wait until a few more salvoes arrive and then continue our route through the poisonous cloud. The eye-pieces become misty and breathing becomes difficult—we cannot see our way. And then gas ! The mask makes freedom of movement impossible with its horrible pressure on the face and the eye-pieces besmirched with mud and gore. Rifles full of water. The ground on which one seeks a foothold, a sliding morass. Impossible to eat ! And day and night the same ! "

These quotations show the harassing effects of gas shelling which, of course, we too experienced ; but in addition there is little doubt that from the middle of 1917, when the 'surprise gas crash' was adopted as our standard tactics, the enemy suffered casualties in a steady and constant stream until the end of the war.

Dr Hanslian, whose historical account of the gas war is seriously marred by patriotic bias, says that the Allied artillery tactics were completely based on German methods. This is quite untrue, and General Schwarte practically admits it when he writes : "Mistakes were made. One used too little gas for too large areas, and too low densities, so that disappointment was the logical consequence. Towards the end of 1916 special artillery gas schools were established to study the use of gas. It was found that

Green Cross shells became less effective, and further research became necessary. Yellow and Blue Cross shells resulted, and there was an improvement of Green Cross in the summer of 1917 and in the use of gas in all calibres of artillery. As the British protection improved it was necessary to change our tactics, and concentrated bursts were employed for surprise and mass effect, and to create high densities of gas—the 'gas surprise attack'—with as many guns as possible." [1]

The French did not suffer from the same shortage of shells that we did, and their artillery used gas as early as in July 1915, and again in August 1915 when supporting our attack at Hooge. At first they employed phosphorus dissolved in carbon disulphide for incendiary effect, and then resorted to the lachrymators, bromacetone and chloracetone.

In February 1916 they succeeded in persuading their Government to withdraw the ban on phosgene, and they employed shells filled with this substance in the early days of the defence of Verdun. Dr Hanslian says that the results convinced the Germans of the value of lethal shells, and General von Dermling, who commanded the XVth German Army Corps, protested to the chief of their gas service that, in comparison with phosgene, the German shells were as harmless as Eau de Cologne!

General Schwarte says: " The French were the first to use gas projectiles without large H.E. bursting charges. This was in open conflict with the wording of the rules of International law.[2] For the gas war it was an important step, because the Germans could now employ similar projectiles." (I would remind my readers that the Germans had introduced gas warfare. They had used lethal gas clouds, and had even employed phosgene in them. They had used lachrymatory gases in their shells, but we are

---

[1] It was only on 1st December 1917 that the Supreme Command issued instructions in a paper called " Gas shelling by artillery " for 'surprise shoots' with a maximum rate of fire for one minute, though I ought to add, in fairness, that M. Daniel Florentin (see p. 31) refers to a German tactical instruction, dated 18/2/17, in which the 'area bombardment' was described, but in which the 'surprise crash' was also mentioned. If this was so, the latter was certainly never put into practice so early in the war on the British front.

[2] Dr Hanslian, too, uses this argument. He says that the French use of phosgene shells was the first contravention of the Hague Convention in the war, so that the responsibility rests with France. He claims that the cloud attack at Ypres was merely a renewal of a very ancient method of warfare, namely fumigation!

asked to believe that they did not feel free to fire lethal gas shells which had small bursting charges until their enemies had committed this dastardly act! One cannot, of course, question the writer's honesty, but one may at least doubt his sense of humour! As regards the first German use of lethal gas shells, see also p. 309.) " The French shells were effective and contained the new substance phosgene against which the German masks gave no protection. It was fortunate that they did not recognise the possible effect of this gas " (this was not the case, as it will be remembered (see p. 115) that in view of its estimated importance they had agreed with us not to release phosgene until we had both accumulated a large quantity of the substance). " They never strove for mass effect and at no time used the gas in connection with a major tactical operation. Their occasional successes were unimportant, on the whole, and resulted in tightening up the German gas discipline. The German Green Cross shells " (phosgene type) " were the answer."

Yellow, Green and Blue Cross Period.

From a glance at the chart it will be evident that it was not until July 1917, when mustard gas was first used, that the enemy achieved undoubted success in the gas war. From that time until the Armistice we suffered 160,970 gas casualties, fully 90 per cent of which were caused by mustard gas ; and although this number was small (14 per cent) in comparison with our total battle casualties in the same period, and the mortality among the gas cases was low ($2\frac{1}{2}$ per cent for 4167 deaths), and troops in action were not affected by the gas until several hours had elapsed, the almost continuous removal of large numbers of men from the front line, especially at critical periods in the great struggle (in March and April 1918 we had 33,000 mustard gas casualties), was a source of serious embarrassment to us.

These numbers might have been still greater but for two reasons : the enemy's supply of the substance was inadequate owing to his employment of the thiodiglycol process of manufacture (upon which we, too, embarked at first until we found a much quicker and less costly one) ; and he declined to take the risk of storing this ammunition at the battery positions, so that it was never available

in quantity at the times when experience showed us that
it would have had its maximum value, namely when our
troops were assembling for attack and all the traffic routes
in rear were congested.

I have mentioned the low mortality amongst mustard
gas casualties ; but it is not so widely known that of the
97½ per cent which survive very few are rendered permanently unfit in the end. Towards the close of the war an
examination of the medical records of 4575 of these cases
which had been sufficiently severe to be sent to England
for treatment (and were therefore rather more severe than
the average) showed that 28.5 per cent were transferred
direct to Reserve battalions and 66 per cent to convalescent
depots—a total of 94.5 per cent—within nine weeks of
their arrival. Out of the total in this series of cases only
0.7 per cent died ; 0.4 per cent were classified as permanently unfit ; and less than 2 per cent were reduced
from Class A. to a lower category. In fact, apart from
about 2 per cent which may be presumed to have died in
France (to make up the average mortality of 2½ per cent),
only about 3 per cent of the remainder were any the worse,
say, after three months. I have reproduced this record
because very mistaken ideas are held, even now, of the
terrible effects of this gas. Even such a careful writer as
Mr H. G. Wells has stated recently (in his ' History of the
next 100 years ') : " It is doubtful if any of those affected
by it " (mustard gas) " were ever completely cured. Its
maximum effect was rapid torture and death ; its minimum,
prolonged misery and an abbreviated life."

The ease with which mustard gas was recognised by
us immediately it appeared in the field (see Chapter XV.)
was due partly to the very efficient chemical intelligence
organisation which I have described and partly to the
fact that it was not entirely unknown before the war, as
its vesicant property was described by Guthrie in the
Journal of the Chemical Society as long ago as in 1859.
The German chemist, Victor Meyer, also drew attention
to its skin-blistering property in 1884, but he said that
the action was selective and affected the skin of some
people and not that of others. French chemists, when
examining the substance in 1916, recognised both the
toxic and vesicant properties, but they considered the
former of less value than that of phosgene or prussic acid,

both of which were already in use, so that the manufacture of it was not thought desirable. In March 1916 a British chemist in the anti-gas department in London mentioned his own experience in Germany, shortly before the war, when a German professor with whom he was working suffered an accidental injury from a drop of the substance, and he proposed its use by the British Army as an offensive agent.

Apparently, however, only the skin-blistering property was known at the time, so that it seemed that shells containing it would have to be burst very close to troops for drops of the liquid to be brought in contact with their bodies, in which circumstances such shells would be less effective than the ordinary high-explosive variety. The persistence of the substance on the ground for days, and even weeks, was overlooked, and the action of minute quantities of the vapour on the eyes, lungs and moist surfaces of the body were, of course, unknown, as well as the valuable property it possessed in its slight odour, which induced men to continue to expose themselves in ignorance of its presence. At this period of the war, too, serious attention was not being paid in England to gas shells owing to the shortage of ordinary ammunition; and as it was estimated that the production of mustard gas on a manufacturing scale would be slow and difficult, and would probably cost a million sterling at least, the proposal was dropped. It was unfortunate that it was not re-examined later.

Actually when Sir Douglas Haig's first request for mustard gas shells was received by the Ministry of Munitions it was calculated that his demand involved a production of 200 tons of the substance per week, a rate which could not be reached in less than fifteen months. This quantity necessitated the use of 800 tons of chlorine per week, and it was thought that the plant would cost four millions sterling, and 10,000 men would be required to erect and operate it! Fortunately, in November 1917, our chemists suggested an entirely new and a much simpler and less costly method of manufacture than that employed by the Germans, and a large plant was assembled at Avonmouth which was capable of producing 500 tons per week; but already six months had been lost in the earlier attempts at manufacture. The new process was adopted by the Americans and the French, and the latter filled, altogether, two and a half million mustard gas shells between April and November 1918, and supplied them for the use of the American, Italian, Belgian and Greek Armies, as well as their own, as the quantity they were producing was greater than the artillery expenditure of their own army. It is claimed that French production commenced in March 1918, British in May and American in July.

We first used mustard gas [1] of our own manufacture on the Fourth Army front on the night of 26th September 1918, when 10,000 shells were fired with very remarkable results. Our artillery reported that many of the enemy's batteries were neutralised and remained silent for the whole of the next day ; and, from information received, there was a steady dribble of gas cases from many of the units opposite to us on the morning of 27th September, which continued until the end of the war, the enemy being faced with the same initial difficulties that we had experienced in July of the previous year. In a report of the 8th German Division, dated 28th July 1918 (Vendhuille sector), it was stated : " The enemy is employing an apparently invisible, odourless gas in shells which he fires simultaneously with H.E. No small losses have been caused by the gas. The type of gas and its particular properties have not yet been definitely established. The strictest gas discipline must be maintained."

A document of the 1st Guard Reserve Division said : " The infantry of the division have suffered heavy losses from Yellow Cross gas " ; and another of the 222nd Division : " In case of night bombardments with Yellow Cross shells the position will be evacuated again at daybreak, even if the effects of the gas are not perceptible, because the gas becomes noxious under the action of the sun's rays."

Prisoners made many sensational statements of the general demoralisation which showed itself among German units that had experienced our mustard gas bombardments. Rations repeatedly failed to reach the troops ; battalions

---

[1] I need hardly say that mustard takes no part in the manufacture of this substance ; but a lady of my acquaintance, when she failed to purchase a tin of the domestic commodity during the latter part of the war, was offered the excuse by the grocer's assistant : " It is very scarce just at present, as so much of it is required by the troops for making mustard gas ! "

lost 25 per cent of their strength ; batteries remained out of action for days, and whole areas were neutralised. Divisions had to be relieved after having been in action for only two or three days, and it was said that it was not possible for the Germans to hold the line if the English continued with these shoots. Herr Hitler himself was one of our victims, and he has stated in a recent interview which appeared in the ' Sunday Chronicle ' (25/6/33) : " The end of it came on 14th October 1918, when with many of my comrades I was knocked out by the new mustard gas which the British were using for the first time."

Civilians in Le Cateau and Bohain were told that the German mask was penetrated by this new gas after only three or four minutes' exposure to it, and to allay the general panic the Germans announced officially that all men with inflamed eyes were suffering from a trench disease, and not from gas.

But General Schwarte endeavours to make light of this situation. He writes : " Great effect was attributed to the enemy's artillery gas shoots in the last months of the war. This was for the greater part exaggerated. The German gas losses at that time, just as previously, were based frequently on irresponsible rumours." [1]

As regards Blue Cross shells there is no doubt that the enemy very much over-estimated their value. The production was said to have amounted to over a million monthly, but the gas effect on our troops was very slight and no cases of poisoning are known to have resulted from their use. They were intended, of course, to be fired simultaneously with Green Cross shells, in order to assist the latter to take effect, but they failed almost entirely in this object, and the reduction of high explosive resulting

---

[1] This pretence finds an echo in General Ludendorff's affected contempt of our tanks : he writes of them, " As to the tanks, opinion was calm : they were not thought particularly dangerous. I purposely made use of the expression ' tank fright,' but the officers from the front would not admit there was any such thing." . . . " They were only effective in masses, and then only when combined with artificial smoke after our infantry had lost its discipline and fighting capacity." " Our own tank detachments suffered losses in the fighting which followed " (in 1918) " without effecting anything." This author appears to contradict himself, as he writes in another passage, " Mass attacks by tanks and artificial fog remained thereafter " (after 8th August 1918) " our most dangerous enemies." General von Zwehl, in ' Die Schlacten im Sommer, 1918, an der West Front,' says : " It was not the genius of Marshal Foch that defeated us, but General Tank."

from the substitution of the chlorarsines for part of the bursting charge was not justified by the results.

The Germans used enormous numbers of Blue and Green Cross shells in their ' coloured shoots ' in all the great battles of 1918. Owing to the non-persistence of their contents they could be fired up to within an hour or two of an infantry advance, whereas the bombardment with mustard gas usually ceased six days beforehand, excepting on the flanks of an attack and on distant targets.

It seems that the faith placed on these ' coloured shoots ' was based on effects obtained previously on the Russian front.[1] In the passage of the Duna on 1st September 1917, and in the capture of the bridge-head at Jakobstadt on 21st September, scores of thousands of these shells were used (116,000 is the figure mentioned by Dr Hanslian for the former occasion) in the preliminary bombardments, which resulted in the complete neutralisation of the Russian batteries. The gunners were said to have abandoned their positions in panic, and although very few gassed men were found, the Germans advanced practically without opposition on both occasions. On the strength of these successes the same tactics were adopted on the Western front. Actually, however, they failed entirely against British troops (as they also did, a little later, against the Italians, on 15th June), and the results must have caused great disappointment.[2] For example, on the occasion of the German attack on Villers-Bretonneux on 24th April 1918, captured German orders showed that for the German counter-battery work on that day, which lasted for two and a quarter hours, none but gas shells were used. (At a G.H.Q. conference on the subject of the future supply of gas shells which I attended a few weeks before this, I was asked for my opinion as to the proportions that should be demanded. I replied, " 100 per cent for counter-battery ammunition," but was told, " Do try and be serious ! ") Owing to the British gas discipline which had by this

[1] Professor Banse, in ' Germany, Prepare for War,' says : " One is almost inclined to suspect that our higher command had grown too much accustomed to the mentality of the Russians whom it had so often brilliantly defeated."

[2] Two privates of the 1st Battalion of the Shropshire Light Infantry who had been taken prisoner on 21st March 1918 escaped from Fontaine on the night of 1st April. They said that the enemy had expected great results from their gas bombardment on the 21st and were very crestfallen at its lack of success. German prisoners made the same statement, and said that they had been told that every British soldier opposite to them would be killed by the gas.

time reached a very high standard, the casualties which resulted were small, though it is impossible to say how the shooting of our artillery was affected. Six days before this attack took place—*i.e.*, on the 17th and 18th April, 20,000 Yellow Cross shells had been fired into the Villers-Bretonneux positions, which caused us 2000 casualties. After the opening of the great attack of 21st March I received reports from twenty-two of the Division Gas Officers in the Third and Fifth Armies who were involved in the action, and summarised them in a memorandum to the C.G.S. on 25th March. The opinions of these officers, of course, varied; but on the whole it was considered that, except for a certain neutralisation of our batteries, the German artillery gas attack had been a complete failure, and that the total number of gas casualties in the two Armies did not exceed 1000 altogether, although 25 per cent to 30 per cent of the vast quantity of ammunition expended during the five hours' intensive bombardment consisted of gas shells. In the Third Army, as a result of the warning issued by G.H.Q. on 24th February (see p. 267), it had been the practice during the preceding two or three weeks for every man to wear his respirator for one hour every day. General Ludendorff accounts for the comparative failure of his gas preparation in the following words : " Unfavourable winds diminished the effectiveness of the gas, fog retarded our movements and prevented our superior training and leadership from reaping its full reward."

Towards the end of May 1918 German gas activity almost ceased on the British front, and in June very little gas was used (see chart) ; but in July there were some heavy Yellow Cross bombardments, and these continued from the opening of the British offensive on the Somme on 8th August till the end of the war, though less and less Yellow Cross ammunition was used owing chiefly to the diminishing supply. German policy also changed, and there was a distinct tendency to increase the H.E. charges in all types of their gas shells, the doubtful advantage being sought of converting them into ' double purpose ' projectiles. It is true that the *severity* of our Yellow Cross casualties also increased at this period, but this was owing to the higher summer temperature which assisted the vaporisation of the liquid, the influx of fresh drafts of troops with no previous experience of gas shelling, and the change to open warfare which, in the absence of trenches, necessitated more frequent contact of men's bodies with contaminated ground. Immense quantities of Blue Cross shells continued to be used, but apart from the damage done by shell splinters few of the gas cases resulting from them required hospital treatment. Apparently in recognition of their failure a number of variations were then introduced in the gas fillings, and a German G.H.Q. instruction dated 9th July 1918 stated that in future all gas shells would contain a considerable H.E. element so as to serve a double purpose, and be more difficult to recognise and more suitable for open warfare conditions.

The importance attached by the enemy to the use of gas shells in the artillery preparations for these attacks was illustrated in a captured order of the Seventh German Army, dated 8th May 1918, which laid down the proportions of gas ammunition to be used in certain natures of guns and howitzers for the attack on the Aisne on 27th May :—

(*a*) Counter-battery and long-range bombardments : Blue Cross, 70 per cent ; Green Cross, 10 per cent ; H.E., 20 per cent.

(*b*) Against infantry : Blue Cross, 30 per cent ; Green Cross, 10 per cent ; H.E., 60 per cent.

(*c*) In the ' box barrage ' : Blue Cross, 60 per cent ; Green Cross, 10 per cent ; H.E., 30 per cent.

As was their custom, no Yellow Cross shells were to be used on the actual front of attack on the day of the battle.

At times the American gas casualties amounted to 65 per cent of their total battle casualties, and of the entire American losses during the war nearly one-third were caused by mustard gas (mortality, 1.6 per cent). It was thought that this number would have been doubled but for the failure of supply of Yellow Cross ammunition to the German artillery in the last stages of the war. The Americans thought so highly of gas that they authorised it for 25 per cent of all their future supplies of artillery ammunition. But they preferred Lewisite to mustard gas. This was an analogous substance which, contrary to the opinion of our own chemists, they considered more valuable, as it was said to be absorbed through the skin and to cause more virulent and deep-seated injuries. They constructed a large factory for its manufacture which was just commencing production at the time of the Armistice, by which date the Americans alone had planned to produce ten times as much of these two vesicants as the total of which the whole of the German plants were estimated to be capable.

The six American gas companies were also to have been increased to fifty-four.

According to Dr Otto Muntsch, the German Head-quarters demanded gas in the year 1918 for 50 per cent of their artillery ammunition ; and the opinion of our own General Staff of the value of gas was reflected in their last demand of the war, dated 9th August 1918, for gas shells and bombs for the 1919 campaign. 20 per cent to 30 per cent of all types of artillery shells were to have contained gas, the majority mustard gas, and pure lachrymators were eliminated entirely. Phosgene shells for the 18-pounder were demanded for the first time, the intention being to employ them in the moving barrage, not because any lethal effect was expected from them, but because it had been so often found advantageous to compel the enemy to meet our assaulting troops with their masks on.

As for Special Brigade stores, 2500 White Star cylinders were demanded per week, and 4000 projector drums and 1000 4-inch bombs filled with phosgene. It was also the intention to fire mustard gas both from the projectors and the 4-inch Stokes mortars, and 500 bombs per week for each were included in the demand. An interesting departure was the contemplated use of phosgene in 5 per cent of the infantry 3-inch Stokes mortar bombs. This had been thought too dangerous up till now, but there was a strong expression of infantry opinion that they would be more useful than H.E. in the attack on ' pill boxes.'

The above programme involved a scale of manufacture per week of 190 tons of phosgene, 250 tons of NC and 520 tons of mustard gas—960 *tons of gas per week altogether !*

The Projector Period.

The adoption of the projector by the Germans was in frank imitation of British procedure. Dr Hanslian says : " As the English gas projector attacks caused considerable losses to the German troops the Supreme Command decided to introduce, with all pressure, a similar projector after the English pattern." But owing to the shortage of steel the existing 18-cm. H.E. bombs, of which there was a large stock, were adapted to hold gas. These only contained half as much gas as the British drum, and as the whole object of a projector attack was to deposit suddenly a dense concentration of gas in the target the effect was correspondingly reduced.

Even with these bombs available it was eight months after the battle of Arras that the first German projectors were fired against British troops. The enemy departed still further from the principle that made our projectors so effective when he adopted a smaller (16 cm.) *rifled* projector in August 1918; and again when he introduced pumice granules into his bombs so as to ensure a slower distribution of the gas. It was not surprising, therefore, that the casualties inflicted were correspondingly small, especially as, in any case, the British mask gave better protection than the German in high concentrations of gas.

In the sixteen projector attacks made by the enemy against British troops we had an average of only 28 casualties in each (mortality, 18 per cent). The French had an average of 65 casualties (mortality, 22 per cent), and in the two most effective of these, both of which took place at Badonvillers, there were 364 and 247 casualties. In the only projector attack against the Belgians the latter had 81 casualties (mortality, 22 per cent); and in the seven attacks against American troops there was an average of 65 casualties (mortality, 11 per cent), the most effective having been made at Apremont, when there were 185 casualties.

Support for my argument that the comparative failure of the German projector attacks was due to the small gas content of their drums (and the inadequate number of them used at a time) is provided in the fact that in the only two attacks made with the rifled projector (the smallest of all) the American losses averaged only 10, including 3 deaths; while in their most effective attack against ourselves, in which we lost 75 men (mortality, 27 per cent), captured British projectors and drums were employed.

Dr Hanslian quotes an instance in which the Italians

used British projectors (they were also employed by French and American gas troops) against the Austrians and Hungarians, when "considerable casualties were caused." All German references to their losses from our own projector attacks are equally vague, so that it is impossible to obtain authentic figures of the total. They can, however, be estimated, and it is certain that the mortality arising from them was very high and that it approached 30 per cent.

My frequent references to percentages of mortality may cause surprise, but it will be evident on reflection that in a prolonged war like the last it is of military value to inflict such injury on one's opponents as to prevent them from reappearing on the battlefield after only a few weeks' hospital treatment.

CHAPTER XIX.

WITH so many facts and data at our disposal it is now possible to review the part played by gas in the war. Probably the total number of gas casualties among all the belligerents in the Western theatre alone amounted to fully a million, and American writers have suggested that considering the small numbers of the special gas troops employed and the low total percentage of the gas shells fired (about 5 per cent), gas was easily the most effective weapon used in the Great War. However that may be, it was certainly one of the factors which led to the Allied victory, and it was increasing in importance and might have played a decisive part in 1919. This also seemed to be the opinion formed at a meeting of a sub-committee of our Government, which I was summoned to attend, when all the factors were being considered before deciding on the terms to be imposed in the Armistice.

As regards the war effort made by the British Empire, probably the principal causes which contributed to the victory were the vigour displayed in the direction of the war from the moment that Mr Lloyd George assumed control, and the example set to the empire by the Royal Family and our political leaders : secondly, the tenacity and self-sacrifice of our people — not forgetting the women [1] : thirdly, the courage and endurance of our troops : fourthly, the blockade of the Central Powers; and fifthly, our overwhelming superiority in tanks. It may be thought that the last-named factor has been given undue prominence in this estimate, but in all the early battles of the war, at the time when our artillery was distinctly inferior both in power and numbers to that of the enemy, our infantry had been given the almost impossible

[1] Professor Banse writes, in ' Germany, Prepare for War ' : " We were not prepared for the incredible tenacity of our Anglo-Saxon cousins in the pursuit of their ends, their tireless energy in thinking out new expedients, and, above all, their unshakeable determination, which nothing but death can overcome, to bring the enemy to his knees."

task of advancing across the open against riflemen and machine-gunners who were under cover, while they themselves received but little, and only indirect support from their own machine-guns. The tanks adjusted the balance : besides sweeping away obstacles in a way which even our stupendous artillery bombardments often failed to do, they enabled direct machine-gun fire to be used for the first time in the assault and gave these weapons mobility and the men behind them comparative immunity. In consequence, the life in battle of our infantry divisions was extended from a few days to weeks.[1]

I am not underrating the part played by our artillery, which, I believe, constituted, with its ancillary services, 40 per cent of the strength of the British Expeditionary Force in the end, and only then established a marked superiority over that of the enemy.[2] Its power was developed to an extent which was not even faintly visualised at the commencement of hostilities ; but the preliminary bombardment and the preparations for it which were necessary robbed an attack of any element of surprise, and it cut up the ground to such an extent that the movement of transport over it was almost impossible. Besides, it had already handed over to aerial bombers many of its long-distance targets, and the reply to it was partly found in the deep dug-out, the wide wire entanglement, ' pillboxes ' and the tactical refusal—the temporary withdrawal of troops from a bombarded area. It is probable that the tank menace, too, would have been met with increasing success by the interposal of physical obstacles, by the use of land mines and by the appearance of an effective anti-tank gun. But no answer was found to gas, which, with tanks, was the only important offensive *innovation* of the war. It is true that the respirator gave partial protection, but only to the eyes and lungs, and

---

[1] General Fuller has calculated that from July to November 1917, the period during which our tanks were not employed to the best advantage, the British casualties per square mile of territory captured from the Germans amounted to 8222 ; whereas from July to November 1918, after the lessons had been learnt, they were only 86.

[2] There was a remarkable illustration of this superiority in the condition in which the two towns, Béthune and La Bassée, were left after a mutual concentrated bombardment in the last days of the war. The former under German fire was left with the walls of buildings standing shoulder high ; but in the streets of the latter, when the British guns had done their work, it was not possible to distinguish where the pavements had been laid !

then only for a while. It was impossible to wear it all
the time, and complete evacuation of gas-infected areas
was the only alternative. I will not fall into the
error committed by so many military writers of ex-
aggerating the importance of the particular arm with
which they were associated, but there is little doubt that
the effectiveness of gas was being more clearly realised by
our own leaders, while there were unmistakable signs in the
last months of the war that the morale of the German
troops, as well as that of their commanders, was seriously
affected by the increasing use that we were making of
it. They were losing faith in the masks which they had
gradually perfected, and this occurred even before we began
to use mustard gas against them. "Regard your masks
as sacred," said a German anti-gas lecturer ; and more
than one instance was reported in August 1918 of German
regiments carrying out two hours of anti-gas training
daily when out of the line. Prisoners constantly expressed
their dread of gas and the belief that their masks were
inadequate. An Alsatian prisoner of the 203rd Reserve
Regiment, captured on 29th July 1918, who had only
arrived in April from the Russian front, said that the whole
of the German infantry was terrified of our projectors
and feared them more than anything else. "They do not
mind gas shells so much" (we had not yet used mustard
gas) "as the artillery always get that ! The men think
they are losing heavily from gas, though the papers say
that they are not. The papers tell lies !"
    In a 'Memorandum sheet for gas Inspection' of the
21st Reserve Division, dated 8th May 1918, the following
words occurred, all of them underlined: "Can you put
on your mask in ten seconds ? Is your mask correctly
packed away ? If not, practise until you can do this.
Only then may you regard yourself as safe from being
surprised by gas."
    A vast number of German documents, captured in
1918, nearly all contained warnings and orders concerned
with gas protection. One of these, after paying a tribute
to the gas discipline of the British Army, said : "We also
must train our troops to an excellent standard of gas
discipline if we expect to avoid the grave dangers which
threaten the fighting forces of our army." Another,
issued by the Seventeenth German Army in July, said :
"Owing to the severe losses we have suffered and to the

impossibility of providing our troops with a more convenient form of protection the Army Commander is
obliged to resort to energetic measures. Close investigation regarding recent projector attacks and the casualties
incurred have furnished the following data," and so on.
" On all nights when a gas attack is imminent—*i.e.*, when
it is neither raining heavily nor blowing hard, a special
gas alert will be ordered. All gas-proof curtains will be
lowered and special sentries will take up their positions
at dug-out entrances. All ration and working parties will
on such nights continue the last 1000 metres of their
journey with the mask adjusted. The extensions will be
put on if a thick gas cloud is encountered. The mask will
be adjusted in principle at every burst of artillery fire,
as latterly the enemy has rarely employed H.E. shell alone.
Although it must be admitted that losses are unavoidable
owing to the heavy concentrations of gas produced in the
case of direct hits, yet the majority of the casualties are
shown by the reports of units to be due to surprise and
carelessness."

Another paper, of the 1st Reserve Division, referred to
215 gas casualties suffered between the 21st and 31st
August 1918, and mentioned drastic steps being taken to
deal with men who either malingered or who wilfully
exposed themselves to gas in order to escape duty. And
an order of the 4th Bavarian Division, dated 12th October
1918, attempted to restore confidence in the unit and to
correct the impression which had apparently obtained
currency that as the result of the action of mustard gas
limbs dropped off ! and the mask only afforded protection
for three minutes. (This latter belief was constantly
expressed by prisoners.)

Even the German War Ministry took a hand in com-
bating the depression, and in a document dated 14th
April 1918 it said : " The opinion is current among all
troops exposed to British projector attacks that the mask,
even when adjusted in time, does not furnish protection,
and that the drum is insufficient. This opinion is not
correct." The paper then goes on to show that it is only
too well founded ! " The men must know that a well-
adjusted mask still offers a full guarantee of protection if
they move away a few paces from the main concentration
of gas and stand up at their full height. At the point of
burst of hostile projector bombs the gas is so concentrated

that no apparatus would afford protection unless it were of such dimensions as would interdict its use in the field. It occurs again and again that men becoming aware of a slight irritation inside the face-piece lose all confidence in their masks, fly into a panic, taking it off or unscrewing the drum, and thus succumb, unprotected, to the effects of the gas. The irritation produced by a little gas penetrating within the edge of the mask and the face must not cause men to lose their heads in this way."

Our total known gas casualties in the whole war, *including slight cases*, were 181,053, among which were 6109 dead. To these must be added about 3000 that were unrecorded, mostly dead, in April and May 1915.

The German losses from our gas attacks are never likely to be disclosed. Although their historians have gained access to all the information at our disposal as regards our own losses we appear to have obtained nothing from them in return.

It has been said that the German battle casualties were compiled in ten-day periods (three per month), and that those retained for treatment in regimental convalescent stations and in hospitals in corps areas (estimated at an additional 30 per cent) were not included at all in the published lists ; that gas casualties were not distinguished from the rest ; and that complete records are not now available as many of them were destroyed during the Revolution in Berlin.[1] I find it difficult to accept these explanations. It seems far more likely that the German authorities adopted the deliberate policy of concealing their gas losses in order to escape the inevitable reflection on their military judgment and the reproach of having come off worse in the gas war.[2]

[1] Dr med. Otto Muntsch, in his book ' Leitfaden der Pathologie und Therapie der Kampfgaserkrankungen,' says : " Statistics are unreliable, especially when the methods of computing them are not uniform : this is especially the case here, as there were a great number of gas casualties among the German missing. Often the published lists include only the cases treated in hospital ; and they exclude light cases of which there are doubtless a great number—men withdrawn from duty and treated in the ambulances. Skin lesions caused by gas are frequently not included in the statistics as such, but are reckoned as diseases of the skin."

[2] Some of the documents that were captured showed the extent to which German Commanders were prepared to go in order to suppress the truth concerning their gas losses. For instance, a statement issued by " Gas Services, Sixth Army,"

CONCLUSION

It was notorious amongst the interrogators on our Intelligence staffs that German prisoners refrained from disclosing their gas casualties whenever possible, though the same men were communicative on every other subject. In fact, they admitted having received special instructions to this effect. Even burial parties, after a gas attack, were warned not to discuss the business on which they had been engaged.

The same reticence is noticeable amongst all the German post-war writers. For example, Dr Hanslian gives, often in exact detail, the losses suffered by the Russians, Italians, French and British, and he can even distinguish between men who died instantaneously and those who succumbed later on from the gas in hospital; but except for the derisory references to the casualties inflicted by the Russians (see p. 313) in three of their cloud attacks he makes no mention whatever of precise German losses anywhere, apart from two instances to which I shall refer presently. Thus, in describing our first projector attack at Arras in April 1917, which " caused considerable losses to the German troops " and created such an impression that the enemy at once decided to imitate this method of gas discharge, no casualty figures are mentioned, though, as no infantry advance took place until five days later, they must have been known. Again, in describing an American projector attack in August 1918 (which was believed to have been very successful), he says, " The German losses are not known." There is no mention of the losses from any one of our cylinder [1]

dated 20th January 1917, contained the following : " In the evening (13/11/16) a cylinder attack in two waves took place between 6.45 and 8 P.M. from the English positions from Blaireville to Ficheux, on the boundary between the First and Sixth Armies. The very dense waves, principally chlorine, were carried by the north-west wind at a speed of 2 to 3 metres per second a long way over the country, so that men at a distance of 50 kilometres from the point of discharge smelt chlorine strongly and were affected with coughing. There were no casualties."

The improbability of the final comment is obvious, especially as the two following quite independent statements of prisoners had been previously published in our Intelligence Reports : " Prisoner put the deaths at 20 per cent of the regiment (the 85th) due to men having masks in which the screw in portion was old and defective." " The 86th Fusilier Regiment's 1st Company had approximately 40 casualties, of which 25 eventually proved fatal." Both these regiments were in the front line of the sector exposed to this gas attack.

[1] Thus, on p. 15 of his book : " The gas activity of the English reached a remarkable development in July and August " (1916) " during the Somme battle. According to English views based on the evidence of prisoners and orders which were found and letters of German soldiers, these attacks were successful."

or projector attacks, though in some cases these were known beyond any doubt to have been striking ; and as regards our biggest projector attack of the whole war, on 21st March 1918 (he gives the date wrongly as the 31st), with 3730 drums, he says, " So far there are no authentic data about the German losses," though here again there was no infantry attack after the discharge, so that it is inconceivable that the losses were not recorded. The figures were merely suppressed.

Five or six hundred German regimental histories have been written since the war. I have, of course, not been able to examine more than a few of them, but I have read through (with the help of a translator) the histories of four of the six regiments mentioned on page 238 which were most frequently subjected to our gas attacks and which were known to have suffered severely from them. The other two have not yet published their histories. I have also searched the pages which deal with certain periods mentioned in the foregoing chapters in the histories of some thirty other German units, but, except in half a dozen instances altogether, no specific mention is made of gas losses in any of them. Very often the gas attacks are not recorded at all, and even when they are, no particulars are given.

Here are some examples. " The gas-mine attacks on September 9th, 1917, and especially on the 13th and 20th, caused considerable losses."

" On August 15th, 1917, there was a gas attack on the left wing of the regiment."

" On October 4th, at 11.45 P.M., a very strong gas attack on the left wing of the regiment, but owing to the splendid discipline there were only a few losses."

" On December 3rd, 1917, gas mines on the front line."

" On April 27th, 1918, a strong gas attack on the left wing of the regiment which caused losses owing to the positions being unfamiliar."

All the above are from the History of the 1st Bavarian Reserve Regiment. (See also the extract from the History of the 10th Bavarian Regiment in the footnote, p. 231.)

It is perhaps too much to expect to find this kind of information in books which have been compiled for the benefit of regimental posterity, and which are chiefly concerned with describing the insuperable difficulties which faced the men and the heroism with which they were overcome. Shortcomings are dealt with kindly when they are not ignored altogether, and gas casualties are, of course, nearly always the result of failure of discipline. It may be that our own war histories are open to the same criticism ! [1]

The two figures given by Dr Hanslian (to which I have previously referred) are as follows : On page 24 of his book he says that the total German gas casualties in the whole war, on all fronts, " are supposed to have been " 78,663. And on page 5 : " According to German statistics, from January 1st, 1918, to September 30th, 1918, during which period exact figures were kept, out of a total of 58,000 gas casualties only 1755, that is 3 per cent, were killed."

From these statements it appears, after all, that gas casualties *were* distinguished from the rest, and that, at any rate during one period, exact records of them were kept. But the total number given is absurd, as, I think, is the suggestion that records were only kept during one period of the war ; while our experience, and that of all of our Allies, showed that a percentage of mortality as low as 3 per cent could only apply to casualties sustained from mustard gas.

However, deducting one figure from the other, it will be seen that according to this authority the total German gas losses during the three years 1915, 1916 and 1917, and in the last few weeks of the war, amounted to only 20,000. So that, conceding half of these to the gas troops of the Russians, Italians and French, and to their artilleries, as well as our own—an estimate which they will not think too generous !—only 10,000 casualties remain which the Special Brigade can claim—say, 5000 in each year, 1916 and

---

[1] A good example of this kind of writing is provided in the history of the 5th Matrosen Regiment which suffered from our cloud attack at Nieuport on 5th October 1916. This attack (see p. 144 *et seq*.), according to all the other accounts collected during the war, took the German Marine Corps, in which gas discipline had been entirely neglected, completely by surprise ; yet this passage occurs : " The gas alarm which had been so often practised with the necessary alarm arrangements, such as gongs, hooters, rattles and yellow flares, was carried out in perfect order ; also the adjustment of the gas masks. The time taken by the cloud to reach our front line was 15 to 20 seconds, but in 8 or 10 seconds the gas masks were in position. The conduct of the troops was splendid : everywhere there was calm and confidence. There was no panic. Gas casualties only occurred through inevitable events, such as masks being caught up or shifted or torn, or through men stumbling and being wounded. It was a brilliant proof of the quality of our gas masks and discipline. Rifles were covered with brown rust and food was spoilt."

1917. This works out to about twelve casualties for each of our gas attacks!

Dr Hanslian's figures cannot be taken seriously—he even seems to give them apologetically and without conviction ("sollen sich belaufen haben")—and I am convinced that in each of the 768 gas operations carried out by the Special Brigade alone the average loss sustained by the enemy amounted to at least 250 men, which gives a total for the whole war of 200,000. Or, taking a more conservative estimate, let us assume that the German losses from each of our 150 cloud attacks amounted to only 500—that is half the average loss sustained by the British and French from German attacks of the same nature (though there is no reason whatever to make this concession); and that we adopt the middle estimate of the "Staff Officer for Gas" of the Fourth German Army (see p. 233) of 100 to 200 casualties for each of the remainder. This gives a total of nearly 170,000 altogether, *a figure which does not, of course, include the casualties inflicted on the enemy by the gas troops and artilleries of our Allies and by the gas shells of our own artillery.* There is little doubt, too, that the percentage of mortality in this total of 200,000 or 170,000—whichever is accepted—must have been between 20 per cent and 25 per cent; and that far fewer of the Germans gassed returned to duty in the field.

To summarise the events of the gas war. The Germans introduced the gas cloud, though they had little faith in its possibilities; and although we suffered nearly 1000 casualties from each of their cloud discharges, even after our troops were provided with adequate protection against them, they believed them to have failed. When we followed the German lead with cloud gas, much sooner than the enemy expected, our own commanders also disbelieved in this method of attack, owing to the absence of visible results. It is not reasonable, however, to suppose that our cloud attacks were any less successful than theirs, while they exceeded them many times in number.

The Germans introduced gas shells, but they soon followed the French lead in substituting lethal for lachrymatory gas fillings. Owing to faulty artillery tactics the results of their bombardments were poor, and they would have been better if H.E. had been employed instead. Even after they had adopted our tactics of the surprise crash H.E. would have given better results as far as casualty production was concerned, though gas shells were far more effective for the neutralisation of batteries.[1]

The Germans imitated us, though feebly, in the projector method of discharge, but we carried out thirty times as many of these operations and liberated far greater quantities of gas in each ; while in seeking the all-important element of surprise, we introduced such variety into our tactics that our enemies accused us of violating all the technical laws of gas warfare !

Their Blue Cross shells were an innovation, but they grievously miscalculated their effect, and they failed to put to the best use the valuable compound which they contained. They depended largely on these projectiles in all the great battles of 1918 and fired millions of them ; but once again the results were less than they would have been if H.E. had been employed,[2] though they seem to have proved more successful against the Russians.

The use of the arsenic compounds in the thermo-generated particulate cloud was our idea, and, as all our gas secrets were well kept throughout the war, we would probably have obtained decisive successes with this one if hostilities had continued.

It was only by forestalling us in the use of mustard gas that the Germans approached equality with us in the gas war. For this they must be given full credit, but the temporary advantage gained in this particular had already disappeared at the time of the Armistice, and it would have rested overwhelmingly with us when the stupendous scale of Allied production of this and analogous substances had been developed.

It is probable that in the year 1919 the whole character of the war would have changed. Particulate clouds of the nature that we were preparing to use would probably have lost a good deal of their value after a few weeks, as soon as a mechanical filter had been incorporated in a new

[1] The counter-battery officer of the Canadian Corps Heavy Artillery reported, in April 1917, " 205 60-pr. gas shells were fired on a group of 3 hostile batteries which were neutralised and absolutely silenced in the first 5 minutes of the bombardment. It is interesting to note that in this case gas shells were effective when 9.2-inch and 12-inch howitzers with aeroplane observation had been found ineffective."

[2] The Blue Cross shell had a *destructive* effect only about a quarter that of an H.E. shell of the same calibre.

German respirator; but the possibilities had been only partially explored, and there would, no doubt, have been fresh developments.[1] Human nature being what it is, no amount of familiarity or tightening of ' iron gas discipline ' would have eliminated entirely the danger of surprise cloud drifts at night, and the probable direction of prevailing winds might have become an important consideration when major tactical movements were being planned. New offensive substances would have been discovered and novel means of liberating them devised. Every smoke cloud would have constituted a potential danger, as it might contain a poisonous element besides concealing an advancing enemy.

The width of No Man's Land would have been gradually extended, and the poisonous fumes hanging over it would have formed a physical barrier between the armies as effective as an inundation. Trench-mortars and projectors would have fallen into disuse, and the ranges of all guns and howitzers would have increased until miles separated the opposing forces, and observation of fire from the ground would have become impossible.

Concealment and camouflage would have become imperative, for without them strong-points and trench systems would have been untenable.[2] For instance, a dozen shells or a single air bomb containing mustard gas, if dropped into places like Forts Douaumont and Vaux, at Verdun, would have compelled their evacuation within twenty-four hours; and though it would have been impossible to occupy them, there would have been no need to sacrifice a single man in their assault.

Even villages beyond the distance of long-range artillery would have been untenable, as they would have been subjected to gas sprays from aircraft.

Perhaps we would have seen combats between fleets of gas-proof tanks, emerging from their own smoke clouds, carrying their own artillery and co-operating with aeroplanes. But in any case the existing deadlock had been loosened and no further stabilisation of armies would have been possible.

From the picture I have attempted to draw it might

[1] " In this war the engineer and the chemist dominated the battlefield " (Mr Lloyd George's ' War Memoirs').

[2] This also applies, in my opinion, to fortified zones constructed in time of peace along a frontier.

seem that further developments in chemical warfare will make future struggles between great nations more terrible ; but that, I think, is hardly possible.

The appearance of gas on the battlefield has, nevertheless, changed the whole *character* of warfare, and there is grave danger in the belief that its continued use can be prevented by agreement : its infinite possibilities in a scientific age preclude any such hope.

I think that nearly everyone must agree with General Groves when he writes, in ' Behind the Smoke Screen ' : " History shows that every new weapon has invariably at first been discredited, sometimes execrated, but that it has always in the end been exploited to the utmost."

" The stark truth is that the application of science and discovery to warfare cannot be restricted."

" No nation fighting for its existence will deny itself the free use of aviation and chemicals."

" Military necessity knows no law, except political expediency."

Other authorities have expressed similar opinions, as follows :—

Mr Lloyd George (' War Memoirs ') : " War is a ruthless business and those who wage it cannot afford to be too discriminating."

M. Voroschiloff, the Soviet Commissar for War, speaking in March 1932 : " Despite the chatter in Geneva, chemistry will play not a lesser but a larger part in the coming war than in the Great War. We can say that as regards the chemical weapon we are not unarmed."

And, finally, Mr Duff Cooper, Financial Secretary to the War Office, said in the House of Commons on 14th February 1934 : " No one liked the idea of warfare or of the latest and most modern weapon, but they must realise that if we were to have an army, a navy, or an air force at all we must have the most modern, the most terrible and the most revolting weapons that science could possibly invent."

There are some who believe that war between civilised communities can be abolished, though they can find little comfort or encouragement in the lessons of history.[1]

[1] A Harvard University investigator has calculated that in the last 1000 years France leads with 185 wars, Britain coming next with 176.

Signor Mussolini said recently, " History teaches us that war is a phenomenon accompanying the development of humanity. War is to man what maternity is to woman."

Nations, moreover, by abandoning the habit of war, are not likely to improve their chances of ultimate survival.

However that may be, it seems far more profitable to make whatever progress is possible towards the abolition of war itself, rather than any particular method of waging it. As a result *some* conflicts, at all events, may be averted.

INDEX.

INDEX

INDEX

INDEX

INDEX

INDEX

INDEX

INDEX

War Museum, the, 91, 111
War Office, the, 97
Warneton, 209, 210
Warsaw, 312 *n*. 2
Watson, Colonel, 37, 250, 276
Wattrelos, German Commandant of, 42 *n*.
Waziristan, 303
Wegener, Professor, *cited*, 21
Weinberg, Major, 298
Wells, H. G., book by, *cited*, 189 *n*., 324
Westende Bains, 150
Westminster, Duke of, 188, 250 *n*. 2
White phosphorus 4-inch bombs, 198 *n*., 216
'White Star' cloud gas, 112 *sqq*., 121, 122 *sqq*., 136, 141, 142, 145, 174, 191, 195, 196, 197, 293, 331
'White Trench,' 164
Wieltje, 182, 308, 310
Willcocks, General, 61
Wilson, Lance-Corporal, 136
Wilson, Sir Henry, 177
Wilson's method of electric discharge of gas cylinders, 99
Wimereux, 2
Wingles, 83

Woker, Dr Gertrud, book by, *cited*, 30
Wolff wireless communiqués, 34
Wulverghem, 181, 310
Wytschaete, 192, 270

Xylyl bromide (T-Stoff), 108.
Shells, 305, 320

Y Ravine, 168
'Yellow Cross' gas, 266, 267, 268, 270, 271, 278, 306, 322, 323, 326, 329, 330
'Yellow Star' gas, 193, 195, 196, 231
Yperite, 263 *n*.
Ypres, 1, 16, 21, 34, 264, 271, 308
Battles of
First, 8, 20, 25, 28
Third, 176, 211, 218, 242, 302
Canal, the, 215
Front, 295
Salient, the, 2, 7, 18, 29, 93, 122, 179, 182, 223, 227, 268, 296, 307
Sector, 233

Zangwill, I., 101
Zeebrugge, 105
Zillebeke, 2, 3, 6, 28, 32
'Zurich bomb and bacilli case,' the, 18

Milton Keynes UK
Ingram Content Group UK Ltd.
UKHW022219131124
451121UK00001B/2